D1560021

THE FATHERS
OF THE CHURCH

A NEW TRANSLATION

VOLUME 111

THE FATHERS
OF THE CHURCH

A NEW TRANSLATION

DIDYMUS THE BLIND

COMMENTARY ON ZECHARIAH

Translated by

ROBERT C. HILL
Australian Catholic University

THE CATHOLIC UNIVERSITY OF AMERICA PRESS
Washington, D.C.

To the Cistercian community,
Southern Star Abbey, Kopua, New Zealand

God is in her midst, and she will not be shaken.
God will help her as day dawns.
(Ps 46:5)

Copyright @ 2006
THE CATHOLIC UNIVERSITY OF AMERICA PRESS
All rights reserved
Printed in the United States of America

The paper used in this publication meets the minimum requirements of the
American National Standards for Information Science—Permanence of Paper
for Printed Library Materials, ANSI Z39.4-1984.

LIBRARY OF CONGRESS CATALOGING-IN-PUBLICATION DATA
Didymus, the Blind, ca. 313–ca. 398.
    [On Zechariah. English]
    Commentary on Zechariah / translated by Robert C. Hill.— 1st ed.
       p. cm. — (The Fathers of the church ; v. 111)
    Includes bibliographical references and indexes.
    ISBN-13: 978-0-8132-0111-5 (cloth : alk. paper)
    ISBN-10: 0-8132-0111-X (cloth : alk. paper)
       1. Bible. O.T. Zechariah—Commentaries—Early works to 1800.
2. Bible. O.T. Zechariah—Allegorical interpretations.   I. Hill, Robert C.
(Robert Charles), 1931–   II. Title.   III. Series.
    BR60.F3D53 2005
    [BS1665.53]
    270 s—dc22
    [224/.98

                             2005010005

CONTENTS

CONTENTS

INDICES

ABBREVIATIONS

AnBib   Analecta Biblica, Pontificio Istituto Biblico, Rome.

BAC   The Bible in Ancient Christianity, Leiden-Boston: Brill, 2004–.

Bib   *Biblica.*

CCG   Corpus Christianorum series Graeca, Turnhout: Brepols.

CCL   Corpus Christianorum series Latina, Turnhout: Brepols.

CPG   Clavis Patrum Graecorum III, ed. M. Geerard, Turnhout: Brepols, 1979.

DBS   *Dictionnaire de la Bible. Supplément,* Paris: Librairie Letouzey et Ané, 1949.

DS   *Enchiridion Symbolorum, Definitionum et Declarationum,* 34th ed., ed. H. Denzinger and A. Schönmetzer, Freiburg: Herder, 1967.

EEC   *Encyclopedia of the Early Church,* ed. A. Di Berardino, New York: Oxford University Press, 1992.

ETL   *Ephemerides theologicae lovanienses.*

FOTC   The Fathers of the Church, Washington, DC: The Catholic University of America Press.

GCS   Die griechischen christlichen Schriftsteller (der ersten drei Jahrhunderte), Leipzig: J. C. Hinrichs, 1897–1949; Berlin: Akademie-Verlag, 1953–.

GO   Göttinger Orientforschungen, Wiesbaden: Otto Harrassowitz.

HeyJ   *The Heythrop Journal.*

KlT   Kleine Texte für Vorlesungen und Übungen, Bonn: A. Marcus und E. Webers Verlag, 1912.

LXX   Septuagint.

NJBC   *New Jerome Biblical Commentary,* ed. R. E. Brown et al., Englewood Cliffs, NJ: Prentice Hall, 1990.

OCA   Orientalia Christiana Analecta, Rome: Pontifical Oriental Institute.

OTL	Old Testament Library.
PG	Patrologia Graeca, ed. J.-P. Migne, Paris, 1857–66.
PL	Patrologia Latina, ed. J.-P. Migne, Paris, 1878–90.
RB	*Revue Biblique.*
SC	Sources Chrétiennes, Paris: Du Cerf.
StudP	*Studia Patristica.*
TRE	*Theologische Realenzyklopädie*, Berlin: Walter de Gruyter, 1976–.
TQ	*Theologische Quartalschrift.*
VC	*Vigiliae Christianae.*
VTS	*Vetus Testamentum*, Supplement.

SELECT BIBLIOGRAPHY

Altaner, B. "Ein grosser, aufsehen erregender patrologischer Papyrus-fund." *TQ* 127 (1947): 332–33.

Balthasar, H. U. von, ed. *Origen, Spirit and Fire: A Thematic Anthology of his Writings.* Translated by Robert J. Daly. Washington, DC: The Catholic University of America Press, 1984.

Bardy, G. "Interprétation chez les pères." DBS 4 (1949): 569–91.

Barthélemy, D. *Les Devanciers d'Aquila. VTS* 10. Leiden: Brill, 1963.

Bienert, W. A. *"Allegoria" und "Anagoge" bei Didymos dem Blinden von Alexandria.* Patristische Texte und Untersuchungen 13. Berlin and New York: Walter de Gruyter, 1973.

Bouyer, L. *The Spirituality of the New Testament and the Fathers.* Translated by Mary P. Ryan. London: Burns & Oates, 1963.

Bruce, F. F. *The Canon of Scripture.* Downers Grove, IL: InterVarsity Press, 1988.

Butler, C., ed. *The Lausiac History of Palladius* 2. Cambridge: Cambridge University Press, 1904.

Crouzel, H. *Origen.* Translated by A. S. Worrall. San Francisco: Harper & Row, 1989.

Daniélou, J. "Les divers sens de l'Écriture dans la tradition chrétienne primitive." *ETL* 24 (1948): 119–26.

Doutreleau, L., ed. *Didyme L'Aveugle. Sur Zacharie.* SC 83, 84, 85. Paris: Du Cerf, 1962.

Ehrman, B. D. "The New Testament Canon of Didymus the Blind." *VC* 37 (1983): 1–21.

Fernández Marcos, N. *The Septuagint in Context: Introduction to the Greek Versions of the Bible.* Translated by Wilfred G. E. Watson. Boston and Leiden: Brill, 2000.

Guinot, J.-N. "Théodoret a-t-il lu les homélies d'Origène sur l'Ancien Testament?" *Vetera Christianorum* 21 (1984): 285–312.

Hanson, P. D. *The Dawn of Apocalyptic.* Philadelphia: Fortress, 1975.

Hanson, R. P. C. *Allegory and Event. A Study of the Sources and Significance of Origen's Interpretation of Scripture.* London: SCM, 1959.

Hill, R. C. "Psalm 45: A *locus classicus* for Patristic Thinking on Biblical Inspiration." *StudP* 25 (1993): 95–100.

———. *Theodore of Mopsuestia. Commentary on the Twelve Prophets.* FOTC 108. Washington, DC: The Catholic University of America Press, 2004.

_____. *Reading the Old Testament in Antioch.* BAC 5. Leiden-Boston: Brill, 2005.

_____. *Diodore of Tarsus. Commentary on Psalms 1–51.* Writings on the Greco-Roman World 9. Atlanta, GA: SBL, 2005.

_____. *Theodoret of Cyrus. Commentary on the Twelve Prophets.* Brookline, MA: Holy Cross Orthodox Press, 2006.

_____. *Cyril of Alexandria. Commentary on the Twelve Prophets.* Fathers of the Church 115. Washington, DC: The Catholic University of America Press. Forthcoming.

_____. "Zechariah in Alexandria and Antioch." *Augustinianum.* Forthcoming.

Jellicoe, S. *The Septuagint and Modern Study.* Oxford: Clarendon, 1968.

Kahle, P. E. *The Cairo Genizah.* 2d ed. Oxford: Blackwell, 1959.

Kannengiesser, C. *Handbook of Patristic Exegesis.* BAC 1–2. Leiden-Boston: Brill, 2004.

Kelly, J. N. D. *Early Christian Doctrines.* 5th ed. New York: Harper & Row, 1978.

Kerrigan, A. *St. Cyril of Alexandria, Interpreter of the Old Testament.* AnBib 2. Rome: Pontificio Istituto Biblico, 1952.

Kramer, B. "Didymus der Blinde." *TRE* 8 (1981): 741–46.

Lubac, H. de. *Histoire et Esprit: L'intelligence de l'Écriture d'après Origène.* Théologie 16. Paris: Aubier, 1950.

Nautin, P. "Didymus the Blind of Alexandria." In *Encyclopedia of the Early Church* 1: 235–36. Edited by A. Di Berardino. Translated by Adrian Walford. With Foreword and bibliographic amendments by W. H. C. Frend. New York: Oxford University Press, 1992.

Olivier, J.-M., ed. *Diodori Tarsensis commentarii in psalmos.* I. *Commentarii in psalmos I–L.* CCG 6. Turnhout: Brepols, 1980.

Petersen, D. L. *Zechariah 9–14 and Malachi.* OTL. London: SCM, 1995.

Pusey, P. E., ed. *Sancti Patris Nostri Cyrilli Archiepiscopi Alexandrini in XII Prophetas.* Oxford: Clarendon Press, 1868.

Quasten, J. *Patrology* 3. Westminster, MD: Newman, 1960.

Redditt, P. L. *Haggai, Zechariah, Malachi.* New Century Bible Commentary. Grand Rapids: Eerdmans, 1995.

Schäublin, C. *Untersuchungen zu Methode und Herkunft der antiochenischen Exegese.* Theophaneia: Beiträge zur Religions- und Kirchengeschichte des Altertums 23. Cologne and Bonn: Peter Hanstein, 1974.

_____. "Diodor von Tarsus." *TRE* 8 (1981): 763–67.

Simonetti, M. "Lettera e allegoria nell'esegesi veterotestamentario di Didimo." *Vetera Christianorum* 20 (1983): 341–89.

_____. "Didymiana." *Vetera Christianorum* 21 (1984): 129–55.

Smith, R. L. *Micah-Malachi.* Word Biblical Commentary 32. Waco, TX: Word Books, 1984.

Sprenger, H. N., ed. *Theodori Mopsuesteni commentarius in XII prophetas.* GO. Biblica et Patristica 1. Wiesbaden: Otto Harrassowitz, 1977.

Ternant, P. "La θεωρία d'Antioche dans le cadre de sens de l'Écriture." *Bib* 34 (1953): 135–58, 354–83, 456–86.

Tigcheler, J. H. *Didyme l'Aveugle et l'exégèse allégorique. Étude sémantique de quelques termes exégètiques importants de son Commentaire sur Zacharie.* Nijmegen: Dekker & van de Vegt, 1977.

Vaccari, A. "La θεωρία nella scuola esegetica di Antiochia." *Bib* 1 (1920): 3–36.

Weitzman, M. P. *The Syriac Version of the Old Testament.* Cambridge: Cambridge University Press, 1999.

Young, F. M. *From Nicaea to Chalcedon. A Guide to the Literature and Background.* Philadelphia: Fortress Press, 1983.

_____. *Biblical Exegesis and the Formation of Christian Culture.* Cambridge: Cambridge University Press, 1996.

Ziegler, J. *Duodecim Prophetae.* Septuaginta 13. Göttingen: Vandenhoeck & Ruprecht, 1943.

INTRODUCTION

INTRODUCTION

1. Circumstances of composition of the Zechariah Commentary

We have Jerome to thank for the *Commentary* on the prophet Zechariah by Didymus, composed at his request by the illustrious Alexandrian scholar a decade before his death in 398.[1] Despite the loss of his sight in early childhood, Didymus not only became a monk[2] but also attained such eminence as a scholar, adversary of heretics, and spiritual director as to win the admiration of a prelate like Athanasius and a hermit like Antony. The Zechariah commentary carries allusions to this early disability, and betrays as well his championing of orthodoxy and his remarkable familiarity with Holy Writ. Born in 313, Didymus's life spanned a period immediately following the persecution of Diocletian and including the ecumenical councils of Nicea and Constantinople I, whose terminology leaves an imprint on his work.[3] And it is ironic that a teacher who attracted to his cell pupils like Rufinus of Aquileia and guests like the historian Palladius as well as Jerome and Paula, and who won the eulogies of church historians like Socrates and Theodoret,[4]

1. Cf. preface to Jerome's own commentary (CCL 76A.747–900).

2. Cf. observations below on internal evidence of the intended readership of this commentary and Didymus's comments on states of life. In view of the mention by Palladius (*The Lausiac History of Palladius* 2.20) of visitors being admitted to Didymus's "cell," P. Nautin concludes ("Didymus," *EEC* 1.235) that "he led a monastic life and that his audience must have been mainly composed of monks."

3. For biographical details see L. Doutreleau, SC 83.13–16; B. Kramer, "Didymus der Blinde," *TRE* 8:741–46; C. Kannengiesser, *Handbook of Patristic Exegesis*, BAC 2, 725–29. At places during the *Commentary* Didymus speaks of the period of persecution (e.g., on Zec 8.6); and we shall find him using conciliar terminology.

4. In commending Didymus's rebuttal of heretical views, Socrates couples

should incur condemnation on charges of Origenism by church councils.[5]

The works of Didymus, dogmatic and exegetical, though in many cases lost as a result of this condemnation, are known to us by name from Rufinus and Jerome and in fragments in the catenae. Palladius tells us that he had "commented on the Old and the New Testament";[6] and Jerome reports that he had "at my request dictated books of commentary [on Zechariah], and along with three books on Hosea had delivered them to me."[7] In 1941 a discovery was made at Tura outside Cairo of the *Commentary on Zechariah* along with those on Genesis, Job, Ecclesiastes, and some Psalms. Didymus mentions some of his other works while commenting on Zechariah (admitting at the outset that it is not a full commentary on The Twelve he is embarking on): commentaries on Leviticus, Psalms, Isaiah, the Final Vision of Isaiah, Matthew, John, Romans, 2 Corinthians, and Revelation; *On the Trinity; On the Son; On Virtue and Vice;* and a work on Ezekiel possibly only projected. The *Commentary on Zechariah* alone, however, enjoys the threefold distinction that it is the only complete work on a biblical book by Didymus extant in Greek whose authenticity is established,[8] that it comes to us not through the catenae but by direct manuscript tradition, and that it has been critically edited.[9] Its appearance in English is overdue.

It seems, then, that Didymus composed the Zechariah *Commentary* soon after Jerome's visit to him in 386; since it was in the latter's hands in 393 when he mentioned it again in the *De viris illustribus*,[10] along with the further work on Hosea, it is rea-

him with Gregory Nazianzen in his *Hist. eccl.* 4 (PG 67.528) as Theodoret likewise couples him with Ephrem in his *Hist. eccl.* 4 (PG 82.1189).

5. J. Quasten, *Patrology* 3:86, attributes the loss of so many of Didymus's works to his condemnation along with other Origenists at the fifth ecumenical council in 553. Cf. also DS 519.

6. *The Lausiac History of Palladius* 2.19–20. Palladius speaks of Didymus as a συγγραφεύς.

7. See n. 1 above.

8. Cf. CPG 2549.

9. The critical edition is that of L. Doutreleau, *Didyme L'Aveugle. Sur Zacharie,* SC 83, 84, 85.

10. *De viris illustribus* 109 (PL 23.705); FOTC 100.142–44.

sonable of editor Doutreleau to suggest 387 as the likely date of composition.[11] More importantly, this date allowed for its availability to a fellow Alexandrian like Cyril,[12] and to two commentators of the school of Antioch:[13] Theodore, contemporary of Didymus, and later Theodoret, in their commentaries on The Twelve.[14] We are thus provided with the markedly diverse approaches of Alexandria and Antioch to this *obscurissimus liber Zachariae prophetae* (in Jerome's words[15]), especially since Origen's two volumes (now lost) did not reach beyond Zec 5 to provide a sample of the former school's hermeneutics;[16] and the opportunity has been taken below to draw the obvious and instructive comparisons of the two schools and of the members within them.

In the course of composition Didymus betrays his attachment to the church of Alexandria as well as to its hermeneutical principles. Athanasius comes in for complimentary reference as the διδάσκαλος (now deceased) of the whole church of Alexandria,[17] and the apostle Peter—mentor of Mark, the local church's patron—consistently receives honorific mention that is much more pronounced than in Antiochene statements. Mary, likewise, is the object of particular regard by comparison

11. SC 83.23.

12. The critical edition of Cyril's *Commentary on the Twelve* is by P. E. Pusey, *Sancti Patris Nostri Cyrilli Archiepiscopi Alexandrini in XII Prophetas* (Oxford: Clarendon Press, 1868). A. Kerrigan, *St Cyril of Alexandria, Interpreter of the Old Testament*, AnBib 2:12–15 (Rome: Pontificio Istituto Biblico, 1952), assigns Cyril's work on The Twelve to the period before 428, thus dating it after Theodore's and before Theodoret's.

13. In the case of the Antiochenes, we might speak of a "school" of Antioch in the sense of a fellowship of like-minded scholars joined by origin, geography, and scholarly principles, with some members exercising a magisterial role in regard to others. To this limited understanding Johannes Quasten, *Patrology* 3:21–23, adds a local sense by speaking of "the school of Antioch founded by Lucian" in opposition to the "school of Caesarea," Origen's refuge after his exile from Egypt.

14. Theodore's commentary has been edited by H. N. Sprenger, *Theodori Mopsuesteni commentarius in XII prophetas*, GO, Biblica et Patristica 1 (Wiesbaden: Otto Harrassowitz, 1977); Theodoret's appears in PG 81.1545–1988.

15. CCL 76A.747–48.

16. Jerome briefly remarks that Hippolytus had also composed a commentary on this prophet. Editor Doutreleau observes that, while he may have read it, "Didyme ne doit rien à Hippolyte" (SC 83.31).

17. SC 83.343.

with Antioch: when commenting on "daughter Sion" in Zec
9.9, the verse cited by the evangelists in reference to Jesus riding into Jerusalem on Palm Sunday, Didymus goes out of his
way to introduce Mary and highlight her virginity. It was doubtless not only Jerome that Didymus had in mind in composing
the work, nor did the former relish its allegorical approach.[18]
Didymus does not specify the readers he thought would principally appreciate his guidance; they are evidently not neophytes,
since he can flatter them with the ability to choose between
conflicting interpretations, as in the case of Zec 1.20, where he
remarks, "I read the interpretation of some commentator taking the *four craftsmen* as the four evangelists; let those reading
the one writing it decide whether this is true." They are possibly
people (men particularly, if not exclusively) interested in
monastic life; he explains the crown on the head of the high
priest Joshua son of Jehozadak in 6.11 in terms of the distinction in Christian living between the active and the contemplative life, and is not prompted to dispel the pejorative implications for married life that he finds in a text like Rv 14.4. While
it is not a polemical work, the commentator is ready to see in
the prophet's words reference to a range of heretical views to
be avoided.[19]

2. *Text of the* Commentary;
Didymus's biblical text

The Zechariah *Commentary* is a unique specimen of Didymus's compendious theological output, for reasons highlighted
above, and of the school of Alexandria in the fourth century,
just as its chance discovery in recent decades is remarkable.[20]
The codex is well preserved, with only eight pages missing of

18. "Its treatment was completely allegorical, with hardly any reference to
the historical background," he wryly remarked, while nevertheless slavishly re-
producing much of its content (CCL 76A.748).
19. Some of these heretical views are itemized below in section 6 of the Introduction.
20. Cf. B. Altaner, "Ein grosser, aufsehen erregender patrologischer Papyrus-
fund," *TQ* 127: 332.

just over 400, though at times throughout the text lines are now missing or illegible; it is the work of a single copyist, but has been liberally corrected by several hands (as editor Doutreleau painstakingly describes).[21] Didymus had divided his work into five volumes on the basis of their length.

The text of Zechariah that formed the basis of his commentary was a form of the Septuagint Greek version in use in Alexandria (despite its differing slightly from Cyril's).[22] Though his visitor from Italy who requested the work could read the Hebrew text, Didymus was like the other Fathers in not having that exegetical skill, nor does he feign such familiarity.[23] The unlikely vision of the flying "scythe" in 5.1, which the LXX offers for the Hebrew "scroll," he properly feels the need to rationalize without being able to correct the solecism (though he will proceed to admit that alternative versions offer "scroll"). On coming to 12.10, which the New Testament will cite in Jn 19.37 with a slightly different verb form, he shows his honesty in admitting his lack of Hebrew (and perhaps his naïveté in seeing the evangelist as a translator with access to Aquila):

The evangelist records the accomplishment of the prophecy that goes as follows: "They will look on him whom they have pierced," which except for a difference in wording is the same as the verse *They will look upon me because they maltreated me.* Those with a good knowledge of Hebrew claim, in fact, that the text of Zechariah was translated as the Gospel verse, either from the evangelist's translating it, since he was a Hebrew, or from the transmission of it by another translator, like Aquila, Theodotion, or someone else, who rendered the Hebrew text into Greek.[24] Now, we have been induced to say this as a result of the attempts of some people to find where in the prophets the verse oc-

---

21. SC 83.139–190.

22. For Cyril's text see Kerrigan, *St Cyril of Alexandria*, 250–65.

23. In this work Didymus cannot be quoted for a statement of the divine inspiration of the Seventy such as we find, say, in the preface to Theodoret's Psalms commentary (PG 80.864).

24. See N. Fernández Marcos, *The Septuagint in Context* (Boston and Leiden: Brill, 2000), 149, for the claim that the evangelist was using an independent revision of the LXX by Theodotion, a conclusion refuted by Alfred Rahlfs, "Über Theodotion-Lesarten im Neuen Testament und Aquila-Lesarten bei Justin," *Zeitschrift für die neutestamentliche Wissenschaft und die Kunde der älteren Kirche* 19–20 (1919–20): 182–99.

curs, "They will look on him whom they have pierced," which is not found anywhere in the available forms of the Old Testament.

Didymus here is perhaps a little disingenuous in implying that he generally checks his LXX version against those ancient versions associated with the names of Aquila and Theodotion (and perhaps Symmachus), or against an alternative form of the LXX or the Hebrew text, both available in Origen's resource, the Hexapla. In fact, he cannot be ranked as a diligent textual critic: only in reference to 1.21 does he cite such alternative LXX forms (ἀντίγραφα); and nowhere else are The Three cited.[25] Some of the readings of Zechariah that he cites differ from the LXX generally (noted in the text below), and these may testify to the existence of a distinctively Alexandrian revised form;[26] predictably his readings differ sometimes from Cyril's and often from those of his Antiochene counterparts— predictably, considering the likely origin of the different local forms of the LXX.[27] As suggested by the instance of the flying "scythe" in 5.1, time and again the LXX does not give an accurate rendering of *our* Masoretic Hebrew text; on other several occasions it is clearly translating a different Hebrew text (all these also duly noted below).

25. With Didymus's tendency to reduce the Zechariah text to a subtext and focus on an associated biblical text, however, it is in reference to the latter that he twice cites alternative readings (e.g., with Zec 7.11–12 and 13.8–9 as the lemmata). M. Simonetti, "Lettera e allegoria nell' esegesi veterotestamentario di Didimo," *Vetera Christianorum* (1983) 20: 346, remarks on "la scarsezza di riferimenti agli altri traduttori del testo ebraico, oltre i LXX, un carattere comune a tutti i commentari didimiani e che li differenzia in modo nettissimo dall'usus di Origene ed Eusebio."

26. Cf. Fernández Marcos, *The Septuagint in Context*, 245: "In the book of Zechariah, Didymus seems to be one of the most faithful witnesses of the Alexandrian group."

27. Jerome, *Praef. in Paral.* (PL 28.1324–25), speaks of three forms of the LXX current in his time, namely, those of Alexandria, Constantinople-Antioch, and "the provinces in-between." While P. Kahle, *The Cairo Genizah*, 2d ed. (Oxford: Blackwell, 1959), 236, would restrict the term Septuagint to the translation made in Alexandria in the second century B.C.E. (the *Letter of Aristeas* speaking in legendary mode of such a translation of the Torah in the third century), others like Fernández Marcos, *The Septuagint in Context*, 57, believe that "in the case of the LXX a process like that of the Aramaic Targums did not occur," though allowing that the LXX is "a collection of translations" (xi, 22).

3. Didymus's approach to Scripture

Readers of the *Commentary* were certainly provided with a rich scriptural fare in the course of a reading of this one prophet. As will be observed in regard to Didymus's hermeneutical procedure, the ready movement by the commentator from the Zechariah verse to a whole series of (in his view) related texts brings to mind in reference to scriptural fare the word "smorgasbord," such being the wide variety (and, to an Antiochene, arbitrary selection) of the material. The Psalms, Isaiah, and Paul, on which he had written commentaries, together with the Song of Songs figure very frequently, the historical books (not grist to his allegorical mill, clearly) hardly at all; when he comes to the word "curse" in his version of 14.11 and is in some haste to complete this huge work, he simply comments, "For the latter sense of the word *curse* many texts can be assembled from the historical books of Scripture, which a scholar will find for himself." What does fall within his day-to-day canon, however, are deuterocanonical books of the Old Testament, like Tobit, Judith, and the additions to Daniel, and early Christian writings like the Shepherd of Hermas, the Epistle of Barnabas, and the Acts of John;[28] Jerome will boggle at the latter group in quoting the works. Unhindered by blindness, Didymus has remarkable ability to recall or access in some other ways the sacred text. It is probably not his disability, however, which gives him license occasionally to manipulate the wording and sense of texts in favor of his line of argument—a tactic not confined to him, of course; editor Doutreleau sees such citation "alteré à souhait."

Didymus, who though obviously an eminent spiritual direc-

---

28. Cf. B. D. Ehrman, "The New Testament Canon of Didymus the Blind," *VC* 37 (1983): 14, who takes account of the Zechariah occurrences and concludes that "Didymus's New Testament canon extended at least to the inclusion of the Shepherd and Barnabas." In the case of Origen's similar flexibility R. M. Grant, *The Formation of the New Testament* (London: Hutchinson University Library, 1965), 171–73, suggests that while he lived at Alexandria he accepted the more comprehensive tradition of the church there and acknowledged Barnabas and the Shepherd, but that after he moved to Caesarea and found that these books were not accepted there, he manifested greater reserve towards them.

tor is never the preacher, is nonetheless not insensitive to a passage like Zec 7.9–10 encapsulating OT morality, which a modern counterpart, Ralph L. Smith, declares "one of the finest summaries of the teaching of the former prophets" with "a strong emphasis on social justice," comparing it with Hos 4.1, Am 5.24, and Mi 6.8.[29] Didymus warms to the prophet's theme as though personally aware of miscarriages of justice, whereas the Antiochenes move briskly on. In no doubt of the charism of inspiration, and having already at the beginning of the work referred to the prophet as "divinely possessed," θεοληπτούμενος (an Aristotelian term),[30] he is further encouraged at the beginning of the second stage of this twofold work in 9.1 to make the connection between the term in his text, λῆμμα, "oracle," with λαμβάνω and speak of divine possession, θεοφορία, as the model of biblical inspiration illustrated here. Theodore, in meeting the term λῆμμα first in Na 1.1, likewise accepted that analogue of inspiration; Theodoret was less willing, Antioch being unhappy with a notion suggesting the behavior of a pagan μάντις, preferring to highlight the human contribution of the biblical author.[31] Consequently, for Didymus Moses is "the great revealer," not the lawgiver as in Antioch's principal understanding of him. The Alexandrian and the Antiochene commentators alike, however, labor under the considerable handicap in interpreting Deutero-Zechariah of having no grasp of the genre of apocalyptic. When Didymus comes to the opening verses of Chapter 12, with their sweeping scenario and the doxology of the Lord as cosmic creator,[32] he is at a loss; and likewise with the "full-blown apocalyptic"[33] of Chapter 14.

29. Ralph L. Smith, *Micah to Malachi*, Word Biblical Commentary 32 (Waco, TX: Word Books, 1984), 225.

30. Cf. *Ethica Eudemia* 1214a23. It is not a term taken account of by J. H. Tigcheler, *Didyme l'Aveugle* (Nijmegen: Dekker & van de Vegt, 1977), 168–71, in his consideration of Didymus's commitment to biblical inspiration as a theological principle underlying his exegesis.

31. Cf. R. C. Hill, "Psalm 45: A *locus classicus* for Patristic Thinking on Biblical Inspiration," *StudP* 25 (1993): 95–100.

32. These verses cause Smith to gasp, "This is Armageddon, the last great battle of earth"; *Micah to Malachi*, 275.

33. P. D. Hanson, *The Dawn of Apocalyptic* (Philadelphia: Fortress, 1975), 369.

4. Style of commentary

By the time he acceded to Jerome's request, Didymus had already composed a commentary on Isaiah, and would proceed to provide his visitor from Rome with another "three books on Hosea,"[34] which the Zechariah work shows he knew well, along with Jeremiah. No stranger to biblical prophecy, he was prepared to tackle Zechariah, even if this book ranked as *obscurissimus . . . et inter duodecim longissimus,* as Jerome observed.[35] Didymus wastes no time coming to grips with the material, sparing just a few words on introduction and the briefest of conventional appeals for prayers for his success. The reader is not offered an opening outline of the structure, character, and purpose of the prophetic book, as modern readers would expect to be given; the commentator himself is unaware of its composition as two works, which has been acknowledged by modern scholars since Joseph Mede in 1653, or of any other editorial work in assembling the present text. If he was familiar with the commentaries on Zechariah by Origen and Hippolytus, he does not acknowledge them, nodding in the direction of predecessors only five times, twice in connection with subsidiary texts (Ezekiel and Hosea),[36] which as ever threaten to reduce the lemma to a subtext. This threat, we shall see, develops from his hermeneutical procedure of interpretation-by-association; when he comes to comment on 8.13–15, he moves to Gn 18.21, and from there to a concatenation of texts, from 2 Timothy to Numbers to Galatians to Matthew to Acts to Daniel 13 to Amos to Luke to 2 Corinthians to John to Ecclesiastes to 1 Samuel, before apologizing for straying, not from the Zechariah text, but from the Genesis subtext that has become the text, with Zechariah left behind.

---

34. CCL 76A.748.
35. CCL 76A.747–48.
36. See commentary on Zec 11.1–2 and 14.13–14 for previous exegetes of subsidiary texts. For his two references to a predecessor in interpreting Zechariah, whom Doutreleau identifies as Athanasius, see commentary on Zec 4.1–3, 11–14, and nn. 10 and 37 on these sections. See also his comment on the four craftsmen in Zec 1.20.

We consider that it is not without benefit to have digressed from the prophetic text in hand: it has been done for the sake of clarifying that obscure text, "I shall go down and see if their actions match the cry reaching [me]; if not, I shall know." There was need, you see, to determine in what sense the statement was made by God, "I shall know."

The reader must often have been bewildered by this lavish provision of a scriptural background to the thought of Zechariah by a commentator without visual resources but with the remarkable gift of having a mind like a concordance. Cyril will not emulate him in this kaleidoscopic exercise; and the Antiochenes prefer to keep in focus Zechariah and the situation of the exiles.[37]

Was this what Palladius had in mind in complimenting Didymus for "commenting on the Old Testament and New Testament κατὰ λέξιν"?[38] No: the compliment probably refers to his moving systematically through the text, engaging with details in it, and even (through a lack of recognition of its apocalyptic character) seeking a clue to the historical situation of the exiles or the restored community, or both.[39] He will generally, if not consistently, devote a few lines to any reference in a verse to the historical situation before moving to another level, and can show a precision that is often found also in the Antiochene commentators; he refuses to shirk the difficulty posed by the obscure term in 11.16 for "ankles/knuckles/hooves" when he might have taken the soft option of a spiritual interpretation, and the "unclean spirit" in 13.2 is also investigated at length.

This interest in history, of course, is predictably less sustained than Cyril's and the Antiochenes', especially Theodore's; and Didymus does not show Theodoret's willingness to elucidate his text by clarifying references that would be unclear to a reader. At the opening of Deutero-Zechariah at 9.1

37. The willingness of Didymus to conduct such an exercise, in the view of Tigcheler, *Didyme l'Aveugle*, 163, comes from his belief that "la Bible entière est alors, pour lui, le contexte synchronique de ce mot ou de cette phrase et peut donc contribuer à la découverte de leur signification profonde."

38. *The Lausiac History of Palladius* 2.20.

39. On the other hand, according to A. Kerrigan, *St Cyril of Alexandria*, 55, n. 2, for the Greek rhetoricians "the term λέξις connoted language unadorned with literary graces."

the author gives a sequence of cities in Syria first and then in Phoenicia, in which a modern commentator like Petersen will see a clue to the author's theme: "Yahweh's purview is international";[40] it is a sense Cyril detects, if not trying as hard as Theodoret to identify the cities, whereas Didymus moves quickly to an eschatological interpretation, finding value in popular etymology rather than topographical precision. Where the Antiochenes, though drilled in the principles of pagan rhetoricians,[41] cannot match Didymus is in his familiarity with the philosophical terms and categories of the Stoics (which he uses to unpack the notion of the flying scythe in Chapter 5), Epicureans, and Pythagoreans, which he frequently invokes; and we have seen his indebtedness to Aristotle in regard to divine inspiration of biblical authors.[42]

5. Didymus as interpreter of Zechariah

Generally, then, today's reader of this commentary would not be inclined to apply Palladius's phrase κατὰ λέξιν to the way Didymus explains this obscure prophet. Though he is not loath to see an obvious historical reference in particular verses, as we have noted, he certainly does not regard the prophetic book as primarily a commentary on the fate of the exiles and the restored community, as Theodore will when he writes with Didymus open before him. Didymus can be unwilling to deal with or even concede such historical reference;[43] when the

---

40. D. L. Petersen, *Zechariah 9–14 and Malachi*, OTL (London: SCM, 1995), 46.

41. Cf. C. Schäublin, *Untersuchungen zu Methode und Herkunft der antiochenischen Exegese*, Theophaneia: Beiträge zur Religions- und Kirchengeschichte des Altertums 23 (Cologne and Bonn: Peter Hanstein, 1974), 158–70, who sees figures like Aristarchus as most influential in the rhetorical education of Theodore, for example.

42. D. S. Wallace-Hadrill, *Christian Antioch. A Study of Early Christian Thought in the East* (Cambridge: Cambridge University Press, 1982), 102–3, claims that Alexandria, putatively indebted especially to Plato through Philo, contributed more to the study of Aristotle than did Antioch.

43. Simonetti, "Lettera e allegoria," 388, sees such concession as rare and deliberate by Didymus, who is "in cuor suo un allegorista," at a time when there was a reaction "contro l'esegesi allegorizzante di tradizione alessandrina in nome di un apprezzamento più letteralista del testo sacro" (342).

prophet has a vision of the high priest Joshua dressed in filthy clothes in 3.3, the commentator reluctantly concedes the possibility of a literal sense before moving at once to a spiritual and Christological interpretation:

It is possible to take at face value [πρὸς ῥητόν] the text quoted about Joshua the high priest, who in figure points to the reality, the faithful high priest who has a lasting priesthood. Since the holy ones are full of love, you see, they have compassion for those suffering misfortune, in their compassion "weeping with those who weep" [Rom 12.15]. Hence, with Israel still suffering its fall into captivity, the priest entrusted with its care, and feeling grief and compassion, is *dressed in filthy clothes*, which the angel at his side bids be taken from him. Now, the filthy clothes are the actions performed unlawfully: after saying, *Take the filthy clothes off him*, he went on accordingly, *See, I have taken away your iniquities*. With the removal of his sins, represented by the filthy clothes, he puts on the long tunic, which is a priestly robe.

Cyril is less reluctant to acknowledge a literal sense here: "The account of the vision, if reported metaphorically, still has a factual basis [ἱστορικός]."[44] Didymus, on the other hand, can even show some impatience with those who would give a literal sense to a text, pointing out its inaccuracy or inappropriateness. When later in that same chapter the promise is made that the exiles will return and enjoy vines and fig trees (3.10), he insists that a spiritual interpretation applies: "The factual basis is not beyond dispute: many people plant a physical fig tree without harvesting or eating its fruit, either prevented by death or being located far from the tree they planted. It is only those who planted a spiritual tree that eat its fruit. As mentioned, on the other hand, the *fig tree* refers to the active life that is productive of good, and the *vine* is to be understood properly as a branch of the true vine." Origen had similarly lectured on the "impossibility" of recognizing a literal sense in some passages of Scripture.[45] A bias is clearly operating, as an opposite bias is

44. PG 72.44. Tigcheler throughout his work *Didyme l'Aveugle* maintains that Didymus distinguishes between a literal sense ("du texte en tant que tel": πρὸς ῥητόν) of a lemma and a factual or historical sense (καθ' ἱστορίαν).

45. See Origen's *On First Principles* 4.3.5: "All of divine Scripture has a spiritual meaning, but not all a corporeal meaning; for the corporeal meaning is of-

found in Theodore, only Cyril and Theodoret deserving the latter's sobriquet "modéré."[46]

One could gain the impression from Didymus's hermeneutic of a lack of a consistent set of principles that could be formulated for a reader, indebted though he was implicitly to his hermeneutical mentor, Origen.[47] In general his hermeneutical procedure is to move quickly from literal/historical comment on a verse to a spiritual level (which may include Christological and—rarely—sacramental reference) by a process of discernment, θεωρία, with the further admission that other interpretations are "possible." His interpretation of the vision of the golden lampstand and olive trees in 4.2–3 provides an instructive example of this procedure:

In saying the lampstand was all of gold, he indicates that the lampstand completely covered in lights is in the mind, immaterial. We do not find everywhere in Scripture that spiritual things are suggested by gold; so perhaps the lampstand in the mind is the spiritual house and temple of God, as is said in the book of Revelation by John, where the one showing the revelation to the neophyte says, "The seven lampstands that you saw with the eye of your mind are the seven churches" [Rv 1.20]. On the completely golden lampstand there is a lamp, the luminous doctrine of the Trinity; from this lamp the wise virgins lit their lamps when in torchlight procession to meet their divine bridegroom [Mt 25.7]. . . .

Since in our way of discernment [θεωρία] of the lampstand, it is not material but spiritual, take note as to whether it is what Moses saw on

ten proved to be an impossibility." R. P. C. Hanson, *Allegory and Event. A Study of the Sources and Significance of Origen's Interpretation of Scripture* (London: SCM, 1959), 241, discounts the efforts of H. de Lubac to defend Origen in the cases where he asserts the impossibility of a literal sense. Of Origen's threefold system of interpretation Hanson says (236), "The result, though it may be methodologically impressive, is to remove the reader one stage further from the original meaning of Scripture."

46. G. Bardy, "Interprétation chez les pères," DBS 4:582.

47. See Doutreleau, SC 83.40–41: "Au terme de cette enquête sur les commentaires orientaux de Zacharie, il nous apparaît que Didyme a surtout été influencé par Origène." Cf. Simonetti, "Lettera e allegoria," 350: "In complesso ZaT ci si presenta come il tipico commentario scritturistico di gusto alessandrino, più specificamente origeniano." To the influence on Didymus of Philo and Origen, that of Clement would be added by É. Lamirande, "Le masculin et le féminin dans la tradition Alexandrine. Le commentaire de Didyme l'Aveugle sur la Genèse," *Science et Esprit* 41 (1989): 164.

the mountain in the type shown him, which is nothing else than what is called the ideal form; in keeping with the invisible and spiritual lampstand, the material one was fashioned according to the design of the revealer Moses [cf. Nm 8.1–4]. It is not inappropriate to add to what was seen also what was said in the Gospel by Jesus, "No one lights a lamp and conceals it under a vessel or a bed instead of putting it on a lampstand for everyone in the house to see the light" [Lk 8.16]. It is possible in this to understand the house as the Church of the living God, which is his house. . . .

It is also possible to speak of the lampstand as the active life, for on it is placed the enlightened mind of the one who sheds the light of knowledge on himself. Let the person who is interested in the present clarification of the inspired text in hand judge whether it should be accepted or another looked for from experienced people, this being the way to gain a precise understanding.[48]

There appear to be no hard-and-fast principles at work here for interpreting the vision—hence the Antiochenes' mentor Diodore's outlawing such use of θεωρία to undermine a text's literal sense.[49] Presuming that the lampstand is to be taken spiritually, Didymus begins flicking through his mental concordance to find similar lampstands, like those in Revelation, Numbers, and the Matthean and Lukan parables of the wise virgins and house lamps, all of which yield an array of meanings for the lampstands and lamps such as the temple of God, "the luminous doctrine of the Trinity," Philo's "ideal form," the Church of the living God, the active life. None "is inappropriate," all are "possible"; "perhaps" they can be nominated if one "take[s] note as to whether" they apply.[50] A modern reader might cavil

48. SC 83.336–44.

49. See the preface to Diodore's *Commentary on the Psalms* (CCG 6.7): "One thing alone is to be guarded against, however, never to let the discernment process (θεωρία) be seen as an overthrow of the underlying sense, since this would no longer be discernment but allegory: what is arrived at in defiance of the content is not discernment but allegory." P. Ternant, "La Θεωρία d'Antioche dans le cadre de sens de l'Écriture," *Bib* 34 (1953): 137, sees Diodore as misrepresenting the position of Alexandria: "Par θεωρία Antioche entendait signifier sa propre position, et par ἀλληγορία celle de l'adversaire." On the other hand, Ternant believes de Lubac is in error in denying that the Alexandrian use of allegory can exclude the literal sense.

50. Tigcheler, *Didyme l'Aveugle*, 166, believes such a procedure is justified by Didymus's theological conviction of the underlying unity of the whole Bible.

about the verse from Revelation being "alteré à souhait," in Doutreleau's words, and the instruction to Moses in Nm 8 being given on the mountain instead of in the tent of meeting.

In fact, in this apparent lack of a methodological approach to interpretation of a biblical text, Didymus is following the guidance of Origen in the pattern he developed for finding a number of senses in Scripture, beginning with the factual; the further senses could be styled moral and (in relation to Christ and the Church) mystical, or mystical and (in relation to the soul as spouse of the Word) spiritual.[51] Not that Origen had at any one place laid out these two different variations of the threefold pattern; nor is the observation of lack of methodology inapplicable: "La méthodologie est une invention moderne."[52] But he did see a pattern of different meanings in Scripture, and in commentary on Zechariah Didymus is only following him.

What an interpreter from another school, like Diodore in Antioch, found particularly unacceptable in this hermeneutical process is its gratuity and arbitrariness (as Eustathius had earlier faulted Origen for attending to ὀνόματα rather than πράγματα[53]); the readers are finally left to select from the smorgasbord of meanings for themselves or look for guidance "from experienced people"—like Didymus himself.[54] Admittedly, the claim has been made that Antiochene biblical interpretation

51. The exposition of Origen's teaching on "le triple sens de l'Écriture," and the "deux façons" is that of H. de Lubac, *Histoire et Esprit: L'intelligence de l'Écriture d'après Origène*, Théologie 16 (Paris: Aubier, 1950), 139–43; cf. R. J. Daly's foreword in translating H. U. von Balthasar's *Origen. Spirit and Fire: A Thematic Anthology of His Writings* (Washington, DC: The Catholic University of America Press, 1984), xvi.

52. J. Brisson, *Traité des Mystères*, 14, cited by de Lubac, *Histoire et Esprit*, 141. J. Daniélou, "Les divers sens de l'Écriture dans la tradition chrétienne primitive," *ETL* 24 (1948), 126, on the contrary, finds it impossible to unify Origen's different senses, his mistake being in attempting to fit the senses of Scripture to categories derived from Hellenic thought and not suited to them.

53. In opening his attack on Origen's homily on the Witch of Endor (1 Sm 28); cf. E. Klostermann, *Origenes, Eustathius von Antiochien, und Gregor von Nyssa über die Hexe von Endor*, KlT 8.16.

54. Daly, op. cit. (see n. 51 above), xvi–xvii, concedes that Origen's hermeneutical schema is open to criticism on the score of arbitrariness and irrelevance. R. P. C. Hanson, *Allegory and Event*, 257, is less tentative: "It seems to me

has been "too naïvely heroicized" by comparison with Alexandrian,[55] and that naïveté should yield to close analysis of texts.
In this text one looks in vain for an exposition of well-rehearsed
principles,[56] such as those de Lubac extrapolates from Origen's
works, and those of a different nature that Diodore had enunciated in the introduction to his Psalms commentary, where he
branded as "self-opinionated"[57] those hermeneuts who adopted
an intertextual approach of interpretation-by-association such
as Origen and Didymus practiced. For Diodore, as we have
seen, only that θεωρία was acceptable which moved from the literal sense of a passage to "an elevated sense" based on it; for
Theodore, any spiritual sense that distorted ἱστορία was self-de-
feating.[58] These Antiochenes would also have repudiated the recourse by Didymus to a numbers symbolism derived from the
Pythagoreans and Philo as a hermeneutical tool;[59] when the

---

that the account of Origen's threefold system of dividing allegory into literal,
'spiritual' and 'moral' given in these pages should persuade anybody that his
method was ultimately self-frustrating. In an effort to distinguish objectively between three different senses of Scripture he only succeeded in reaching a position where all distinctions were dissolved in a 'spiritual' sense which was in fact
governed by nothing but Origen's arbitrary fancy as to what doctrine any given
text ought to contain." Theodore had said as much long before. Of Didymus's
approach Tigcheler concedes, *Didyme l'Aveugle*, 165, "Le danger d'arbitraire et
d'interprétation subjective est considérable."

55. R. E. Brown, "Hermeneutics," *NJBC*, 1154. By others, of course, Antiochene exegesis was dismissed for association with theological views thought heterodox.

56. Cf. Simonetti, "Lettera e allegoria," 347: "Manca in ZaT, come del resto
anche negli altri commentari, una presa di posizione teorica, sulla *ratio* da
seguire nell'interpretazione della Sacra Scrittura." Tigcheler, *Didyme l'Aveugle*,
152, studies "quelques présuppositions herméneutiques que Didyme n'a jamais
formulées théoriquement."

57. *Diodori Tarsensis Commentarii in Psalmos* I, *Commentarii in Psalmos I–L*, 7,
CCG 6.7.

58. Cf. Theodore on Gal 4.24 (according to the fifth-century Latin version
edited by H. B. Swete, *Theodori Episcopi Mopsuesteni in epistolas B. Pauli Commentarii* I [Cambridge: Cambridge University Press, 1880], 74–75): "When they
turn to expounding divine Scripture 'spiritually'—spiritual interpretation is the
name they would like their folly to be given—they claim Adam is not Adam, paradise is not paradise, the serpent is not the serpent. To these people I should say
that if they distort *historia*, they will have no *historia* left." Cf. R. P. C. Hanson's
sentiments quoted in n. 54 above.

59. Simonetti, "Lettera e allegoria," 348, refers to Didymus's "simpatia tutta
particolare per le simbologie numeriche, a volte complicatissime."

opening vision of the man on the red horse occurs, in the reading of his text of 1.7, "on the twenty-fourth day of the twelfth month," the reader is given a lecture on these significant numbers, a lecture that rests on the false reading "twelfth" ("eleventh" in other forms of the LXX and the Hebrew) and that contributes little to explication of the vision (a judgment with which Cyril evidently concurred). And though they did not know enough Hebrew to question them, the Antiochenes would have found excessive the weight put upon etymologies (often false) as another hermeneutical device; Diodore insists that "we far prefer τὸ ἱστορικόν to τὸ ἀλληγορικόν."[60] And Jerome, though much indebted to Didymus throughout, rejects his etymology of Benjamin in 14.10 as "son of days" when Gn 35.18 already offered "son of the right."[61]

Allegory, predictably, is employed frequently by this commentator bent on finding at all points a spiritual meaning in the text ("We must also read the text spiritually" is his frequent directive); we saw Jerome in introducing his own work criticizing his mentor's for being totally allegorical,[62] scarcely at all touching on factuality—a shortcoming Jerome claimed to have avoided. Their modern counterpart Petersen warns about the opening to Chapter 11, "It would be improper to treat the poem as an allegory,"[63] whereas Didymus asserts that an allegorical approach is sanctioned by Jesus, and proceeds to support the claim by quoting at great length one of Ezekiel's celebrated allegories at 31.3–9 and other parts of the Bible. In his development of the text's spiritual meaning Didymus will also have recourse to what he refers to as ἀναγωγή, not always clearly distinguished from allegory. Doutreleau admits that the terminology in regard to spiritual meaning employed by Didymus and by the whole Alexandrian school is "si peu précise," and that in the use of these two terms in particular "on confondit l'une et

60. From a fragment of Diodore's work on the Octateuch; cf. Schäublin, "Diodor von Tarsus," *TRE* 8.765.

61. CCL 76A.887.

62. See n. 18 above. Cf. Simonetti, "Lettera e allegoria," 343, in reference to the *Commentary on Zechariah:* "L'interpretazione di Didimo è soltanto allegorica."

63. *Zechariah 9–14 and Malachi*, 81.

l'autre."[64] When 8.3 reads, "I shall go back to Sion and shall dwell in the midst of Jerusalem, and Jerusalem will be called a true city," Didymus concludes his commentary thus:

With these things explained in an initial spiritual sense [πρώτη ἀναγωγή], there is need also for an allegorical interpretation with elevated understanding of Sion's going back and Jerusalem's being called true. This is the explication arrived at in the epistle to the Hebrews by the one speaking in Christ, who writes, "You have made your approach to Mount Sion and the city of the living God, the heavenly Jerusalem . . ." [Heb 12.22].

Does Didymus believe he is making a necessary distinction here? It is one that Frances Young (on the basis of the work by Tigcheler) offers to support her claim that "Didymus assumes a *consistency* of reference," namely, "ἀλληγορία leading to the recognition of a figurative sense in the language, ἀναγωγή to the reality to which the figurative language refers."[65] Consistency of usage, however, is hardly the impression one gains from a reading of the whole *Commentary.*

6. *Theological accents of the* Commentary

For a monk in his cell, Didymus is very familiar with a litany (perhaps by then conventional) of figures and groups professing heretical trinitarian and Christological views, and ready to rehearse the list; over a dozen times he gratuitously finds a reference to them either in his lemmata or in the many loosely associated texts he adduces. When Zec 12.8 mentions "house of David," he sees a hint at "the one born of the immaculate virgin Mary," and takes issue with those entertaining false Christological opinions:

64. SC 83.61, 58. Simonetti agrees, "Lettera e allegoria," 346: "I due termini praticamente coincidono per il senso."
65. F. M. Young, *From Nicaea to Chalcedon. A Guide to the Literature and Background* (Philadelphia: Fortress Press, 1983), 87–88 (Young's emphasis). Tigcheler, *Didyme l'Aveugle,* 173, would thus allow no eschatological element to the allegorical meaning in Didymus's usage (a claim denied by Simonetti). His citation of a genuine anagogical meaning (a term's "portée") usually rests on these senses given to Jerusalem.

We should study the precision of the prophecy that reveals to us the infant's birth from Mary and the giving of the only-begotten Son from the bosom of the Father. A son was not given without a child's being born for us [Is 9.6], as is impiously supposed by the docetists, nor again was the child born of a virgin without the Father's giving the only-begotten Son, as taught by Paul of Samosata, Photinus the Galatian, and their equally impious companions Artemas and Theodotus.

And he proceeds to add Apollinaris and Marcellus of Ancyra to the list. Mention of "thirty pieces of silver" in 11.13 leads Didymus to ignore any historical reference and speak rather of worthless potsherds, beginning with the Jews and proceeding, "Are not the words worthless of those who posit two uncreated principles, a good and an evil (these people being the Manicheans)? and of those who claim the Son is a creature, and who separate the Holy Spirit from Father and Son? and the words of those who show no reverence for the Incarnation of the savior, maintaining that the savior came in appearance and not in reality?" And he goes on to include the Gnostics in this rogues' gallery.

Writing in the wake of the councils of Nicea and Constantinople, and with sympathy for Athanasius's stand against Arian subordinationism, Didymus not unpredictably takes issue with such positions by citing conciliar terminology, as in his comment on the term "Lord almighty" in 2.8–9.

It is not surprising that the almighty is from the almighty: he is also God from God and light from light, being consubstantial with the one who begot him and one with him who begot him, as the verse says, "I and the Father are one"; and so all the Father has belongs to the Son [Jn 1.3; Col 1.17; Jn 10.30; 17.10]. Now, what the Father has is being God, being light, being holy, being almighty, all of which belongs to the Son. The Son is thus almighty from the almighty, being king of all from the one who reigns over all.

It has been remarked that, along with the Cappadocians, Didymus makes the three hypostases rather than the one divine substance the starting point of his trinitarian thinking.[66] In opposi-

66. J. N. D. Kelly, *Early Christian Doctrines*, 5th ed. (New York: Harper & Row, 1978), 262.

tion to Origen's subordinationist thinking on the procession of
the Spirit,[67] he is anxious in this work to uphold the *homoousion*
of the Spirit,[68] whereas Theodore in his commentary will consistently deny any knowledge of the Holy Spirit to people of the
Old Testament.

Didymus, therefore, would not have relished the fact of his
later inclusion in a similar rogues' gallery for Origenist views, as
he appears in canon 18 of the Lateran council of 649 (in company not only with Origen and Evagrius but also with Diodore
and Theodore).[69] Unfounded though such blanket condemna-
tions may have been, it would seem that he shares some of Origen's opinions, such as the pre-existence of souls,[70] as emerges
from his comment on a phrase in 10.8: "So a spiritual interpretation must be given to the multiplication of those with the
promise of becoming *as numerous as they were:* it is not at this
point that the righteous began to be multiplied and become
numerous in the sense explained, for they were numerous even
before the present life." Doutreleau also finds a trace of Origen's condemned teaching on *apocatastasis*[71] in the comment
on v.10 of that chapter, "I shall bring them back from the land
of Egypt," which Didymus takes spiritually: "Clearly, when all receive the fullness of divinity, there is no one left who is cut off
from this unity, outside and alone; then all 'grief, pain, and
groaning will disappear,' and likewise in place of great numbers all will be combined in one single man." When the text
shows Didymus using the term "God the Word," more typical of
the Antiochenes, editor Doutreleau finds it "surprenante"[72]
and would like to amend the text—though this usage is not a
unique occurrence in the *Commentary*.

7. *The significance of the* Commentary on Zechariah

As students of patristic exegesis, we are in the fortunate position of having four complete works extant in Greek from the
fourth and fifth centuries on this "most obscure book," as also

67. Ibid., 261.
69. DS 519.
71. DS 411.

68. E.g., in his comment on Zec 4.6.
70. DS 404.
72. SC 85.808–9.

the longest, of the Twelve (minor)[73] Prophets; other works, like those of Hippolytus and Origen and possibly Chrysostom, have not survived. Though coming from the "schools" of both Alexandria and Antioch, the four clearly illustrate markedly different approaches, particularly those of Didymus and Theodore, while Cyril's and Theodoret's may be said to preserve elements of both.[74] As noted above, the four commentators labor under an inability to recognize the literary genre of apocalpytic, which so characterizes this prophet's expression in particular, the flaw seriously impairing interpretation of the work in the case of all four. The attempt of Didymus is the most comprehensive of them, the author not being committed to an overall treatment of The Twelve; he is never satisfied with a brief paraphrase of a verse or chapter, moving through the book at a slow pace and detailing the levels of meaning he sees in Zechariah's cryptic statements.

It is, in fact, for his hermeneutical approach to this challenging material that we are particularly grateful for the survival of the *Commentary*. If Theodore, in fidelity to the norms he learned from his mentor Diodore, does his best to offer us a window onto the world of Zechariah, the exiles, and the restored community (with Zerubbabel to the fore), Didymus, with equal fidelity to Origen, uses the text to provide his readers—perhaps religious men like himself—with a mirror in which they can see reference to their own lives. Though he will usually introduce comment on a passage with a brief reference to Zechariah's situation, he is principally concerned to write for the reader who looks beyond that; "the person who understands it is a seer," he claims on 3.8–9. For such a reader he will tease out the other

73. The term, unknown to Didymus, is Augustine's, who spoke of *prophetae minores* in the *De civitate Dei* 18.29 (CCL 48.619), implying nothing pejorative, only brevity: "quia sermones eorum sunt breves."

74. Kerrigan, whom we saw dating Cyril's *Commentary on the Twelve* prior to 428, and who recognizes some Antiochene features in his approach, believes he had access to the similar works of both Theodore and Theodoret (*St Cyril of Alexandria*, 250). But there seems little doubt that Theodoret only began his exegetical career in the wake of the council of Ephesus, his own *Commentary on the Twelve* following three others. To the commentaries of Didymus and Theodore, on the other hand, Cyril would have had access, and possibly Theodoret to Cyril's (as also, of course, to Theodore's).

meanings Origen had taught him to find in Scripture, through use of allegory and—more rarely—typology.[75]

With the Antiochenes and even Cyril intent on explicating for a reader the historical reference in Zechariah, an effort often frustrated by the apocalyptic character of the material, Didymus's readers probably stood to gain more from the "possible" spiritual meanings to be found. The obvious sense of the reference in 7.14 to the desolation of the land left behind by the exiles is clear but meager; Didymus finds in it more for the benefit of the reader. "As well as the factual sense, the devastated land can be taken in an allegorical sense as the good and upright heart: from bearing good crops it is transformed into bearing thorns and producing prickles and weeds. . . . It could also be expressed in this way by tropology: our body is the chosen land, containing self-control and purity, so that sober and proper habits pass that way and abide in it on account of its bearing the produce of purity and edible fruits which the trees of virtue bear."[76] At times, however, this movement from literal to a range of spiritual meanings proves arbitrary and even bewildering as the commentator follows his procedure of interpretation-by-association, where a reader would look in vain for attention to the author's σκοπός, as in Cyril, or for some clear hermeneutical principles of the kind that Antioch had formulated for itself. All in all, our thanks are due both to Jerome for prompting Didymus to turn to Zechariah, and to the soldiers who in 1941 unearthed the codex, allowing it now finally to appear in English.

75. Cf. Tigcheler, *Didyme l'Aveugle,* 183: "Pour Didyme, il n'y a là aucune différence: il appelle les deux choses ἀναγωγή et les considère toutes les deux comme importantes pour ses auditeurs."

76. Didymus could not be held guilty of the charge leveled against Alexandrian spiritual direction generally by L. Bouyer, *The Spirituality of the New Testament and the Fathers,* trans. Mary Ryan (London: Burns & Oates, 1963), 449: "A fervent piety unsatisfied by mere moralism fell by the nature of things into a deceptive 'mysticism.'"

COMMENTARY
ON ZECHARIAH

PREFACE

HE TEXT REQUIRING explication, namely, Zechariah, is the eleventh of the Twelve Prophets.[1] With the
eye of his mind enlightened, and being divinized by
the word that came to him, he had wonderful visions and proclaimed a prophetic word in many ways and under many forms.
Desirous of grasping it, let us set about clarifying him, begging
"for a message to be given in the opening of my mouth," and
thus confident of attaining what we aspire to if you endorse our
request by your prayers.[2]

---

1. Didymus is not embarking on a complete commentary on the "Book of
the Twelve."
2. Eph 6.19. Didymus with typical conciseness embarks on his work of commentary with only a conventional expression of reliance on divine help, eschewing any initial treatment of the book's structure (much debated by his modern
counterparts), character, and purpose.

COMMENTARY ON ZECHARIAH 1

N THE EIGHTH MONTH *of the second year of the reign of Darius, a word of the Lord came to Zechariah the prophet, son of Berechiah, son of Iddo, in these terms* (Zec 1.1). In the second year of the kingship of Darius, king of the Persians, in the eighth month of the second year of the ruler's reign, the word of the Lord came to the prophet Zechariah, declaring that an awful wrath had come upon the ancestors of those who were under accusation; God was angry with those under censure. The one to whom the word of God came is referred to as Zechariah, a Hebrew name that in Greek means "reminder of God"; after all, how could it be that the one with God's . . . would not prove to be a reminder of God? Berechiah, Zechariah's father, . . . Iddo.[1]

It was a tradition, which has come down to us, to mention the prophets' parents in the case where they also were servants of God. Now, the fact that the prophet in question and his parents were from the priestly tribe emerges in particular from the Gospel according to Luke also: the father of John the Baptist was called Zechariah, and his father Barachiah.[2] As a general

1. Not surprisingly, the bottom of the first page of the manuscript found at Tura is defective. After correctly tracing the etymology of the Heb. name (though unfamiliar with the language, unlike Jerome, who similarly renders it *memoria Domini*), Didymus repeats the textual statement of Zechariah's family details without detecting and pursuing the discrepancy involved: whereas the Heb. text of Zec 1.1, 7 declares Zechariah to be "son of Berechiah, son of Iddo" (as though father and grandfather), in Ezr 5.1 and 6.14 he is called only "son of Iddo." Didymus does not bother to specify the location of the prophet at the time, later assuming he is still in Babylon (in comment on 4.4–9), which is not the view of the Antiochenes or of modern commentators.

2. These details come to us from Lk 1.5 (as Didymus notes), but also from Mt 23.35 ("Zechariah son of Barachiah, whom you murdered between the sanctuary and the altar"), the latter reference apparently in error, as the prophet is not known to have been slain—unlike Zechariah son of Jehoiada in 2 Chr 24.20–22, or the Zechariah mentioned by Josephus, *Jewish Antiquities* 4.5.4.

practice, you see, later family members take the name of their forbears, especially when they are holy. In the introduction to the prophetic writings, mention is made of the ancestors of those called by God to prophesy and the time of their prophecy. Mention is made of their family for reasons also of veracity, in case confusion should occur as a result of names that sound alike or are incorrect.[3]

The word of God comes to people when they have a share in it, just as virtue and knowledge come to a man who is zealous and knowledgeable.[4] On the other hand, what the word of God communicates and declares to the one under the influence of the prophetic word will become clear from what follows. The text goes on, *The Lord Almighty says this: The wrath of the Lord against your ancestors was extreme* (vv.3, 2). Extreme wrath is directed at people guilty of extreme sins and acts of impiety. Since God as judge repays all "according to their works,"[5] you see, and according to the behavior of the one transgressing the divine laws, not everyone is threatened with the same punishment: it is commensurate with the sins and befits them. On the other hand, the threat is redolent of great kindness: had God in vengeful fashion punished those liable to suffer this fate, far from giving prior warning he would have inflicted the penalty without hesitation.

The recipient of the divine word is ordered to urge the captives to repentance in these words: *The Lord almighty says this, Turn back to me* (v.3), keeping my commandments and acknowledging my truth; this in fact is the way you will find me turning back to you. Though subject to no change or alteration,[6] you see, ever the same and invariable, I give the impression of turn-

3. Theodoret is indebted for this same observation to Didymus, who has not bypassed historical details in the text. The former will go further, as we would expect of an Antiochene, in commenting also on the reference to the year of the reign of the Persian king Darius I, that is, 520 B.C.E.

4. This accent on human effort one would expect rather in the Antiochenes.

5. Rom 2.6.

6. The term employed here for God's being proof against change will appear in its adverbial form as ἀτρέπτως in the Chalcedonian formula regarding the hypostatic union (DS 302). The symbol of Nicea in 325 had already declared anathema those who claimed the Son to be τρεπτός (DS 126).

ing from you and staying far from you when you have that experience. In other words, he is saying to all the accused, as
though addressing them individually, "Because you rejected
knowledge of me, I shall also reject you from my priestly service; you have forgotten the Law of your God, and I shall forget
your children."[7] Such an impression is gained also in the case
of some material things: though the land does not move from
its position, people who leave it by ship get the impression that
it is moving away whereas it is they who are moving away.

The one who betrays the great extent of his kindness by saying this says that he will do all this in his omnipotence. After all,
it is a mark of his compassion and extreme kindness to invite
to conversion and familiarity those who have distanced themselves from God and virtue so that they may enjoy eternal salvation by approaching him and having him near, in keeping with
the scripture, "Approach the Lord and he will approach you."[8]
Now, the withdrawals and approaches mentioned involve not
place but disposition and attitude. Return to me, and I shall to
you. Do not live evil lives like your forbears, whom the prophets
censured in the past, lest you suffer the same fate as theirs. For
what did they censure them, if not for them to turn from their
vile pursuits and evil ways? Giving no heed or attention, however, they perished along with the deceptive false prophets, with
the result that neither the impostors nor those taken in by their
chicanery would exist any longer.

Since the prophets and their victims are no more, therefore,
you for your part, to whom I offer the word of God, follow the
divine ways and take no interest in the evil ones. They are, in
fact, divine and salutary pursuits that are proposed to you by
our Spirit—that is, the Holy Spirit—by my servants the prophets, who possess it. It is they, you see, possessing the Spirit of
truth and made ready by him to declare it, who are beneficial

7. Hos 4.6. Resistance to knowledge of God and his "truth" is seen as the
capital sin of the people and their ancestors, less so moral failings, as also
(against the text) Didymus sees the ancestors deceived by false prophets.
(Doutreleau, SC 83.196, remarks on the blind commentator's acquaintance
with a visual effect, which he puts down to conventional scholastic usage.)

8. Jas 4.8.

to those who heed them.[9] Your forbears had experience of them in receiving their censure; but since they did not hear or heed them, they were judged on their actions. As the Lord proposed to do, so will it be done to them, despite God's urging them to repentance lest they meet with the fate that was threatened.

On the twenty-fourth day of the twelfth month, which is Shevat, in the second year of Darius a word of the Lord came to the prophet Zechariah, son of Berechiah son of Iddo (v.7). All God's actions and gifts have an order and harmony in keeping with mathematical proportions, since "in doing wonderful and imponderable things, he arranges everything by norm and number."[10] To be sure, the word of the prophet before us, for example, which was the result of an informed insight, is a matter of vision rather than hearing,[11] and is expressed with a numeral of great force, "twenty-fourth day of the twelfth month" in Hebrew. The number 24 has the force of 36, the latter being the sum of its parts—its half 12, its third 8, its quarter 6, its sixth 4, its eighth 3, its twelfth 2, its twenty-fourth 1. The number made from 24 by the addition of its parts is a square, six times 6. Now, of all the geometrical figures none has as much force as a square; and the present one is exceptional in that each of its sides consists of a perfect numeral, 6. Like the numeral 24, the numeral

9. Didymus attributes a role in association with the prophets to the Spirit with the encouragement of the LXX, which includes a phrase in v.6 not found in our Heb.

10. Jb 5.9; Wis 11.20. Having shown some attention earlier to the prophet's background, if not to the extent of the Antiochene commentators, Didymus now parts company with them completely by going off in the direction of numbers symbolism. The contrived scriptural basis he cites for this hermeneutic is further undermined by the second half of the Job verse, which proceeds to describe God's "wonderful things" as being "beyond number."

11. Certainly the following λόγος that came to Zechariah is rather a vision than a word, and requires ἐπιστημονική θεωρία, as Didymus claims; and both Theodore and Theodoret discuss which bodily sense is best adapted for interpreting it, admitting the need for θεωρία. But while Didymus (without LXX support, and unlike Cyril) reads—conveniently—"twelfth month" (instead of "eleventh") and goes off on the numerological tangent without identifying the date indicated, Theodoret examines the chronological clues and finds Shevat (a Babylonian name occurring only here in the OT) to be the eleventh month (our January) in the Hebrew calendar.

12 makes a square when you add up its parts: half of it is 6, a third is 4, a quarter is 3, a sixth is 2, a twelfth is 1; and all these parts added up make 16, which itself is a square, four times 4. It also has something exceptional as to its sides, the square having the force of 10: 1 + 2 + 3 + 4.

I saw by night and, lo, a man mounted upon a red horse, and he was situated between the two shady mountains, and behind him horses: red, dapple-grey, piebald, and white (v.8). When the word of the Lord came to Zechariah by night, a man appeared to him mounted upon a red horse, positioned between the two shady mountains. Now, the man mounted upon the red horse is the incarnate savior, and the red horse the body in which he is clothed, human flesh being red by nature on account of the blood circulating in it.[12] But where did the divinely possessed one see the man positioned?[13] Between what? When? Let us pause at this point.

Well, for one thing, he saw him *between the two shady mountains.* These are the two testaments, bearing fruit and providing shade with dense growth of thoughts and the generous extent of their texts concerning the divinity and Incarnation. And since each of the pronouncements in the two testaments is characterized by deep obscurity along with riddles and profundity, it was by night that he saw the man mounted upon the horse, in the manner similar to what is said of him, "He set darkness as his concealment," a verse in which there is reference to the "concealment" arising from obscurity, as is the case also in the verse, "The depths his covering like a garment."[14]

12. Again the basis for the identification of the rider as Christ is flimsy, though Jerome and many commentators after him accepted it—unlike Theodore, who rudely rejected it. It is not even worth considering, in Theodoret's view. Antioch would require further scriptural support for arriving at such an identification.

13. Didymus's term for the inspired author, θεοληπτούμενος (which he may have taken from Aristotle; see Introduction), which perhaps prompts Theodore's development of the term λῆμμα (from λαμβάνω) for "oracle" occurring in Nahum, Habakkuk, and Zechariah 9, accentuates possession rather than Antioch's model of "a shipwright building a ship" (Chrysostom). See my article, "Psalm 45: A *locus classicus* for Patristic Thinking on Biblical Inspiration," *StudP* 25.

14. The arbitrariness of interpretation of the set text and citation of other

As well as the vision of the man mounted upon the red horse, the subject of our commentary, he perceived also in a manner conveying true doctrine of God the horses coming behind him. Those following him come behind him; Moses, for example, the great revealer, being unable at the time to have a clear vision of his face, was allowed to see "his back," that is, what came after him, which was nothing other than God's creation. When what came after God was shown him, which, to be sure, is referred to as "his back," he wrote Genesis, which begins with the verse, "In the beginning God made heaven and earth."[15]

Now, the text mentions the difference in color of the horses behind the one who appeared, especially since some of them were human beings while others were "divine spirits sent to serve for the sake of those who are to inherit salvation."[16] That is to say, all who have transmitted the human actions of the Word, who stayed with us and was made flesh, are red for the particular reason that the one they follow wears "the scarlet of garments from Bozrah," making those seeing him say to him, "Why are your garments crimson?" (by "garments" meaning the flesh clothing him and the blood flowing in it). This has been fully clarified in the commentary on the prophet Isaiah.[17] After the red horses behind the celebrated one, horses that were piebald, dapple-grey, and white were seen. Perhaps the piebald and dapple-grey ones are the people who in many ways

---

texts (here Pss 18.11; 104.6 [modern numbering]), without reference to their original context, predictably earns the scorn of Antioch, despite its similar admission of the obscurity of the OT in particular. On the other hand, an openness to allegory leaves Alexandrian commentators at less of a loss before apocalyptic with its visionary material than is true of Theodore and Theodoret, who must ever be looking for a factual basis (ἱστορία).

15. Cf. Ex 33.23; Gn 1.1, Genesis being referred to as κοσμοποιΐα (Theodore speaking also of κτίσις). For Didymus, Moses is pre-eminently the great revealer (ἱεροφάντης), this Exodus verse being repeated in commentary on 2.8, whereas for Antioch he is predictably the lawgiver.

16. Heb 1.14.

17. Is 63.1–2. Jerome refers to a commentary by Didymus on Second and Third Isaiah. Theodoret in his *Commentary on Isaiah*, looking for further support for seeing in these Isaian verses a reference to Jesus, makes the mistake of relating Bozrah to Heb. *basar;* Didymus needs no such support.

are involved in teaching on material and spiritual things, which the divine words say are "visible and invisible,"[18] the white horses being people announcing the true doctrines of God apart from any matter. It should be mentioned that in another sense the piebald and dapple-grey ones are those who in their teaching adapt themselves to the varied nature of those under instruction. Was not Paul a piebald horse, attentive as he was to Christ speaking in him, when he became a Jew to the Jews so as to win them over, but like a man without the Law to those without the Law so as to draw them away from the morals of those without the Law, and like a man under the Law to those under the Law so as to win them over as well, persuading them to go beyond "the law of the shadow"?[19] At any rate, after saying this he goes on, "I became all things to all people so as to save everyone."[20]

It is not only those after his stay with us, however, but also those before it who had this piebald color, sharing in "God's wisdom in its rich variety."[21] Suffice it to mention two of them, lest the treatment become lengthy; one can call to mind others as well. Isaiah, who received divine visions from God, exercised at the same time the various styles of beneficial discourse: in one case, as prophet and visionary of the future with a prophetic eye, he said, "Lo, the virgin will conceive and bear a son"; in another, as lawgiver, he gave orders and pronouncements in the words, "Cease your wickedness, learn to do good." He also wrote an account of Sennacherib, king of the Assyrians, and Hezekiah, ruler of the Hebrews. In addition to this he also adopted the style of a singer in saying, in one case, "Let me sing for my beloved a love song about my vineyard," in another, "On that day they will sing this new song: Lo, a fortified city and our

18. Col 1.16. There seems no norm in this style of interpretation: the interpreter chooses any referent that appeals to him.

19. Cf. Heb 10.1.

20. 1 Cor 9.20–22 (Paul speaking of "saving some" in most manuscripts). The notion of Paul as a piebald horse, if ingenious, seems fanciful and equally gratuitous.

21. Eph 3.10. Didymus speaks of the Incarnation as ἐπιδημία as well as ἐνανθρώπησις (but never οἰκονομία, Doutreleau tells us, SC 83.77). His following remark shows that he flatters his readers with some familiarity with the Bible.

COMMENTARY ON ZECHARIAH 1   35

salvation."[22] David likewise spoke as a musician, "O God, let us sing to you a new song"; as a lawgiver, "Turn away from evil and do good"; as a prophet of the future he cried aloud, "The God of gods will appear on Sion."[23] Nor did he neglect the historical account, recounting in many psalms much of what was visibly done for the Israelites against both the Egyptians and Pharaoh.

Now, as to what the spiritual horses behind the man mounted upon the red horse achieved, let us see in the following verses of the prophet before us. *I asked, What are they, Lord? The angel who was speaking in me said to me, I shall show you what they are* (v.9). The prophet himself asks the angel speaking in him a question, *What are they, Lord?* Now, "the angel speaking in him" is either the angel in charge of prophecy or, in another interpretation, the savior himself, of whom the prophet says, "His name is angel of great counsel."[24] The teacher speaks in the listener when he has some share in him or he is in him by disposition. A text illustrating the former is this: "Christ lives in me," and again, "Christ speaking in me"; in the same sense also the psalmist said, "I shall hear what the Lord God will say in me," and Habakkuk, "I shall be on the alert to see what the Lord will say in me." Illustrating the latter is this: "Priests, speak to the heart of Jerusalem,"[25] not every teacher speaking to the heart of the listeners—only the one who brings the mind of the learners into line with the sense and level of the lessons. There are, in fact, teachers who have the effect of only making the ears buzz, with no benefit to the learners' understanding, whereas the one who speaks *in* someone also speaks *to* them,

22. Is 7.14; 1.16–17; 5.1; 26.1 LXX. If the nomination of Isaiah as a piebald horse is also gratuitous, Didymus at least shows an ability to distinguish the range of literary forms to be found in First Isaiah (even if we have no guarantee that he commented on Isaiah of Jerusalem; but see n. 25 on chapter 7).

23. Pss 143.9; 34.14; 84.7 (to which Theodoret in his Psalms commentary also gives an eschatological sense). Didymus proceeds to admit that many of the psalms can be taken historically. The numbering of the Psalms throughout this translation conforms to the Hebrew and modern systems.

24. Is 9.6. Didymus has no trouble allowing an interpretation of the angel as Christ despite having taken that view of the rider of the red horse. He insists on taking the LXX phrase "speaking in (ἐν) me" literally, and proceeds to see what is its force.

25. Gal 2.20; 2 Cor 13.3; Ps 85.8; Hab 2.1; Is 40.2 LXX.

while everyone who deafens the eardrums does not speak in the heart.

The man positioned between the mountains replied, saying to me, They are those whom the Lord sent to roam the earth (v.10). Since the prophet had seen the red, piebald, dappled-grey, and white horses coming, you would doubtless ask why on earth the angel who was speaking in him promises to show him what has been seen. Perhaps, then, since there are two ways of looking at the same things, elementary and more advanced, the divine teacher promises the more perfect to the one acquainted with the elementary, for the recipient of revelation enjoys perfect love. The man positioned between the above-mentioned two mountains replied, *They are those whom the Lord sent to roam the earth.* In terms of the second way of seeing, the two shady mountains represent the people of the Hebrews and the people of the nations,[26] between which is positioned the man already commented on, who introduces the prophet to the identity of those sent to roam the earth. They are the best teachers from human beings and angels, as has just been said. Not without purpose is the further remark, that it was by the Lord that they were sent to roam the earth: not all those who profess to teach or who roam about are sent by the Lord. The devil, for one, is "roaming the earth," as he himself said, to test Job and the other athletes of God,[27] and does so not by God's commission, but by his own malicious choice. Now, what those sent claim to have seen in their roaming is the fact that *all the earth is inhabited and is at peace*, as appears in the following verse.

They replied to the angel of the Lord positioned between the mountains, saying, We roamed all the earth, and lo, all the earth is inhabited and is at peace (vv.8–11). Since not every angel is the Lord's, those who abandoned the heavenly habitation being no longer his,[28] consequently the reply to the angel of the Lord by those

26. As Didymus allows Christ to be represented by both the rider and the commenting angel, so the "two mountains" (appearing in the LXX for Heb. "myrtles") can be both the two testaments and also Jews and Gentiles—allegory at two levels.

27. Cf. Jb 1.7, where the LXX had already transformed the loyal-opposition figure Satan into a malicious demon, διάβολος.

28. Cf. Jude 6; Gn 6.3.

roaming was that *all the earth is inhabited and is at peace.* The fact that the apostates are not styled the Lord's, even if called simply angels, still emerges clearly from the Scriptures, where in one case it says, "God did not spare the angels who sinned," where it does not say, note, that they are his, and in another case it is said by the apostle speaking in Christ, "We shall judge angels."[29]

There is need to discern the meaning of the statement that *all the earth is inhabited and is at peace.* Since the rational soul of itself has the power of independent and constant movement, it is at peace and unaffected by any disorderly turmoil when it moves properly and in a blessed manner, and it is from reverence for the divine that it attains this stability. Scripture says, remember, "Earth feared and was at peace when God arose to judgment," and, "The person who dwells in hope is free of every problem," according to the inspired text of Proverbs.[30] In keeping with this interpretation, God said to the vengeful Cain for being moved unjustifiably, "You have sinned; be at peace," as if to say not only, By sinning you act in disorderly and riotous fashion, but to say also, put an end to the disorderly behavior; then commendably you will be at peace "by turning from evil and doing good."[31] *Dwelling* follows upon being at peace in this way. Because this is so, the loose woman appearing in Proverbs, whoever she is, "does not keep her feet at rest in her own home," keeping them on the move outdoors, vulgar and restless as she is, whereas the refined woman of good stock dwells at home, discharging her wifely duties to her spouse, an immediate consequence of which is having a family. It is said in the Psalms, remember, in regard to the spouse who is God the Word, "He gives the barren woman a home, so that she becomes a mother rejoicing in children born in wedlock."[32]

29. 2 Pt 2.4; 1 Cor 6.3.

30. Ps 76.9; Prv 1.33. Didymus concedes that Proverbs is θεόπνευστος; by contrast, the Antiochenes are inclined to speak of the sages merely as σοφοί, not προφῆται (the usual term for inspired OT authors, including the Latter Prophets).

31. Gn 4.7; Ps 34.14. The LXX version of the Genesis verse is based on a text that almost perfectly adheres to the letters of our Heb. but divides words differently, leading to a range of versions.

32. Prv 7.10–12; Ps 113.9 loosely cited. For a concise commentator it has

The angel of the Lord replied in the words, Lord almighty, how long will you have no mercy on Jerusalem and the cities of Judah you have overlooked? This is the seventieth year (v.12). Having seen with foreknowledge all the earth inhabited and at peace, all the nations having come to faith in the Lord who had come to dwell there, the angel of the Lord almighty asks the sovereign king to let him know how long until both the Jerusalem of that time and the cities of Judah subject to it will be the object of mercy, as it is the seventieth year of the captivity that leads them to think they have been ignored. Since Jerusalem has often been interpreted in many ways, the cities of Judah would also be taken in each sense. If, then, Jerusalem were taken as the perfect soul that has been enlightened, surveying everything in peace and serenity ("vision of peace" being its meaning),[33] the cities of Judah are souls that are inferior because of progress yet to be made. If, on the other hand, the name Jerusalem suggests the Church, "presented to Christ in holiness," the cities of Judah should be interpreted as the souls not yet in that state. In writing to the Corinthians the apostle highlights such a difference, blessing that church along "with all those who call on the name of the Lord," Jerusalem in an allegorical sense representing the Church, and the cities of Judah those who call on the name of the Lord.[34]

According to both interpretations Jerusalem at some time has been neglected, and the cities subject to it suffer the same fate as the mother city, so that on experiencing the neglect they may bestir themselves so as no longer to suffer captivity, *this being the seventieth year.* In other words, on completion of the sabbatical year, hardship will no longer distress them. The number seventy, you see, made up of seven tens, conveys perfect rest, since the one who provides it has come "to proclaim release to captives," having sprung from Judah. It is about the savior, in

---

been a lengthy development of a single clause—and a moral one, hardly respecting the apocalyptic character of the passage.

33. Though Jerome confirms this etymology, modern scholars are less certain. Nonetheless, Didymus is familiar with a range of allegorical meanings of Jerusalem, which can then give similar significance to "the cities of Judah," finding some support in Paul.

34. Cf. Eph 5.27; 1 Cor 1.2.

fact, that the announcement is made, "Judah my king," and to him the word of blessing is addressed, "Judah, may your brothers praise you, your hands on the back of your foes, and all your father's sons will bow down to you."[35] These divine verses proclaim who is the soul that possesses insight (bearing the name Jerusalem), and who are those that confess (the cities of Judah, Judah meaning "confessing"); so let them know of Jesus that he is "meek and humble of heart, so that they may find the rest"[36] that is due to pure souls with the completion of the seventieth year of the cycle of "the sun of justice,"[37] who encircles minds that are pure and transparent.

The Lord almighty replied to the angel talking in me, with fine words and consoling expressions (v.13). In reply to the angel asking, *How long will you have no mercy on Jerusalem and the cities of Judah?* the Lord almighty replied in fine words and consoling expressions about mercy being bestowed on Jerusalem and the cities subject to it, manifesting and conveying deep consolation. After all, how would they not comfort and endear those returning from captivity, leading them to say in thanksgiving, "When the Lord brought back captive Sion, we were like people enjoying consolation, we were gladdened"?[38] May the Lord almighty reply in fine words also to us through his angel of great counsel so that we may attain all that is commendable and be perfectly consoled by his perfect words and bring ourselves to a blessed life of freedom.

The angel speaking in me said to me, Cry out in these words, The Lord almighty says this: I am extremely jealous for Sion and Jerusalem. I am extremely wrathful towards the nations who have conspired be-

35. Lk 4.18; Is 61.1–2; Pss 60.7; 108.8; Gn 49.8. One wonders which approach to the number seventy is more productive (once the apocalyptic nature of the passage is overlooked): that of Didymus in seeing a perfect number, or that of Theodoret in trying (unsuccessfully) to relate it historically to the reigns of Hezekiah and Darius.

36. Mt 11.9. The derivation of "Judah" is disputed, Zorell suggesting *laudatus*, not unrelated to Didymus's ἐξομολογούμενος; see Franciscus Zorell, *Lexicon Hebraicum et Aramaicum Veteris Testamenti* (Rome: Pontificium Institutum Biblicum, 1963), s. v.

37. Mal 4.2.

38. Ps 126.1, 3. The following parenetic remark suggests movement from one section to another.

cause of the fact that while I was slightly wrathful, they conspired with evil intent (vv.14–15). Speaking on his own behalf, the prophet says that a command had been given him by the angel of the Lord almighty to cry out with voice raised, Thus says the Lord: I am extremely jealous for Jerusalem and Sion, I bear deep anger against the nations who are their oppressors, since at the time when their protector imposed slight and brief punishment with a view to correction and conversion, they for their part hatched a savage and fierce conspiracy. Whereas they should have been afraid on seeing God's friends abandoned to chastisement for their evil behavior and should have been on their guard lest they suffer the same fate, they hatched an evil conspiracy instead, swaggering and mocking with malevolent glee, abusing and treading upon those who had been surrendered to them. Those who behaved with such inhumanity and ferocity to the ones surrendered to them God reproaches by saying in the prophet Isaiah, "I gave them into your hands, but you did not show them mercy; you made the yoke weigh heavy on the aged and said, I shall be ruler forever."[39] I am enraged at this, and so there will suddenly come upon you what I threatened to impose on those I surrendered to you, not for their ruin but for them to sense the threat coming upon them and turn back to me, who cares for them.

Now, what were the boasts that arose from their arrogance and audacity? "I am, and there is no one besides me. I shall not sit as a widow or know the loss of children."[40] For making these arrogant and harsh pronouncements they were suddenly by God's judgment shown to be without protector, the object of care not even of father or husband. Taking this to heart, let those entrusted with power take pains not to treat harshly those made subject to them by a decree of the providence to which they are responsible.

What does the Lord almighty mean by saying, *I am extremely*

39. Is 47.6–7. Concise at times, Didymus is ready also to give several paraphrases of the one verse.
40. Is 47.8. Being the author of commentaries on Isaiah and the Psalms as well (also recovered at Tura), Didymus liberally documents his work from those books.

jealous for Sion and Jerusalem? Sion and Jerusalem are called bride and partner of God the Word in a spiritual sense, and he abandoned it for a while for violating its marital duties to its husband, so that he says to it as its partner, "As a wife sets aside her partner, so the house of Israel set me aside, says the Lord."[41] When the woman who was once espoused to him in noble and solemn fashion became neglected in this way, many of those bent on her ruin subjected her to abuse, demeaning her, treating her with abuse like a woman with no husband to protect her. Taking pity on her at this, the one who by nature is merciful began once more to be jealous of her. When this happened, you see, those intent on maltreating her had no further opportunity, since her jealous husband drove off from his spouse those moving to harm her; once more he took sincere care of her and dwelled with her in love as he had done previously before abandoning her.

Now, the fact that this interpretation has force you can learn also from the prophet Ezekiel: God at any rate was angry with the Hebrew populace; "I shall no longer spare you," he said, "nor shall I be jealous of you."[42] He gave vent to this sentiment to stir them up so that they might not become liable to the threats, and might instead begin to maintain undefiled the duties of partnership. It is because of the virtues it possesses that he refers to Sion and Jerusalem as the object of jealousy to the point of no longer being maltreated by those joined in evil conspiracy against it. Sion, in fact, means "watchtower for implementing a command," and Jerusalem "vision of peace"; in a spiritual sense it is called Sion for watching not for temporary but for eternal things in implementing the commands that have been given, and on this attitude there follows the serenity and orderliness of good actions.[43] The peace that is seen is that of which Jesus speaks, "My peace I leave with you," and has

41. Jer 3.20.
42. Ezek 16.42.
43. Though Didymus has no difficulty accommodating this etymology also of Sion, which is hardly his own, and though Jerome will adopt it as *specula*, again modern scholars would not support it. A lengthy digression arises from the etymology of Jerusalem (equally disputed; see n. 33 above).

been given with divine grace "from God the Father and the Lord Jesus Christ," as Paul teaches. The savior is both of these, namely, peace and grace: it is said of him, "He is our peace"; and again the one who performs good actions from it and through it admits, "It is not I myself" who have performed any good deeds of this kind, "but grace with me."[44] While it is God the Father who provides this grace and peace, Jesus also lays them as a foundation in imparting himself to those who acknowledge him as grace and peace. Let us also have this character through goodness of will so that we may never forsake him like the woman who set aside her husband, proving instead zealous and loving.

Hence the Lord says this: I shall return to Jerusalem with compassion, and my house will be rebuilt in her, says the Lord almighty, and the measuring line will still be extended over Jerusalem (v.16). Since nothing is done by chance by the one who has oversight of everything, therefore the causal links in what happens are frequently determined in advance, God telling those subject to his governance, Because this is what you said and did, this is what will be imposed on you. In the present verse as well, for instance, the text reads as follows: *Hence the Lord almighty says this.* What it means is nothing other than *I am extremely jealous for Sion and Jerusalem.* Since *while I was slightly wrathful,* the foes of the object of my jealousy *conspired with evil intent, I shall return to Jerusalem with compassion,* having compassion for it as its protector and sincere ally, being in actual fact "the father of compassion."[45]

The manner of having compassion on Jerusalem is proclaimed at once: *My house will be rebuilt in her* and in her midst, so that by dwelling within and parading among her citizens, I may have entire compassion for her, leaving her the victim no longer of devastation and pillage, showing her to be a worthy object of jealous love and remembrance, once my measuring line is extended over her as before when she enjoyed prosperi-

44. Jn 14.27; Rom 1.7; Eph 2.14; 1 Cor 15.10.
45. 1 Cor 1.3. The accent on divine pre-ordination placed here by Didymus rests on a misreading of Heb. tenses by the LXX (as often), unbeknownst to him.

ty and fruitfulness. Since a country that is desolate and neglected is not measured, the land now shown compassion by God is
measured like a fruitful country. The city that is measured is
spread out in streets and thoroughfares, shrines and parks. The
measuring line placed on her will be indicated in what follows
when an angel appears holding a cord for measuring.

The house being built in the midst of Jerusalem, the city that
is the object of compassion, is the Church of the living God, in
which the servant of God should live in keeping with the law of
sanctification. This is announced to Timothy by the apostle,
speaking in Christ, when writing in these terms: "If I am delayed, you may know how one ought to behave in the Church
of God, which is the Church of the living God, the pillar and
bulwark of the truth." In another sense the house being rebuilt
in Jerusalem is Jesus, who was born of Mary and built by the wisdom of God, according to the oracle from Proverbs that runs as
follows: "Wisdom built a house for herself." Of him Wisdom
said to the adversaries on building him, "Destroy this Temple,
and in three days I shall raise it up," the text adding, "He said
this of the temple which is his body," in the evangelist's words.[46]
In addition to what has been said, each of the faithful is also a
house raised up so as to be a temple of God: "Do you not know
that you are God's temple, and that God's Spirit dwells in you?"
And the savior himself says as much openly, "If they love me,
they will keep my word, and I shall love them, my Father and I
shall love them and come and make our home with them."
Now, temple and house and home . . .[47]

The angel speaking in me said to me, Cry aloud, The Lord almighty
says this: Cities will still overflow with good things, the Lord will still
have mercy on Sion and choose Jerusalem (v.17) . . .[48]

One must understand that it also deals with the good things

46. 1 Tm 3.15; Prv 9.1; Jn 2.19, 21. Zechariah's reference to the rebuilding
of city and Temple has been developed at length in a spiritual sense to the point
of disappearing from sight.

47. 1 Cor 3.16; Jn 14.23. There then occurs in the text a lacuna of about ten
lines.

48. A further ten lines are missing, including the text of v.17 (reproduced
from Rahlfs's ed. of the LXX). There follow two pages of scarcely legible commentary on v.17, part of which can be pieced together by reference to Jerome.

mentioned in the text: "If you are willing to obey me, you will eat the good things of the land," and "You will trust in the Lord, and he will make you ride upon the good things of the earth." Of them the sage to whom "the obscure and hidden things of wisdom" were revealed by God says, "I believe that I shall see the good things of the Lord in the land of the living."[49]

I lifted up my eyes and saw and, lo, four horns. I said to the angel speaking in me, What are these, sir? (vv. 18–19)[50] . . . "I lifted up my eyes to you, who dwell in heaven." And the savior, "Lift up your eyes and see how the fields are already white for the harvest."[51] . . . He went on with a question in his wish to know what they are. The horns are the four kingdoms besetting the citizens of Sion and Jerusalem, and are none other than those enemies of whom the apostle and the other believers say, "Our struggle is not with blood and flesh, but with the rulers and authorities, the cosmic powers of this present darkness and the spiritual forces of evil." In harmony with this reference to the multitude of the evil powers against whom the saints struggle, the psalmist also speaks of the one rising up against the enemies: "You will step on asp and basilisk, and tread underfoot lion and dragon." And since each of the aforementioned evil beings established its power by usurpation, he says it rules unlawfully. These horns, described obscurely, the prophet saw on raising the eyes of his mind, the purpose being that from the vision of their equipment and power he might don the invincible armor of God.[52]

Now, who the craftsmen were who were sharpening the horns in question you can learn from the sequel. *He said to me, These are the horns that scattered Judah and crushed Israel* (v. 19). After showing the prophet the four horns and their meaning, the angel in reply enlightens him about the purpose and the value for which they were brought to the fore. The horns were brought to the fore, he says, for no other reason than to disperse Israel and Judah away from the holy city so that by their

49. Is 1.19; 58.14; Ps 51.6; 27.13. A further lacuna occurs.
50. This text also has been supplied from Rahlfs's ed. of the LXX.
51. Ps 123.1; Jn 4.35.
52. Eph 6.12; Ps 91.13; 86.14; Eph 6.13.

being scattered in captivity they would forfeit unity and con-cord together. As was mentioned before, Judah means "confess-ing," while the one who sees God in the mind is given the name Israel.[53]

The Lord showed me four craftsmen, and I asked, What are they coming to do? He replied to me, These are the horns that scattered Ju-dah and crushed Israel with no one of their number raising their head; they went in to sharpen with their hands the four horns that are the na-tions raising a horn against the land of the Lord to scatter it (vv.20–21). To console the one who saw the advancing multitude of enemies, he shows him those summoned to assistance to be of a number equal to the adversaries and in fact excellent crafts-men. Not all those exercising that trade are excellent, you see, some being blameworthy; as the proverb puts it in prophetical-ly distinguishing the one from the other, "Mercy and fidelity are the crafts of the good, while those who craft wickedness have no appreciation of mercy and fidelity."[54] These wicked machinations of the craftsmen differ in no way from the four horns, a product of utter infidelity and cruelty. The advancing craftsmen whom God shows are workers of mercy and fidelity, practicing the virtue of mercy towards their fellows, loving their neighbor as themselves, and producing fidelity in pious and in-formed insight. The one who presents and reveals them to the person lifting up the eyes of the mind is none other than God, who calls to good works those able to help the suffering.[55]

After perceiving those shown to him as sent by God, he puts to the one showing him a question as to what they are coming to do. God replies to him that they are coming to sharpen the four nations brought against God's land to take charge of those

53. See n. 36 above for the etymology of Judah. Relating "Israel" to a vision of God (not the usual etymology) may have suggested itself to Didymus from the incident at Peniel in Gn 32.29–31. The relevance of either derivation here is not obvious except as an index of desperation.

54. Prv 14.22 LXX. Comment on v.21 is hindered by the LXX's reading "sharpen" in a similar Heb. form for "terrify," a critical error.

55. Didymus again takes the prophet's vision as "lifting up the eyes *of the mind*," thus avoiding any reference in horns and craftsmen and nations to the peoples of the prophet's time, a concern occupying the Antiochene commenta-tors.

surrendered to captivity with a view to scattering Judah and crushing Israel, with none of those abused capable of lifting their head to challenge or gainsay the foe besetting them. On the other hand, the verse presents the weakness of the horns to be worse, in that even after the sharpening they were incapable of destroying those surrendered to them, despite the presence of the craftsmen sharpening them. The passage presents the one scattered being broken in pieces, sustaining a fracture akin to that suffered by the man who went down from Jerusalem and fell foul of spiritual brigands, the result being that he was left half-dead by them, especially when they stripped him of the divine vesture which he wore while living in the sacred city and which was of a potency equal to armor, the apostle writing of it to those being roused to battle, "Put on the armor of light."[56]

In place of the clause *They crushed Israel* there occurs in some manuscripts "They brought Israel down," which shows in this reading as well the sinner moving down from above. There are many texts to confirm this, like the following: "How did the morning star fall from heaven, the one that rises at dawn?" and "They will go to the depths of the earth"; and countless other texts suggest that the devout person ascends and rises, whereas the one with a taste for pleasure and a materialistic attitude sinks downwards, so as to be "of the flesh, sold into slavery under sin."[57] I read the interpretation of some commentator taking the four craftsmen as the four evangelists; let those reading the one writing it decide whether this is true. It is possible to say the four craftsmen are the angels "sent to gather God's elect from the four winds," that is, the four corners of the world.[58]

56. Rom 13.12. Is it the obscurity of the text in hand that prompts Didymus to see a connection with the Lukan parable (10.30) taken spiritually (in a manner reminiscent also of the gnostic Hymn of the Pearl)?

57. Is 14.12; Ps 63.9; Rom 7.14. Though blind, this exegete reveals a familiarity with alternative LXX readings, ἀντίγραφα (found in the Hexapla?), as also with other commentators whom he claims to have "read." But see Introduction for the rarity of such reference.

58. Cf. Mt 24.31. Didymus is flexible in allowing his readers to decide on the plausibility of reference to evangelists. Antiochene commentators would have regarded as gratuitous these interpretations (with which Jerome had no problem)—though Doutreleau, SC 83.243, does less than justice to Theodore in denying him an interest in the possibility of reference to the four corners of the

In whatever way the four craftsmen are taken, however, it is by the provident God of all that they are revealed and brought to bear on the impudence and arrogance of those oppressing the people made subject to them by God's judgment. With the sacred craftsmen ranged against them, neither the captor nor the captives raise their head; as the saying goes, the wretched do not raise their head. If, on the other hand, it is "mind" that is suggested by the term *head*, not even it is raised up when a person is "surrendered to a debased mind for not seeing fit to acknowledge God." After all, how could one under the influence of a debased mind give thought to things on high, or have one's heart in heaven when not having one's treasure in heaven? In keeping with Israel's being crushed or brought down is the mournful announcement by those scattered by the force of the conquerors, "Our bones are scattered in Hades."[59]

Since the inspired text seems confused as a result of the incoherence of composition, there is need to rephrase it as follows.[60] While living a good life, Israel and Judah had a dwelling in the land of the Lord; but on forsaking their attachment to the Law and attention to it day and night, they turned to wickedness and thus became subject by a sentence of Providence to four nations (referred to as *horns* on account of their bid for power). These aforementioned horns in their cruelty and pride beset the Israelites and Judah so as to bring down and crush the people of God. Since God was only slightly angered, these instruments of anger were used for evil purposes, but they were sharpened by the good craftsmen already commented on so as to emerge weak and vanquished after this sharpening, no longer able to have a firm grip on those surren-

---

earth (not so much "winds"), Theodore's unwillingness being only to limit the biblical author's thought to the number four.

59. Rom 1.28; Col 3.2; Mt 6.19–20; Ps 141.7. The approach to a difficult text is completely intertextual, not historical, no attempt being made to consider a historical referent.

60. Like many a commentator after him, Didymus is prepared to admit the ἀκαταλληλία of the thought in this chapter (unlike a later reader of the manuscript, who inserted a qualification), and so summarizes it—if not from a historical perspective, at least omitting the spiritual elaboration he had previously supplied.

dered to them. The four horns, already commented on, were
of one mind in their hostility to the captives, and so are spoken
of as one horn besetting the land of the Lord. There are many
scriptural texts referring to kings and kingdoms as horns, especially in the prophet Daniel, as will be clear to you in your reading.

COMMENTARY ON ZECHARIAH 2

LIFTED UP MY EYES *and saw, and, lo, a man with a measuring cord in his hand. I said to him, Where are you going? He replied to me, To measure Jerusalem to see what are its breadth and its length* (Zec 2.1–2). It has often been mentioned before that people raise the eyes within them to understand the visions affecting them. In the same way as referred to, the prophet in this case also raised his eyes and saw a man holding a measuring cord in his hand with which, like a good architect, to measure the breadth and length of Jerusalem to see how to lay its foundations and ensure its rebuilding after experiencing destruction by the enemy.

It is time to see who is the one who appeared to the prophet. See whether it is the same person as the one *mounted upon a red horse and positioned between two shady mountains.* According to one of the interpretations mentioned, he is the savior, whom the prophet Jeremiah indicated in saying, "Lo, a man, Dawn is his name" (called Dawn in being the true light). John the Baptist also said of him, "A man comes after me, though he is before me."[1] This man, builder of Jerusalem, who in the manner of an architect first established and laid its foundations, and, after the destruction it suffered with the onset of the enemy, who also enslaved it, measures its breadth and length so as in an orderly and coordinated fashion to lay the groundwork in the proper places where its walls should be raised.

To the prophet he was shown holding a measuring cord, plaited of various architectural rules, for the accomplishment of what was stated in the verse *a measuring line will still be extended over Jerusalem.* In keeping with the expression *the city of the*

---

1. Zec 1.8; 6.12 (not Jeremiah); Jn 1.9, 15. The LXX sees "Dawn" in the Heb. form for "shoot" in Zec 3.8; 6.12.

Lord of hosts, the verse "God established it forever" is not inapplicable to the savior as architect.[2] Similarly, the apostle Paul writes of this divine city, to which all those look forward who are pleasing by their faith, in these terms. "They set their sights on the city with foundations, God being its architect and builder." As the aforementioned measuring cord he holds the angels and holy men, who like excellent architects build with him by the practice of virtue (referred to as his *hand*). Paul at any rate says of himself, "I laid a foundation like a skillful architect." In fact, in Ezekiel a man is seen holding a builder's tape and rod for measuring and laying foundations for God's holy Temple.[3] Now, how he measured and designed the building you can learn from reading the prophet.

Since, then, it is also the savior who is indicated as builder of the spiritual Jerusalem on high—something that is still clearer from the Father's reference to him in the words, "He will build my city"[4]—and since the angels and human beings are also assigned to the rebuilding of the city, it is in accord with all the clarification provided that we are to understand the man shown by Zechariah in the prophet's words, *Lo, a man with a measuring cord in his hand* and *Where are you going?* so as to obtain a response about the one holding the measuring cord for measuring how wide and long Jerusalem is. After all, it is characteristic of one planning a building properly to know about the site and suitability of the layout so that all parts of the city—shrines, temples, passageways, corners, streets—be placed in accord with suitable breadth and length. The result is that the wisdom of God will move confidently through these streets, making herself heard on the pinnacles of the city walls in keeping with the sage advice in Proverbs that God personally gives to the guardians of this holy city to proclaim in it and on its walls day and night, never keeping silent but ever saying what concerns the welfare of its citizens.[5]

---

2. Zec 1.16; Ps 48.8.

3. Heb 11.6, 10; 1 Cor 3.10; Ezek 40.3. Do holy *women* also play a part in this construction? Does Didymus envisage women readers of his commentary?

4. Is 45.13.

5. Prv 1.20–21; Is 62.6. Didymus, who has left commentaries also on Job and

Jerusalem has often been given an anagogical interpretation at three levels: the virtuous soul, "the glorious Church without spot or wrinkle" as a result of the fullness of holiness, and the heavenly city of the living God.[6] So it is in keeping with all these figures that the person who takes account of wisdom and knowledge[7] should interpret the measuring of the length and breadth of Jerusalem by the man holding the measuring cord in his hand.

Lo, the angel speaking in me was at hand. Another angel came to meet him and said to him, Run and say this to that young man (vv.3–4). He says he saw the angel speaking in him standing by, and another angel coming forward and saying to him, Run and say to this young man what is opportune to say. There were various ways before of interpreting what was said in the prophet by the divine angel and how it was made plain, especially when the announcement came from another angel who emerged. It is not possible, you see, for the message to be heard which stays within and by itself—only when someone emerges as a gesture of considerateness.[8] At any rate, the introduction to the mystery was given not to a man but to a young man; to the divine angels, you see, the holy man is a young man, especially when he is clad in the new man,[9] as the saying goes in the divine Proverbs, "A young person is no stranger to holiness, and his way is straight." After all, how could the way of the one walking in holiness not be straight? Of those who enjoy such a share in virtue John said in the epistle on the subject when addressing them, "I am writing to you, young people, because you are strong and have conquered the evil one."[10] All those, and only

Ecclesiastes, likes to cite sapiential material from the Bible, as one might expect of his condition and parenetic avocation.

6. Eph 5.27; Heb 12.22. Antiochene commentators on this verse, predictably, are not interested in taking Jerusalem κατὰ ἀναγωγήν at any of these levels.

7. Cf. 1 Cor 12.8.

8. Considerateness, συγκατάβασις (a term we associate particularly with Chrysostom, Origen speaking rather of συμπεριφορά), carries no patronizing connotation such as is suggested in its frequent translation "condescension," a mere calque.

9. Cf. Eph 4.24.

10. Prv 20.11; 1 Jn 2.13.

those, who are young in spirit are instructed by the angel who
emerged to say what the sequel clarifies.

Take note as to whether the angel's coming has the same
force as the statement by the band of the saints, "You came
forth for the salvation of your people, to save your anointed
ones," and the verse, "I came from God and am here." In other
words, salvation and divine revelation come to the human race,
driven out of paradise for transgressing the divine laws, when
the angel of God's great counsel came to reintroduce them after expulsion, thanks to obedience and divine correction, saying, "Today you will be with me in paradise."[11] The one who
came promises to reveal great things concerning the spiritual
Jerusalem, which the next verse indicates in the following
terms.

*Jerusalem will be inhabited as a fruitful city on account of the num-
ber of people and cattle in its midst. I shall be, says the Lord, a wall of
fire for it round about, and I shall be as glory in its midst* (vv.4–5). In
the way that all the trees in paradise produce much fruit, so,
too, the holy city of Jerusalem is inhabited *fruitfully*, with vast
numbers of people and cattle in its midst. It is, in fact, beyond
the realms of propriety and possibility for anyone to prove un-
fruitful in this divine and holy city, the tree without fruit being
cut down and consigned to fire outside. This was the case with
the person of whom the holy one cried aloud in these terms:
"For this reason God will do away with you forever, pluck you
up and move you from your tent, and your race from the land
of the living," whereas everyone abiding in God's house will
give expression to thanks: "I am like a fruitful olive tree in
God's house." After all, how do those who dwell in God's house
not bear fruit from the nourishment of the divine light by doing their duty and pondering the pious teachings? Similarly,
the man declared "blessed" in the first psalm was a fruitful tree:
"He will be like the tree planted by the water channels, which
will produce its fruit in due season, and its leaf will not fall."

11. Hab 3.13; Jn 8.42; Is 9.6. The application of Lk 23.43 to the whole human race would be thought by Antioch to be typical of Alexandrian arbitrariness in the use of Scripture.

The verse in Jeremiah is similar: "Blessed are those who trust in the Lord; the Lord will be their hope. They will send out their roots for moisture and not cease bearing fruit."[12]

Then, since, on account of the great goodness of the one who founded the holy city of Jerusalem, it is inhabited by people of the kind who not only are motivated in action and thought by reason but also are simple in their tastes and of a lowly attitude, it follows that it is *inhabited as a fruitful city on account of the number of people and cattle in its midst.* I mean, how would there not prove to be in its midst people and cattle of whom the psalmist says to God, "People and cattle you will save, O Lord"? People are the beneficiaries of eternal salvation from God, and each of them can say, "The word of the Lord was addressed to me as follows," while cattle that are saved are the sheep that listen to the voice of Jesus. To people of this mentality, acting and thinking with reason and insight, the Lord Jesus says, "You call me Lord and teacher, and you are right: I am that,"[13] especially since you serve me sincerely, doing as you ought, and instructed in what it is good to know. Along with people of the kind we have suggested, there will dwell fruitfully in Jerusalem also those able to say of the king of the heavenly city Jerusalem, "He will shepherd us forever." Of this kind of flock belonging to God the author wise in God's ways says, "The Lord will stand and see, and he will shepherd his flock in might," the result being that each of the objects of his care will joyfully sing hymns of this sort: "The Lord will shepherd me, nothing will be wanting to me; he settled me there in a green pasture, near restful waters he reared me."[14]

The guard and sentry of Jerusalem, *fruitful on account of the number of people and cattle in its midst,* will be none other than the Lord, who personally surrounds it like a fiery wall, providing both warmth and flame, enlightening and warming those inside the guarded city to make them fervent in spirit; Scripture says of them, "like people fervent in spirit." Those advancing

---

12. Pss 52.5, 8; 1.1; Jer 17.7–8.

13. Ps 36.6; Jn 10.27; 13.13. The tissue of citations is strung together without heed to their original contexts.

14. Ps 48.14; Mi 5.4; Ps 23.1–2.

from without, on the other hand, he scorches to their detriment, "being a consuming fire," especially those producing thorns and thistles, which are cut down and thrown away for producing fruit that is not good but harmful and lethal. Like the holy city, the people also are said to be surrounded by the Lord in one of the Songs of the Steps: "The Lord surrounding his people."[15]

Just as a wall of fire surrounded the fruitful Jerusalem, he is in its midst as a source of glory: they are glorified with divinity and blessedness who inhabit the holy city surrounded by God, and the psalmist in his singing said of them—or, rather, to them—"Glorious things are said of you, O city of God," and, "Great is the Lord and much to be praised in the city of our God on his holy mountain."[16] It will be our lot also, by the grace of the beneficent God, to bear the fruits of the Spirit, so that the Lord will surround us like a fiery wall, enlightening and protecting us, on the one hand, and on the other consuming the enemy who advance to destroy us. The effect will be that we shall cry aloud triumphantly in pointing to the indestructible city, "Behold a fortified city and our salvation."[17]

O, O, flee from the land of the north, says the Lord, because I shall gather you from the four winds of heaven, says the Lord. Escape to Sion, you inhabitants of the daughter of Babylon (vv.6–7). To stir up those scattered "to the north, before which troubles break out for the inhabitants of the land," the verse in short refers to an escape from the disasters (suggested by the term "north"), duplicating the encouraging watchword *O, O, flee from the land of the north.* Now, the person who stays clear of evil by an ardent repentance flees from disasters that bring with them retribution. The same meaning as fleeing from the land of the north is found in "Turn away from evil" and "Put an end to your wicked ways." This advice is followed when there is detachment from every form of wickedness, and a hold kept only on what is desirable

15. Rom 12.11; Heb 12.29; 6.8; Ps 125.2. Pss 120–34 have been referred to as Songs of the Steps, possibly for structural reasons, and also as Pilgrim Songs for their traditional association with the captivity and return.

16. Pss 87.3; 48.1.

17. Is 26.1, commentary on vv.4–5 concluding with a brief parenesis.

and praiseworthy, according to the recommendation in the apostolic encouragement, "Test everything, hold fast to what is good, abstain from every form of wickedness."[18] All those, and only those, flee what is harmful who consider the good desirable and do it.

Flight from the north is unhindered when the one who is everyone's benefactor and provider gathers from the four winds the citizens scattered by them from the beautiful city Jerusalem. To facilitate flight, he makes clear where and in what city salvation is available to those fleeing from the harsh, cold north wind, of which Scripture says, "Wind from the north is harsh," and again, "A cold wind will blow from the north."[19] It is the sacred place Sion, where it is possible for the previous inhabitants of the daughter of Babylon to escape in safety, her daughter being the vast number of her inhabitants. And since the name Babylon means "confusion," everyone alarmed and confused in mind is a Babylonian, which is a condition and disposition to be avoided by the person with the desire to find escape in Sion with a view to singing God's praises, since that is the place where praise of God is fitting and it is pleasing to sing in his honor. Scripture says, remember, "A hymn of praise befits you, O God, in Sion," and, "Sing to the Lord, who dwells in Sion."[20]

Since it is not possible for those dwelling in the daughter of Babylon and in the north to sing God's praises, the Holy Spirit cries out with full voice in the words, *O, O, flee from the north, says the Lord, escape to Sion, you inhabitants of the daughter of Babylon, because I shall gather you from the four winds,* that is, from all the regions of the earth. Similar in meaning to the phrase *I shall gather you from the four winds* is what the savior said in the Gospel about "sending the angels to gather the elect from the

18. Jer 1.14; Ps 34.14; Is 1.16; 1 Thes 5.21. Once again plenty of moral references to Scripture, but no comment on what lies to the north and who have reason to fear it. Theodoret, by contrast, simply and briefly refers to those who have returned or are yet to return from exile in Babylon, having established this historical context at the beginning of commentary.

19. Prv 27.16; Sir 43.20.

20. Pss 65.19; 9.11. We have seen Didymus capitalizing on etymologies, true or false, as a substitute for focusing on the historical context.

four winds."[21] With Sion and the daughter of Babylon being taken allegorically, there is need to see a spiritual sense also in the four winds, whether as the incorporeal powers or the different currents of the so-called teaching, which toss and turn to godless attitudes and futile actions those who are immature in mind to their own discredit. The apostle, for instance, writes of such a condition, "lest we be immature, tossed and turned by every wind of doctrine through trickery."[22]

The winds are sometimes taken to be trials and tribulations, as for instance in the Gospel they are mentioned beating down with rain and raging torrents to strike and severely buffet the houses of those listening to the words of Jesus, but unable to harm or upset those who put the Master's teachings into practice, since they set their foundation on the saving rock. But they overturned the building of those who listened to the divine teaching without practicing it because they laid its base down on sand.[23] In whatever way the winds are interpreted, from them all God gathers those inhabitants of the daughter of Babylon who are fleeing from the north to give them rescue on Sion, of which the apostle writes, "Make your approach to Mount Sion and city of the living God, the heavenly Jerusalem." This, in fact, is the only way the inspired text in hand will also be understood in an elevated fashion.[24]

For the Lord almighty says this: In the wake of glory he has sent me to the nations despoiling you, because the one touching you is like the one touching the apple of his eye. For this reason, lo, I raise my hand against them, and they will be spoil to their slaves, and you will know that the Lord almighty sent me (vv.8–9). The Lord God almighty gives the reason for his being sent in the wake of glory to the nations despoiling the true Israelites. And since God almighty

21. Mt 24.31.
22. Eph 4.14. Didymus obviously has no qualms about settling for an allegorical approach to the verses, eschewing an examination of the ἱστορία underlying them.
23. Mt 7.4–27.
24. Heb 12.22. The hermeneutical priority here enunciated Diodore would contest: "The historical sense, in fact, is not in opposition to the more elevated sense; on the contrary, it proves to be the basis and foundation of the more elevated ideas" (CCG 6.7).

is the one saying this, the terms "in the wake of" and "in front of" should not be taken corporeally: "in the wake of" God is to be understood as what comes after his transcendent being. Being uncreated and eternal, after all, he is before everything, and after him and "in his wake" comes what is planned for his creatures and his government, like his Incarnation and descent, of which men of godly wisdom can conceive and imagine. Moses the revealer was one of them: he asked God to allow him to see him clearly when God had manifested himself, but on being asked he replied, "You will see what is behind me, but my face will not be seen by you"; "I shall first pass by in my glory." In regard to the descent of God the Word, *in the wake of his glory* means his becoming flesh and being seen in the flesh, whereas before such glory was visible, there was that of "the Only-begotten of the Father, full of grace and truth."[25]

This insight is implied also by the statement of the apostle and those of one mind with him, "Even though we knew Christ according to the flesh, we know him no longer in that way,"[26] his first glory being that of the Son according to which he is Only-begotten God the Word, the second—from the Incarnation—being after that, and in that capacity *he was sent to the nations despoiling* God's people, the nations despoiling those belonging to God being the ones taking it captive. This was done with great goodness, however: if he judged the impious as God eternal and uncreated, everything would disappear; but acting with considerateness and not observing all the offenses of those under judgment, he acts as benefactor rather than punisher. In fact, in his goodness and longsuffering the actual threat and prediction of the impending punishment gives room for repentance to those willing to abandon the impiety they committed. The descent of the savior, who became visible in the flesh, was due to the same goodness and lovingkindness, the purpose being that in the wake of this there might be seen "the glory of

25. Ex 33.23,19; 1 Tm 3.16; Jn 1.14. Again Didymus ignores the contemporary referent of the verses to seize upon "the most puzzling phrase in the book" (Ralph Smith, 196) for its spiritual potential. Cyril and even Theodoret (but, typically, not Theodore) will see a reference to the Incarnation in the phrase.

26. 2 Cor 5.16.

the Son from the Father, full of grace and truth," so that by his journey and burial "he might be manifested in the flesh, justified in the spirit, seen by angels," thus "becoming visible in the world, heralded among the nations, and will be taken up in glory."[27]

Take note as to whether this interpretation is suggested by a verse from Jeremiah to this effect: "This is our God, no other will be compared with him. Afterwards he appeared on earth and lived with humankind,"[28] such living with humankind being a sending *in the wake of* the glory of the God who is confessed to be almighty. He was not sent as almighty, note, but as one who had "emptied himself" in a gesture of considerateness, "taking the form of a slave."[29]

Now, what fate does he predict for those still subject to the nations despoiling them? *The one touching you is like the one touching the apple of his eye*, harming himself in striking the righteous rather than those he intends to abuse, like the one striking the apple of his eye. It is possible to support this way of seeing it from many places in Scripture: by wishing to harm Abel, Cain brought death on himself before the treacherous murder he had planned; the same thing happened also in the case of Saul when pursuing David to kill him, and to Absalom when bent on taking power from his father. In the inspired text in hand he implies harming by *touching*, and especially in what God himself says to those with murderous intentions against his own, "Lay no hand on my anointed ones, nor abuse my prophets."[30] *Touch* has the sense of culpable handling in the text, "It is good for a man not to touch a woman," suggesting a shameful and lustful approach. Proper handling is suggested by this word in the sense of making contact by touch, as in the remark by Jesus, "Someone has touched me,"[31] when the woman with the flow of blood ran up in her desire to be healed and touched the hem of Jesus' garment.

27. Jn 1.14; 1 Tm 3.16.

28. Bar 3.35, 37 (somewhat slanted to suit Didymus's purpose by the omission of v.36, referring to wisdom, who "appeared on earth").

29. Phil 2.7.   30. Ps 105.15.

31. 1 Cor 7.1; Mk 5.30.

Such for the moment being the background to the term for *touching*, the inspired text in hand suggests malicious harm. The one bent on abusing those protected by God touches the apple of the eye of the interior man. It indicates how the one touching God's servants touches the apple of his eye by saying, *I raise my hand against them*, that is, his chastising power, with the result that they themselves became the spoils of those they were previously despoiling in taking them off into captivity, so that they became enslaved to those whom they had dominated tyrannically. When this happens, you will know that I am *the Lord almighty*, sent by the Lord almighty for the fulfillment of what was foretold. God the Word is the almighty sent by the almighty, coming to human beings by the Father's pleasure; the principle by which the Father rules as king over all that he has made through his Word is that by which the Son also rules and reigns over all that subsists in him and to which he has precedence. Hence the apostle's saying that in Christ were created things visible and invisible, since he exists before them and all things subsist in him: "He is before all things, and all things subsist in him."

It is not surprising that the almighty is from the almighty: he is also God from God and light from light, being consubstantial with the one who begot him and one with him who begot him, as the verse says, "I and the Father are one,"[32] and so all the Father has belongs to the Son. Now, what the Father has is being God, being light, being holy, being almighty, all of which belongs to the Son. The Son is thus almighty from the almighty, being king of all from the one who reigns over all. In John's Apocalypse the savior is undeniably confessed to be almighty, personally saying of himself, "This is what the faithful witness says, the ἀρχή of God's creation, the one who is and who was and who is coming, Lord God almighty."[33] The one saying this

---

32. Jn 1.3; Col 1.17; Jn 10.30; 17.10. Choosing to give the passage a Christological interpretation, Didymus senses possible overtones of subordinationism, which he rebuts by citing terms from the creed of Constantinople of 381, including ὁμοούσιος.

33. Rv 1.5, 8; 3.14. The ambiguity of a term like ἀρχή, offering both "beginning" and "rule" as meanings, made such texts grist to the mill of both orthodox and heterodox in Christological debate, as well as some texts from Colos-

is almighty, and is no creature such as does not have power over itself; it would be absurd, in fact, for the same person to be creator and created by itself, both ruler and subject. Even if the one we confess as God is called in the passage cited "ἀρχή of God's creation," he is "ἀρχή of creation" because of his ruling as king and being almighty, which is the same thing—in other words, his kingship controls and governs all creatures.

Rejoice and be glad, daughter Sion, because, lo, I am coming, and I shall dwell in the midst of you, says the Lord. Many nations will take refuge in the Lord on that day, and will be a people for him, and will dwell in your midst, and you will know that the Lord almighty has sent me to you. The Lord will take possession of Judah as his portion in the holy land, and will still choose Jerusalem (vv.10–12). Just as in the case of the people of the Hebrews being enslaved there was weeping and wailing on account of the Lord's keeping his distance from the captives, so on their returning to their spiritual mother, referred to as Sion, the order is given for them to rejoice and be glad on account of the Lord's coming and dwelling in their midst, the Temple having been erected and the Lord dwelling in it. *Rejoice and be glad, daughter Sion,* says the prophet, "daughter" being a term used of any city in many places of Scripture in reference to the citizens occupying it.

The joy and gladness which the divine word orders them to have is the same as the happiness which is fruit of the Holy Spirit, in keeping with the love of God and blessed peace to which the sacred apostle points in writing in these terms: "The fruit of the Spirit is love, happiness, peace." Enjoying this security, those redeemed from captivity say, "When the Lord reversed the captivity of Sion, we were like people enjoying consolation; then our mouth was filled with happiness, and our tongue with rejoicing." And in another psalm the sentiment is identical, "When God reverses the captivity of his people, Jacob will rejoice and Israel be glad."[34] After all, it is logical that those who were grief-stricken in being snatched from their homeland

---

sians and John. Theodore avoids this by not bringing Jesus into focus, simply confining himself to "the events themselves"—πράγματα in preference to ὀνόματά, as Eustathius had reminded Origen's followers (KIT 83.16).

34. Gal 5.22; Pss 126.1–2; 53.8.

by the norm of captivity should on returning to it rejoice and be glad on account of the Lord's dwelling in its midst, the cause of rejoicing and gladness.

Now, what is the cause of gladness and rejoicing other than enjoying the torrents of the river filled with water, of which it is written, "The river of God was filled with water," and again, "The torrents of the river give joy to the city of God; God is in its midst, it will not be moved," since he no longer keeps his distance or abandons them, choosing in his goodness to abide in it? Now, what is the good and saving effect of the Lord's dwelling in the midst of the beautiful city if not the repentance of *many nations* and their *taking refuge in the Lord on that day* illuminated by the sun of righteousness? The patriarch Abraham had a longing for it and rejoiced to see it, and with him those who by faith and works became his sons and his children, thus exclaiming in thanks, "This is the day the Lord has made; let us rejoice and be glad in it."[35] The fact of *many nations taking refuge in the Lord* will result in their being styled the people of the one in whom they have taken refuge, no longer remaining godless and hopeless. God says of them in the prophet, "What was not my people I shall call my people, and they will say, You are the Lord my God," so that they will bear the name "holy nation, holy priesthood, God's race." In other words, in the sense indicated he says to those taking refuge in God what was said by the one in whom they take refuge: "You will be my chosen race, holy nation, royal priesthood, my people whom I have made my own to recount my virtues."[36]

Now, what follows from their becoming God's people other than his dwelling in the midst of the heavenly and blessed Sion? Then it is that by a divine and accurate insight they *will know that the Lord almighty sent* its redeemer, who says of his Father, "The Spirit of the Lord is upon me; hence his anointing me to bring good news to the poor, to proclaim release to cap-

35. Pss 65.9; 46.4–5; Mal 4.2; Jn 8.56; Gal 3.7; Ps 118.24. After dwelling to an unusual extent on the situation of the returned exiles, Didymus is not inclined to examine a historical basis for the advent of "many nations," moving instead to a spiritual level with employment of a string of loosely related texts.

36. Hos 2.25; 1 Pt 2.9; Ex 19.5–6.

tives."[37] It was, in fact, to bring good news to the poor that Jesus, who dwells in the midst of Sion, was anointed by the Holy
Spirit and the power of God to proclaim release to its children
held captive by invisible foes, this being the way that its benefactor the sovereign king will take possession of Judah, the con-
fessors (Judah meaning "confessing"). He will therefore first
take possession of those called to salvation, since from the beginning they were his portion, even before enduring dispersal
and captivity.

Where will he *take possession of* Judah, his portion, if not in
the holy land in which he will spend a long and pleasant time
honoring God his Father and his mother Jerusalem, which is
the Church? He will choose it yet again to assist it and reign in
its midst, aware as it is that he has come to dwell in its midst,
sent by the Lord almighty when he lowered heaven and came
down to us human beings, saying, "I have come down from
heaven so that I may do the will of the one who sent me," and
"to seek and to save what was lost."[38] Thus, they will not remain
in a state of ruin for whom he came to be the source of eternal
salvation. It will also be the fortune of Jerusalem, the Church of
the living God and composed of ourselves, to have such great
faith and works productive of happiness that it will still be chosen by him who with his own blood washes it and gives it splendor.

*Let all flesh show reverence before the Lord, because he has roused
himself from his holy clouds* (v.13). The term *flesh* is ambiguous,
and has many meanings, as emerges from divinely inspired
Scripture itself. In the Psalms, for instance, when it says, "God
gives nourishment to all flesh," it presents all mortal creatures
depending on nourishment for life, as also in the verse, "All
flesh associates with its own kind."[39] When, on the other hand,
the apostle writes, "Who ever hated his own flesh? Instead, they
nourish and care for it," there is reference to the body linked

37. Is 61.1–2; Lk 4.18.
38. Ps 18.9; Jn 6.38; Lk 19.10. A bishop of a gentile church like Theodoret
will accentuate the reference he sees in v.11 to the entry of gentiles into the
Church.
39. Ps 136.25; Sir 13.16.

to the rational soul, as is the sense occurring also in the same passage from the apostle that goes on, "Husbands should love their wives as they do their own bodies. After all, who ever hated his own flesh" and so on.[40]

There are also cases, however, where human beings alone are referred to by "flesh," as in the verse, "Hearken to my prayer; all flesh will come to you." Now, it is not the brute beast that comes to God in attitude and disposition—but only humanity, accorded the generous gift of the Holy Spirit by the one who says, "I shall pour out my Spirit on all flesh, and your sons and daughters will prophesy." In this usage flesh is rational and capable of reverence for God; for instance, it is directed to *show reverence before* the one who manifests himself to it, to whom the pure in heart offer a prayer in these words: "Show your face, and we shall be saved."[41] The text supplies the reason for all flesh being obliged to show reverence before the Lord God, *because he has roused himself from his holy clouds.*

Now, the holy clouds are not those that discharge a downpour that we feel, but those that bring the spiritual rain, in keeping with the Lord's saying in Isaiah about Israel, referred to in an allegorical mode as a vineyard, "I shall direct the clouds not to shed rain on it," because of its producing thorns and not a bunch of grapes. You see, as the vineyard is presented allegorically, so, too, in keeping with it are the clouds to be understood, which sometimes send rain to water it, and at others are prevented from performing that function. It is in connection with such showers that the same prophet is again directed by God, "Let the clouds rain down righteousness,"[42] righteousness being a virtue of the rational soul—not rain-bearing clouds that you can see, but the divine prophets, referred to as clouds in an anagogical sense.

40. Eph 5.28–29. Very helpfully and didactically Didymus distinguishes senses of σάρξ; not all terms need to be taken spiritually.

41. Ps 65.2; Jl 2.28; Ps 80.3.

42. Is 5.6; 45.8. Predictably Didymus finds "clouds" in his text harder to accommodate to the sense of the passage, this meaning being found by the LXX in a similar Heb. form for "dwelling"; so he immediately turns to allegory and a spiritual level of meaning.

Since, then, the savior has come and *has roused himself from these clouds* to fulfill the Law and the Prophets, hence *let all flesh show reverence before the Lord* God, who has become visible and manifest at the fulfillment of the prophecy expressed in these terms: "The God of gods will become visible on Sion," and he was so resplendent that "we saw his glory, that of the Only-begotten of the Father."[43] Having *roused himself from the holy clouds* (we have commented on the interpretation of these as Moses the great revealer and the prophets, who were under the influence of the Holy Spirit), he descended, riding on a light cloud, into our world, referred to anagogically as Egypt. This is the sense of the prophecy that begins thus: "Lo, the Lord is seated on a light cloud, and will come into Egypt, and its idols will be shaken." With Egypt taken in a transferred sense as this earth, accordingly the light cloud will also be given the spiritual sense of the Incarnation of the savior, since God the Word is seated on the one who comes forth from Mary. I mean, what is the light cloud that carries no heaviness of sin if not the flesh of Jesus, which derives not from the heavy union of man with woman, but from the Holy Spirit, who came in the virgin without her experiencing a man, the force of the Most High overshadowing her, with the result that what was born without intercourse is styled holy?[44]

The light and buoyant quality of the cloud of the Lord, however, is demonstrated further from the fact that the soul of Jesus did not personally commit or know sin; nothing, in fact, drags down and weighs upon the human soul as does iniquity, which is comparable to a lead weight, weighing upon and drawing downwards those committing it. Jesus' soul, by contrast, did not experience this weight: "loving righteousness and hating iniquity," he had "no guile in his mouth,"[45] which of all sins is

---

43. Mt 5.17; Ps 84.7; Jn 1.14. Didymus again gratuitously applies texts in a sense suiting his purpose (itself based on the LXX's misreading of the text). The following expression, "God the Word seated on the one who comes forth from Mary," on the other hand, does less than justice to the hypostatic union (in his fellow Alexandrian Cyril's later terminology).

44. Is 19.1; Lk 1.35.

45. Ps 45.6; Is 53.9; cf. 1 Pt 2.22.

the undoing of the soul guilty of it. It was therefore necessary that the savior, *rousing himself from his holy clouds* after fulfilling the prophecies about him, should be established in regal manner on the light cloud of which we have spoken, which showers the evangelical rain for the world to produce saving fruits and provide covering from the heat from which the understanding person is preserved, according to this proverbial oracle: "An understanding son is protected from the heat." It provides covering also from the cold of sin, of which Scripture says, "As a well keeps its water cool, so her wickedness keeps cool." The text, "The cold north wind will blow," is to be taken allegorically in this sense.[46]

Interpreting what has been said above in a discerning way, and with a fleshly heart obedient to God's ordinances and commands, let us practice reverence for God so that God may be still more favorable to hearts of flesh and not of stone, and may engrave on them divine characters with his living Spirit. Feeling the benefit of this, we may thus be made perfect so as to come face to face with the truth, surpassing a vision of it that is indirect or partial.[47]

46. Prv 10.5; Jer 6.7; Sir 43.20. This commentator's readiness in the name of θεωρία to take verses of Scripture in any sense that suits (even in cases where they are based on a mistranslation) explains the belief of Eustathius and Diodore in Antioch that for Alexandria allegory entailed no respect for the literal sense.

47. Ezek 36.26; 2 Cor 3.3; 1 Cor 13.12.

COMMENTARY ON ZECHARIAH 3

HE LORD SHOWED ME *Joshua the high priest standing before an angel of the Lord, and the devil standing at his right hand to oppose him* (Zec 3.1–2). What God reveals is wonderful and extraordinary, and beyond human powers to perceive. This being so, God shows the prophet the high priest Joshua, not in a human manner but standing in a godly way before an angel of the Lord. It was not so much the son of Jozadak as the one suggested by him,[1] the truly great high priest descended from heaven, made a priest "according to the order of Melchizedek," not in virtue of a fleshly command binding for a time, but according to permanent priesthood. It was said of him, in fact, "You are a priest forever." Jesus the high priest[2] was revealed by the Lord, not in a casual posture but serenely standing and firmly established, like the description in the Gospel: "Standing there Jesus cried aloud, Let anyone who is thirsty come to me and drink."[3] Anyone coming to him drinks, you see, for the reason that his position is immovable.

In addition to the sight of him standing there, God presenting him before an angel of the Lord, the devil also appeared, *standing at his right hand to oppose him.* Now, whom did the devil have to oppose and resist if not those on the right of the one revealed by the Lord standing in front of the angel of great counsel? Judas also stood on the right, as is said in Psalm 109, "Appoint a sinner over him, and let the devil stand at his right hand." Note, however, the great difference in the passages: the savior's betrayer stands at his right, occupying that position "af-

---

1. Joshua son of Jozadak is the priest referred to as a leading figure in the restoration; cf. Ezr 3.2. Didymus does not allow, as Cyril will, a historical basis for the vision.

2. The names Jesus and Joshua are identical in Greek: Ἰησοῦς.

3. Ps 110.4; Heb.7.17, 24; Jn 7.24 cited loosely—and inconsequentially?

ter making room for the devil." It is said, remember, that "he put it into his heart to betray" the person who had chosen him, both excellent teacher and savior; and after putting it into his heart, he entered into him so as to set in motion the plan of betrayal in him as in the sons of disobedience, Scripture saying, "After the morsel, Satan entered into him."[4] In the case of the high priest, on the other hand, he stood on his right for no other purpose than to oppose him, especially because he tries to undo those being assisted and instructed by him. Is it not with hostile intent that he stands on the right when he makes demands on those called to faith and the other virtues, according to the verse, "Lo, Satan has made demands on you to sift you like wheat, but I prayed for you," O Peter, our disciple, "lest your faith fail"?[5]

In addition to the fact that no harm is experienced by those he opposes, they even receive power against him so as to trample on every hostile force, not sustaining harm of any kind, thanks to their hope in the one crushing under the feet of the holy ones the rebellious and pernicious devil. It is written, remember, "Everyone with hope in God" remains unharmed and unmoved, the evil one being incapable of reaching or touching the person assisted by God's protective right hand. Note, for example, what the psalmist leaves ringing in the ears of those who find themselves under God's hand, "You made the Most High your refuge, trouble will not befall you nor the scourge come near your dwelling, because he has given his angels orders about you," and a little later, "You will tread on asp and basilisk, and tread underfoot lion and dragon."[6]

The one called lion and dragon here is called "the ancient Satan" in the Apocalypse of John. It would seem in that interpretation that "devil" and "Satan" are used interchangeably, the Hebrew term "Satan" meaning "adversary" in Greek. When they are understood in that sense, we are better off having the devil as a foe and adversary than as a friend: companionship

4. Ps 109.6; Eph 4.27; Jn 13.2, 27.
5. Lk 22.31.
6. 1 Jn 3.3; Wis 5.3; Ps 91.9–11, 13.

with him is harmful and productive of ruin. For example, he was close to Judas and made him "son of destruction," his own child to share even his name. The savior in fact says of him to the twelve disciples, "Did I not choose the twelve of you? And one of you is a devil."[7] In the case of Jesus himself, as a human being after assuming a human soul and body, he stood at his right as an adversary while he fasted in the desert for forty days and an equal number of nights. Was it not as an adversary that he took him up to the pinnacle of the Temple and said to him deceitfully, "Throw yourself down from here," showing him all the kingdoms of the world and their splendor with the words, "All this I shall give you if you fall down and worship me"? Despite his speaking with guile, he was undone, thrown down, and vanquished by the one who "was put to the test in everything" like other human beings.[8]

May God, help of the helpless, grant that we, too, whose "struggle is with the powers, the masters of this world of present darkness, and the spiritual forces of evil,"[9] remain protected from blows and falls, the evil one laying no hand upon us.

The Lord said to the devil, The Lord rebuke you, devil, and the Lord who has chosen Jerusalem rebuke you. Lo, is not this man like a brand snatched from the fire? (v.2) The Lord said to the devil, May he rebuke you, devil. And in the present verse the Lord speaks of the Lord, the Father of the Son, as was mentioned before. There is need to understand how the Lord speaks to the devil and what he says. It is not by use of any overt language in one of the human idioms that the Lord of all communicates to the devil, nor does he employ vocal organs, incorporeal and spiritual being as he is, nor does the devil to whom the words were addressed have a sense of hearing affected by sounds composed of syllables, especially when it is God who is speaking. Reading the book of Job, for example, and finding there God speaking to

---

7. Rv 12.9 and 20.2 (where "ancient serpent" is the phrase); Jn 17.20; 6.70. Though Didymus is aware of the Heb. sense of *satana* as simply "adversary," as distinct from the demonic sense found in NT usage of διάβολος, he does not check the text to find that it lies behind the LXX's διάβολος here, too.

8. Lk 4.9; Mt 4.9; Heb 4.15.

9. Eph 6.12.

the devil and the devil to God,[10] we are not so naïve as to think that questions and answers were delivered overtly in human discourse, a different mode being suited and appropriate to the persons in question. In other words, God speaks by indicating what he wishes to those he decides will hear him, as likewise he hears those conversing with him by knowing what they have in mind.

In the present text, at any rate, the Lord spoke to the devil, indicating to him the message in the following terms: *The Lord rebuke you, devil,* as if to say, You will be a vessel of wrath, in which and through which those to be chastised are rebuked in a manner worthy of their vile behavior. If, on the other hand, it were to him that *you* is addressed, the sentence would have the following meaning:[11] though you sin within yourself in secret, you do not escape notice in doing so; God rebukes you for your hidden sin and that of everyone else preceding you, aware as he is of the evildoing hidden within you. Now, because in this way evildoing is committed by the devil and many of those raised by him in wickedness, God says to him in Isaiah, "You said in your mind, I shall ascend to heaven," and so on to the point, "I shall be like the Most High." What is said in the psalm is also consistent with this, "The lawless person proposes within himself to commit sin." By sinning within himself, you see, and saying in his mind, "I shall ascend to heaven," he does not escape notice, becoming liable instead to rebuke. Similar in effect to these statements is the verse, "A fool said in his heart, There is no God."[12]

After showing that even the one sinning in secret does not escape punishment, he goes on to show who it is who rebukes, namely, he who chose Jerusalem. God's chosen city is presented under many guises: referred to as "Jerusalem" is the pure soul, who sees "peace surpassing all understanding," or the glorious Church of Christ, "holy and blameless, without spot or

10. Jb 1.7–12; 2.2–6. Again Didymus shows didactic skills in clarifying the process of divine communication.

11. Didymus is able to develop the notion of secrecy because for "(rebuke) you" the LXX reads ἐν σοί.

12. Is 14.13–14; Pss 36.1; 14.1.

wrinkle," or by a transcendent allegory the heavenly city of the
living God, as in the following verse, "You have made your approach to Mount Sion and the city of the living God, the heavenly Jerusalem, and to countless angels, and to the festal gathering."[13]

He makes clear what follows on the Lord's rebuking the devil: *Lo, is not this man like a brand snatched from the fire?* The brand
is a half-burnt piece of wood, close to being turned into char-
coal, no longer having the value and firmness of wood. In this
condition also were the foes of the king of the Hebrews, of
whom God said to him, "Do not be afraid, or let your heart
grow weak in the face of these two smoking brands."[14] As people subjected to punishment by fire appear to be weak, so, too,
the one who received a rebuke from the Lord, who chose
Jerusalem, proved so weak as no longer to bear fruit, losing vi-
tal force, like the brand snatched from the fire; the branch
burnt like this cannot any longer bear fruit, even if snatched
from the fire without being completely consumed and turned
into ashes. It is useful for other purposes to which God puts it
for the benefit of what is being manufactured, silver and gold
vessels being molded or beaten.[15] This, in fact, was the way the
one was pulled from the fire of captivity who was redeemed
from it by the person proclaiming release to captives[16] and giving return to their homeland, where they previously dwelt before the enemy attacked, capturing and uprooting them.

*Joshua was dressed in filthy clothes and standing before the angel,
who said in addressing those standing before him, Take the filthy clothes
off him. He said to him, See, I have taken away your iniquities. Put on
him a long tunic, and place a clean turban on his head. They clothed*

13. Phil 4.7; Eph 5.27; Heb 12.22. Didymus's third example is allegorical
like the preceding ones, but ὑπεραναβεβηκυία because realized at a higher level. He will proceed in comment on vv.3–5 (cf. n. 17) to speak of the reality, ἀλήθεια, and the image, εἰκών, pointing to it; the literal referent (the earthly
Jerusalem in this case) is only a shadow.

14. Is 7.4, the king in question being Ahaz of Judah, facing attack by King
Rezin of Aram and King Pekah of Israel.

15. Cf. 2 Tm 2.20.

16. Is 61.1. This time Didymus stays with the historical situation of the returning exiles, not developing the Christological application of the Isaian verse
by Lk 4.18.

him in garments (vv.3–5). It is possible to take at face value the text quoted about Joshua the high priest, who in figure points to the reality, the faithful high priest who has a lasting priesthood.[17] Since the holy ones are full of love, you see, they have compassion for those suffering misfortune, in their compassion "weeping with those who weep."[18] Hence, with Israel still suffering its fall into captivity, the priest entrusted with its care, and feeling grief and compassion, is *dressed in filthy clothes*, which the angel at his side bids be taken from him. Now, the filthy clothes are the actions performed unlawfully: after saying, *Take the filthy clothes off him*, he went on accordingly: *See, I have taken away your iniquities.* With the removal of his sins, represented by the filthy clothes, he puts on the long tunic, which is a priestly robe, clothing the wearer to his feet, and places a clean turban on the head of the one serving in priestly fashion *the Lord who has come and dwells in the midst* of Sion and Jerusalem. In the restoration and rebuilding of the city and the Temple, the leader of those freed from captivity wears "a garment of salvation and tunic of joy,"[19] casting off the soiled garments because he is suffering no longer, and instead feeling joy and happiness, now that those who experienced captivity are rescued from it.

Those ordered to remove from him the garments of mourning, referred to as *filthy*, are those who by sinning are responsible for his wearing such clothing. It is possible to understand those receiving the commands as the divine angels, surrounding those who fear God for their protection lest they any longer be downcast and depressed in their current misfortune.[20] In addition to what has been said regarding the historical narrative, there is also something to be said on the sense derived by dis-

17. Cf. Heb 2.17. Almost reluctantly, Didymus concedes that the text is susceptible of a literal interpretation, πρὸς ῥητόν, though this is but a *figure* of the *reality* in Jesus (the terms εἰκονικῶς and ἀληθῶς occurring, as mentioned in n. 13).

18. Rom 12.15.

19. Zec 2.14; Is 61.10. While the Antiochenes do not see a personal moral sense in the filthy garments, their text alone has Joshua wearing a headband (like Aaron's in Ex 8.9) as well as a turban.

20. While again Didymus looks for a "possible" interpretation at the historical level, he is more than ready to get beyond the literal to a more elevated sense derived by discernment, θεωρητέον.

cernment. Jesus the great high priest, of whom Joshua represents a type in figurative mode, living in Babylon as he did
along with the captives, put on as *filthy clothes* the sins of all human beings without sinning himself or experiencing sin. To
put off and remove the weave of sin that he put on for our sake,
he mounted the cross, so that the theologian Peter, Christ's
apostle, writes, "He who bore our sins in his body on the cross
so that, rid of sin, we might live by his righteousness."[21] In keeping with this, Paul, "the chosen instrument," writes a letter in
these terms: "He disarmed the rulers and authorities, publicly
triumphing on the cross, erasing the record against us by tear-
ing it up and setting it aside,"[22] so as publicly to triumph and remove the rulers and authorities previously encumbering us. After all, what is the alternative but for us to be invested again in
even worse notions by the one responsible for our subjection to
them?

The interpretation should be established by considering its
opposite. The person whose actions and attitudes are those
taught by the savior puts him on—namely, Christ—in keeping
with the statement, "Put on Christ Jesus," and, "All you who
have put on Christ." The person whose actions and thoughts
are from the evil rulers and authorities, against whom people
contesting for salvation direct their struggle, puts them on, accepting an identification with them. These are what our Lord
and savior put off by taking on our sins, Scripture saying of
him, "He bears our sins and suffers for us," and after other
statements in the prophecy of Isaiah, "He will take on the sins
of many."[23]

Even if Joshua[24] was seen clothed in filthy garments, therefore, they were not his, not woven or tailored by him: it was on
behalf of those who made them and were the principal wearers
of them that he put them on by the grace of the good God so

21. 1 Pt 2.22, 24 (or "for righteousness," Didymus's text including "his"). If
Paul is frequently referred to as "the apostle," Peter is a θεολόγος, and is given
particular mention at times by Didymus (unlike the Antiochenes).
22. Acts 9.15; Col 2.14–15 loosely cited.
23. Rom 13.14; Gal 3.27; Is 53.4, 11.
24. Or "Jesus": the movement from one level to another makes even the
commentator ambiguous.

that "by tasting death for everyone"[25] he might deliver from
death those for whom he tasted it, simply by touching it and approaching it. At any rate, even while clad in the filthy attire, he
stood before the angel, not keeping his distance from him.
Now, what does the angel say to those standing before Joshua?
Take the filthy clothes off him: they are not his, they are yours;
since it was because you did what was forbidden that he has
been clothed in defiled garments, repent of the sins you committed, and deliver him from the defilement of sin. There is
need to say yet again, "Though not acquainted with sin, Jesus
was made sin by God for your sake," taking up the cross "so that
in him we might become the righteousness of God." When this
happens, being made sin ceases to be his lot, the result being
that he will no longer have the filthy clothes of others. Similarly, he wears soiled clothing when he becomes a curse for the
sake of us all so that we may gain a blessing; he takes it off when
we receive the blessing, agreeing to become a curse and despising the shame so that we may live according to God.[26]

With the removal of the filthy garments, he puts on as great
and true high priest the priestly tunic called *long*, dons a *clean
turban*, and is invested by us with the *garment* of a human body;
in being responsible for his using such clothing, we invested
him in it. Yet even if he is invested with the afore-mentioned
garment while saying to God, "A body you have formed for
me," he still continues as high priest to wear the priestly tunic,
that long tunic, which served as a model for weavers, who were
filled with a spirit of wisdom, in making the material one; the
whole tabernacle, in fact, its vessels and the finery in which the
high priest was invested, were prepared on the model shown to
the revealer on the mountain.[27] The clean turban covers the
head—that is, the mind—of the high priest, the turban being
the summit of the divine doctrine about Christ, since it has
nothing of matter or defilement, while the tunic is the discernment of his Incarnation.

The angel of the Lord was standing by. The angel of the Lord as-

25. Heb 2.9.
26. 2 Cor 5.21; Gal 3.13–14; Heb 12.2.
27. Heb 10.5; Ps 40.6; Is 11.2.

sured Joshua, The Lord almighty says this: If you walk in my ways and keep my commandments, you will judge my house. If you guard my halls, I shall also give you those living in the midst of these attendants (vv.6–7). The angel who was standing firm and immobile assured Joshua in these words: *The Lord almighty says this: If you walk in my ways and keep my commandments.* Now, the Lord's ways are his virtues practiced in keeping with the observance of his commandments, of which the holy one says to God, "Make your ways known to me, Lord, and teach me your paths."[28] The one who walks and treads them in constant passage will gain divine rewards, receiving from the Lord the role of judging his house and guarding his divine halls. The *house* in this text is to be understood not as a place or a building but as the assembly of those occupying it, as the apostle suggests in saying, "Christ over his house as a son, we being his house"; and to Timothy he writes, "If I delay, it is for you to know how you must behave in God's house, which is the Church of the living God, the pillar and bulwark of truth." Now, this house is judged by Jesus, who has appointed in the Church "apostles, prophets, shepherds, teachers, for perfecting the saints"[29]—not casually, but with careful judgment and discernment, for one person to be appointed in the role of an apostle, another in the place of a prophet, while others are for pasturing Christ's flock and developing the divine teaching for those with a holy disposition for learning. Resembling these people is what occurs in the Psalms: "God has taken his place in an assembly of gods, in the midst he judges gods."[30]

What is thus styled God's *house* is in another sense Christ's body composed of and furnished with many limbs: its eyes are those who have opted for the contemplative life, as likewise its hands are for action, performing the deeds of virtue, the body's ears being the name for the intelligent listeners, who will individually say, "The Lord's instruction opens my ears." In an appropriate sense "those not wanting in zeal" might be called the

28. Ps 25.4.

29. Heb 3.6; 1 Tm 3.15; Eph 4.11.

30. Ps 82.1—a relevant and helpful reference? Scripture is once more a smorgasbord.

feet of Christ's body. It follows that *judging the house* of the Lord
is judging the divine body, so that one person is the eye (as
mentioned above), another the hand for performing what is
good to do and put into practice, and similar comment will be
made on the remaining limbs as well. In a way resembling the
judgment of God's house he also guards his divine halls, of
which the Holy Spirit cries aloud to those eager to live in them,
"Adore the Lord in his holy halls."[31]

Now, the return for judging God's house and guarding his
halls is presented in the verse *I shall also give you those living in
the midst of these attendants.* Those firmly set in holiness are the
ones presented as *standing by,* taking a stable position through
faith, whom the apostle addresses in writing, "Because you
stand firm in faith." In the Gospel in reference to those who in
this way are "founded and rooted" perfectly "in love," the savior
says, "There are some of those standing here."[32] Among those
standing in this way are those given to Jesus by God who are living according to a divine way of life and discernment of the
truth. Of the people who are faithful to the image and likeness
of God there lived Jesus, who received them from the Father,
and who "appeared on earth so as to live among human beings," providing a type and model for those choosing to imitate
him.[33]

In a second sense you could say that those shown *standing by*
are the angels assembled in choir in "thousands of thousands
and ten thousands of ten thousands" singing the praises of the
sovereign savior and ministering to him. Those who have become like angels after the resurrection and live amidst those attending on their creator are given to him, no longer marrying
and being given in marriage, no longer liable to death, when
the succession of marrying and raising a family has come to an
end, especially since their "corruptible element has put on incorruptibility and the mortal element immortality."[34] I mean,

31. Is 50.5; Rom 12.11; Ps 29.2. Predictably, these levels of meaning are not
found in the more jejune commentary by the Antiochenes, who simply see the
verses as a directive for proper behavior, dismissing them in a few brief lines.
32. 2 Cor 1.24; Eph 3.17; Mt 16.28.   33. Gn 1.26; Bar 3.37.
34. Rv 5.11; Mt 22.30; 1 Cor 15.53.

how is it possible that amidst the immortal angels and the other
divine powers standing by, there would not be living the one
who practices celibacy, "attentive to the things of the Lord,"[35]
ever attached and devoted in choosing the priestly service,
committed to his noble service, so to say? Similarly, the virgin
"holy in spirit and body" is devoted to pleasing the divine bridegroom, reluctant to be parted from him even for a moment. In
brief, all who have approached the savior by being in commun-
ion with him live among those who ever and without interruption *stand by* in holiness. One of those living this way sang the
praises of the sovereign king by proclaiming, "I shall sing to you
in the presence of the angels."[36]

Listen, Joshua the high priest and your intimates seated before you,
because they are seers. Because, lo, I bring my servant, Dawn by name.
Hence a stone which I have set before Joshua, and on the one stone are
seven eyes (vv.8–9). The angel of the Lord assuring Joshua the
high priest says this: Listen, Joshua the high priest, and let your
intimates and those seated before you listen, seers as they are: I
summon my servant Dawn, because on the stone I set before
Joshua there are its seven eyes. In what went before, Joshua the
high priest represents the one who serves as priest in the order
of Melchizedek, of whom the apostle writes in the letter to the
Hebrews, "Thus, holy brethren, partners in a heavenly calling,
consider that Jesus, apostle and high priest of our confession,
was faithful to the one who appointed him."[37] And note that
those capable of understanding that the apostle and high priest
of our confession is faithful to the one who appointed him are
the holy ones, partners in a heavenly calling. It is not for everyone, in fact, to perceive how Jesus, apostle and high priest, is
faithful to the one appointing him—but only for anyone
among the mature who is capable of speaking wisdom, able to
say, "I have seen Jesus"[38] with the eyes of my heart open to the
true light.

35. 1 Cor 7.32, 34, 35.
36. 1 Cor 7.34–35; Ps 138.1. We have lost sight, of course, of Joshua the high
priest.
37. Heb 3.1–2. Why does Didymus proceed to comment on this, and not the
Zechariah verses?
38. 1 Cor 9.1.

Of course, those not partners in a heavenly calling are, on the basis of this text, both deceivers and also themselves deceived in advance, claiming that the Son of God is creature and artifact. The fools are mindlessly astray in taking the phrase "who appointed him" of creation and bringing into existence, a sense the writer of the letter did not intend.[39] Being faithful apostle and high priest, you see, indicates that he is shown to be lasting and unchangeable apostle and priest: Jesus has not always been apostle and priest—only from when they came to be to whom he was sent and for whom he acts as priest. It was for them and on account of them that the descent to them occurred of the one sent by the Father, when "he bent down the heavens and descended" to those to whom he was sent and whose priest he is.

There are many texts suggesting by use of "faithful" lasting and unwavering: the statement about God, that "all his commandments are faithful, confirmed forever," and "I shall give you the holy promises made in faith to David," and even further, "I shall raise up for myself a faithful priest," implying lasting and immovable, that God's commands under the law of the Spirit are faithful on account of their unchangeable character, whereas the commands under the shadow of the Law are subject to change, passing from letter to Spirit and from shadow to reality.[40] By this process of discernment it is possible to understand also the story of the real David, the man with power in his hand—namely, the savior in his humanity, whose holy promises are faithful because they abide forever, his words abiding even if heaven and earth pass away.[41] Hence he is also faithful priest, with a priesthood that never passes away, being and shown to be in the order of Melchizedek.

To this high priest the angel of the Lord says, *Listen, Joshua*

39. It now emerges that Didymus has a Christological axe to grind, and has chosen this moment to do so with the rather contrived introduction of the Heb. verse, where the ποιήσαντα for "appointed" has led some "mindless" commentators to see a suggestion of subordination.

40. Ps 18.9; Ps 111.7–8; Acts 13.34; cf. Is 55.3.

41. Mt 24.35. Again Didymus dabbles in popular etymologies, another resource to support his argument, modern scholars not supporting his interpretation of "David"—and not agreeing among themselves.

the high priest and your intimates, those who are priests in a spiritual sense, ranked under you as the high priest, righteous people to whom it is said also in Isaiah, "You will be called priests
who serve God." Those in particular who as unmarried people
minister to God in complete chastity are the object of this
promise.[42] It is not only those, however, who hear the angel
with Joshua the high priest, but also those seated before him.
These are the ones who by rebirth in the resurrection of the
dead are seated before the savior, who is judge and king, and
judge the twelve tribes of Israel. They who with Joshua hear the
divine words of the angel are no different from the apostles, being close to him and seated before him; they are not infants or
children, but mature men, face to face with a man who is mature with the fullness of the knowledge of the Son of God.[43]
Hence they are also *seers*, in their wisdom enjoying an understanding of the portentous acts of power of the Lord so as to
grasp what is meant by them. Such knowledge was possessed by
Moses the great revealer and his brother Aaron the high priest,
Scripture saying that God "proposed to them the words of his
signs and his portents."[44] Now, how is the person not a *seer* who
enjoys not only the vision of divine portents and signs but the
very words by which they are performed?

This insight can be confirmed by one or two readings from
the Gospels. The bringing to sight of the man blind from birth
was a sign and portent, when his eyes were rubbed with mud
composed of soil and the benefactor's spittle.[45] Since this happened in unprecedented fashion, the one who discerns the
prototype indicated in it is a seer: the people from the nations,
who previously had no sight because they had been reared in

42. Is 61.6. Also in comment on v.7 Didymus saw those practicing celibacy
given precedence in service of the Lord.

43. Mt 19.28; Eph 4.13–14.

44. Ps 105.26. Still no attempt to relate these verses of Zechariah to events
of his time.

45. Jn 9.1–7. Didymus sees typology operating in this Gospel incident, the
gift of sight to the blind man pointing to the archetype, or πρωτότυπος, the enlightenment of the nations. Editor Doutreleau, SC 83.322, notes that this incident of the gift of sight, and in fact the theme of light generally in the Scriptures, is dear to this blind commentator, as also to other Fathers.

godlessness and ignorance of God, are to be taken as the man blind from birth gaining sight at the time when they knew Christ and had their eyes rubbed with the mud made from the spittle of Jesus, experiencing the Incarnation of the one who brought them to sight. In addition to this the woman with a flow of blood for twelve years was delivered from the flow of unclean blood, which prevented her from having children, by touching Jesus' hem. It was a portent that was without precedent: the person who understands it is a seer, interpreting what happened in portentous fashion to the woman in a transferred sense as the purifying of the Church from the nations.[46]

After bringing out everything seen in the text in hand, he goes on, I the Lord almighty *bring my servant, Dawn by name,* by his servant referring to the one from David's offspring according to the flesh, "who took the form of a servant, emptying himself though being in the form of God." This servant of God being introduced is that dawn of which it is said in the Gospel, "A dawn from on high to enlighten those seated in darkness and a shadow of death," being no other than "the true light."[47] In showing his servant, the Father says, "See, a man, Dawn is his name," calling him "a man" as a result of the Incarnation, and "Dawn" on account of his rising, sun of justice as he is; there is mention of him, for example, at the end of the Twelve Prophets on the part of the Father who sent him, "The sun of justice will arise for you who fear my name, and healing is in his wings."[48]

---

46. Mt 9.20–22. Implicitly Didymus commends readers of Scripture who (unlike the ideal proposed to readers in Antioch) take it in a transferred sense, thus becoming "seers." By contrast, the Zecharian term means to Theodore those "capable of discerning and understanding the causes of what is done in puzzling fashion by God"; see his *Commentary on Zechariah* 3.8, ed. H. N. Sprenger, 343; trans. Hill, FOTC 108.344.

47. Phil 2.6–7; Lk 1.79; Jn 1.9. Without, of course, checking as to whether the LXX has correctly rendered the term "Dawn" (which it sees in the Heb. form for "shoot," found also at 6.12), Didymus confirms his accreditation as a "seer" by at once moving to a transferred sense of the clause. He is not interested in any historical referent for this man, unlike the Antiochenes, who see Zerubbabel ("shoot of Babylon") in focus.

48. Zec 6.12; Mal 4.2. Evidence of the accuracy of the term Dawn is intertextual, not linguistic. Didymus knows the Twelve as a unit in the manner of Sir 49.10 and the Hebrew Bible; Augustine is yet to refer to them as *prophetae minores* (on grounds only of length, not stature).

To supply the reason for introducing his servant Dawn, the text goes on, *Hence the stone in front of* the one providing enlightenment *has seven eyes.*[49] Now, this person can be no one but the savior, who has descended, with a nature endowed with a seven fold capability of seeing. At any rate, in Isaiah it is said of him, "A rod will come forth from the root of Jesse, and a flower spring up from the root; a spirit of God will rest upon him, a spirit of wisdom and understanding, a spirit of counsel and strength, a spirit of knowledge and piety, and it will fill him with a spirit of the fear of God."[50] Note, in any case, the seven eyes of the Lord on one stone, one being a spirit of wisdom and another of understanding; the shining eye of this kind, in fact, surveying everything good and great, is nothing other than the spirit of wisdom, and likewise the spirit of understanding.

The spiritual stone endowed in this way with eyes is counsel and strength, perceiving everything in a manner suggesting counsel and strength, and was filled with the Spirit of God in a knowledgeable and pious manner especially at that time when it assumed the form of a servant. For example, it did not receive from an external source the spirit of wisdom and understanding, of counsel and strength, of knowledge and piety, that rests upon it (it is said to "rest upon" it, in fact); in other words, each item mentioned is specific and appropriate to it, the spirit of fear alone coming so as to complete it. This spirit of fear is referred to by another term, reverence, applicable to the one born of Mary, of whom the apostle writes in the following text: "In the days of his flesh he offered up prayers and supplications with loud cries and tears to the one capable of rescuing him from death, and he was heard because of his reverence."[51] It is not as God, however, that he has reverence, but as man.

49. Playing upon the identity of his name and priestly role with Joshua's, Didymus has no hesitation in reading the Zechariah verse to refer to Jesus ("the one providing enlightenment" deriving from a unique reading of his in the Lukan verse above).

50. Is 11.2–3. Strangely, Didymus does not proceed to develop the significance of the number seven, which, while puzzling modern commentators (and dismissed by Theodore as involving an "idle chase after detail"; see his *Commentary on Zechariah*, ed. Sprenger, 343), might be thought to have appealed to an Alexandrian.

51. Heb 5.7.

Now, proof that the one with the sevenfold faculty of vision is called *stone* comes from the divine Scriptures. Peter, the apostle chosen before the others, cites the verse from the Psalms that runs as follows, "The stone that the builders rejected was turned into the head of the corner," and directs it against the teachers of Israel as highly critical of them: "This is the stone spurned by you the builders, but proving to be the head of the corner." After all, did it not join the two walls and make a single corner, when it was built of Jews coming to the Gospel and of those from the nations who believed? The Church, in fact, is composed of both Jews and Greeks, with Christ as its head making a single corner. Those who are fitted into one building were then in harmony in one faith, all human beings being made into a single new human being from two peoples after accepting the divine Gospel.[52]

The stone announced in those terms, "a cornerstone, chosen, precious, God has laid as the foundations of Sion, no one ashamed any longer" for any sin, since everyone believing in him has become an expiatory sacrifice. Those who make their approach to the living Word that is never to die are alive themselves, and built into the house, ceasing to attract notice as stones, so that a spiritual house and spiritual altar are formed, on which are offered the sacrifice of praise and all similar spiritual ones. May we, too, become living stones that are holy, rolling on God's land, so that "built on the foundations of the apostles and prophets of Christ Jesus" we may form a spiritual temple and house for God to live in us.[53]

Lo, I shall dig a pit, says the Lord almighty, and I shall take hold of all the injustice in that land in one day. On that day, says the Lord almighty, each of you will invite your neighbor under your vine and under your fig tree (vv.9–10). I shall dig a pit, says the Lord almighty, to reveal all that is hidden, and to touch and take hold of all the injustice of that land—namely, that which is dug up—on one bright day, the time when the Lord God almighty "sheds light on things hidden by darkness, and reveals the

52. Ps 118.22; Acts 4.11; Eph 2.14–21. Peter once more gains honorable mention; see n. 21 above.

53. 1 Pt 2.4–7; cf. Is 28.16; Zec 9.16 LXX.

plans in people's hearts" so as to condemn those guilty of every iniquity.[54]

The moment of our savior's descent can be referred to as *one day*, since on it the one who sheds light, at once benefactor and judge, took hold of all the iniquity of the world as revealed by "taking away the sin of the world." With that achieved, and with the removal of iniquity, which is mother of every revolution and every war, there will be profound peace, so that there will be no one to fear any longer. Demons who stirred up revolutions and wars will be put down along with the other hostile powers, called "cosmic powers of this present darkness," the result being that all people from then on live without fear and even invite their neighbors under fig tree and vine. Outlining this restoration of peace and stability, Micah the prophet also makes the following forecast with advance knowledge of that day: "Each person will invite his neighbor and his brother under his fig tree and vine, with no one to cause alarm."[55] After all, how could there still be anyone to cause alarm when all those who stir up revolutions and wars are put down?

The reference in the plants mentioned—I mean vine and fig tree—is none other than the contemplative and the active life: the vine because it bears the fruit of knowledge and understanding that is productive of happiness; the fig tree the fruit of action, bitter as it is and harsh on account of the sweat and toil expended in the acquisition of virtue. It is of the fig tree thus portrayed that the Solomonic oracle in Proverbs speaks: "The one who plants a fig tree eats its fruits, and the one who attends to the Lord will be honored." The factual basis is not beyond dispute: many people plant a physical fig tree without harvesting or eating its fruit, either prevented by death or being located far from the tree they planted. It is only those who planted a spiritual tree that eat its fruit. As mentioned, on the other hand, the *fig tree* refers to the active life that is productive of

54. 1 Cor 4.5. As he often does, Didymus paraphrases the text (though without exploring its historical reference) before acting as a "seer" in moving to an elevated sense.

55. Jn 1.29; Eph 6.12. The citation of Mi 4.4 is rather that of Zechariah, itself differing slightly from the LXX.

good, and the *vine* is to be understood properly as a branch of the true vine. Each of Jesus' disciples, remember, is a branch of the savior, who says, "I am the vine, you are the branches; every branch abiding in me bears abundant fruit."[56]

Those who cultivate the trees mentioned love their fellows and their family, and they invite one another under their vine and fig tree in peace to live enjoyably. For example, when you see the man gifted with knowledge showing an interest in bringing his neighbors to the sage contemplation of God and his teachings and attitudes, you consider how he invited the neighbors, whom he loves as himself, under his own vine so as to celebrate and be happy together. Similarly, the one perform-ing good deeds brings his friends under the fig tree he plant-ed—namely, the practice of virtue—so as to be at leisure to-gether, entering into the joy of their master.[57]

56. Prv 27.18; Jn 15.5. While the factuality, ἱστορία, of proverbs and other scriptural statements may be disputed, Didymus says, there is no disputing their spiritual sense.

57. Cf. Mt 25.21.

COMMENTARY ON ZECHARIAH 4

HE ANGEL SPEAKING *in me approached and woke me in the way a person is woken from sleep, and said to me, What do you see? I replied, I see and, lo, a lampstand all of gold, on top of it a lamp, seven lights on top of it, seven spouts of the lights on top of it, and two olive trees above it, one on the right of its lamp and one on its left* (Zec 4.1–3). The angel speaking in me moved from one revelation to another vision, waking me up to see it by raising me up like someone who was asleep. He *said to me, What do you see?* For my part I replied to him, *I see and, lo, a lampstand all of gold, on top of it a lamp, seven lights,* and the same number of spouts carrying oil to the lights. I also saw *two olive trees above* the lampstand, *one on the right* of the lamp and *one on the left.*

It is time to see what each thing shown to the prophet means. The angel constantly speaking in me without interruption, who returned and woke me (the holy one says), is probably none other than "the angel of great counsel." He woke me like a man waking from sleep and coming to his senses. This waking is commendable, the result being that the one who looks forward to it exclaims with confidence, "I shall awake at dawn"; and when the expectation has been fulfilled by the implementation of the prophecy, he cries out in thanksgiving, "I awoke because the Lord will defend me."[1] Now, this verse is applied to the savior awoken from the dead after having been asleep in respect of his humanity. After all, how was he not awoken from sleep when he rose from the dead after spending three days and three nights in the heart of the earth, bringing benefit to the souls in Hades, gladdening them and filling them with the enjoyment experienced there? He says, at any

1. Is 9.6 LXX; Pss 57.9; 3.5.

rate, "I intoxicated every thirsty soul, and satiated every hungry soul," providing "wine to gladden people's hearts and bread to strengthen the spirit of the one being nourished." I awoke and saw that the souls that had drunk were enjoying a sober intoxication and were satiated, as it were, with saving nourishment. Hence "sleep was pleasant for me," that is, "the death I tasted on everyone's behalf," thanks to God's benevolence.[2]

Awakened like this "person in distress and accustomed to bearing weakness,"[3] the divine prophet listens to the angel awakening him with the words, *What do you see?* Having seen with the enlightenment of the eyes of his heart the vision that came into his ken, he replied to him, *I see a lampstand all of gold.* In saying the lampstand was all of gold, he indicates that the lampstand completely covered in lights is in the mind, immaterial. We do not find everywhere in Scripture that spiritual things are suggested by gold; so perhaps the lampstand in the mind is the spiritual house and temple of God, as is said in the book of Revelation by John, where the one showing the revelation to the neophyte says, "The seven lampstands that you saw with the eye of your mind are the seven churches."[4]

On the completely golden lampstand there is a lamp, the luminous doctrine of the Trinity; from this lamp the wise virgins lit their lamps when in torchlight procession to meet their divine bridegroom. Enlightened with the light of knowledge, they themselves have a share in God's light, in which there is no shadow of evil or ignorance; they share also in the "true light,"[5]

---

2. Jer 31.25–26; Ps 104.15; Heb 2.9. The extended Christological development, resting on a slim basis surely, is predictably ignored by the Antiochenes. Doutreleau, SC 83.336, observes that the theme of "sober intoxication" is found in a eucharistic and eschatological sense in Gregory of Nyssa and Symeon the New Theologian.

3. Is 53.3.

4. Cf. Rv 1.20, Didymus inserting the subordinate clause. His method of explication emerges here: faced with the detail of a golden lampstand, he shows no interest in any factual basis, proceeding at once to recall other occurrences of "gold" in Scripture (as we might consult a concordance); then, failing to find an entry under that head, he lights upon the lampstands in Revelation. It is exegesis by association, the association being often slim and contrived. Theodore was content to make the obvious remark that "gold [is] the most precious of all earthly materials" (Sprenger ed., 345; Hill trans., FOTC 108.346).

5. Cf. Mt 25.1–13; Jn 1.9. While the trinitarian interpretation is gratuitous,

while by having a share in the Holy Spirit they form a choir of lampbearers. Just as the lamp appeared atop the lampstand, on which we have commented, so, too, seven lights appeared on top of the lampstand itself, providing a sevenfold illumination. In other words, in the same way that seven eyes represent the perfect light of the mind and seven pillars support Wisdom's house,[6] so, too, the seven lights are positioned on the lampstand.

In another sense the latter represents the soul and flesh which the savior assumed in his descent: how could this lampstand not be completely golden, having committed or experienced no sin, and supporting as it did seven lights, the spirit of wisdom and understanding, the spirit of divine counsel, strength, knowledge, piety, and fear of God? How each of these relates to the one springing from the root of Jesse, on whom they rest, was clarified before at the occurrence of the verse, "A rod shall emerge from the root of Jesse," and the whole prophetic passage from the text dealing with them.[7] This sevenfold efficacy of the seven lights on the lampstand is nourished and increased from the oil running through the seven spouts bringing oil to nourish and maintain the flame. Now, the oil is nothing other than meditation on the knowledge of the truth;[8] from meditation we gain remembrance and a more powerful insight.

In addition to all that was seen—the lampstand, the lamp, the seven spouts and equal number of lights—there also appeared two olive trees on top of the lampstand, one located on the right of the lamp and the other on the left. Take note as to whether the oil obtained from the olive tree on the right means meditation on the spiritual realities and the gifts of the Holy

---

Didymus—fascinated again with the theme of light—brings out the virgins' trinitarian share in the lamplight. Cyril, by contrast, gives the passage an ecclesiological interpretation, his normal practice; see P. E. Pusey, ed., *Sancti Patris Nostri Cyrilli Archiepiscopi Alexandrini in XII Prophetas*, vol. 2, 330.

6. Prv 9.1.

7. Cf. comment on Zec 3.9.

8. Didymus does not trouble to establish this spiritual sense; the readers must just take his word for the gratuitous identification, as is the case also in the following interpretation of the two olive trees.

Spirit, and oil pressed from the olive tree on the left means meditation on the world, its composition, and God's providence for it. Some people believe, following another way of discernment, that the olive tree on the right of the lamp represents contemplation of the only-begotten Son of God, while that located on the left nourishes consideration of the Incarnation, the latter also giving light but not in the same fashion as the discernment on the right, which has pride of place.[9] I personally once heard a teacher who presides over the whole Church clarifying the present passage to the effect that the lamp on top of the lampstand is the light shed on the Father, while the olive trees on its right and left are the considerations about Son and Holy Spirit.[10] The person who offered this interpretation, however, did not explain why one is on the right and the other on the left.

Since in our way of discernment of the lampstand, it is not material but spiritual, take note as to whether it is what Moses saw on the mountain in the type shown him, which is nothing else than what is called the ideal form; in keeping with the invisible and spiritual lampstand, the material one was fashioned according to the design of the revealer Moses.[11] It is not inappropriate to add to what was seen also what was said in the Gospel by Jesus, "No one lights a lamp and conceals it under a vessel or a bed instead of putting it on a lampstand for everyone in the house to see the light." It is possible in this to understand the house as the Church of the living God, which is his house; those staying and living in it with attitudes in line with its teachings are illuminated by the lamp placed on the lamp-

---

9. Didymus clearly gives precedence to θεωρία, contemplation, over λόγος, rational thought, as a means of accessing spiritual realities, like the true meaning of the lampstand—the historical reference of which, of course, not being of interest to him. Diodore would not see an antithesis, and in fact would give a priority to the latter.

10. For Doutreleau, SC 83.343, this διδάσκαλος of the "whole [local] Church" (of Alexandria) would be Athanasius, who died in 373, a dozen or so years before this work.

11. Cf. Nm 8.1–4 (though the instructions were given in the tent of meeting, not on the mountain). Doutreleau, SC 83.343, remarks on Didymus's use of philosophical terms like ἰδέα as well as biblical notions.

stand, which is lit by the one who instructs those living in God's
house according to the laws, norms, and teachings of the
Church's judgment. This teacher sheds light when he raises his
mind like a lamp, not concealing it under bed or vessel, but
proposing it in his public discourse (the allegorical meaning of
"lampstand"), using "the language of instruction when there is
need to speak."[12]

It is also possible to speak of the lampstand as the active life,
for on it is placed the enlightened mind of the one who sheds
the light of knowledge on himself. Let the person who is interested in the present clarification of the inspired text in hand
judge whether it should be accepted or another looked for
from experienced people, this being the way to gain a precise
understanding.[13]

*I put a question to the angel speaking within me in these terms:
What are these things, Lord? The angel speaking within me replied to
me in these terms:*[14] *This is the word of the Lord to Zerubbabel: Not by
great power, nor by strength, but by my Spirit, says the Lord almighty*
(vv.4–6). The prophet says he put a question to the angel
speaking within him, wanting to learn the meaning of the divine visions given him, whether all the revelations or those immediately preceding the text in hand have to do with the completely golden lampstand and what was on top of it, the lamp
and the seven spouts and equal number of lights, and the two
olive trees, one on the right and the other on the left of the
lamp. To this question about the vision of these things, immaterial as they were, the one who was asked immediately said in reply that they were God's word to Zerubbabel. Hence it emerges
that what was shown were spiritual visions and that it was true.
The communication of the revelations came to the prophet
when he was still in Babylon where there was no house of God

12. Lk 8.16; Is 50.4.
13. If Didymus shows considerable flexibility in allowing his readers to
choose from the smorgasbord of interpretations of the lampstand he has arrived at, his only norm for selection is guidance from a trusty mentor. He could
not offer them precise hermeneutical principles.
14. At this point Didymus's text omits the clauses, "Do you not know what
they are? I said, No, Lord. He replied to me," as does his commentary.

built containing vessels, including the lampstand and what was above it.[15]

With this being seen, we must confine ourselves to the explanation given of it, or look for greater significance. The message that the angel gives to the prophet is not given with great power or with human strength or anything else: it is said and made clear by the Spirit of the Lord. Now, the Holy Spirit of the Lord is repeatedly mentioned in the Scriptures, including the Scriptures beyond the passage in hand. The statement is made of him also in Isaiah, for example, in these terms, "The Spirit of the Lord is upon me, for whose sake he anointed me." In similar terms the apostle Paul writes in his letter to the Corinthians, "What human being knows what is human except the human spirit that is within? So also no one comprehends what is God's except the Spirit of God, who searches even the mystical depths of God." And again in Isaiah the one who is the origin and caretaker of all things says, "A spirit will come forth from me."[16]

It was by this Spirit that what was shown in the sight of Zerubbabel was made clear, not by the *great power or strength* of any created person; of a different kind is the power conferred with the Spirit to those who are worthy, the savior saying of it to his disciples in the Acts of the Apostles when ascending to heaven and to his Father, "You will receive power from the Holy Spirit coming upon you." In similar terms at the end of the Gospel according to Luke, the savior on going back to where he came from gave the Holy Spirit to the apostles with the words, "For your part, stay in the city until you are clothed with power from on

15. As was remarked above, if Didymus is going to show any interest in the historical *Sitz im Leben* of the verses cited, it will be in this opening paraphrase of a passage, before he moves to another level of meaning. The reader, however, might have expected something on the role of Zerubbabel in the restoration and his background as acknowledged even in the New Testament (cf. Lk 3.27); he looms large in the Antiochene commentaries.

16. Is 61.1; 1 Cor 2.11, 10 ("mystical" probably Didymus's own insertion); Is 57.16 LXX. It is perhaps in the light of this anxiety of Didymus to establish that πνεῦμα here and in other OT passages refers to the Holy Spirit (to refute opponents like the Macedonians, Doutreleau suggests; SC 83.348) that Theodore will vigorously (and more properly) deny knowledge of the Holy Spirit to the people of the OT (as in his comments on Jl 2.28 and Hg 2.5); see Sprenger ed., 95, 310–11, and Hill trans., FOTC 108.117, 313–14.

high."[17] No different is the actual power of Christ, "the wisdom and power of God," in virtue of which the evangelical preaching was delivered by the apostles, one of whom, Paul, writes, "My speech and my preaching were not in cloquent words of human wisdom, but with a demonstration of the Spirit and with power." These attributes, though stemming from God, are sometimes styled the qualities of the possessor, as in the case of John in the Gospel, who went before the Lord "with the spirit and power of Elijah." Examine precisely whether the annunciation to Mary by the holy angel Gabriel has the same sense, "The Holy Spirit will come upon you, and the power of the Most High will overshadow you."[18]

It was with the Spirit of God mentioned in the passages cited and in many others that the announcement was made in the presence of Zerubbabel and of the power associated with him, and not with any other *great power and strength*, which would be inferior, even if divine and much to be desired.

Who are you, mighty mountain before Zerubbabel, to achieve anything? I shall bring forth the stone of the inheritance, its grace an equality of grace (v.7). The prophet in his vision or the angel speaking in him directs a question to someone, as it were, rational and receptive of the divine voice. What does he say to him? *Who are you, O mountain before Zerubbabel, to achieve anything?* What is *the stone of the inheritance* that I shall remove, *its grace an equality of grace?* Whichever way it is taken, both terms are equally applicable to the savior in his descent, many texts calling him *mountain* and *stone*. For example, in the verse, "The mountain of the Lord will be visible on the last day," it is God's Son through whom he has spoken on the last day after having spoken through Moses and the prophets. It is also he who is pointed to in the verse, "Ascend Mount Sion, you who bring good news to Sion"; and there are many other texts about him that we must pass over now lest our treatment be drawn out endlessly, especially since the identification of the mountain with the savior was frequently the subject of com-

17. Acts 1.8; Lk 24.9.
18. 1 Cor 1.24; 2.4; Lk 1.17, 35.

ment in our notes on the divine Psalms and the final vision of Isaiah.[19]

The savior, however, who is called *mountain,* is also spoken of as *stone* in the verse, "The stone which the builders rejected has become the head of the corner." Recalling this text in the Acts of the Apostles, Peter, the most eminent disciple of the savior, spoke with greatest reproach against Pharisees, scribes, and Sadducees for priding themselves on the Jewish teaching, "He is the stone scorned by you the builders that has become head of the corner." And since he is not only head of the divine building but also its foundation, God makes a promise about him in the words, "Lo, I am placing a cornerstone as Sion's foundations, chosen, precious, on whom the believer places his hope without fear of shame." After citing these texts, Peter, disciple of Christ, on whom the Church is built, exhorts and advises those to whom he composed his letter, "Come to him, a living stone, and be built into a spiritual house in which spiritual sacrifices are offered."[20]

Of what sort of inheritance is the stone? Of the kind described in Isaiah, "It is an inheritance for the servants of the Lord," and of which the psalmist said, "My inheritance is the finest for me; you are the one to restore my inheritance to me."[21] See whether it is the stone of that inheritance which is filled with those who are godly in every respect, chosen and loved by the author of all things in the terms announced by those spirit-filled men, apostles, evangelists, prophets, and the great revealer of all things, Moses: "He chose for us his inheritance"—God, that is—"the beauty of Jacob, which he loved." Of

19. Mi 4.1; Heb 1.1–2; Is 40.9. Of the two works of his own that Didymus cites here, only the former is extant. The Antiochenes see no reason to take these verses Christologically (even Jerome demurring, and Origen having preferred to see the devil in focus; see Jerome on Zec 4.7, CCL 76A.780, and Origen on Jer 28.25, GCS 3.129).

20. Ps 118.22; Acts 4.11; 1 Pt 2.4–6—texts which (despite his insistence on not repeating himself) Didymus cited shortly before on Zec 3.9 to make the same point. Peter again receives honorable mention; he is now also the one "on whom the Church is built."

21. Is 54.17; Ps 16.6, 5.

equal force with the psalm verse is also the one in the great song of Deuteronomy, which runs as follows: "Jacob became the Lord's part, Israel the cord of his inheritance." In particular the celebrated stone of the inheritance is the one indicated in the second psalm by the stone himself, "The Lord said to me, You are my son; this day I have begotten you. Ask it of me, and I shall give you nations for your inheritance."[22]

In addition to the interpretation already given, that the mountain and the stone refer equally to the same person, it must also be said from another point of view that the mountain signifies one thing and the stone another. The mountain of achievement is Mary, who had no experience of marital intercourse, and the stone issuing from her is the son she bore without man's involvement. The book of the most wise Daniel initiates us in these matters;[23] in it there is mention that the stone striking the various kingdoms and the statue composed of them was cut without human hands and separated from it without the customary action of parents that is directed at generation. In other words, all people owe their generation to both parents; by their "hands" in the sense of marital acts they are separated and cut from the mother. Only the one born of the virgin who did not know a husband was separated and cut from her without hands.

It is *before Zerubbabel* that the stone is cut from the mountain without hands because the genealogy of Jesus is drawn from him as well. In any case, his name is rendered "change of process" because the customary process of the parents was changed, being completed by a virgin alone without a man being involved. The stone removed from the inheritance has *grace from grace*, this being the understanding of John the Baptist in saying, "Of his fullness we have all received": the coming of the savior and the salvation resulting from it are entirely the effect of grace, as the theologian announces to those to whom he ad-

22. Ps 47.4; Dt 32.9; Ps 2.7–8.
23. Cf. Dn 2.34, 45. This figure of the stone cut without use of human hands taken from Daniel is invoked by other Fathers, including Theodoret (*Commentary on Daniel*, PG 81.1303), though not at this point. For Didymus Mary is the mountain of κατόρθωσις, from the verb in v.7.

dresses his letter, "By grace you have been saved, and this is not from us: it is God's gift."[24]

The word of the Lord came to me saying, The hands of Zerubbabel laid the foundations of this house, and his hands will complete it. You will thenceforth acknowledge that the Lord almighty has sent me to you (vv.8–9). The prophecy is not referring to material construction of a visible house. It has already been said, remember, that this prophet was in Babylon when in the course of the seventieth year of the captivity he was initiated into the present revelations. The material house was built not in Babylon, however, but in Jerusalem and after the captivity. Hence this present verse does not refer to it: he uses the demonstrative of it as though of a temple already in existence, *this house.* The house erected in Jerusalem after the return from captivity was not before his eyes while in Babylon.[25]

Even if this does not refer to the material building, however, at least it indicates the archetype of the visible one, one that is spiritual and as it were the ideal form providing a likeness of the one being constructed. It has also been mentioned before that just as the tabernacle and the furnishings in it were prepared according to the model of the invisible tabernacle shown on the mountain—that is, the archetype on high—so the physical house erected from material stones is an imitation and image of the one shown to Zechariah the prophet under the form of a vision, not by sensory experience. The implementation of this archetype the hands of Zerubbabel initially began and his active powers will complete; when it happens, you will know, as the recipient of the promise, *that the Lord almighty has sent me to*

24. Mt 1.13; Lk 4.27; Jn 1.16; Eph 2.8 (reading "from *us,*" as some manuscripts read, "*we* have all been saved). The Johannine text, along with its preceding verse 15, is attributed to John the Baptist in Alexandrian exegesis from Origen's time (Raymond Brown informs us; see *The Gospel According to John I–XII,* Anchor Bible 29 [Garden City, NY: Doubleday, 1966], 15). Didymus's popular etymology is again wide of the mark, Zerubbabel meaning instead "shoot of Babylon."

25. As some modern commentators see these verses as part of an interpolation, so Didymus sees grounds for ruling out reference to a material building and taking the reference to be to a spiritual temple. At the opening of commentary he had not specified the prophet's location, but on 4.4–6 he had opted for Babylon (against the Antiochenes and modern commentators).

you for you to be enlightened and gain insightful understanding of what was prophesied in a divine vision.

Now, the prophet under discussion could also say the same as Paul, speaking in Christ, when he writes in these terms: "I shall come to revelations and visions of the Lord." In keeping with God's communication by revelations to people who discern interiorly, the psalmist says in the Psalms, "Then you spoke in a vision to your sons,"[26] since God the Word does not speak by ears and voice to those in possession of the spirit of adoption. As the true light, you see, he enlightens the mind of those he wishes to receive his divine communications, speaking by vision rather than by hearing; for example, when God spoke this way also in Isaiah in the verse, "A vision which Isaiah saw," it was not visible things that followed but words. I mean, what is visible about the verse, "Listen, heaven, and give ear, earth, for the Lord has spoken: I have begotten sons and elevated them, but they set me at naught." To the same effect is what is said in connection with the fifth of the Twelve Prophets: after the statement, "Vision of Obadiah," no sensory vision occurs, only words in this vein: "The Lord says this to Idumea: I heard a message from the Lord, and I sent a notice to the nations, You have been severely dishonored," and so on.[27]

Because who was scornful for a brief time? They will rejoice and see the tin stone in the hand of Zerubbabel. These seven eyes are looking down on the whole earth (v.10). Because who was the one briefly despising? This is the time after which comes the restoration, when those in Babylon as a result of captivity make the return journey to their homeland. Now, the *brief time* means days few in number, and especially days cut short, the sun not remaining long in the vault above the earth. The former sense should be taken in light of the giving of the revelations to the prophet in the seventieth year of the captivity, so that the prophet himself says to God, *How long will you have no mercy on Jerusalem and the cities of Judah you have overlooked? This is the seventieth year.* Consis-

26. 2 Cor 12.1; Ps 89.19 LXX.
27. Is 1.1–2; Ob 1–2 (fifth in the order of The Twelve in the Alexandrian LXX, fourth in our Heb. and the Antiochene LXX).

tent with this vision is what was said in the Gospel by the savior, "If those days had not been shortened, no one would be saved."[28] Shortening the days of tribulation implies that the distress will not last a very long time, quickly coming to an end, so that the strength of those being maltreated will be sufficient for them to compete nobly to win prize and crown. No credence, in fact, should be given to the heretic Tatian, who falsely claims that the days of yore were shorter than now because the hours of day and night were fewer in view of the proclamation to God by the psalmist, "At your command the day will continue."[29]

Since it is impossible for days to be literally shortened, however, the Gospel text about the shortening of the days and the verse about the *brief time* occurring in the inspired text should be taken spiritually. Because the spiritual days get magnitude and number from the sun of justice,[30] there is need also . . . from the difference of those who are enlightened and not . . . of the divine light. You see, when the Lord says, "I shall fill them with length of days," in respect of the righteous "dwelling with help from the Most High," we do not claim that long life is promised to the righteous person so anxious "to be dissolved in order to be with Christ" as to say, "Alas that my sojourn has been prolonged." The facts, of course, are also at odds with such an interpretation, since those who honor their parents do not reach a great age in every case, despite its being said to everyone, "Honor your father and your mother so that it may be well with you and you may be long-lived in the land that the Lord your God gives you." It is possible, in fact, to find people who keep this commandment dying early after a short life.[31]

Since, then, the literal sense is not as the general run of people suppose, the statement in the Psalms or some other place

28. Zec 1.12; Mt 24.22.
29. 1 Cor 9.24; Ps 119.91. Tatian, who in the second century departed from orthodoxy for his sect of Encratites, developed a series of *Quaestiones* on scriptural problems like Theodoret's, now lost. Didymus seems to have saddled himself with an unnecessary problem in understanding "brief time."
30. Mal 4.2.
31. Ps 91.16, 1; Phil 1.23; Ps 120.5; Ex 20.12. It is grist to Didymus's mill to find scriptural texts lacking a factual basis, ἱστορία, that then require a different interpretation from the literal, τὸ ῥητόν.

in the inspired Scripture about the length of days is of that kind: "He asked for life, and you gave him length of days for ever and ever," and in Proverbs, "The righteous will pass many years in riches." Now, the fact that length of days means extended illumination Moses the revealer of the divine laws tells the godly person: "This is life and length of days for you, to love the Lord your God with your whole soul and your whole heart."[32] In other words, since intense love of God is illuminating, it is also productive of length and quality of days, so that the person practicing it lives a long and fruitful life. Compared with these days the initial enlightenment involves brief days, but whoever does not scorn it will very easily experience further illumination after the initial stages; at that point they will rejoice "with an indescribable and glorious joy," which is "the fruit of the Holy Spirit."[33]

Now, what follows for the person rejoicing in this way is nothing else than the sight of the *tin stone in the hand*—that is, in the actions—*of Zerubbabel* by his being included in the genealogy of Jesus from Abraham, David, and finally Mary;[34] on account of his complete power of illuminating, Jesus renders those near him people of discernment. He mentioned *seven eyes* surveying and observing the whole earth, particularly when the inhabitants of the earth learned to practice righteousness, living blamelessly and practicing righteousness. The fact that they were observed by the Lord can be learned from the psalmist's words, "The eyes of the Lord are upon the righteous, and his ears open to their appeal." The one who is completely discerning has seven divine eyes; this, at any rate, was the case with the all-holy cherubim on whom God was carried in the vision of Ezekiel, being completely covered with eyes; they were said to

32. Ps 21.4; Prv 13.23 LXX; Dt 30.20, 6.
33. 1 Pt 1.8; Gal 5.22. With the text of Zechariah only in the background, Didymus moves to apply a phrase, whose literal sense he sees as inapplicable, in a different sense and then apply it to his readers' growth in spiritual enlightenment.
34. This is Matthew's genealogy (Mt 1.1–16, Zerubbabel occurring at v.13). Though in fact the genealogy arrives at Joseph in establishing Jesus' Davidic descent, we note the readiness of Didymus to give Mary by name a position of prominence, something the Antiochenes are generally reluctant to do.

be so full of eyes that their back and front had eyes observing
the marvelous, supernatural sights. Now, "cherubim" means
"fullness of knowledge," from which it emerges that they see
what they understand and they gaze on what they encounter.[35]
See if the phrase *Who was scornful for a brief time?* suggests not
the odd viewer but a particular person, referred to by some
people as ἰδίως ποιόν and by others as ἄτομος, as in the verse
by the apostle to this effect: "Every house is built by someone."[36]

In reply I asked him, What are these two olive trees on the right of the
lampstand and on its left? I asked a second time and said to him,
What are the two branches of the olive trees in the hands of the two gold-
en pipes that pour out and bring back the golden cups? He said to me,
Do you not know what they are? I said, No, Lord. And he replied, These
are the two sons of plenty, who stand in attendance on the Lord of all
the earth (vv.11–14). When the angel speaking in the prophet
asked, "What do you see?" he replied with a question, "What
are the two olive trees on the right of the lampstand and on its
left?" When no reply was given him, he asked a second time
about the two branches of the olive trees in the hands of the
two pipes pouring out and bringing back the golden cups. The
angel replied to him, "Do you not know what they are?" When
the prophet replied, "No, Lord," the angel said, "These two
sons of plenty stand in attendance on the Lord of all the earth."

It is impossible for someone at the beginning of initiation to
know what the olive trees are to the right and left of the lampstand—hence the second question about the branches of the
two olive trees. In what went before, it was explained[37] that
there are processes of divine meditation that are called olive
trees on account of their fruit augmenting and nourishing the
light. Since it is impossible, then, for the one who "knows and

35. Ps 34.15; Ezek 10.12, Didymus again essaying a popular (and again incorrect) etymology. While he manages to account for the mention of Zerubbabel (without reference to the historical situation of the restored community),
he gives up on the tin stone.

36. Heb 3.4. Didymus here employs Stoic and Epicurean terminology to in-
sist that the pronoun in the text is indefinite (i.e., someone was scornful), not
interrogative (implying no one).

37. In comment on Zec 4.3, though there it was the oil that was referred to
in that way.

prophesies in part" to have complete insight into the stumps and the shoots of the trees in question, he poses a question a second time about two branches of the olive trees, since only with difficulty is it possible for one encountering truth "through a mirror, dimly"[38] to gain knowledge of this; his hope is to benefit from these parts of the trees so as to succeed eventually in knowing what the olive trees are. And since one of the explanations comes from an interpreter of the text who took the two olive trees in reference to Son and Holy Spirit, see if the branches of these olive trees should be taken as the knowledge attainable to the person who "knows in part." With Christ as an olive tree, the Word becoming flesh would be a branch, whereas in the case of the Holy Spirit it would be initial insight into him, referred to as his "pledge."[39]

On putting the second question about these things, the divinely-possessed one heard the angel's introduction to the mysteries, *Do you not know what they are?* On his admitting, *No, Lord,* he continued, *These are the two sons of plenty, who stand in attendance on the Lord of all the earth.* That is to say, in the same way as there is reference to the Father in the one on the right, he being the lamp on top of the lampstand, which was the interpretation given a little before,[40] so contemplation of the Father is called *plenty,* and its *sons* refers to Son and Holy Spirit, in so far as it is possible to know while one is still in a body. In another interpretation it is the mystical understanding of the inspired Scriptures that is the *plenty* of God's house according to what is read in the thirty-sixth psalm addressed to the Lord God, "They will be inebriated with the plenty of your house," and it is clear that "the human beings trusting in God's wings"[41]

---

38. 1 Cor 13.9, 12.

39. 2 Cor 5.5. Again without giving a thought to any historical persons or realities as possible referents (the Antiochenes see Zerubbabel and Joshua as candidates for the two olive trees), Didymus considers an alternative view (of Athanasius, Doutreleau believes; SC 83.372) and rationalizes it.

40. In fact, as Doutreleau points out, SC 83.374, in that earlier comment it was the Son who took his place "on the right." The interpretation, in any case, seems contrived. See n. 13 to chapter 1 on Didymus's notion of inspiration suggested by the Aristotelian term "divinely possessed" used of the prophet.

41. Ps 36.8, 7. Didymus, having no clear hermeneutical principles, offers his

are human sons, two sons, one becoming so by circumcision, the other according to the Gospel of Christ.

Decide whether you are able to take the *two sons of plenty, who stand in attendance on the Lord of all the earth,* as those who appeared in glory with Jesus on the mountain, Moses and Elijah, referring obviously to Law and Prophets. That is to say, just as the spiritual law is a son of plenty in the sense given, so, too, is the word of a prophet in a spiritual sense. I read in an apocryphal book that Enoch and Elijah are the two sons of plenty, presumably on account of their privileges relative to other people; Enoch, remember, "was taken elsewhere so as not to experience death," and Elijah was taken up when a fiery horse and chariot took him up "to heaven, as it were."[42]

Having pondered these ideas to the extent of our powers, limited though they be, let us expound the following section of the prophet in our desire to understand it as well, with the proviso, of course, that the one who enlightens the prophet by revelations "may give a message by an opening of our mouth."[43]

---

readers any interpretations he is aware of (which do not include any deriving from ἱστορία), leaving them to choose.

42. Heb 11.5; 2 Kgs 2.11. It is interesting that, while Didymus is not concerned to relate Zechariah's prophecy to events and characters of his time, he is prepared to look to apocryphal literature for clues to its interpretation.

43. Eph 6.19. Edifying though this admission by Didymus is of his limitations and dependence on divine grace, Diodore would recommend that he work harder at plumbing the information available in the text.

COMMENTARY ON ZECHARIAH 5

TURNED AROUND, *lifted up my eyes, and looked, and, lo, a scythe flying. He said to me, What do you see? I replied, I see a scythe flying, twenty cubits in length and ten cubits in breadth. He said to me, This is the curse that issues forth on the face of all the earth, because every thief will be punished from this point to the moment of death, and every perjurer will be punished from this point to the moment of death. I shall bring it forth, says the Lord almighty, and it will enter the house of the thief and the house of the one swearing falsely in my name; it will cause destruction in the middle of his house and topple it, its timbers and its stones* (Zec 5.1–4). Turning from the previous vision, I lifted up the eyes of my mind, and I saw a flying scythe twenty cubits long and ten cubits broad.[1] Of the scythe the one showing the vision said, "It is the curse—that is, the punishment—imposed on the whole earth to cut down and destroy the thief and perjurer."

Note, for one thing, the extent of the instruction given through revelation, making clear what is not clear from what is clear, spiritual things from material ones. I mean, as by his verdict the just judge examines the righteous and the impious, dealing with all individually according to their behavior and actions, [Scripture] uses for the penalties imposed on unjust and impious people the terms sword and arrows in some cases, axe and scythe in others. For example, when "wicked people and impostors" and along with them the vengeful demons prove hostile and rebellious in their cruelty, swords and javelins are the terms used of the punishment deservedly imposed on them, wielded by the Lord who says of them in the great song in Deuteronomy, "I shall make my arrows drunk with blood,

---

1. The LXX has seen "scythe" in the Heb. form for "scroll"; Didymus, if unaware of the solecism, at least pauses to rationalize the unlikely metaphor of a flying scythe.

100

and my sword will devour the blood of the fallen," and again, "I shall inflict my sword on them, and my arrows will destroy them."[2]

Since the punishment falls not only on those on earth who sin, but also on the angels who fell into wickedness (Scripture saying, "God did not spare the sinful angels," who abandoned their heavenly abode), in Isaiah it is said in the person of God, "My sword was intoxicated in heaven." The painful judgment passed against the impious is conveyed especially in Amos, the second of the Twelve Prophets, in these terms: "All sinners of the people will meet their end with a sword";[3] the prophetic text does not, in fact, refer to a physical weapon of enemies, since in no circumstance were all sinners of the people annihilated by a visible sword. To similar effect in the seventh psalm as well, the singer makes a threat in saying to those summoned to repentance: "Unless you be converted, he will brandish his sword; he has drawn his bow; with it he has also prepared deadly weapons, and made his arrows into flaming shafts." And in Jeremiah there is mention of the deadly weapons: "How long will you strike, sword of the Lord, how long until you rest? Return to your scabbard."[4]

Now that sufficient comment has been made on the weapons of war striking and injuring cruel and rebellious human beings and demons, let us look also at the obscure statements about the trees that do not bear good fruit but are objects of wrath or actual punishment. For instance, "Produce fruits worthy of repentance," and a little further on, "Already the axe is set at the root of the trees; so every tree not bearing good fruit will be chopped down and thrown into the fire." It is against plants taken in this sense that the curse is inflicted like a scythe to chop down those said to bear lethal and harmful fruit. "Our enemies are fools: their vine comes from the vinestock of Sodom, and their branches from Gomorrah; their grapes are

2. 2 Tm 3.13; Dt 32.42, 23.

3. 2 Pt 2.4; Jude 6; Is 34.5; Am 9.10 (Amos placed second by the Alexandrian LXX). Didymus, bent on proceeding to a spiritual level, is always quick to note when scriptural texts are not literally correct.

4. Ps 7.12–13; Jer 47.5–6.

grapes of bile, their clusters bitter to them, their wine the anger
of dragons, incurable anger of asps."[5] Since it is a perverted will
that produces poisonous fruits like a noxious vine, there is
need to chop it down with a sharp scythe and remove the
grapes and the clusters.

While this is the picture in general, note also the details to
the extent it is possible to clarify them. Having turned away
from what he had previously seen and conveyed, the prophet
lifted the shining eyes of his heart and saw a flying scythe—not
a material one, obviously, but a spiritual one, twenty cubits long
and ten cubits broad, chopping down "every plant which the
heavenly Father did not plant." Everything cut out is impure;
the cutting was done with a scythe twenty cubits long, the number twenty not being a pure number, consisting of two tens. It is
not a question solely of length, however, there being in addition a breadth of ten cubits; and this number resembles a unit.
He brings out through the exposition of these numbers that an
auspicious and beneficial end awaits those purified by the
scythe.[6] Now, the scythe is called a *curse* on account of the affliction and hardship imposed on those being purified, exacting
vengeance on every thief and everyone who swore falsely by the
Lord's name. Lest you experience this, then, keep the commandments phrased this way in the teaching of Moses: "You
shall not commit adultery, you shall not steal"; and in the teaching of the apostle: "Let thieves thieve no longer; rather, let
them labor and work honestly."[7]

In the same way that theft is to be deprecated on account of
the curse referred to as a scythe, so perjury is to be avoided by
"not taking the name of the Lord in vain." A little further on in
the text, at any rate, perjury is condemned in these terms: Do

5. Mt 3.8, 10; Dt 32.31–33. Didymus has now turned the (false) scythe into
an axe for chopping down bad trees that produce bad fruit, proceeding to
moral implications not present in the text.

6. Mt 15.13. Didymus is interpreting the (non-existent) scythe by invoking
number symbolism to extract a spiritual value from measurements (themselves
unlikely in a scythe). The whole edifice, of course, would come tumbling down
if a reader knew some Hebrew—something the Antiochenes avoided by settling
for a simpler (if still faulty) commentary.

7. Ex 20.14–15; Eph 4.28.

not love those taking the name of the Lord in vain or "false oaths."[8] In reference to such a curse, the meaning of the scythe, the Lord says, *I shall bring it forth* by a verdict of judgment, *and it will enter the house of the thief and the perjurer; it will topple it, its timbers and its stones.* Now, if the house that is destroyed is not a material building, likewise the wood and stones composing and completing it are not visible things. (In the other translators who used the Hebrew text the curse is referred to as a parchment scroll, obviously because it conceals the thief and perjurer who are caught by it.)[9]

Now, this scythe *flies*, rapidly advancing on all the earth. In a second sense it flies because it reaches upon not only those on earth who are sinners, but also those being punished for impious behavior in the air and anywhere else. The scythe destroys those in the midst of the house—that is, in the faculty of reason—like the dagger that cut a swathe through the judge in Israel who was adulterously besotted with Susanna; in this passage cutting a swathe through the man convicted of adultery signifies dividing his faculty of reason.[10]

The angel speaking in me came out and said to me, Raise your eyes and see what it is that is issuing forth. I replied, What is it? He answered, It is a measure that is issuing forth, and he said, This is their iniquity in all the earth. Lo, a leaden weight lifted and, lo, a woman seated in the middle of the measure. He said, She is iniquity. He pushed her into the middle of the measure, and thrust the leaden weight in her mouth (vv.5–8). The angel who was constantly speaking in the prophet, instead of remaining within, emerged so as to demonstrate iniquity by the measure and the weight of lead lifted up.

---

8. Ex 20.7; Zec 8.17.

9. As a mere aside, Didymus cites the version of Aquila and Theodotion, which of course invalidates his elaborate development of the "scythe." For that reason, or because he is not in a position to validate either version, he quickly returns to further spiritual development of the scythe. Only in one other place, in comment on 12.10, will he consult these alternative versions; textual criticism is not his forte nor (considering his preference for a text's spiritual meaning) his interest.

10. Dn 13.55. Doutreleau suggests, SC 83.384–85, that the beings "in the air" are angels, and identifies "the faculty of reason," τὸ ἡγεμονικόν, as a Stoic term.

What each of these things signifies it is good for an understanding person to grasp.

The emerging *measure* that was shown, then, is the plenitude
of every vice and impiety. As this was not true of "the Amorites"
and the other nations, he did not punish the nations thus designated, who were punished at the time when their sins
reached plenitude, with no type of offense lacking, as is said of
some such, "Woe to a nation of sinners, a people full of sins."[11]
There was reference in the same way to those filled with adulterous lust towards the most chaste Susanna: "The two old men
came, full of lawless intent." And in reference to Elymas the
magician, the apostle spoke directly, forthrightly confronting
him with accusations: "O son of the devil, full of deceit and
every vice, enemy of all righteousness, will you not stop pervert-
ing the straight ways of the Lord?" This interpretation is gained
especially from what the savior said to Jews who claimed, "If we
had lived in the days of our ancestors, we would not have taken
part with them in shedding the blood of the prophets," namely,
"You thus testify that you are sons of those who killed the
prophets; so fill up the measure of your ancestors in your case
as well."[12] In other words, even if they were guilty countless
times of the murder of the prophets, there yet remained for
the completion of the *measure* of the offenses the outrage committed against Jesus for speaking this way, by which they crucified him; this, in fact, this was the moment the measure of their
impiety was filled up, when they condemned to death along
with those prophesying the one they had prophesied.

Just as there is a measure of sins, then, for those who are to
be punished, so, too, there is a measure of good deeds and
thoughts for those who opt for a zealous life lived in piety. This
measure, too, is completed when no righteous attitude or holy
action is lacking. Regarding the two measures, the good and
the bad, the savior said, "With the measure you measure, it will
be measured to you": to those who complete the praiseworthy

11. Gn 15.16, the term "Amorites" being used in a general sense of the original peoples of Canaan (as Didymus perhaps proceeds to imply); Is 1.4 (addressed to Judah, however).

12. Acts 13.10; Mt 23.30–32.

measure there will be measured promises which no human being "has seen or heard, nor has it entered the heart of a human
being what has been prepared by God for those who love him."
On the other hand, to those with the culpable and execrable
measure of vile deeds, words, and thoughts there will be measured in return the punishment duly inflicted, one proceeding
to "exterior darkness," another departing into "the fire prepared for the devil and his angels."[13]

Decide whether the savior addresses both measures or only
the measure of good actions in saying, "A good measure,
pressed down, shaken together, flowing over they will pour into
your lap," . . . your heart. There is probably reference only to
the measure of zealous acts when the judge gives a hundred-
fold recompense, more than "we ask or imagine." There is no
reason for a measure to be given to those whose offenses are
not all noted by the one who knows the hearts and understands
the minds of all; to such people he gives, not a measure that is
"pressed down, shaken together, flowing over," but one that is
deficient and incomplete, so to say, out of mercy and goodness
on the part of him "who with his eyes examines humankind."[14]

Seated in the middle of the condemnatory measure a soli-
tary woman appeared, who was none other than iniquity and
the hostile force underlying it. The prophet himself, in fact, in
identifying this woman, said, "This is the iniquity of the whole
land"—namely, of humanity, which is also called injustice:
"Everyone who commits injustice is guilty of iniquity, and iniquity is sin."[15] Following on this, the one being introduced to the
revelations sees *a leaden weight lifted*, and the woman raised up
and pushed down in the midst of the measure, because she was
iniquity. The woman appeared not simply in the measure but
in its midst because in her bid for power she had presumed to
occupy the central place in wickedness of all kinds. Into her

13. Lk 6.38; 1 Cor 2.9; Mt 8.12; 25.41.
14. Lk 6.38; Eph 3.20; Ps 129.3; Acts 1.24; Jb 7.20; Ps 11.4. The spiritual
and moral development of "measure," again by association inter-textually (without any reference to the prophet's overall message in his situation), has been
prolonged.
15. Zec 4.6, according to Doutreleau's note, but the quotation is closer to
Zec 3.9b (in his Didymus edition) or 3.10 LXX; 1 Jn 3.4.

mouth was thrust the leaden weight uplifted, representing
speech which is dull, heavy, and bare of brilliance by contrast
with the speech of someone in possession of virtue; "the language of the righteous," Scripture says, "is silver tried in the
fire." In other words, speech dealing with orthodox views and
the practice of virtue has much that is rich and brilliant, unlike
the speech in the mouth of iniquity, which is dull and heavy, especially because it is deceitful and crafty. The speech of the magician Elymas was like that, "full of deceit and every vice."[16]

Now, it need not be thought unusual for the woman's name
to be identified with a perverse disposition, a petty attitude,
and the evil force responsible for such things. After all, just as
the woman is referred to as iniquity in this case, so in the divine
Proverbs folly is given the name "woman," the passage on the
topic going like this, spoken in the person of the sage to the listener: "Son, give heed to my wisdom, incline your ear to my understanding so as to retain a sound attitude; attention to the
words on my lips is what I bid you. It is honey, you see, that
drips from a loose woman's lips, and for a while it sweetens
your throat; but later you will find it more bitter than bile." And
a little further on, "For the feet of the foolish woman lead down
to Hades in the company of death." And in the same book of
Proverbs there is a description of lust as a woman lying in wait
at the corner when there is darkness and gloom so as to lead
astray and do harm to the young man of little sense. She appears in the trappings of a prostitute, making idle chatter (the
text says) to the one she intends to deceive by addressing him
with a bold mien, aflame and intemperate, her purpose being
to arouse the young man's heart. "This day," she says, "I have
made a peace offering, I have paid my vows; hence my coming
out to meet you; in my desire for your presence I have found
you." And a little further on, "Come now, let us give free rein to
passion; come now, let us enjoy our love till daybreak." After
such loose talk and what follows, the sage remarks, "She seduced him with much inducement"[17] (or ὡμυλία, as appears in

16. Prv 10.20; Acts 13.10. The Antiochene commentators are also forced to
give the leaden weight an arbitrary interpretation.
17. Greek, πολλῇ ὁμιλίᾳ.

some of the manuscripts), "and with the noose from her lips she brought him down." Nevertheless, even if the youth was deceived, the master still urges him, "Do not take that path with her: her house is the way to Hades, leading down to the chamber of death; she has fastened upon many and brought them to ruin, without number those she has destroyed."[18]

In the same way that the vices are referred to as women, so, too, the virtues. The sage, for example, says of wisdom, "I became infatuated with her beauty, and took her to live with me." In reference to the one who in this way took her as a partner, this proverbial oracle declares, "Wisdom gives birth to good sense in a man"; to this man the advice is given, "Hold her fast, and she will uplift you; honor her so that she may embrace you." The devout man who, thanks to his virtue, has had children the Holy Spirit addresses in the words, "Your wife like a fruitful vine in the recesses of your home, your sons like olive shoots around your table." Now, the fact that it is not in reference to a mortal wife and her sons that the oracle makes this promise, the following verse indicates: "Lo, this is the way the person who fears the Lord will be blessed."[19] You see, if you were to take such statements in human fashion, many of the great saints, devout though they were, would not have attained the blessing, since they did not have relations with a wife and had no children at all. For proof of this it suffices to cite the great prophet Elijah and Elisha his spiritual son in regard to piety, and the same could be said of John the Baptist; and there are many others who live unmarried lives so as to "attend to the things of the Lord." John in the Apocalypse, remember, saw countless numbers of virginal men who have not defiled themselves with a woman; even if the passage about the virgins mak-

18. Didymus has cited almost all of chapter 7 of Proverbs on the loose woman, even providing what seems a copyist's error in some other forms of the LXX for ὁμιλία. Doutreleau, SC 83.394, would take this as an index of his respect for the text; but with only such rare citations and but two references to the alternative versions his textual criticism seems patchy.

19. Wis 8.2; Prv 10.23; 4.8; Ps 128.3–4. The excursus on spiritual fertility is quite removed from the text of Zechariah, even if a favorite theme of the hermit mystagogue, who (Doutreleau observes, SC 83.396–97) is familiar with the vocabulary for instruction on vices and virtues.

ing up the number one hundred and forty-four is taken spiritually, yet that does not prevent the text being taken literally with respect to a pure and chaste life.[20] In the book of catechesis entitled *The Shepherd* much of the contents is conveyed through wives and virgins, some of it to do with virtues and blessings, and some vices and punishments, which the reader of the book will interpret.[21]

I lifted up my eyes and saw and, lo, two women issuing forth, and wind in their wings. They had wings like a stork's wings. They lifted up the measure between earth and heaven. I said to the angel speaking in me, Where are they taking the measure? He replied to me, To build a house for it in the land of Babylon and furnish it; they will set it down there on its furnishings (vv.9–11). He now lifted up the eyes of the inner man as in the preceding visions, and saw two winged women issuing forth, with wind in their wings. Their wings were like the wings of the creature called a stork. The women issuing forth in this way took up the measure we have commented on, in the midst of which was the woman called iniquity, and took it up between earth and heaven. When this had thus been perceived, I asked the angel speaking in me, "Where are they taking the measure?" He replied to me, "To build it a house in the land of Babylon, and they will set it down there on its furnishings."

There is need to understand who the two women are. Note whether they can be anything else than the two vices, either actual transgression of the divine commandments or false views on ideas, as well as the evil forces themselves at work. They were seen with wings filled with wind, of which the apostle writes, "At one time you also lived among them, following the course of this world, according to the power of the air, the spirit that is now at work among the sons of disobedience." There is proba-

---

20. 1 Cor 7.32; Rv 14.3–4, which speaks of 144,000 such virginal men. Didymus likes to retain some contact (even if tenuous) with the obvious sense (κατὰ πρόχειρον) of a text.

21. *The Shepherd of Hermas*, a work belonging to the second century, contains visions, commands, and parables of a moral nature. Doutreleau, SC 83.396, observes that Jerome avoids making reference to the work, unlike Didymus, who cites it more than once.

bly a relationship between the vile spirit in the aforementioned wings and the unclean spirit driven out of the man by Jesus; if the one driven out by Jesus finds on returning the place from which it was driven out empty and swept clean—empty in the worst sense, and swept clean with the rejection of all its good contents—it brings in seven other spirits worse than it, gains entrance and dwells there, "and the last state of that person is worse than the first."[22]

By way of presenting the women's wings in a bad light, they were compared also with the wings of a stork. It is an unclean creature, fond of carrion and human offal, by foraging among graves, for instance, and making nests for itself from human dung so as to lay its eggs in this unhealthy and evil-smelling refuge and produce chicks like itself. It got its name from flying over and observing human activities. Women use it in cooking for evil purposes, to produce deception or miscarriage, or potions directed at lascivious and lustful ends. There is need to consider how this creature should be taken in a spiritual sense, and see if it is possible. It signifies either the devil or the Antichrist, nor should a reference also to all unorthodox people be passed over. The devil, the godless Antichrist, and the word of heretics like to graze around tombs, being the same as tombs (in allegorical terms) "whitened on the outside but within full of all kinds of indulgence" and of similar thoughts that separate one from God on account of their perverse nature; it is said in the excellent Wisdom of Solomon, in fact, "perverse thoughts separate one from God."[23]

In addition to the bird in question flying around tombs on

22. Eph 2.1; Mt 12.44–45. Like other commentators, Didymus is left to give the women and the wind a spiritual/moral interpretation, again using association to find in Scripture other malevolent πνεύματα.

23. Mt 23.25; Wis 1.3. While the Antiochenes saw only the stork's leanness and speed in focus (Theodoret, *pace* Doutreleau, being as keen a naturalist as Didymus; cf. Theodoret's *Commentary on Zechariah*, PG 81.1904), the Alexandrian finds other habits of the bird relevant (perhaps confused with vultures?) and as well a supposed etymology of its name (ἔποπος) and scriptural associations to develop a spiritual meaning. Doutreleau cites sanctions imposed by a council of Ancyra in 314 on women guilty of such abortions. For Doutreleau see SC 83.400–401.

account of its being unclean and being attracted by stench, it builds its roost out of human excrement. The consequence of this is that the bird itself—the stork, I mean—and its chicks live in uncleanness. Beyond this it gets this name from surveying human affairs—by human affairs meaning quarrels, disputes, and culpable rivalry, of which the apostle writes in censuring those guilty of these things, "For as long as there are rivalry and quarreling among you, are you not being human and walking according to the flesh?"[24] You may claim by way of jest that those people thus referred to as "flesh" are women who use the stork spoken of in an allegorical sense for evil purposes, probably when cooked and eaten, so as to abort what is conceived out of fear lest it go full term, and to administer potions that lead to licentiousness. Those who have taken on the wings of a dove, as it were, ought to keep their distance from these women and their wings; one who flies with the former enjoys repose in finding "the rest reserved for the people of God," thoughts of the Holy Spirit descending in the form of a dove at the Jordan. That person, and only that person, has them who finds repose between the two testaments, called "lots" in the verse, "If you lie down among the lots, a dove's wings covered in silver."[25] It is a blessed thing to have wings of this kind, for they lift on high the person who has them up to heaven and beyond worldly things.

The two women with wings of a stork raise the measure on which iniquity is seated between heaven and earth, something attempted by the sinful angels, the earthly demons, and all human beings who "bear the image of the man of dust."[26] When the visionary saw the measure raised and carried off with iniquity seated on it, he said to the angel speaking in him, "Where are they taking the measure?" In reply the angel says, "To build a house for it in the land of Babylon, and there they will put it down on its furnishings." After all, what other place was suited to the measure holding iniquity, or "confusion," for it to be found ready for those longing for it? Hence the need for Baby-

24. 1 Cor 3.3.
25. Heb 4.9; Ps 68.13 (where Theodoret also remarks, "'Lots' is the word he applies to the two testaments").
26. 1 Cor 15.49: a relevant citation?

lon to be avoided and shunned on account of the placement there of the measure in readiness to be found by those interested. At full volume, therefore, the divine word proclaims to the person wanting to be devout, "Leave Babylon, flee the land of the Chaldeans."[27]

Let us grasp the meaning of the prophet's vision, and feel revulsion for having a stork's wings, bearing instead the wings of the Holy Spirit. This in fact is the easiest way to be able to pass to regions above heaven.

---

27. Is 48.20 (more to the point). The meaning of the stork's taking the basket to Babylon—the point of the vision—which the Antiochenes concisely see as an index of the city's punishment, Didymus hardly touches on, being satisfied again with a play upon words ("confusion"/Babylon) instead of developing the challenge delivered to the exiles. Whatever the value of the closing parenesis for the reader, the prophet's thought in his own situation is given scant attention.

COMMENTARY ON ZECHARIAH 6

 TURNED AROUND, *lifted up my eyes, and saw, and, lo, four chariots coming out between two mountains, and the mountains were mountains of bronze. In the first chariot were red horses, in the second chariot black horses, in the third chariot white horses, and in the fourth chariot piebald horses of dapple-grey. I asked in reply to the angel speaking in me, What are they, Lord? In reply the angel speaking in me said, They are the four winds of heaven issuing forth to attend on the Lord of all the earth. The chariot with the black horses issued forth to the north country, the white issued forth after them, the piebald issued forth to the south country, the dapple-grey issued forth and searched where to journey and roam the earth. And they roamed the earth. He cried out and spoke to me thus: Lo, those issuing forth to the north country have set at rest my anger with the north country* (Zec 6.1–8). The prophet turned around to be given even a further revelation, and saw four chariots emerging between two bronze mountains. The first chariot was drawn by red horses, the second by black, the third by white, the fourth by piebald horses of dapple-grey. On perceiving the four chariots he wanted to learn their meaning, and asked the angel speaking in him what the visions meant. He replied that they were the four winds of heaven, that is, the four quarters of the world. The black ones were seen to issue forth from the north land, the white coming behind them, and the dapple-grey and piebald came from the south.[1] I spoke about all the horses to

---

1. Didymus, *pace* Doutreleau, is not concerned about textual discrepancies in these verses. Our Heb. text has only three lots of horses going on errands; the LXX in vv.6–7 also loses sight of the errand of the red horses from v.2 and instead divides the fourth group of piebald and dapple-grey into two (a discrepancy Cyril will note; see Pusey ed., vol. 2, 363). Furthermore, against the text (unless he is reading a different text from the lemma) Didymus sees the horses coming from, not moving to, the points of the compass, which alters Zechariah's thought in his historical context considerably.

COMMENTARY ON ZECHARIAH 6   113

the extent of my ability when they appeared in the first vision following the man mounted upon a red horse;[2] content with that, therefore, let us see what is now said that was not conveyed in the first vision.

There is mention of two bronze mountains, between which the chariots emerged. Note that by *bronze* there is reference to clear utterance with a loud report. Those who teach with sophistry and peddle heretical views employ this style, becoming "echoing bronze and a clanging cymbal" through being bereft of divinely inspired love for God. Suspicious of this, the inspired apostle writes, "If I speak the language of human beings and angels but do not have love, I have become echoing bronze and a clanging cymbal." This material implies also brazen behavior, as iron also suggests lack of submission and flexibility, such that God censures in the harshest terms the impudent person with deportment of a courtesan, shameless in everyone's sight and resistant to the kindly yoke of Jesus: "I know that you are obstinate, your forehead of bronze and the sinew of your neck of iron." Now, there is mention of *two* bronze mountains on account of the double obstacles raised against the knowledge of God: it is possible to have false views regarding both the practice and the theory of virtue, the latter being simply the knowledge of truth. People are ungodly when under the influence of heresies regarding both forms of virtue.[3]

The horses that were black on account of their being instruments of wrath issued forth from the north, "whence will be enkindled troubles for all the earth's inhabitants."[4] Behind them were shown the white horses coming, these being productive of joyful events and happiness, and ministers of beneficial developments. Since, you see, chastisements are inflicted for the improvement of those consigned to them, it was appropriate that they should come behind them—that is, after them—

2. Cf. Zec 1.8.
3. 1 Cor 13.1; Jer 3.3; Is 48.4.
4. Jer 1.14. Is it this citation, and its different historical situation, that has misled Didymus into thinking that his text is speaking of troubles coming from Babylon, not going in that direction—a critical error?

to prepare and announce bright and shining things. The soul
with experience of being in these situations cries out most
clearly to the one taking satisfaction in the loss of those sustaining harm, "Do not exult over me, my foe, because I have fallen;
I shall rise up once more"—by repenting, to be sure; if I fell
and suffered punishment through God's wrath, yet I also suffered the wrath imposed and bore it nobly, arriving at a joyous
restoration and happy life, and now I say, "For sinning against
him I shall bear the Lord's wrath until he is satisfied with my
sentence; he will set aside the judgment against me, and lead
me to the light, and I shall see his righteousness." In other
words, even if God is angered for the sake of improvement and
benefit, he will not always be that way, saying, in fact, "If the
wrath of my anger comes to pass, I shall in turn give healing."
Those who have benefited from such wonderful providence say
gratefully to the one who briefly subjected them to misfortune
for the sake of their welfare, "I shall bless you, Lord, for being
angry with me to my benefit; you turned away your face and
had mercy on me."[5]

When the black horses came from the land of the north to
allay the Lord's anger, the piebald and dapple-grey ones were
seen coming from the south.[6] It was doubtless from the quarter
to which the bride in the Song of Songs referred in saying to
her bridegroom, "Come, south wind," after the cold, harsh
north wind was dismissed by her. The bride's statement goes as
follows: "Awake, north wind; come, south wind; blow upon my
garden and let my fragrance be wafted,"[7] the fragrance being
good words and pious thoughts. Comment was made in the
previous section on what the piebald horses were and why they
were spoken of that way.[8] All the horses attend on the Lord of
all the earth, standing ready to roam all the earth and execute

5. Mi 7.8–9; Is 7.4 LXX; 12.1. Zechariah's announcement of vengeance on
Babylon has now been reduced to a moral lesson on the value of punishment
for sin.

6. Again the text has been misread: only the piebald horses "issued forth *to*
the south," the dapple-grey "roaming the earth."

7. Song 4.16. Needless to say, the Antiochenes do not find in Zechariah's
text any reference to fragrances of Solomon's garden.

8. Cf. comment on 1.8.

the commands of the Lord of all the earth, or rather of all creation.

This completes the first tome written on the visions given to the prophet Zechariah, who enjoyed luminous insight. A beginning is thus to be made to the second with the following verses in these terms:[9] *A word of the Lord came to me saying, Take from the rulers among those in captivity, from its useful ones and those familiar with it. On that day enter the house of Josiah son of Zephaniah, who comes from Babylon. Take silver and gold, make a crown, put it on the head of Joshua son of Jehozadak the high priest* (vv.9–11). As it is impossible for someone who is not learned to discourse on or convey learned matters, so it is impossible to foreknow in truth and according to God or to prophesy spiritual prophecy without the word of God coming to the one who foreknows and prophesies. It was to such a one, in fact, that the word of the Lord came, giving him sight and enlightenment for beholding the beauties and mysteries of the truth and wisdom of God.

The word that came to the prophet is none other than God the Word, a word that comes to holy men and to angels, principalities, powers, thrones, and dominations, being ever at the side of the Father, who begot him. In reference to the Father, in fact, is the statement that the Word was with him, the text saying, "He was with God," being God the Word.[10] It comes to Spirit-filled men without remaining, since it is there at the time it comes to them; then, in fact, then is the time they will also be gods whom he enlightens by coming, as the savior himself says in the Gospel to those complaining that he said he was God's Son: "If it calls those people gods to whom the word of God came, the one whom the Father sanctified and sent into the world"—namely, myself who is saying this—"your charge is blasphemy for saying, I am God's Son."[11] And since those people

---

9. The five tomes comprising the work are generally divided on the basis of length rather than the prophet's movement of thought—though in this case it happens that Origen's two lost volumes on Zechariah concluded at this point (Jerome says; see CCL 76A.748). Doutreleau's first SC volume also concludes here.

10. Col 1.16; Jn 1.1.

11. Jn 10.35–36, where Jesus cites Ps 82.6.

are shown to be gods to whom the word of God comes, we must understand and interpret as God's statements what the blessed prophets report under divine influence.

There is need to grasp what Zechariah, to whom the word of the Lord has come, is bidden to say: *Take from the rulers among those in captivity, from its useful ones and those familiar with it* from experience. Now, what is to be taken from those in captivity when given by the rulers, the useful ones, and those familiar with it, is nothing other than the priestly vessels which the captors took from Jerusalem and the Temple there; they were taken to Babylon along with the people of the Hebrews by the tyrannical men who were in charge of it. He bids him take them not from anyone at all but from the duly appointed rulers and captives who were useful;[12] the latter were the people who were transported usefully and to advantage from their own country to a foreign land, not for any sins of their own but for the people's impiety. Just as in human conflict, you see, physicians accompany military forces to attend to the soldiers who are wounded, so the sages taken captive to advantage by way of helping the people in matters of encouragement and legislation are referred to as *captivity's useful ones*, including Daniel, Ezekiel, Haggai, and many other prophetic men. In addition to them there were also those who were familiar with the end of the captivity, the return to the country from where they had been led into captivity, leading them to sing a hymn of thanksgiving: "When the Lord reversed the captivity of Sion, we were like people enjoying consolation; then our mouth was filled with joy, and our tongue with rejoicing."[13]

The rulers and those named with them as useful and familiar with captivity brought back from it not only the physical vessels of the Temple but also the virtues and wise thoughts they

12. Didymus has chosen an unfortunate moment to dwell on the meaning of phrases in the text with reference to the exiles' return. The LXX has seen in three Heb. proper names personal attributes, and Didymus—unaware of this—rationalizes the nomination of these attributes, as does Cyril (see Pusey ed., vol. 2, 363). (The Antioch text, as often, includes both.)

13. Ps 126.1–2. Having persisted for an atypically long time with the historical reference in these verses, Didymus now moves to another level of interpretation.

acquired there; gaining benefit from their unpleasant and distressing condition, they drew good from what was said in one of
the Songs of the Steps to the person blessed by the Lord, "May
you see the good things of Jerusalem," and again, "You will trust
in the Lord, and he will make you ride upon the good things of
the land," the inheritance given to those who learned of Jesus
that he is "meek and humble of heart." The psalmist cried
aloud about it, "I am confident of seeing the good things of the
Lord in the land of the living." In similar terms also the blessed
prophet Isaiah recommends desire to receive the good things
already commented on: "If you are willing and responsive to
me, you will eat the good things of the land."[14]

Having taken the possessions of the captives after being giv-
en the command, the one in receipt of the word of the Lord is
bidden to enter the house of Josiah, a name meaning "the one
who is saved." After all, it is appropriate for the one who is
saved by the Lord, of whom Scripture says, "Our God is a God
who saves," having come "to seek out and save what is lost," to
be a son of Zephaniah, which means "Yahweh's extended stay,"
an extended stay being granted by God to the one given eternal salvation, for which the savior was responsible. The apostle
writes of it in saying of the savior, "Being made perfect, he became for all who obey him the source of eternal salvation."[15]

To the person ordered to enter the house of the one who has
come from Babylon to the holy city of Jerusalem the order is
given to take silver and gold and make crowns to place on the
head of the high priest, Joshua, since the true Joshua is the salvation from God, his name meaning "salvation of Yahweh," that
is, of God, Yahweh being one of the names of God in Hebrew.[16]
Let us study the meaning of the gold and silver from which sev-

14. Ps 128.5; Is 58.14; Mt 11.29; Ps 27.13; Is 1.19—a lengthy tissue of citations selected from the scriptural smorgasbord to elaborate a spiritual meaning
of the text gratuitously nominated.
15. Ps 68.20; Lk 19.10; Is 45.7; Heb 5.9. Again Didymus capitalizes on popular (or conjectured) etymologies to develop a spiritual meaning of the text,
Jerome suggesting instead "the Lord's visitation" for Zephaniah.
16. Didymus makes legitimate play upon the use in Greek of Ἰησοῦς for both
Joshua and Jesus. Perhaps the readers deserved a less simplistic comment on
the significance of Yahweh.

eral crowns were made by the one given the order. By the norms of allegory silver is understood to be speech and gold to be understanding; in the Song of Songs, for instance, in reference to these spiritual treasures there is a statement to the bride by the friends of the groom, who is her king, "We shall make you gold figurines with silver markings while the king is on his couch." The figurines of the spiritual gold are probably the teaching given through shadow and image in Scripture before the coming of the savior; the apostle speaks of "the shadows of the good things to come" and "the image of the surpassing realities," these being the future goods guaranteed by the life-giving Spirit. And since the figurines of the aforementioned spiritual gold owe their variety and formation to the divinely inspired sayings, the figurines of the spiritual gold are given variety by the silver markings. Now, the silver from which the figurines of gold are adorned with markings is nothing other than "the pure words of the Lord, which are silver that is tested in the furnace, proven in the ground."[17]

In reference to the gold given this spiritual meaning and the silver understood in like manner there is a statement in the bridal song itself about the peaceable spouse, "King Solomon made himself a litter of timber from Lebanon. He made its posts of silver and its back of gold." The posts of this spiritual bed were made of the aforementioned silver, and its back was of spiritual gold. And since the practice is for the athletes of piety to be shown to be victorious with the aforementioned treasures, "having struggled unto death for truth," it is from the same spiritual treasures that the crowns are made for the martyrs for truth to put them on their heads along with everyone who has been involved in the incorporeal contests, trampling underfoot those against whom their contest has been waged, known as "rulers, authorities, cosmic powers of this present darkness, spiritual forces of evil."[18]

17. Song 1.11–12; Heb 10.1; Ps 12.6. See nn. 13 and 17 on chapter 3 for usage of σκιά and εἰκών for OT scriptural references pointing to fulfillment (ἀλήθεια, πράγματα) in the NT.
18. Song 3.10; Sir 4.28; Eph 6.12. The reference to Solomon as "the peaceable spouse" represents another use of etymology.

The contests being many and varied, it follows that the prizes are many and varied. Hence it is not one but many crowns that are fashioned by the person receiving the order: each virtue and the deeds performed in keeping with it have their own crown. For instance, the person who listens to the laws of God his Father and "has not spurned the dictates of his mother," "the free Jerusalem on high" and "the glorious Church," is awarded a "crown of graces" for his head, adorning with "a golden collar" the power of his submissive soul, referred to allegorically as his "neck." In this text the golden collar is not made of the stuff of matter, having instead the raiment of divine intelligence. There are graces in what is woven into the crown bedecking the head of the one who listens to the words of God, who gave him birth from his practice of righteousness; "everyone practicing righteousness is born of God," remember, and observing the dictates of the mother in the sense given without spurning any. These are the virtues which lend grace to the person crowned and which "save by grace" the person practicing them.[19]

There is a different contest, where the contestant "delights in the Lord," partaking of him as of living bread, and drinking the chalice, "inebriating like finest wine," which he offers to those anxious to drink, so that the drinker says in gratitude to the offerer, "You have given joy to my heart."[20] The one who partakes of this excellent fare in an innocent and pleasing manner in obedience to the word of the prize-giver, "Be innocent and pleasing in my sight," receives a crown of delight, which is at once an ornament and an instrument of salvation, in the words of wisdom, "Bedeck yourself with a crown of delight." In his desire for prize and crown the apostle Paul "fought the good fight and finished the race" of which the psalmist says, "Free of iniquity I ran the race and directed my steps," and in

19. Prv 1.8; 6.20; Gal 4.26; 5.27; Prv 1.9; 6.21; 1 Jn 2.29; Eph 2.5. With an allegorical approach admitted, the scriptural fare is rich, only the Zechariah text missing. Cyril will be briefer in commenting on the crown(s), having first examined the historical situation.

20. Pss 37.4; 23.5; 4.6; the spiritual interpretation is now extended to include the Eucharist.

another psalm, "I ran the way of your commandments when you gave me largeness of heart." Appropriately, those completing this race also "keep faith" in the Trinity, not losing their footing but made resolute in it according to the commendation given to some, "You have stood firm in the faith."[21]

Now, the reward that will be given to the contestant who has made a good contest of it, completing the race in the sense given and keeping the faith "reckoned as righteousness," is the crown of righteousness. The one who has acquitted himself in this way claims to have "fought the good fight" and adds the sequel, "There is now reserved for me the crown of righteousness, which the just judge will award me, and not only to me but to all who long for the appearing" of our savior Jesus Christ. It is also the crown of eternal life, as James in his epistle describes it in saying, "Blessed the man who endures testing, because when he is found to be true, he will receive the crown of life which God promised to those who love him."[22] And since the steadfast endurance of testing is the same as fighting the good fight, running the race, and keeping the faith, it follows that the crown of righteousness is the same as the crown of life.

The many crowns made of the spiritual gold and silver are placed on the head of Joshua, the son of righteousness ("righteousness" being the Greek version of the Hebrew Jehozadak). Note how the one head—that of Jesus—is given many crowns; "he was tested in every respect without sinning,"[23] remember, being involved in the contests. There is need to grasp another sense in which the head of Joshua the high priest is given the crowns of everyone. All the believers are the body and members of Christ; it is said in regard to those who compose the assembly of the Church, "You are the body of Christ and individually members of it." Of these members of the body those who are active are the hands, "those not lagging in zeal" are the feet, those of a perceptive mentality are the eyes, those duly appoint-

---

21. Gn 17.1; Prv 4.9; 2 Tm 4.7; Pss 59.4; 119.32; 2 Tm 4.7; 2 Cor 1.24.
22. Rom 4.3; 2 Tm 4.7–8; Jas 1.12. The development of the silver and gold crown has now gone beyond eucharistic and trinitarian interpretation to general parenesis on the Christian life.
23. Heb 4.15. The play upon Joshua/Jesus continues.

ed and ruling as they ought are the head. Those thus acting as head penetrate and give ear to the parables of Jesus, and since there are many who in this way are referred to allegorically as head on account of the active and contemplative life they lead, consequently it is the head of the high priest that is given all the crowns. Now, a high priest is described in these terms in the epistle to the Hebrews: "Since, then, we have a high priest in Jesus, who has passed through the heavens, let us hold fast to our confession."[24]

It is not surprising for the head of one man to receive all the crowns. You see, if there is a crown for every virtue—or, rather, every virtue is a crown—and if people who are perfect have all the best dispositions, the virtues being connected to one another, the person with them all is bedecked with all the crowns, in first place the human being assumed by God the Word, then those imitating him and also called Christs on account of being sharers in him of whom it is said, "Christ the wisdom and power of God."[25]

You will say to him, The Lord almighty says this: Here is a man, Dawn by name, and it will rise beneath him, and he will rebuild the house of the Lord. He will receive virtue, will be seated and rule on his throne; the priest will be at his right hand, and a counsel of peace will be between them both. The crown will be for those who endure, its useful ones and those familiar with it, and as a gift for the son of Zephaniah and as a psalm in the house of the Lord. Those far distant from them will come and rebuild in the house of the Lord; and you will know that the Lord almighty has sent me to you. It will happen if you really hearken to the voice of the Lord your God (vv.12–15). The text says, *You will say to him*—that is, to the son of Zephaniah—*The Lord almighty says this: Here is a man, Dawn is his name.*[26] This is in ref-

24. 1 Cor 12.27; Rom 12.11; Heb 4.14. For Didymus the Church is composed of duly appointed leaders and those in active and contemplative life.

25. 1 Cor 1.24. By contrast with this lengthy spiritual development of Joshua's crown, Theodore simply sees it as "an ornament and embellishment of priesthood," and moves on; see Sprenger ed., 355, or Hill trans., FOTC 108.355.

26. As has happened before, Didymus's commentary is undercut by textual errors or his misreading. He sees the words being addressed to Josiah instead of the high priest Joshua; and his LXX version has wrongly read "Dawn" in place

erence to our savior's coming: a man, on the one hand, as the
one born of Mary and temple of God the Word,[27] and true light
and sun of justice, on the other. In keeping with the text in
hand is the verse in the prophet Jeremiah running as follows:
"Lo, the days are coming, says the Lord, and I shall raise up to
David a righteous dawn, and he will reign as king, be understanding, and execute justice and righteousness on the earth.
In his days Judah will be saved and Israel will dwell in confidence. This is the name by which the Lord will call him, Jehozadak among the prophets."[28] In other words, the one raised
up from David as a righteous dawn is the one shown to the revealer in the verse *Here is a man, Dawn is his name.* This same
man called Dawn on account of being "sun of justice," a righteous dawn raised up from David, we claim is none other than
the one born of David's offspring according to the flesh, of
whom the sacred herald Isaiah cries aloud in prophetic tones,
"The root will spring from Jesse, raised up to govern nations; in
him will nations hope, and his rest will be glorious." In writing
to his "true disciple" Timothy, the apostle pens the same words,
"Remember Jesus Christ raised up, of David's offspring."[29]

   These citations, in fact, indicate that the one born of the immaculate virgin sojourned here so as to be called by the name
"God with us," the sense in translation of the term Emmanuel.
In keeping with this is what was forecast by the great patriarch
in connection with the blessing of Judah, beginning thus: "Judah, may your brethren praise you. Your hands on the back of
your foes, and all your father's sons will bow down to you. Lion

---

of the Heb. "shoot" (the name of Zerubbabel—a candidate for this person in
the view of the Antiochenes—meaning "shoot of Babylon"), prompting a Christological interpretation.

   27. The text of Didymus himself is uncertain here, Doutreleau informs us
(SC 84.444); one reading could refer "temple" to Mary.

   28. Jn 1.9; Mal 4.2; Jer 23.5–6, where this time "righteousness" would be a
better rendering for Jehozadak, and where Didymus has included the phrase
beginning the next verse, "among the prophets," prompting him to look for
prophetic support for his Christological interpretation (see n. 36 below).

   29. Mal 4.2; Is 11.10; Rom 15.12; 1 Tm 1.2; 2 Tm 2.8. Again there is no effort by Didymus, especially by comparison with the Antiochenes and modern
commentators, to look for a contemporary figure who might fulfill the role out-
lined in the verses from Zechariah.

cub, you have grown from a shoot, my son."[30] After all, how could the one born of an immaculate virgin without a man's involvement not have sprung from a shoot? His majesty and preeminence are presented in the praise and adoration of his brothers and sons of his own mother. He is also shown to be a triumphant king from his having his hands on the back of his foes, who are put to flight.

Consistent with the writings about the rising of the celebrated person, there is also what is promised by God in Ezekiel the prophet, when he speaks to those he intends to help and save, "I shall raise up for you one shepherd, my servant David," the one who says in the Gospel, "I am the good shepherd. The good shepherd lays down his life for the sheep," whose leader he is and excellent pastor, risking his life for them; he goes to his death, in fact, "having by God's grace tasted death for everyone"[31] so as to make them live and give glory to the Lord almighty. It is of him, you see, that the holy prophet Micah prophesied in the manner of a hymn of praise in saying, "The Lord will stand and see and shepherd his flock in strength, and they will live in the name of their God almighty," that is, by sharing in the one who says outright to Moses the revealer, "I am who am."[32] Now, just as the one who is the true David with strength in his hand rises as an excellent shepherd to pasture the sheep that listen to the voice of Jesus, "the sheep of his hand," that is, of Jesus' hand, and "people of his pasture," so an excellent general was sent in the person of the one risen from the shoot, as has just now been established, to rout the terrified enemy, putting his hands on their back. Having been revealed as their firstborn, he is praised and glorified by his own brothers, in keeping with the apostle's statement, "Those whom he foreknew and predetermined"—God, that is—"to be fellow sharers in the image of his Son so that he should be the first-

30. Mt 1.23; Gn 49.8–9.
31. Ezek 34.23; Jn 10.11; Heb 2.9.
32. Mi 5.4; Ex 3.4. Doutreleau, SC 84.448, seems concerned at Didymus's altering the Micah text at will, though he might have noted his reeling off a host of citations with loose thematic connection without respect to their original setting and purpose—or to that of the Zechariah text in hand.

born of many brethren." Of them the firstborn says to God, "I shall proclaim your name to my brethren; in the midst of the assembly I shall sing your praises."[33] Now, this refers to the one who is glorified on the basis of being descended from Abraham and David, as Matthew writes, "A book of the genealogy of Jesus Christ, son of David, son of Abraham." In keeping with his brothers praising him, the sons of his mother—obviously the Jerusalem on high—bow down to him "in spirit and in truth" in a fashion identical to that of the angels, of whom it is said, "Let all God's angels bow down to him."[34]

All the deeds of valor were accomplished, and there was a fulfillment of the prophecy that reads, "There will be a root of Jesse who will rise up to rule nations; in him nations will hope." Account should be taken of the verse of Jeremiah lately cited in the same sense as the words on the root of Jesse rising to rule all the nations: "the king of the nations rising from the root of Jesse" has the same meaning as "See, the days are coming, says the Lord, and I shall raise up for David a righteous dawn, and he will reign as king, and in his days salvation will come" to the one confessing (a word that is Judah in Hebrew), and the mind that sees God (Israel its name) "will dwell in confidence" according to what is said by those professing faith in the Lord of all, "Have mercy on us, Lord, because we have trusted in you." Of the person who shows confidence and courage in this way Scripture says, "Blessed be those who trust in the Lord: the Lord will be their hope."[35]

Now, what name will be given to the reigning king who rises from David, enjoying understanding because God's Spirit rests on him, a Spirit of wisdom and understanding, a king who exercises justice and righteousness over the earth, if not "Jehozadak among the prophets"? Jehozadak, rendered "righteousness," is among the prophets, forecasting to us its coming,

---

33. Jn 10.3; Ps 95.7; Rom 8.29; Ps 22.22.
34. Mt 1.1; Jn 4.24; Ps 97.7 LXX.
35. Is 11.10; Jer 23.5–6; Is 33.2; Jer 17.7. For the accuracy of the etymologies of Judah and Israel, see nn. 36 and 53 on chapter 1; proper recourse to Hebrew in connection with "dawn" would have made much of this spiritual development otiose.

according to what is announced in one place in the hymns, "Righteousness looked down from heaven," and in another place, "He will cause righteousness to arise in his days."[36] Now that we have clarified the prophetic texts cited as proof of the inspired verse of Zechariah, it is time to study its meaning as well.

Here is a man, Dawn is his name. In addition to what has been said in highlighting the Incarnation in the words, *Here is a man. Dawn is his name,* there is need to examine whether it is the bridegroom with the bride who is the man referred to here. The apostle suggests as much in writing to the Corinthians, "I intend to promise you all in marriage to one husband as a chaste virgin." It is to this man that those can expect to be introduced who are filled with the knowledge of the Son of God, as Paul himself again writes when speaking in Christ, "Until all of us are introduced to a perfect man, to the measure of the full stature" of the Son of God, to this perfect man, described by John the Baptist, than whom "no one greater has arisen among those born of women," in these terms: "A man is coming after me who has been before me." This is the man he indicates in saying, "He who has the bride is the bridegroom. The friend of the bridegroom rejoices greatly at the voice of the bridegroom."[37]

The man indicated by the prophet is called *Dawn,* the one of whom the Baptist's father, Zechariah, pronounced in the Gospel when filled with the Holy Spirit, "A dawning from on high" of the true light and the sun of justice "has shone upon those seated in darkness and a shadow of death," so that, with the darkness dissipated and the shadow of death no longer in existence, we may move from death to life, be illuminated and become a light in the Lord, casting off the darkness of ignorance of God and other vices, becoming a light in the Lord ac-

36. Jer 23.6; Pss 85.11; 72.7. As observed in n. 28 above, Didymus is developing his thought from a misquotation of the phrase "among the prophets" in the Jeremiah verse, which encourages him to find in many prophetic texts a Christological reference to Zechariah. He admits it is time to return to the latter—if return he does.

37. 2 Cor 11.2; Eph 4.13 ("alteré à souhait," as Doutreleau would say); Mt 11.11; Jn 1.30; 3.29.

cording to the sound values of the writer to some people, "For once you were darkness, but now light in the Lord." In reference to this dawn rising from David, the Baptist's father, in addition to other things regarding God, says this as well: "He lifted up a horn of salvation for us from the house of David," meaning a king of salvation; in many places in Scripture, not least in the wise Daniel, kings and kingdoms are called horns. Adopting this notion of the one rising in the house of David, the sages say to God, "Through you we shall gore our foes."[38]

What *will rise beneath* the man called Dawn is either a light or a plant bearing fruits of salvation (the word *rising* being applied equally to lights and plants). They will rise beneath the great teacher, lawgiver, and king. What is underneath him are the rational beings subject to divine laws and to teaching germane to them. After all, how could everyone properly called man not be underneath Christ as their head? All the members of Christ that compose the Church, the body of Christ, are underneath Christ, who is head of the Church. This is also the way in which you could say subjects and pupils are under a king and a teacher, since from them comes a dawning of a light of the knowledge of the truth and of a tree bearing good fruit. Speaking of the latter, God the vine-dresser says, "I planted you as a quite choice fruit-bearing vine"; may the sequel not be true of every devout person, "How did you turn bitter, becoming a wild vine?" Underneath the spiritual farmer you could say there rise also different kinds of virtues and their works, produce of justice, of whom the apostle writes, "May God sanctify the produce of your righteousness," while the prophet Hosea says, "Seek out the Lord until the produce of justice reaches you." "Those who sow it in tears"—that is, with labor and sweat for the sake of their religion—"will reap with rejoicing" this produce.[39]

---

38. Lk 1.78; Eph 5.8; Lk 1.69. Didymus makes the same remark about usage in Daniel at the close of comment on Zec 2.4.

39. 1 Cor 11.3; Eph 5.23; Jer 2.21; 2 Cor 9.10; Hos 10.12; Ps 126.5. Though admittedly the clause "It will rise beneath him" is obscure, Didymus's "you could say" approach suggests a gratuitous interpretation, especially when Zechariah's historical situation has not been probed.

It is possible to take the clause *It will rise beneath him* this way as well: the Word made flesh, "born of a woman," Jesus, rose beneath "the dawning from on high" of God the Word, the true light. Furthermore, this must be said as well: when the Son was seated at the right hand of the Father, "his enemies like a footstool were placed"[40] under him, all of whom benefited from being under his feet and rose like a light and like produce. The person rising beneath the one confessed to be God *will rebuild the house of the Lord*, the Church of the living God—in particular, the human being rising beneath God the Word in his coming. As well, however, those *rising beneath* according to the other interpretations, subjects of the great king and good teacher, putting into action the commands of the one commanding and instructing them, built their lives like a house on the rock which is Christ, establishing the base and foundation of the house on firm and indestructible faith in the Trinity. The name "rock" is given to the one making a confession of the one confessed, according to this saying: "You are Peter, and on this rock I shall build my Church, and the gates of hell will not prevail against it." The enemies who according to the third interpretation, however, were placed under the feet of the great king will become friends instead of adversaries, and rebuild the house of the Lord so that "he will dwell and walk among them," having summoned and transformed them.[41]

The one who in his coming rose from beneath in a manner like the text, "Truth rose from the earth," *will receive virtue* since those saved by him and brought to a high degree of glory produce it as fruit. After all, how does he not receive it from those who become God's righteousness through him when he became sin for them, according to the apostle's sound observation, "The one who did not know sin he made sin for our sake so that through him we might become God's righteousness"? I mean, how does he not receive as virtue the righteousness and

40. Gal 4.4; Ps 110.1.
41. Mt 7.24; 1 Cor 10.4; Mt 16.18; 2 Cor 6.16; Ex 25.8. One would surely expect that mention of rebuilding the Temple would bring to mind the key figures in the restored community involved in this task, like Zerubbabel. Didymus seems as loath to take an OT perspective as Theodore is to take a NT one.

abundance of peace occurring in the days of his Incarnation? Since he does agree to receive the virtue found among human beings, however, let each of the faithful bear fruit and make an offering of it—the one committed to being continent produce modesty and continence, purity, and virginity; the one committed to controlling himself, self-control—"always carrying about in the body the death of Jesus." They also make an offering of virtue who are sharers in the honorable state of marriage and an undefiled marriage bed, the condition of Joseph, Susanna, Anna the prophetess, Elizabeth the mother of the Baptist, and all other such men and women who were distinguished for purity. They demonstrated a deep and unfailing faith, a supernatural virtue, in "fighting to the death for truth," confessing by their own conduct the Son of God before human beings so that he in turn would in them confess them before the heavenly Father and the holy angels.[42]

The man called Dawn *will be seated and rule on his throne.* It is a twofold throne, a royal one and a priestly one, as can be shown from the texts of Scripture. The throne of the Almighty is suggested by that oracular proverb that goes as follows: "When a righteous king sits on a throne, no evil opposes him," and also by the verse, "Your throne, O King, is forever and ever; a scepter of uprightness the scepter of your kingship"; and from the saying in the Psalms, "The Lord will sit as king forever." To the priestly one, on the other hand, there is reference in the epistle to the Hebrews, the author writing in these terms: "It was fitting that we should have such a high priest, holy, blameless, undefiled," and he goes on, "Let us therefore approach with confidence the throne of grace so that we may receive mercy and find grace as assistance," by "throne of grace" referring to that of the holy, blameless, and undefiled high priest.[43]

42. Ps 85.11; 2 Cor 5.21; Ps 72.7; 2 Cor 4.10; Heb 13.4; Sir 4.28; Mt 10.32. The phrase "He will receive virtue" is admittedly obscure, the Antiochenes passing over it—but not Didymus, who can find a range of scriptural associations. His acknowledgment of "the honorable state of marriage" is unqualified.

43. Prv 20.8; Ps 45.6; Ps 29.10; Heb 7.26; 4.16. Again a reader might have expected Didymus to consider if there was a likely candidate for this regal role in Zechariah's time (the Antiochenes both seeing Zerubbabel eligible, though mistaken about his royal status). Joshua, of course, qualified as the priest in question.

Since the person referred to, then, *will be seated and rule on his throne*, he took the throne of David his father so as to reign forever, his kingship having no end, and his priesthood being permanent, Scripture saying of him, "You are a priest forever." On the twofold throne he will sit and rule, he alone having a throne of kingship and priesthood. When he is seated on the throne and rules with a steadfast reign, that is the time when there will be *the priest at his right hand, and a counsel of peace between them both.* This is none other than Melchizedek, of whom the apostle writes that he remains a priest forever, resembling the Son of God; the apostle's statement to the Hebrews runs as follows: "Without father, without mother, without genealogy, having neither beginning of days nor end of life, but resembling the Son of God, he remains a priest forever."[44] And since he is God's servant not in shadow but in truth and in spirit, he will be *at the right hand* of the one seated and reigning on his throne. Being at his right, resembling God the Son and remaining a priest forever, he has a counsel of peace in respect of the one whom he resembles, the Son of God also being likewise at peace with the king of Salem—"peace," that is[45]—and the king of righteousness, namely, Melchizedek. After all, how could he not have a counsel of peace towards him when he is priest in his order, lasting forever?

Now, the true and divine crown is awarded to those who with patience and magnanimity bore the captivity, according to the text we cited a little before as well, "Blessed the man who endures testing, because on being proven he will receive the crown of life that God has promised to those who love him." Let whoever longs to receive it and to have his head so bedecked practice endurance, of which James writes, "When you encounter all kinds of trials, brethren, consider it all a joy in the knowledge that the testing produces endurance," with the result that the practitioners sing thanks for it, at times in unison and harmony, all having one heart and one soul, "I waited

---

44. Ps 110.4; Heb 7.3.

45. Again a popular etymology—disputed by modern scholars, but encouraged by Heb 7.2 (cf. Gn 14.18)—is adduced to allow Didymus to ignore an identification with a contemporary figure.

on the Lord with endurance; he hearkened to me and heard
my petition," at other times, "And now what do I wait for? Is it
not the Lord? My being is for you."[46] This sacred and beautiful
crown is not only for those who endure, however, but also for
its useful ones and those familiar with it.

In view of the prophet's present vision or the previous exposition of the virtue, what is this crown, which was said to be of
utmost value in what was stated before because it is made of silver and gold? It is the Lord of hosts, as is said in the prophet
Isaiah: "On that day the Lord of hosts will be the crown of glory." It is a prize of glory, in fact, because it will be given to those
who have glorified God with their body, and to those who have
a pious attitude both in their thinking and still more in religious teachings; on this basis we who have ecclesiastical learning are said to be orthodox.[47] This crown is woven not of gold
and precious stones, but of correct views on the truth; it is the
same as the imperishable one of which the apostle writes in the
following verse, "Athletes exercise self-control in all things,"
but while the one involved in human contests here below
strives even "to receive a perishable crown, we an imperishable
one." It is "incorruptible" in the terminology of the chief of the
apostles, Peter: in the letter to the flock being guided by the
true shepherd, whom God promised to give to his spiritual
sheep in the words, "I shall give you shepherds after my own
heart, and they will shepherd you with understanding," the
verse from Peter goes this way: "I exhort the elders among you
to tend the flock in your charge not under compulsion but willingly, so that when the chief shepherd arrives, you will win the
incorruptible crown of glory" that will be given to those who
keep the faith in orthodox fashion and to those who have put

---

46. Jas 1.12, 2–3; Acts 4.32; Pss 40.1; 39.7. Didymus is moralizing about the
value of endurance rather than showing interest in the recipient of the crown in
Zechariah's vision.

47. Is 28.5; 1 Cor 6.20. The requirement of orthodoxy for award of the
crown is likewise gratuitous, like the moralizing; *noblesse oblige* is Didymus's advice to pastors like himself, for whom ὀρθὴ δόξα should accompany γνῶσις.
Doubtless there were pastors of Didymus's acquaintance who at that time failed
to meet this requirement.

into practice the command given thus, "Give glory to our God," and again, "Offer the Lord glory and honor."[48]

This crown is given *as a gift for Zephaniah and as a psalm in the house of the Lord*, of whom the songwriter says, "Take a psalm and beat a drum, a pleasing harp with a lute." Now, the psalm which is to be taken is the account of those whose actions and thoughts are reputable, in response to which one ought to play a drum, a pleasing harp, and lute. The person hearing the account of self-denial plays the drum by "putting to death the songs of this world—fornication, impurity, passion, evil desire," by "carrying about the death of Jesus in the body," which he has subjected and mortified (the drum being made of the skin of a dead animal).[49] This is what the five wise virgins hold and play when carrying their lamps, in keeping with the refrain in the sixty-eighth psalm, "At the head come rulers in the wake of singers, in the midst of young girls playing drums." Drums in this sense were employed after the exodus from Egypt and the crossing of the Red Sea by the Hebrew women with their drums in hand, led by the prophetess Miriam, sister of Moses and Aaron; in harmony they sang in triumphal fashion with their choir leader in the words, "Let us sing to the Lord, for he has triumphed gloriously; horse and rider he has thrown into the sea," and so on to the end of the song.[50] It is not plausible, in fact, to think so many drums could be provided for such countless numbers of women in a completely desolate place, whereas it is quite possible for drums spoken of allegorically to be found for women advanced in years of pious living, especially when spurred on to spiritual dancing by witnessing the remarkable events worked for their leaving Egypt.

As well as the drum, "a pleasing harp with a lute" is also

48. 1 Cor 9.25; Jer 3.15; 1 Pt 5.1–4; Jer 13.16; Ps 29.1. Peter is again accorded a position of eminence.

49. Ps 81.2; Col 3.5; 2 Cor 4.10; 1 Cor 9.27. Is it wrong to see Didymus here citing "the μελή of this world" in the sense of "songs" (rather than "limbs") after describing the psalmist unusually as a μελόγραφος?

50. Ps 68.25; Ex 15.1. Greater attention is given to justifying an allegorical interpretation of a piece of scriptural documentation than to the precise sense of the Zechariah text in hand. A text that is the subject of commentary is only

played by those adopting a psalm, adapted to the divine recital by the powers of the soul and the senses, and also with recourse to sober restraint lest someone employ unacceptable instruments and songs which God abhors in saying, "Take away from me the din of your songs, I shall not listen to the melody of your instruments." The person who forsakes what is abhorrent to God plays and sings commendably, in keeping with the recommendation of the apostle, who writes, "Speak to one another with psalms and spiritual songs, singing and playing in your heart."[51]

After the giving of a wreath *as a gift for Zephaniah and as a psalm in the house of the Lord,* those of the captives who are still far off will come so as to be near the one proclaiming release to them. Giving praise, *they will rebuild in the house of the Lord* so as to provide constant service like priests, in the manner of the blessed prophet Samuel. All the details of the vision will be brought to fulfillment when *the useful ones and those familiar* with the cause *will really hearken to the voice of the Lord . . .*[52]

---

an occasion for spiritual and moral development that bears little connection to the original author's thought. (No mention is made of reference in this verse 14 to Zephaniah—or, rather, "the son of Zephaniah," as originally quoted.)

51. Am 5.23; Col 3.16.

52. There follow ten lines of closing comment on the chapter that are badly mutilated. It is doubtful if readers have been given a clear picture of what the vision in vv.9–15 requires to be done by way of contributions to the leading figures of the restoration and to the rebuilding of the Temple; the commentator has gone off in other directions of an allegorical nature.

COMMENTARY ON ZECHARIAH 7

N THE FOURTH YEAR *of King Darius the word of the Lord came to Zechariah on the fourth day of the ninth month, which is Chislev. The king sent Sharezer and Arbeseer to Bethel, and his men with him, to placate the Lord, telling the priests in the house of the Lord almighty and the prophets, Sanctification was initiated here in the fifth month, as I have already done for enough years now* (Zec 7.1–3). . . .[1]

The word of the Lord of hosts came to me: Say to all the people of the land and to the priests, If you fasted and lamented in the fifth and the seventh months, and this for seventy years, surely you did not fast for me? If you eat and drink, is it not for yourselves you eat and drink? Are not these the words the Lord spoke by means of the prophets in former times when Jerusalem was inhabited and prosperous along with the cities round about, and the mountain country and the plains inhabited? (vv.5–7) . . .[2] These are the people who were given over by God to degrading passions and a deprived mentality by showing reverence for creation rather than the creator, forfeiting God's truth and judging God to be of no account, thus becoming guilty of unseemly behavior.

Just as it is salutary to abstain from the flesh of serpents, therefore (the flesh of the serpent being godless teachings and wrong ideas), so it is beneficial and preferable to abhor and shun "the grapes gathered from the vine of Sodom" and the

---

1. The text of Didymus's commentary on these verses is corrupt; and, as it happens, the text of Heb. and LXX is also suspect, the sense depending on division of Heb. words and recognition of proper names. Jerome also despairs of its condition, and Theodore avoids direct textual citation. The overall sense is clear, a delegation arriving to ask advice on continuing penitential practices (though only Theodoret testifies to the precise question about fasting included above); a fragment containing a reference by Didymus to Heb 10.5–6 and Ps 40.6–8 suggests he has grasped the author's drift.

2. A further lengthy section of Didymus's commentary is mutilated.

wine drawn from it, which is "the wrath of serpents and the lethal wrath of asps."[3] There is need to practice fasting performed in this way, and thus with weeping and wailing to practice a like penitence. Quite abhorrent and harmful, on the other hand, is the fasting practiced by those who abstain from the bread of life and the flesh of Jesus, which is the bread of life, the bread of truth come down from heaven, from which no one should abstain, food of life as it is.[4] There are references to this twofold fasting scattered throughout the divinely-inspired Scripture, including a direction about the commendable kind in Joel the prophet, "Sanctify a fast, proclaim a service," and elsewhere there is an announcement, "Fasting with prayer and almsgiving delivers from death."[5] Of the culpable kind, on the other hand, vile and impious men make this complaint to God: "Why did we fast without your noticing? Why did we humble ourselves without your knowing?" In response to those making the impious complaint he says, "It was not this fast I chose," but abstinence from harmful foods accompanied by good works. He is saying, "Break your bread with the hungry; if you see someone naked, clothe them, and bring the threadbare poor into your house. Then your light will break forth like the dawn, and your healing will spring up quickly."[6]

To those who fasted and mourned improperly *in the fifth and seventh months*, the Lord says, Lo, you spent all of seventy years in Babylon, deported by the actual norms of captivity. The fast you held was not acceptable to me, eating and drinking at your pleasure, not regulating your conduct by the words given by means of the prophets of former times when Jerusalem was in-

3. Rom 1.24–28; Dt 32.32–33.

4. Jn 6.33, 35, another eucharistic reference in the spiritual development of Zechariah's thought.

5. Jl 1.14; 2.15; Tob 12.8–9. Again Didymus's hermeneutical procedure is clear: instead of focusing on the situation of Zechariah's restored community and its penitential practices, he checks his scriptural concordance (physical or intellectual) for references to fasting, good and bad (his Alexandrian canon, incidentally, including many deuterocanonical works like Tobit and sapiential books). Cyril, by contrast, embarks on a study of events surrounding Judah's fall in 2 Kgs 25 to construct a historical basis for the months nominated for fasting, something beyond even the Antiochenes; see Pusey ed., 371–74.

6. Is 58.3–8.

habited and prosperous before the captivity along with the
cities of Judah surrounding it of which it is the capital, and
when mountain and plain were inhabited. After all, how could
it not be prosperous, being the capital with cities subject to it,
and adjoining mountain and plain inhabited, enjoying a deep
peace and being ruled with proper laws, with every enemy and
foe driven far off? With Jerusalem and its surrounding cities
thus enjoying peace and great prosperity, there were good seasons, the land on plain and mountain being inhabited. Such
places are usually inhabited when there is fertility and great
prosperity, since people are able to live securely in mountainous terrain on account of abundant growth of fruit-bearing
trees, and the plains yield wheat, barley, and other crops.
Crowds of people, you see, love to live in places abounding with
fertile growth, some as farmers, others enjoying the produce.

Jerusalem prosperous and inhabited along with its surrounding cities represents in a spiritual sense the Church and
the orthodox beliefs: the mountainous terrain abounding in
fruits represents the teachings of piety and orthodox faith,
while the produce on the level plains is the abundant outcome
of moral instruction. There is reference to such spiritual fertility in the sixty-fifth psalm, "You visited the earth and bedewed it,
you spared nothing to enrich it. Bedew its furrows, multiply its
produce; in its drops it will enjoy growing up. You will bless the
crown of the year of your bounty, and the plains will rejoice
with everything in them. The mountain spots of the wilderness
will be enriched, and the hills encircled with joy. The rams of
the flocks were clad, and the valleys will abound with grain;
they will shout and sing hymns."[7]

With this spiritual abundance and fruitfulness existing, how
will mountain and plain not be inhabited with people behaving
completely in accord with upright thinking, the result being

7. Ps 65.9–13, with some departures from the LXX text and particular omission of v.9b (about "the river of God"), which exercises ancient and modern
commentators. Didymus insists the psalm can be taken, like the Zechariah passage, κατ᾽ ἀναγωγήν, as does even Theodoret in his Psalms commentary, who
also mentions the preference of some for an application to the situation of the
returned captives.

that everyone will cry aloud with thanksgiving and sing the praises of God, who bestowed such things? Now, the sign that dwelling on mountain and plain is secure is that fact that even "the rams of the flock are clad" in thick fleeces as a result of the dense growth springing up on the pastures of mountain and plain. Let anyone desiring to access and enjoy this spiritual fertility hearken to the words given by God by means of the prophets and put them into action so that there may arise even from its active force a spring of life "gushing up with water to eternal life,"[8] thanks to the savior who provides all this.

The word of the Lord came to Zechariah: Thus says the Lord almighty, Deliver a just judgment; show mercy and pity, all to their brethren. Do not oppress widow and orphan, sojourner and poor person, and hold no grudge in your hearts, each of you against your brethren (vv.8–10). The word of the Lord that came to the prophet, as was said before, announces what the Lord almighty ordered, beginning thus: *Deliver a just judgment, show mercy and pity, all* of the listeners *to their brethren;* further, *Do not oppress widow and orphan*, and further, *sojourner and poor person*. In this way, you see, it will be easy to *hold no grudge in your hearts, each of you against your brethren*. It is time to see what is the meaning of this—the commands, I mean.

The word of the Lord, as often happened in the case of Zechariah, is now also in him, declaring the following: *Thus says the Lord almighty* to each of the rulers of the people, *Deliver a just judgment*. As it is possible also to judge unjustly with judgments given in defiance of right reason as a result of bribery and favoritism, it is possible also when judgments are given out of hostility to people. Subject to such accusations are those against whom the divine word exclaimed in loud tones, "How long do you deliver unjust judgments and take the part of sinners? Judge in favor of orphan and poor; give justice to lowly and needy." Such, too, are they of whom the prophet Isaiah says, "They judge in favor of the impious for bribes, and wrest justice from the righteous." Of those who offend in this way, Habakkuk the prophet cries aloud to God, "The judgment was

8. Jn 4.14.

given against me when the judge was bribed; the law was mocked and justice not put into effect for the reason that the impious oppressed the righteous."[9]

Now, it should be admitted that those who in this way examine the affairs of people in dispute, far from being law-abiding judges, are nothing but unjust and unlawful arbiters. The judge, after all, must not have friendship in mind, or wealth, status, family ties, love, nor have regard to enmity—only evidence for the case in hand. The divinely possessed revealer makes this declaration to those commissioned to judge: "You will render justice to mighty and to lowly, making no account of persons," and you "will not have pity on the poor in giving judgment," "because judgment belongs to God."[10] What belongs to God must not be accorded and assigned to anyone; you may enjoy the privilege of granting to whomever you please what is yours, whereas judgment in keeping with the divine Law is not yours but God's. It fell to one of the ancients to describe the judge as "justice in person,"[11] being alive and personal, fashioned perfectly in accord with justice, the purpose being that just as in the other acts of virtue he pursues justice justly, so, too, in the act of judging.

The force of this insight will be grasped by its contrary: just as it is the person with both intention and action conformed to righteousness who pursues justice justly, so it is the person who has adjusted his will and deed to inequity and malice who pursues injustice unjustly. All such people are those to whom the verse is addressed, "How long do you deliver unjust judgments and take the part of sinners?" whereas the divine lawgiver says, "You will render justice to mighty and to lowly, making no account of persons," be the defendant rich or enjoying reputa-

9. Ps 82.2–3; Is 5.23; Hab 1.3–4.

10. Dt 1.17; Ex 23.3. On the use of "divinely possessed" of the biblical authors (Moses in this case), see n. 13 on Zec 1.8.

11. Aristotle, *Ethica Nicomachea* 5.4.7. Didymus is not insensitive to the encapsulation here of OT morality in a passage that Ralph L. Smith, *Micah to Malachi*, 25, declares "one of the finest summaries of the teaching of the former prophets" with "a strong emphasis on social justice," comparing it with Hos 4.1, Am 5.24, Mi 6.8. Didymus warms to the prophet's theme as though personally aware of miscarriages of justice, whereas the Antiochenes move briskly on.

tion or status. The law, in fact, is not to be administered to those liable to judgment according to their affluence or poverty, status or lowliness, but according to deeds and actions performed in keeping with virtue or vice. Just as, therefore, regard must not be had to the wealth and status of the parties, neither must it be to indigence or lowly condition; Scripture says, remember, "You will not have pity on the poor in giving judgment"—in other words, the poor person's case must also be conducted in accordance with justice. This, in fact, is the way that widow and orphan, poor and needy will be judged, not by awarding them the verdict if they are guilty, lest justice according to law be perverted.[12]

After ordering that a just judgment be rendered, the upright word goes on to declare, *Do not oppress widow and orphan, sojourner and poor person:* there should be no tyrannical imposition on those bereft of human help; on the contrary, a right hand should be extended them in keeping with the direction, "Be like a father to orphans, and take the place of a husband to their mother," "rendering just judgment to orphan and widow." This behavior, in fact, is beyond reproach and in accord with the will of the one who keeps all things in being, as James writes in the epistle to the faithful, "Religion pure and undefiled before God the Father is this: to care for orphans and widows in their distress, and to keep oneself untainted from the world."[13] How could the one who serves God in this fashion judge unjustly those whom he cares for in their tribulation, meeting their needs with almsgiving and other forms of assistance and patronage required by the beneficiaries? And just as widow and orphan should not be oppressed on account of having no husband or parents, nor should the sojourner who makes a claim on those to whom he has fled, and who treat him as a compatriot and fellow citizen. Even if any of the aforementioned—widow, orphan, or sojourner—are bereft of resources, they should receive equal treatment and not be oppressed or abused in any other way.

12. The parenesis has taken on a momentum and length of its own, extending beyond commentary on the biblical text.

13. Sir 4.10; Is 1.17; Jas 1.27.

While it is therefore a fine thing pleasing to God to assist those who are in this situation in reality, it is especially so in a spiritual sense. The woman who has cast off the evil husband she had, who was nothing other than the devil or some other wicked spirit, is commended as a widow in a spiritual sense.[14] Likewise, the one whose father generated him in sin and is now dead to him is a true orphan; a sign of this is his leaving his father's house when called by God, like the woman referred to in the Psalms, "Forget your people and the house of your father," who is dead to you already. Those souls widowed and orphaned in this fashion are transported on high by the heavenly bridegroom, who is father as well, according to the statement about him in the Psalms, "He will welcome orphan and widow," "being father and judge of orphans and widows," as is said in another psalm. He cares also for the sojourners who have abandoned idolatry and devoted themselves to the true religion, and enriches every poor and needy person by the poverty which he has accepted for our sake, according to the apostle's statement recommending thanksgiving to those lucky enough to experience it, "You know the generous act of our Lord Jesus Christ, that though he was rich, yet for our sake he became poor so that by his poverty we might become rich."[15]

Having given instruction that those lacking patronage and help should not be oppressed, he went on in similar terms to forbid holding a grudge, not only in word but also in the depths of one's mind, *Hold no grudge in your hearts, each of you against your brethren.* What is said by the savior in the Gospel has the same inspired import, "If you forgive people their faults, your heavenly Father will also forgive you your faults." In harmony with the present text also is Jeremiah's statement on God's part, *Hold no grudge in your hearts, each of you against your neighbor.*[16] This is the perfect ungrudging attitude to others' sin-

---

14. Extended though the parenesis on justice in judgment has been, Didymus now proceeds to take the plight of the disadvantaged in a spiritual sense. Doutreleau, SC 84.491, notes that Jerome does not follow his lead in this (not surprising, considering the license Didymus accords longsuffering wives).

15. Pss 45.10; 146.9; 68.5; 2 Cor 8.9.

16. Mt 6.14, following which, of course, is simply the same verse of Zechariah

ful behavior which the savior highlights in the parable of the slave with the debt of ten thousand talents: the advice to all of us, given by the master who forgave "the worthless slave" the debt, is as follows: "So will the Father treat you as well if each of you forgives your debtors from your heart."[17] With the whole of this parable in hand, you should make careful study of its expressions and meaning so as to turn it to your good, and with your whole heart forgive the debts to all who owe them, holding no grudge for any sin committed against you unjustly. By understanding *brother* in a twofold sense, in one a relation in a physical way, in the other someone born of God who gave birth also to you, you ought to hold no grudge against one another in your heart.

They refused to give heed, they stupidly turned their backs, they blocked their ears against hearing, and made their hearts resistant to hearkening to my Law and the words the Lord almighty issued in his Spirit by means of the prophets of old (vv.11–12). After God gave the divine Law to the people of the Hebrews, an exhortation was offered by the one who gave it in the seventy-eighth psalm to this effect: "Give heed, my people, to my Law." The person responding to this exhortation "meditates on the Law of the Lord day and night," according to the sound values proposed in the first psalm, which Moses the revealer had previously uttered in an oracle on God's part, "Let all these words I command you today be in your heart and in your soul; you shall recite them when seated in your home and when traveling in the way, when resting and when getting up, and you shall attach them as a sign on your hand, and they shall be unfixed" (or "fixed," both forms occurring) "before your eyes."[18]

In the case of the person who thus observes the commandment that was given, there follows attention and obedience to the Law; after all, how could the one who keeps the holy words in heart and soul not show obedience by giving heed so as to re-

---

repeated, not of Jeremiah. Jerome's close dependence on Didymus is proven by his repeating this incorrect attribution; see CCL 76A.804.

17. Mt 25.30; 18.35, Didymus again recalling loosely and confusing the parables of The Unmerciful Servant and The Talents, respectively.

18. Pss 78.1; 1.2; Dt 6.6–8.

cite them when at home or when walking in the way, going to bed and getting up? Are they not given utterance on going to bed by the person who says to the Lord of all, "When I thought of you on my bed at dawn, I meditated on you"? And the person getting up does the same thing, keeping God's sayings in mind so as to make the confident claim to God, "O God my God, I watch for you at break of day." This devotion the prophet Isaiah also had when saying, "By night my spirit watches for you, O God." Note whether the same sense emerges also from this statement: "I roused myself at midnight to confess to you."[19]

The person who thus has a devout disposition towards God's words and puts them into action attaches them to his practical faculty (referred to allegorically as "hand") so as in this way to hold them before his eyes and perceive the beauty of their meaning, keeping them "unfixed" or "fixed" (I mentioned there are two forms of the term). The expressions and the words formed from them are left unfixed before the eyes of the heart when we take action in conformity with the law that has been laid down. Are not the words attached to the hand unfixed when understood and acted upon? The other reading, suggesting that the law laid down is fixed before the eyes, implies the stability and permanence of the statements, as is consistent with this inspired verse: "The word of the Lord remains forever," and the expression of the psalmist, "All his commands are reliable, established forever." In the same sense the words of Jesus "will not pass away, even if heaven and earth pass away."[20] The person who is made secure by all these thoughts, who keeps the words of the Lord in heart and soul, recites them when at home and when traveling on the way, when going to bed and when getting up, will never be guilty of heedlessness or disobedience, nor on the other hand *scornfully turn his back.*

19. Ps 63.6,1; Is 26.9; Ps 119.62.
20. Is 40.8; Ps 111.7–8; Mt 24.35. Has the (otherwise unattested) difference in readings been highlighted out of precise textual criticism, or in a desperate attempt to develop a spiritual meaning? Antioch by contrast finds the meaning of the Zechariah verses self-evident.

Now, the meaning of *the one refusing to give heed will scornfully turn his back* must be examined. It happens when someone is so vile that the worst charges, as leveled in the fiftieth psalm, are brought against him, beginning thus: "To the sinner God said, Why do you declare my right judgments and take up my covenant in your mouth? You hated discipline and cast my words behind you." In other words, in turning his back on them he forsook the divine commandments, "consorting with a thief and throwing in his lot with adulterers," guilty of the same offenses as the lawless who forsook the laws "You shall not commit adultery, you shall not steal" and the laws given with them.[21] Now, it happens that those who have turned their back on the divine words lose their wits and act scornfully to the extent of even forsaking the one whose words they are; everyone so deranged and unbalanced dishonors the God who made the laws by transgressing them, as the apostle says to the one who falsely and with guile gives the impression of having the truth and observing what God laid down, "boasting in the Law yet dishonoring God by transgression of the Law." The result is that it is said by God himself when dishonored to those who twist their mind to the point not only of casting the divine words behind them but also of turning their back on him whose words they are, thus taking a turn for the worse: "They have turned their back to me and not their faces." They should have shown the illuminated face of the interior man to the one responsible for all good things in keeping with the saying of the sage to the one to whom all the secret and hidden wisdom is clear, "I lifted up my eyes to you, who dwell in heaven," and again, "My eyes are always directed to the Lord, because it is he who will pluck my feet from the snare." The wretches were guilty not only of this: in following all the rites of the Baal and every form of idolatry they also turned their back on the one who observes them with unsleeping eye.[22] The result was that they reverenced and adored wicked demons that were ranged alongside the lifeless images, and that took satisfaction in smells and smoke, cakes

21. Ps 50.16–18; Ex 20.14–15.
22. Rom 2.23; Jer 2.27; Pss 122.1; 25.15.

and libations consumed on altars lawlessly constructed with grave impiety.

How it was that these possessed people scornfully turned their back the sequel clarifies: *They blocked their ears against hearing, and made their hearts resistant to hearkening to the divine Law and the words the Lord almighty issued in his Spirit.* It is not the ears of their body that people block, since this is not up to us, but those of the soul, which by choice are blocked and by choice gain sharper hearing. The psalmist, remember, goes to some length in saying of some people, "Sinners were estranged from the womb, they went astray from birth, they spoke falsehood. Like an asp that is deaf and stops its ears, that will not hearken to the command of the charmer, drugged with drugs from a sage."[23] In other words, how are they not deaf and unhearing who block and stop their ears, who are estranged from God from the womb, both deceived and deceptive from birth? This could be said regarding moral teaching in connection with those estranged from the womb of the Church who bore them, and who have been both deceived and deceptive from the time they emerged from their mother, blocking their ears like an asp, the effect of which is evil and poisonous.

Regarding such people the most wise John, Jesus' beloved disciple, says in the holy epistle he wrote, "They went out from us, but they did not belong to us; for if they had belonged to us, they would have remained with us." In other words, they appeared to come from the apostles and disciples of Christ, attached to the same Gospel and born of "the bath of rebirth"; but they left the holy mother who bore them and those born of her who continued to have "the spirit of adoption."[24] What followed their apostasy was their stopping their ears and blocking them, like the murderous asp that never heeds those who chant

---

23. Ps 58.3–5. On these verses (classed by Mitchell Dahood as "some of the most difficult phrases in the Psalter"), the text of Theodoret's commentary includes a lengthy (and apparently later) digression on heretics (identified as Arians, Eunomians, Macedonians, and others) in the Church—polemic resembling Didymus's development here. See Dahood, *Psalms* II, Anchor Bible 17 (Garden City, NY: Doubleday, 1968), 57; Theodoret, PG 80.1297–1300.

24. 1 Jn 2.19; Ti 3.5; Rom 8.15.

the sacred words of God and prepare a rational potion capable of putting them to sleep and sedating them, the purpose being for them to recover and reject the lethal poison so as to graze on God's holy mountain, now that the blessed and holy rod has emerged from the root of Jesse. An explanation has been given of these people at greater length by us, however, in our commentary on the passage of the prophet Isaiah when we came to the verse, "A nursing child will put its hand in a nest of asps, and they will not hurt or harm anyone on my holy mountain, because everything is filled with the knowledge of the Lord."[25]

Now, proof that the blocking of the ears of the interior man is a matter of choice, as has just been said, comes from the prophecy of Isaiah, which addresses in the following terms those committed to this evil practice: "The heart of this people has been dulled, they have become hard of hearing and have closed their eyes lest they see with their eyes, hear with their ears, understand in their heart, and be converted, and I heal them." Content to persist in the vice and impiety they have chosen to exhibit, he is saying, they blocked their ears and closed their eyes, their heart being dulled, lest they hear the words about virtue and the knowledge of the truth, become better, and undergo conversion to the one they abandoned, who heals their deafness and blindness. Many examples of such cures occur in the Gospels, where Jesus even heals the ailments in a physical sense: he brought the deaf and blind to sharpness of hearing and sight, healing "every disease and malady" of body and much more of soul.[26] Just as in the Isaiah text the people who were dull in heart blocked their ears so as not to hear and were guilty of depraved deeds to their own detriment, so, too, in the present passage from Zechariah those who made their heart disobedient, so as not to hear the Law and the words sent them by the Spirit of the Lord almighty, blocked the ears of their mind lest they receive the salutary and beneficent teach-

25. Is 11.8–9. The commentary has been lost.
26. Is 6.10; Mt 4.23. Didymus, who takes Zec 7.11–12 as general morality not specific to the community of the time, and sees the deafness referred to there as a spiritual ailment, would like to see Jesus' miracles as also directed at spiritual diseases, conceding only that some were "even" healing in a physical sense, αἰσθητῶς.

ings and the words sent them by the Spirit of the Lord almighty, which is the Holy Spirit.

Let censure be directed at the heretics for introducing in their ignorance and considerable naïveté the notion of different kinds of people, their doctrine being that some are incapable of virtue and others by nature not liable to vice, from which it follows that neither law nor admonition, censure, exhortation, nor prayer directed to God counts for anything.[27] These most impious of people have arrived at this doctrine without taking the least notice of the New and the Old Testaments. In the Gospels, in fact, it addresses people as though in possession of a free and independent will: "If anyone wishes to come after me, let him deny himself, take up his cross, and follow me," and again, "Come to me, all you who labor and are heavily burdened, and I shall give you rest; take up my yoke, and learn of me that I am meek," the verbs "come," "take," and "learn" being addressed to independent people. At any rate, he makes a beginning to his own teaching in this way in speaking to acquaintances: "Repent: the kingdom of heaven is at hand";[28] repentance for what has been done improperly occurs in the case of people with free will, not with a nature unacquainted with virtue or vice. According to the impious notion of those introducing the different natures, in fact, the scoundrel will never be devout, nor the good person wicked.

It is appropriate, in addition to the texts cited from the New Testament on the human being's independence, to quote also some from the Old; firstly, we should mention Mosaic texts, then some from the prophets. Firstly, there is the statement from the Decalogue given by God through Moses, "There shall be no other gods but me," and the sequel, "You shall not make yourself an idol or an image of anything in the sky above or in the waters below the earth"; and shortly after, "Honor your father and mother so that it may be well with you," and further

27. Though Zechariah does not examine especially this question of free will, Didymus here begins building a case against its opponents, the Valentinians, presenting evidence from New and Old Testaments. Jerome will omit the digression, as will the Antiochenes. Cyril also avoids theological polemic in commenting on Zechariah.

28. Mt 16.24; 11.28–29; 4.17.

on, "You shall not kill, you shall not commit adultery, you shall not steal." Supported by these, the apostle Paul, learned in the Law beyond all others, writes, "Let the robber rob no more, instead exerting himself to do honest work." Now, he, too, is writing this as to people of independent will: "Set aside falsehood and speak the truth, each to his neighbor."[29]

We should go on to cite also the proclamations of the prophets to people of independent will. Isaiah says to those guilty of sin and hence lacking experience of the practice of commendable actions, "Cease your evildoing, learn to do good," since cessation of evildoing and learning to do good belong to those of a free and unconstrained will. To such people the Lord says in Isaiah, "Remove from my sight the wickedness of your souls," for I see your hidden thoughts. Hence be zealous for the removal of wickedness from the hidden depths of your souls, not in word and in appearance but in reality. Of a similar character is the direction given by Jeremiah to the soul bent on having recourse to evil and yearning for depraved potions, "Keep your feet away from the rough path, and your throat from thirst. But it replied, I shall be bold, because it has loved foreigners and gone after them." The rough path is the one that is forbidden or filled with thorns, the thorns being base desires, licentious pleasures, and "the cares of this life," which grow up particularly in the pathways of those not practicing virtue, as the proverb has it, "The ways of the lazy are strewn with thorns, while the ways of the brave are level." In other words, people of maturity and courage, who are in the habit of walking without interruption, make the places they travel level, so that as a result of the leveling no thorns or prickles grow. Since there are countless statements in all the prophets rebutting the impious fiction of those who concoct the idea of different natures, and confirming the independence of rational beings, let us be content with those cited lest our treatment, commentary as it is, be extended to unnecessary length.[30]

With these matters behind us, there is need to return to the

29. Ex 20.3, 4, 12, 13–15; Eph 4.28, 25.
30. Is 1.16–17; Jer 2.25; Lk 21.34; Prv 15.19. Didymus is happy to aspire to brevity of treatment while nevertheless embarking on a doctrinal digression. In

text in hand referring to *the ones scornfully turning their backs and blocking their ears against hearing;* in rendering their heart resistant and unresponsive to the Law, they fell foul of the sins involved. It was, you see, not without warning and by chance, and not to the unwilling, that the veto was issued: it was delivered before their malevolent attitude, and in light of it they rendered their heart resistant. In fact, they acted by choice, without pressure from fate or any other necessity, as the inspired text suggests to the same effect: *they made their hearts resistant to hearkening to my Law.* The case is similar to that of the invisible tyrant of Egypt taken in a spiritual sense, who made his heart hard and unresponsive, as Scripture says of him often in Exodus.[31] Perhaps the heart of the scornful man is made hard and unresponsive by becoming guilty of iniquity, which was compared to a lead weight. The apostle addresses the person scornful of God, the fountain of kindness, in writing thus: "Do you scorn the riches of his goodness, forbearance, and longsuffering in your ignorance that God's goodness leads you to repentance? In your hard and impenitent heart you store up wrath for yourself on the day of wrath." This is the way Pharaoh's heart also was hardened: the mighty portents of the one rich in goodness that happened in succession urged him—or, rather, pressured him—to have recourse to repentance; but the wretch persisted in his audacity and cruelty, he proved inflexible, and his heart was weighed down with the lead weight, which was nothing else than iniquity. Hence, in a description identical to the lead weight of iniquity, "He sank like lead in the mighty waters," as the saying goes in the song sung in triumph against him.[32]

It is not of God's doing, therefore, that anyone's heart is in this condition, those possessing one such having it of their own accord, the name "stony" also being given it on account of its hardness and resistance because they have this guiding principle of themselves. Let us likewise by choice make our approach to the one who removes hearts of stone so as to put in their

omitting the latter, Jerome endorses the former principle, *praeterire manifesta, obscura disserere.*

31. Ex 7.13, 22; 8.15, on Pharaoh.
32. Rom 2.4–5; Ex 15.10.

place hearts of flesh that are compliant and docile, so that we may be able to observe his commandments and ordinances in response to the spiritual law,[33] our heart changed from disobedience and lack of response to the divine Law to doing in obedience all we should perform in accord *with the Law and the words the Lord almighty issued in his Spirit*—namely, the Holy Spirit, as has just been said. Consistent with this also is the statement made elsewhere in these terms: "What I command in my Spirit to my servants the prophets." To explain what are these words issued, how they are given and where, he says they are given "by means of the prophets."[34] The sense of this expression has been clarified a little above. So lest we repeat ourselves in studying the same things many times, let us be content with what has been said and move on to the following passage from the prophet.

Great wrath came from the Lord almighty. It will happen this way: just as he spoke and they did not listen to him, so they will cry out and I shall not listen to them, says the Lord almighty. I shall expel them to all the nations that they have not known. And the land behind them will be bereft of anyone passing or abiding; they turned a chosen land into a wilderness (vv.12–14). The Lord repays everyone according to their behavior, greatly wrathful with those whose sins are many and grave, but less so with those whose failings are light and short-lived. It is said by him, for example, of those who were punitive instruments of his wrath, "While my wrath was slight, they conspired with evil intent." And those who accuse themselves of their transgressions cry aloud to the compassionate and merciful Lord, "Do not visit extreme wrath on us"; just as he is "a just judge, powerful and longsuffering, and does not inflict wrath each day," so he is less wrathful with those judging themselves, and does not take account of all their iniquities. If we have this understanding of things, and the text says, *Great wrath came from the Lord almighty*, we do not say it is *great* for all alike: "He will no longer forget to show compassion, nor will he in his anger withhold his pity."[35] After all, he is father and

33. Ezek 11.19–20. With the restored community well out of sight, Didymus is content to develop general parenesis.

34. Zec 1.6; 6.12.

35. Zec 1.15; Is 64.8; Pss 7.11; 130.3; 77.9.

source of compassion and pity, and imposes punishment only to the point of bringing his threats to our notice; if, on the other hand, sinners were to spurn the threat, they would also be the object of punishment in actual experience.

Those who have this pious attitude to their benefactor cry aloud, "Do not be wrathful with us forever, nor maintain your wrath from generation to generation," and again, "O God, when you turn to us, you make us live; turn your anger from us." With Scripture making such statements about God, let us not fall into such awful impiety and stupidity as to attribute human passions to the one who says, "I am not subject to change," and to whom the theologians say, "You are the same" in one case, and in another, "With whom there is no variation or shadow due to change."[36] In other words, if he is the same, subject to no change or alteration, without variation or shadow due to change, how could he yearn for punishment? Wrath, after all, is nothing other than the yearning for punishment. God has no such yearning, not being subject to passions, instead inflicting troubles on those in need of them as an aid to their improvement with a view to their putting an end to sin and every ailment and failing. It is possible, at any rate, to hear him, "who wants everyone to be saved and come to the knowledge of the truth," saying, "When my wrath and anger come, I shall proceed to give healing," the result being that the person experiencing healing through this painful process may say in thanksgiving, "I shall bless you, Lord, because you have been angry with me; you turned away your anger and had mercy on me." The soul who benefits in this fashion sings the praises of the one who invested it in misfortune, "Do not exult over me, my foe, because I have fallen and shall rise up; I shall bear the Lord's wrath for sinning against him until he accords me justice; he will deliver a judgment on me and bring me out to the light. I shall see his vindication, and my foe will see and be covered in confusion for saying to me, Where is the Lord your God? My eyes will see her; now she will be dust under my feet."[37]

---

36. Ps 85.5, 6, 4; Mal 3.6; Ps 102.27; Jas 1.17.
37. 1 Tm 2.4; Is 7.4 LXX; 12.1; Mi 7.8–10.

The Lord's wrath, productive of so much good, is beneficial, not harmful, being applied in a skillful fashion by the physician of souls, who "cures every disease and ailment."[38] After all, how could it not be a salutary experience for the one with whom the compassionate Lord is angry to be brought out to the light so as finally to perceive the evil force that is the enemy covered in confusion and brought down to the point of being dust under the feet? Now, as proof that the one responsible for every good inflicts what is unpleasant and painful like a skillful surgeon, the prophet states in his theologizing, "He, too, is wise when he brings troubles on them, and his word will not be set at naught." If the purpose in his inflicting troubles is to prevent the word of God, who alone is wise, from being set at naught, God's wrath in inflicting them is not a matter of passion or change. Proof that the wrath of the one who alone is compassionate is not a yearning for punishment emerges also from what was said by the revealer Moses to the one whom he confesses in the triumphal song against Pharaoh and his army: "You dispatched your wrath, and it consumed them like stubble."[39] Now, wrath dispatched for the purpose of consuming those presented as stubble on account of their infertility is not a passionate yearning arising in someone who is angry, and disappearing when given vent by the wrathful person. Hence what is dispatched is not a passion but a corrective process. The reason for the great wrath coming from the Lord almighty is given in what follows: *It will happen this way: just as they did not listen to him,* transgressing his Law, thrusting his words behind them, *so they will cry out* when encountering misfortune, *and I shall not listen to them, says the Lord almighty.* Resembling this is what is said by the righteous judge in the composition of Moses, "They left the straight and narrow to go against me, and I shall go against them by indirect anger."[40]

Now, what will the objects of the great wrath suffer? *I shall ex-*

38. Mt 4.3.
39. Is 31.2; Ex 15.7.
40. Lv 26.27–28. A reader might expect that it is time for some reference to be made to the fate of the people of the time, to whom Zechariah is referring.

pel them to all the nations that they have not known, whose ferocity
and cruelty they have not experienced—Assyrians, Babylonians, and all other barbarians to whom Israel in its sin and impiety was surrendered, falling into their hands by the norms of
captivity. In addition to these people's qualities of cruelty and
savagery, in a spiritual sense Assyrians, Babylonians, and Egyptians represent also incorporeal hostile powers treating the
prisoners in their control in an inhumane fashion; it is not
mortal Assyrians whose leader is called "haughty pride" in the
description of Isaiah, "The Lord will afflict the haughty pride,
the leader of the Assyrians." Of him it is said also in the
prophet Nahum, the seventh of The Twelve, "Alas for them,
your shepherds have fallen asleep, the Assyrian king has put to
sleep his nobles."[41] Now, the king of the Assyrians is given the
name "haughty pride" because of his involvement in such evil
and base knavery that not many people detect his craftiness,
but only those capable of saying, "We are not ignorant of his designs," able as we are to grasp and deplore them. This, in fact,
was the way the man who was not ignorant of the devil's designs
detected also the sophistry of his henchman Elymas the magician, and boldly confronted him with the charge, "You son of
the devil, you enemy of all righteousness, full of every deception and villainy, will you not stop making crooked the straight
paths of the Lord?"[42] This "haughty pride," commanding and
ruling the Assyrians, taken in an allegorical sense, ruled the
wickedness of the Babylonians in another sense, and in another
the Egyptians, those who in an allegorical sense are spiritually
Egyptians and Babylonians.

It is to the nations in this sense that Providence expelled
those being surrendered to them: had they persisted in remaining faithful to the divine laws, conforming their thoughts and

41. Is 10.12; Na 3.18. Despite the readers' expectations touched on in the
previous note, Didymus still passes up the opportunity to refer to the plight of
the returned exiles by moving to a range of "nations" not all immediately relevant (and even a NT magician) and showing that they are capable of allegorical
interpretation. He is not content to bring out Zechariah's thought, preferring
to exploit it for a less specific and more wide-ranging agenda.

42. 2 Cor 2.11; Acts 13.10.

observance to them, they would not have been expelled, a fate they suffered for choosing and implementing what was the cause of their expulsion and surrender. The apostle commented on this in a variety of ways, in one place writing, "Claiming to be wise, they became fools, and exchanged the glory of the immortal God for an image representing a mortal human being or birds or four-footed animals or reptiles; so God gave them up in the lusts of their heart to impurity," and in another place, "They exchanged the truth about God for a lie, and worshiped and served the creature rather than the creator; so he gave them up to degrading passions by way of degrading their own bodies, with the result that their men were disgracefully inflamed with unbridled lust for one another, men committing shameful acts with men, and likewise their women giving up natural intercourse with women for unnatural." They also experienced a third kind of surrender in being "surrendered to a debased mind in not seeing fit to acknowledge God," as a result of which "they were filled with every kind of wickedness" and its forms, which the apostle went on to list in writing the letter.[43] Those who were expelled to the nations experienced these forms of surrender on account of the great wrath coming to them from the Lord almighty; they were surrendered to foreign nations they had not previously known by experience.

The objects of the great wrath were expelled to all nations they did not know, leaving the land they abandoned *a wilderness behind them, with no one to pass that way or abide there.* With no one left in residence, it also lost all growth, there being no vegetation, no growth of trees, with the result that there were no longer any herds of animals on it, either. Devastation spread because the land once chosen on the basis of "flowing with milk and honey"[44] was turned into barren countryside. As well as the factual sense, the devastated land can be taken in an alle-

---

43. Rom 1.22–29. Having decided to give a spiritual interpretation to Zechariah's reference to the nations among whom the Jewish people were expelled, Didymus now accounts for the expulsion by numbering the people's sins as cited in Paul's list—which, however, is a list of *the nations'* sins. Doutreleau's phrase of Didymus's approach to texts, "alteré à souhait," comes to mind.

44. Ex 3.8.

gorical sense as the good and upright heart: from bearing good crops it is transformed into bearing thorns and producing prickles and weeds, with the result that no longer does any upright thought pass that way or abide there since it is reduced to a wilderness, even after formerly being chosen and having inhabitants, farmers, and flocks. It could also be expressed in this way by tropology: our body is the chosen land, containing self-control and purity, so that sober and proper habits pass that way and abide in it on account of its bearing the produce of purity and edible fruits which the trees of virtue bear. At times it happens as a result of aggravated wickedness that the land chosen for its purity is reduced to wilderness and devastation, to avoid which everyone who has opted for the perfection of celibacy to please God keeps his land chosen—in other words, the flesh is mortified in praiseworthy fashion, "bearing about the death of Jesus."[45]

In the twofold sense, tropological and allegorical, the land worthy of blessing flows with milk and honey, from which come spiritual nourishment and good cheer, honey being the result of the bee's display of God's wisdom, according to the proverb recommending the industrious man in these terms: "Go to the bee and learn that it is a worker; it is held up as a model of esteem for wisdom, since both princes and peasants turn its labors to their good health; it is an object of desire and commendation." It is with this sweetness and milk that the holy land flows, the apostle giving the latter as a drink to the infants in Christ. The holy bride of God the Word brings both of them into her discourse, and so they are mentioned in praise of her, "Milk and honey are under your tongue."[46] Paul at any rate, like a bride joined in spirit to the heavenly bridegroom, with milk

45. 2 Cor 4.10. Didymus feels he has taken the Zecharian phrase in three senses, by ἱστορία, ἀλληγορία, τροπολογία, his preference lying with the latter two (which Doutreleau, SC 83.59, has difficulty distinguishing, taking a cue from Jerome to see a more moral accent in the second of the two).
46. Prv 6.8 LXX; 1 Cor 3.2; Song 4.11. The digression on honey and the bee, which do not appear in Zechariah, is developed on the basis of a LXX text that departs considerably from the Heb. (where, in fact, it is the ant that is held up as a model of industry).

under his tongue—that is, his discourse—gives it as a drink to those of whom it is said, "You have need of milk, not solid food," whereas to those who were mature he supplied honey, giving them wisdom in the words, "But among the perfect we speak wisdom."[47]

The person who forfeits the title of chosen land has that honey of which Scripture says in proverbial style, "Honey drips from the lips of the loose woman, or for a time sweetens your throat, but later you will find it more bitter than bile." Like this honey from the lips of the loose woman, milk flows from the teats of the dragons, which are the evil powers, as the prophet Jeremiah says of them, "Even dragons bared their breasts and nursed their young. Daughter of my people like an ostrich in the desert." Commentators interested in studying the habits of so-called "horned serpents" claim that in the sandy desert they cover their whole body, leaving their horns above the surface, which they move about to poison the ostriches; the latter fly down to what has the appearance of grubs, and are stricken by the poison injected into their mouth by the horned serpents. Hence the verse says of those who are given the dragons' poison from what they use for suckling that, even if they are part of the people of God, they are as dry as the "ostrich in the desert," snared by the aforementioned serpents.[48]

47. Heb 5.12; 1 Cor 2.6.
48. Prv 5.3–4; Lam 4.3, which in the Heb. refers to a jackal's nursing habits, and where Didymus has omitted a phrase in the LXX about the ostrich. As we have seen him doing before, he goes to some lengths to make a point from a piece of scriptural documentation, even citing naturalist authorities (Doutreleau identifies Philumenos of Alexandria; SC 84.528–29), while leaving the precise reference in Zechariah unplumbed.

COMMENTARY ON ZECHARIAH 8

HE WORD OF THE LORD *almighty came to me saying, The Lord almighty says this: I am jealous for Jerusalem and Sion with a great jealousy, and am jealous for it with a great anger. The Lord says this: I shall turn back to Sion, and dwell in the midst of Jerusalem; Jerusalem will be called a true city, and the mountain of the Lord almighty a holy mountain* (Zec 8.1–3). The text cited is explained in this way: *The word of the Lord almighty came* saying what is indicated in what follows: *The Lord almighty says this: I am jealous for Jerusalem and Sion,* recalling it to myself after repelling and rejecting it so that abuse by foreigners was heaped on it. It is not lightly that I *am jealous for it,* but *with a great anger.*

The comparison is drawn with wives living with their husbands. The wife who sets aside her marital obligations and through love for outsiders abandons the conjugal home no longer enjoys the care of her former partner and is then ignored. The result is that it is said to her by her abandoned husband, I no longer care for you nor feel any jealousy for you. After all, how could anyone feel jealousy or solicitude when the marriage is over? So even if the woman who scorned the conjugal home is driven off, she becomes the object of jealousy once more if she seizes the opportunity for repentance and returns to the man she abandoned, once her former partner with extreme generosity lets her come back.

Now, we must move from the situation of the wives to the consideration of Sion and Jerusalem—by *Jerusalem and Sion* referring not to the places but to their inhabitants. In bringing them up from Egypt God entered into a relationship with them and provided them with laws and ordinances like a dowry; the result was that he showed his betrothed care and consideration, and shared his bed with her as was proper for a husband with his partner. After agreement was reached in this way according to law, she set aside the marriage laws and set aside her husband, who was her protector and ally. Hence the saying, "As a wife sets aside her partner, the house of Israel set me aside"[1] and thus went off to sinful demons and impure spirits, and became the object of lustful abuse. Her companions in an allegorical sense are Babylonians and Assyrians.

When this had gone on for a long time, Jerusalem, or Sion, came to her senses and recalled the one who had taken her as a companion, the result being that she decided to go back to the one from whom she had been separated. At any rate she uttered these words: "I shall go back to my husband of former times because at that time I was better off than now." The one to whom she began to come back and return accepted this kind of repentance on her part, and said, "On that day"—namely, when her return is confirmed—"she will call me 'my husband,'"[2] as a result of which he will from then on be jealous for her as protector and provider *with a great anger,* punishing those who heap abuse on her. Since he was jealous of her with such a great anger as to long to be with her as before when she had not abandoned the conjugal bed, hence he turns back to her and says, *I shall dwell in her midst.* (He speaks of Sion and Jerusalem as one, Sion being a part of the capital.)

Now, what will happen when *I shall turn back and dwell in her midst* if not her once again being styled a *true city,* no longer desolate but full of citizens and buildings, the Temple rebuilt along with the houses one by one, the result being that there will now be lanes and roads as before, shrines and squares and streets? When Jerusalem taken literally is given this name, the mountain of the Lord almighty will also be *holy* as it was before the captivity: the customary rites will be celebrated there, and songs and hymns performed in accord with the words of the psalmist when he says in one case, "A song of praise befits you, O God, on Sion," and in another, "Sing to the Lord who dwells on Sion."[3]

1. Jer 3.20.
2. Hos 2.9 LXX, 16.
3. Pss 65.1; 9.11. While Theodore sees Jerusalem to be once more "true" in the sense of "having real value," and both Antiochenes investigate the physical

After the exposition of this in a factual sense, it would be appropriate to plumb the meaning in an anagogical sense. The contemplative soul is spoken of as Jerusalem, Jerusalem meaning "vision of peace"; she stumbled and hence was banished from the divine conjugal chamber and alienated from the one who formerly lived with her. As a result, lustful abuse was heaped upon her by hostile powers, anagogically referred to as Assyrians and Babylonians, so that the partner who showed her consideration no longer cared for her. The vagaries of her free will do not remain set in that direction: as movement occurs from virtue to vice and from piety to impiety, so there is likewise a change from pernicious and harmful things to good and useful things. Thus the one who had abandoned the divine conjugal chamber is acquainted with it again, so that her former carer drives off her adulterous abusers and is jealous for her. He does so with a great anger, extremely incensed with her mockers, to the point of now saying openly, *I am jealous for Sion and Jerusalem.*

Anagogically, Sion, or Jerusalem, is a soul that has an eye for things that are unseen and eternal, a soul perceiving peace, feeling the bonds of the interdependence of the virtues and godly attitudes. The one who is jealous for her with a great anger makes her turn back to him, as he likewise does to her by acceding to her pleas and providing what she prays for unceasingly. Reformed in this way, she could be called *true* Jerusalem because she no longer hankers after the shadows and images of the Law, but only the good things prefigured by them. Of these things the divinely inspired apostle writes, "The Law has a shadow of the good things to come, not the actual image of the realities," and again to the believers from the nations, "Do not let anyone condemn you in matters of food and drink, nor in connection with festivals, new moons, and sabbaths, which are a shadow of what is to come."[4] The future good things in the

---

restoration after the return, Didymus's moral accent is more in keeping with modern commentaries. He touches on physical recovery without descending to historical details of the restoration under Zerubbabel, and soon opts for a spiritual meaning to the verses.

4. Heb 10.1; Col 2.16. With constant insistence on the ascending levels of significance of OT things, words, and events, it is not surprising that Didymus does not trouble to root the text in the facts of Zechariah's time.

texts cited are the evangelical teachings, which the savior called "mysteries of the kingdom" in speaking to the initiated: "To you it has been given to know the mysteries of the kingdom of heaven." The soul that has an eye to them and that has a vision of the peace of their concord is Sion, or Jerusalem, in a spiritual sense, and bears the name *true* because she is living according to the truth prefigured by the shadow of the Law, and "studying the inspired Scriptures."[5]

Consistent with the reference to the sacred city as *true*, the mountain of the Lord almighty will also be *holy* and given that title. Note whether the mountain of the Lord almighty is the doctrine of the descent of the Son of God, who is referred to in one of the Songs of the Steps in these terms: "Those who trust in the Lord are like Mount Sion."[6] After all, our mind is not so impoverished as to think that those who trust in the Lord are compared or likened to a material mountain when they have such extraordinary virtue as to prove blessed like people possessing spiritual blessings. It is written in Jeremiah the prophet, remember, "Blessed are those who trust in the Lord; the Lord will be their hope"; and in the Psalms, "It is better to trust in the Lord than to trust in human beings."[7] Since those who trust in the Lord are not portrayed as a material mountain, then, which is something thrust up from the earth, we must think of it in the way Isaiah said of it, "At the end of time the mountain of the Lord will be conspicuous," splendid and manifest "at the end of the ages so as to bring sin to naught," destroying and eliminating it in being sacrificed like a lamb. The mighty John sheds light on this mystery in presenting Jesus in the words, "Behold the lamb of God, who takes away the sin of the world." It is also in reference to the aforementioned mountain that one must take what is announced in the forty-eighth psalm, "Great is the Lord and highly to be praised, in the city of our God, on his holy mountain."[8]

5. Mt 13.11; Jn 5.39.
6. Ps 125.1. Didymus constantly uses ἐπιδημία to refer to the Lord's coming, as does Cyril.
7. Jer 17.7; Ps 118.8.
8. Is 2.2; Mi 4.1; Heb 9.26; Jn 1.29; Ps 48.1. The movement of thought from Mt. Sion to the faithful to Jesus proceeds by association and concatenation of

With these things explained in an initial spiritual sense, there is need also for an allegorical interpretation with elevated understanding of Sion's going back and Jerusalem's being called true.[9] This is the explication arrived at in the epistle to the Hebrews by the one speaking in Christ, who writes, "You have made your approach to Mount Sion and the city of the living God, the heavenly Jerusalem and assembly of the firstborn gathered in festal assembly with innumerable angels" and hence "enrolled in heaven," listed with the citizens of a holy and heavenly city. Included among them are the apostles, who heard it said by the sovereign king, "Rejoice that your names are inscribed in heaven."[10] This list is the "book of the living." Some blessed ones, at any rate, the vessel of election describes this way: "With Clement and the others, whose names are in the book of life."[11]

The Lord almighty says this: Old men and women will again sit in the streets of Jerusalem, all with their sticks in their hands from their advanced age. The streets of the city will be filled with boys and girls playing in its streets (vv.4–5). At the literal level the prediction of the prophet suggests that Jerusalem is restored to profound peace and an undisturbed way of life. With such tranquillity, and all the enemy expelled far from the beautiful city, dread of foes is no longer a preoccupation. So those of advanced age from length of life and fullness of time, both men and women, will take their place in the streets as before the captivity, holding sticks in hand, old men taking precedence (though we should make up our minds as to whether old women are also there). The stick is a mark of respect. With those advanced in age taking pride of place in this way, the streets will be filled with boys and girls at play, whereas the very young were not allowed out of doors in the streets when foes were threatening and enemies expected.

---

texts. In this process Zechariah's point of God's return to Jerusalem with the rebuilding of the Temple goes without accent.

9. If Doutreleau sees allegory proving "le moyen d'excellence" of arriving at the spiritual meaning (ἀναγωγή) of texts, he also admits of Didymus that "on confondit l'une et l'autre" (SC 83.58). Here, too, the relation of the two is unclear.

10. Heb 12.22–23; Lk 10.20.

11. Acts 9.15; Phil 4.3.

After giving this factual statement, we must also read the text spiritually.[12] The spiritual city with its streets is the Church in its glory; in reference to it the announcement is made to the sovereign king in charge of it, "Wonderful things are said of you, O city of God." After all, how could it fail to be celebrated and exalted when it partakes of the divine draughts from "God's river full of water"? There is mention also in the forty-sixth psalm of the royal city and the favors it receives from its royal ruler: "The river's currents give joy to the city of God. The Most High sanctified his tabernacle; God is in its midst, he will not be moved."[13] In other words, the Most High dwells in the midst of the peaceable city to sanctify his tabernacle, and is in no way outside of it, instead remaining steadfastly within it. The streets of this beautiful city are the individual virtues and their practice, described by the sage in proverbial form in giving this picture of wisdom: "Wisdom sings in the lanes, she parades confidently in the streets, atop the walls she proclaims her message." After all, how could God's wisdom not parade confidently in the streets of the spiritual city when a further saying states, "If you long for wisdom, keep the commandments, and the Lord will bestow it on you," referring by each commandment to the streets on account of their peculiar breadth, so that the psalmist says to God, "Your commandment is exceedingly broad."[14]

There is need to consider whether reference is made in the same sense by the bride of Christ in the wedding story, "On my bed at night I sought him whom my soul loves and did not find him, I called on him and he did not hearken to me. I shall get up and go about the city, in the market places and the streets,

12. This maxim could be Didymus's hermeneutical rule of thumb (though the balance between ἱστορία and another level of διάνοια is somewhat one-sided).

13. Pss 87.3; 65.9; 46.4–5.

14. Prv 1.20–21; Sir 1.26; Ps 119.96. The spiritual meaning of the text is again developed by loose association, Didymus leafing through his mental concordance to discover scriptural references to cities and then to rivers and wall tops (not items in Zechariah's text). The trail leads to mention of streets in the Song of Songs and wall tops in Isaiah. Cyril is much more restrained in finding a spiritual meaning in these verses, and only after an attempt to identify a historical basis.

until I find him."[15] In other words, at the time of lying in bed together and getting up, which in allegorical fashion she called "night," after thinking the divine bridegroom was close to her, she searched without finding, and called without getting a response from him. He kept his distance from her for the beneficial reason that she might be further smitten with love for him, love for him being further aroused by distance from the object of her affections. Feeling this way, then, she awoke and got up, looking for him nowhere else than in the churches, these being public places of a sacred nature where those appointed as apostles, prophets, and teachers expound the sacred rites of truth and mysteries of the kingdom of God.[16]

Beyond looking for him in the public places she is anxious to meet the object of her search even in the aforementioned streets so that in her love for him she may find repose in him. Wisdom, by whom the creator brought everything into being,[17] and who paraded confidently in the streets of the beautiful city, proclaims her message nowhere else than atop the walls to the nightwatchmen and guards of the divine city, according to the statement from Isaiah in the person of the sovereign king, which goes this way: "On your walls I set guards by day and night, who to the end will not be silent in recalling the Lord."[18]

In the aforementioned divine streets of the blessed city, devoted old men and women will still take their place as before, with their sticks in hand, symbols of both kingship and priesthood as well as corrective instruction. We should understand the old men as those who have gone grey with understanding, according to the statement in the commendable Wisdom of Solomon to this effect: "Distinguished old age consists not of length of life, nor is it measured by number of years; with human beings grey hair means understanding, and old age an unblemished life."[19] Age in this spiritual sense applies to the one styled a friend of God; faith in him "was reckoned as righteousness" in Abraham's case; it was said by Moses the revealer in Genesis, "His strength failing, Abraham died, having reached a

15. Song 3.1–2.
16. 1 Cor 12.28.
17. Ps 104.24.
18. Is 62.6.
19. Wis 4.8–9.

ripe old age, advanced in years and full of days."[20] There is not
in this, in fact, a reference to the number of annual cycles of
the material sun; though before him there were people born
who had longer lives, none of them was said to be "advanced
in years and full of days": the father of Isaac was the first one
of the elderly to be called "advanced in years" on the basis of
virtue.

In reference to people with such an attitude, lifestyle, and
spiritual maturity, the cause of all things and provider of every
good says to his faithful servant, "Appoint seventy elders to be
with you whom you personally know to be elders." It emerges
from this that it is not appointment or mandate that makes
an elder of one who was not so before: they only prove and
demonstrate it. The precise command, in fact, was for those to
be appointed whom the appointer knew to be already of that
caliber. The command in Joel, one of the Twelve Prophets, may
be taken as of equal import: "Choose as elders" those who already are so, where the choice does not anticipate but acknowledges the fact of their demonstrably possessing already the
virtue and its seniority. It is written in Proverbs in reference to
those in possession of this distinction, "Grey hair is the glory of
elders," that is to say, the hair that obviously stems from understanding.[21]

Enjoying a status and authority equal to the elders mentioned above are those also of the new covenant. In writing to
his own disciple Titus, for instance, the apostle expressed this
thought in addition to others: "I left you behind in Crete for
the express purpose of settling outstanding matters as I directed you, and appointing elders in each city." He lists the charac-
teristics of those being promoted, who were given a position in
the church hierarchy: monogamy, faultless rearing of children,
and behavior in accord with the other virtues.[22] He calls them
overseers in ancient parlance, as we mentioned also in other

20. Gn (Κοσμοποιΐα) 15.6; Rom 4.3. Didymus's geocentric cosmology is not
remarkable, of course, nor his acceptance as factual of the great ages of figures
that are cited in the Bible's primeval history (and in extrabiblical accounts).
21. Nm 11.16; Jl 2.16; Prv 20.29.
22. Ti 1.5–9.

places; for example, in the Acts of the Apostles it is reported that "Paul summoned the elders of the Church," and said to them, "The Holy Spirit has made you overseers to shepherd the Church, which he acquired with his own blood," and so on. To those of this rank, Peter, the head of Christ's disciples, announces in his epistle, "I urge the elders among you." Now, let us see what it is that he urges if not "to tend Christ's flock, not under compulsion but willingly," so that "when the chief shepherd appears, they may win the crown of glory that does not fade."[23]

The aforementioned elders in both covenants are kings in the style of Abraham according to what was said by those who acknowledged his superiority: "You are a king from God among us."[24] Yet they also sincerely attend in priestly fashion on the one who chose them, and bear the scepter of twofold preeminence, seated in the streets of the city just described, each holding his own stick, which serves as scepter and also for corrective teaching. In regard to the accusations facing the guilty, remember, it is said in a letter by Paul, "Which do you prefer—that I come to you with a stick or with love?" In keeping with this the divine text of the Proverbs also declares in one case, "The one who has wisdom to offer on his lips strikes the heedless man with a stick," and in another, "Spare the rod and hate your own son; correct him assiduously and love him."[25]

Females also share in the respect shown elders if it is through faith and the practice of virtue that they attain to old age. Describing such a life, Paul, speaking in Christ, writes thus to Timothy: "Honor widows who are truly widows," implying that such women are rid of all human concerns, cultivating the growth of commendable actions, raising children as duty requires, showing generous hospitality, ministering to God's servants, meeting the needs of the poor, and adorned with all similar works of virtue. The apostle's teaching refers to this in actual detail, beginning this way: "Let a widow be put on the list who is not less than sixty years old, the wife of one husband,

23. Acts 20.17, 28; 1 Pt 5.1–4.   24. Gn 23.6.
25. 1 Cor 4.21; Prv 10.13 LXX; 13.24.

well-attested for good works, provided she has brought up her children, shown hospitality, washed the feet of the saints, helped the afflicted, devoted herself to doing good in every way."[26]

In confirmation of the aforementioned virtues the need was felt also for mature age as an ornament for the virtues acquired, for a woman to be no less than sixty if she was to have achieved maturity. The prophetess Anna was like that in actual fact, having lived with a husband for seven years after her maidenhood, and long continued as a widow to the age of eighty-four, the number being appropriate to a chaste widowhood, on which remark has been made elsewhere.[27] It is possible to see women committed to this option in the Old Testament as well; the valiant Judith was one such, bearing a name to this effect (Judith meaning "commendation").[28] It is not unlikely that you would also find many others adorned with age and honor, especially those of whom it is said in a prophet on God's part, "I shall pour out my spirit on all flesh, and your sons and your daughters will prophesy," and so on to the point, "Even on my servant men and women I shall pour out my spirit and they will prophesy."[29] Ponder the question yourself and consider whether the reference is only to old men holding sticks in their hands, or to old women as well. While it is possible that the statement applies to both categories, however, it seems more likely to refer only to the men.

In the streets (a reference we have clarified) where those have taken their place who have grown old in understanding and reached advanced age by an unstained life, boys and girls

---

26. 1 Tm 5.3, 9–10. Though women do not usually figure in Didymus's commentary (ἄνδρες frequently occurring when reference is to people in general), the Zechariah text here allows for a digression on female virtue. But he will conclude—against the text, in fact—that only men are being referred to.

27. Lk 2.36–37; Anna's case κατὰ τὴν ἱστορίαν confirms what might otherwise have seemed mere speculation. Didymus had spoken of the virtues of the number 12 (a factor of 84) in commenting on the date in 1.7.

28. The book of Judith seems to occur in Didymus's canon and to be accepted as historical, though he does not develop its spectacular contents for his purposes. The name is usually taken to mean simply "Jewess." Didymus does not exert himself to list a range of valorous women in the OT.

29. Jl 2.28–29.

are also engaged in praiseworthy games for which David was distinguished, a man after God's own heart, who did all the bidding of the one who chose him, and who uttered with great confidence, "I shall dance and play before the Lord."[30] You can interpret children playing in the streets of the glorious city of God as those so dedicated to temperance from their tender years as to enjoy incorruptibility along with unimpaired gravity and sound speech beyond reproach. Of this kind were the disciples of the apostles, "born anew, not of corruptible but of incorruptible seed, through the living and enduring word of God," "like newborn infants who long for the pure, spiritual milk." It is relevant to cite also the verse from Proverbs, "so as to communicate shrewdness to the innocent, and good sense and prudence to the young child"; and in the same book the man of godly wisdom said, "Listen, children, to a father's instruction, and pay attention so as to learn prudence." Now, there is reference here not solely to those who are physically male: souls in a female body are male in their way of thinking.[31]

Following on comment on the boys there is need also to interpret the girls at play. Note whether it is in reference to them that in the forty-fifth psalm there is a hymn of praise about the bride and the groom that goes as follows: "Maidens will be brought to the king in her wake"—namely, the bride and queen, who is positioned at the right of her partner—"her companions will be brought to you, they will be brought in joy and gladness." The virgins who will be brought in the wake of the Church, who is conducted as a bride to her sole husband, Christ, are those without corruption of spirit or body, and who are chaste in thought and action. As it was said that there are children who are male not solely in body but especially in soul, likewise the virgins who have holiness in thought and action do not necessarily have a female body. In the Apocalypse of John, for instance, the hundred and forty-four thousand virgins are

30. Wis 4.9; 1 Sm 13.14; 2 Sm 6.21.
31. Ti 2.7–8; 1 Pt 1.23; 2.2; Prv 1.4; 4.1. If the closing remark is meant to indicate an attitude inclusive of women, it succeeds in being no less condescending than the closing statement of the gnostic Gospel of Thomas, "Every female that makes herself male will enter the kingdom of heaven."

not of that condition in a bodily way, the qualification being added, "They are those who were not defiled with a woman: they are virgins, and in their mouth there is no guile, for they are beyond reproach."[32]

There is reference in one of the Psalms to all those living in the streets of the celebrated city as though in a single group: "Let young men and maidens, the old along with the young, praise the name of the Lord." In reference to the different ages of the interior person, the disciple whom Jesus loved writes, "I am writing this to you, children, because your sins are forgiven on account of his name"—the savior's, obviously—"I am writing to you, fathers, because you know what was from the beginning; I am writing to you, young people, because you are strong, and the word of God abides in you, and you have overcome the evil one."[33] Now, by "children" he refers to those who have just gained forgiveness of sins, whatever their age in terms of the exterior person; he gives the name "fathers" to those with an understanding of the elements of the true doctrine of God; and "young people" to those of strength from the word of the one who abides in them and exhorts them to remain invincible, even if their contest is "with rulers, with authorities, with cosmic powers of this present darkness, with the spiritual forces of evil." After all, how could they not be strong when they have received from the savior, the sovereign king, "authority to walk on snakes and scorpions and on every power of the foe" without suffering harm? The phrase, "Nothing will wrong you," in fact, means, "Nothing will harm you." For instance, in reference to the person who receives the power to walk on venomous creatures and all the power of the foe, a triumphal hymn is uttered, the text of which goes thus: "He will tread on asp and basilisk, you will tread underfoot lion and dragon."[34]

With sufficient comment made on the text in hand, let us deal with what follows.

---

32. Ps 45.14–15; 2 Cor 11.2; 1 Cor 7.34; Rv 14.1, 4–5. Here, too, Didymus is not concerned about the disparaging attitude to marriage in the passage from Revelation that concerns modern commentators. He is, of course, at some distance from the thought of the Zechariah text.

33. Ps 148.12–13; 1 Jn 2.12–14.

34. Eph 6.12; Lk 10.19; Ps 91.13.

The Lord almighty says this: If it will be impossible in the view of the remnant of this people in those days, surely it will not be impossible also to me? says the Lord almighty (v.6). The material Jerusalem here below had been subjected to such ruin by the enemy that its citizens had endured a cruel captivity, and had no faith in promises of its restoration. Seeing it reduced to ruins, they believed it impossible for it to be rebuilt anew in splendor, with mountains and plains inhabited, old men and old women again occupying its streets, and boys and girls in large numbers playing in them. Since "all things are possible to God,"[35] however, including bringing breadth out of narrowness and abundance out of shortage, and even if in view of the remnant of the people who to this point had survived the death of large numbers it seemed to them impossible, it was not impossible to God.

In the capital of Judah, then, which was captured and suffering extreme desolation, it was considered impossible by the people who had no resilience of soul for it to be restored to its former glory and prosperity, despite God's promise and ability to put it into effect. Likewise, those of no faith and of impoverished thinking, who saw the Church so reduced to extremities in the persecution against the Christians that its fall seemed to exceed recovery, believed it was impossible for it to be restored and recover the deep peace of the one who had said to the disciples, "My peace I give you, my peace I leave with you." He thus instilled confidence in those to whom he had promised to give a stable and tranquil peace, saying, "Have confidence, I have overcome the world": hence, even if you now have distress, be confident in expecting relief.[36]

Those who attacked the Church and Christianity were guilty of such savagery as to demolish all the places of assembly and consume by fire the sacred books. With such awful cruelty be-

35. Mt 19.26. Didymus neatly, if briefly, paraphrases Zechariah's statement of the relative impossibility of the city's restoration by the disheartened populace, before moving to comment on the similar situation of the Church under persecution (the persecution under Diocletian being in force up to the time of his birth).

36. Jn 14.27; 16.33. At this point occurs a brief phrase, "fulfillment (ἀλήθεια) being welcome," which editor Doutreleau (SC 84.562) admits is unclear, and could be either retrospective or prospective.

ing in force for a short time, pusillanimous people thought it
was impossible for it to recover its glorious condition once
more. But even if in their view what happened was beyond solu-
tion and repair, what they despaired of proved possible and
easy. You can see, for instance, the places that were formerly
razed rearing on high in a more splendid condition than before, covered in gold and bedecked with all carefully worked
ornaments, and the books that were damaged by fire gilded
and inlaid with gold, and exposed to view in the royal halls.
God's power against the odds emerges also in the fact that the
renewal of Christianity was achieved by those by whom it was
persecuted—though by them I mean not the same people but
those who exercise the same government. Of these matters,
however, more complete mention has been made in the *Commentary on Isaiah.*[37]

To give confidence to look forward to what seemed beyond
hope, the text says that the Lord almighty promised to do it.
*The Lord almighty says this: Lo, I shall rescue my people from the land
of the east and from the land of the west. I shall bring them back and
shall dwell in the midst of Jerusalem, and they will be my people and I
shall be their God in truth and righteousness* (vv.7–8). Just as the title "man of God" is given to the person who worships and
serves him, so the people that comprises only those who are devoted to God in every way is styled God's people. It is his people
whom he rescues from all over the world and its limits, his
promise stating, *Lo, I shall rescue my people from the land of the east
and from the land of the west, says the Lord almighty.* This people is
not only the one of the circumcision, but the one of all the nations who believe in the savior in keeping with the Gospel.

In former times, remember, one single nation, that of the
Hebrews, was the people of the one who created everything, his
lot and portion, according to the testimony of the revealer
when he said, "When the Most High apportioned the nations,
when he scattered the sons of Adam according to the number
of God's angels, Jacob became the Lord's portion, Israel the

37. Doutreleau (SC 84.564) believes that Didymus finds such details of persecution and restoration in Eusebius's *Church History.*

cord of his inheritance" on account of the beauty of its behavior and life in keeping with the text of the forty-seventh psalm, uttered by the saints in these terms: "He chose us as his inheritance, he loved the beauty of Jacob." Of similar intent is the direct statement in the teaching of Moses, "Lo, this great nation is a wise and discerning people," devout and resistant to sin, according to the verse in the admirable Wisdom of Solomon, "The one whose soul is unfamiliar with vice and whose body is not a victim of sin" is a recipient of God's wisdom and the sacred discernment corresponding to it. Consistent with this view is the statement by a God-fearing man to a person of real worth about God's word: "Lo, fear of God is wisdom, and resistance to vices is discernment."[38]

In company with this wise and discerning nation that is "a royal priesthood, a people as a special possession," all the nations rejoice at the birth of the savior, which they ardently looked forward to in accord with the blessing that spoke of a savior's rising from Judah, which is consistent also with what is expressed this way in Isaiah: "There will be a root of Jesse which will rise to command nations; in it nations will hope." In reference to the common pleasure and satisfaction of all human beings, Scripture says, "Rejoice, nations, with his people," which is no longer composed only of the one nation of the Hebrews, but of all who together adore and worship God according to the statements in the Psalms, in one place, "All the nations will serve him," and in another, "All the nations you made will come and bow down before you, and they will glorify your name," Lord, and again, "The ends of the earth will remember and will return to the Lord, and the families of the nations will bow down before him, because kingship is the Lord's and he is master of the nations."[39]

In reference to the calling of everyone, both Jews and Greeks, as a single people, the present text of the prophet makes the pronouncement in the words of the Lord of all, *Lo, I*

38. Dt 32.8–9; Ps 47.4; Dt 4.6; Wis 1.4; Jb 28.28. The privileges of the ancient Israelites are not understated.

39. Ex 19.5–6; 1 Pt 2.9; Gn 49.10; Is 11.10 LXX; Dt 32.43 LXX; Pss 72.11; 86.9; 22.27–28.

shall rescue my people from the land of the east and from the land of the west, says the Lord almighty. Regarding an assembly of a group from all the regions of the world, the Gospel speaks in reporting the savior's words, "Many will come from east and west, and will take their place in the kingdom with Abraham and Isaac and Jacob." In accord with the calling from all quarters, the psalmist says in loud tones in the fiftieth psalm, "The Lord God of gods has spoken and summoned the earth from the rising of the sun to its setting."[40]

Now, when did this calling come if not when "the comeliness of his charm" was made manifest "from Sion"? Another prophecy was then fulfilled that ran thus: "The deliverer will come from Sion," or "for Sion," as the vessel of election writes, Paul speaking in Christ. When did the God of gods speak and summon from east to west if not when the people of the circumcision were rejected for denying the sovereign savior in the words, "We have no king but Caesar," and "his blood be upon us and upon our children"? For having crucified the savior, remember, they were rejected, and the worship in shadow and letter came to an end, so that God said to them, "I have no pleasure in you, and I shall not accept a sacrifice from your hands, because from east to west incense is offered to my name in every place and a pure offering." Now, what is the "incense" and "pure offering" made "in every place" for glorifying God? The psalmist makes it clear when he says to the great king, "Let my prayer be directed like incense in your sight, a lifting up of my hands like an evening sacrifice." In former times, remember, when the shadowy worship held sway, in Jerusalem was "the place where one had to adore," offer prayers, and perform sacrifice. But now that the true light is shining and illuminating the whole world,[41] in every place the incense commented on is offered as well as the sacrifice associated with it, with oratories everywhere on earth erected through devotion to God, so that the name of God may be glorified among all the nations east and west.

40. Mt 8.11; Ps 50.1.
41. Ps 50.2; Is 59.20; Rom 11.26; Jn 19.15; Mt 27.25; Mal 1.10–11; Ps 141.2; Jn 4.20; 1.9.

In another sense those glorifying God are those on whom the "sun of justice" rose and on whom the light of the impious set, of whom it is said in Proverbs, "The light of the impious will be extinguished."[42] But when this has taken place, *the Lord almighty will rescue his people from the land of the east and from the land of the west* so as to bring in the nations, not leaving them to stay outside like the crowds listening to the discourse on perfection in parables, but with the purpose of their being admitted to the mystical and spiritual courts of Jesus, and becoming hearers of the clarification and knowledge of the parables, as the guide says, "To you it is given to know the mysteries of the kingdom of heaven." Now, just as anyone on the outside—with respect not to location but to disposition—hears words superficially, so, too, the listener to the Old Testament in letter and shadow is culpable; it is said of such people who listen to the Law in a veiled fashion, remember, "They read out the Law superficially, and invoked a confession"—not reading out superficially the teaching when the life-giving Spirit came to them. This happens when prayer is offered in this form: "Unveil my eyes, and I shall understand your marvels from your Law." This veil that he asks to be removed is the obscurity of the contents and the ignorance inherent in the understanding of the one who reads improperly. It is possible, in fact, to learn about these matters in an understanding way, according to the apostle, who writes, "For to this very day, when Moses is read out, a veil lies over their reading; but when there is a turning to the Lord, the veil is removed. Now, the Lord is the Spirit."[43]

What will happen, by the grace of God, when the nations are introduced in the manner we have mentioned, other than the Lord's making his dwelling in Jerusalem, when the Temple is filled with the glory of the Lord God almighty *in truth and in righteousness?* Not only here, in fact, but also in other texts righteousness is mentioned along with truth; for example, in the fifteenth psalm it is said that "the one who walks in innocence

---

42. Mal 4.2; Prv 13.9.
43. Mt 13.11; 2 Cor 3.15; Am 4.5 LXX; 2 Cor 3.6; Ps 119.18; 2 Cor 3.15–17. The direction of the thought is not that arising out of Zechariah's text, nor is his reference to east and west explored.

practices righteousness and speaks truth in his heart," and in another psalm, "Mercy and truth have met, righteousness and peace have kissed; truth rose from the earth, righteousness descended from heaven." Consider whether *truth* suggests the mystical and spiritual insight into the doctrines of the true religion, whereas *righteousness* is the name given to virtue of a moral and practical nature, in keeping with the saying about it to those with a desire for salvation, "Learn to practice righteousness, you inhabitants of the earth."[44]

There is need to study what is involved in the virtues mentioned. "Mercy meets truth, righteousness and peace have kissed." In other words, since God's truth is something great and elevated, there is need for mercy to be shown by God, the source of goodness, for people to receive it. Righteousness, on the other hand, which does away with all iniquity, the mother of all discord and all hostility, is the harbinger of peace and harmony. One of this world's philosophers has said that concord keeps peace and righteousness together:[45] when everyone in a righteous manner goes after what is righteous, should this happen, all discord and enmity are eliminated, just as when peace obtains, equality and righteousness reign. This being the case, the Almighty is Lord of truth and righteousness. In the thirty-first psalm, for instance, it is said by the one with hope in the Lord at the opening of the song, "You have redeemed me, O Lord, God of truth," and in the fourth psalm, "When I called, you hearkened to me, O God of my righteousness." Consequent upon his being God of truth, he is also God of knowledge, as the blessed mother of the holy Samuel said, "Let not arrogance issue from your mouth, because the Lord is a God of knowledge."[46] When we show zeal in good works and in true and pious knowledge to be styled God's people, then it is that he for his part will be our God, related to us in truth and in righteousness.

44. Pss 15.2; 85.11; Is 26.9.
45. If the sentiment cannot be directly traced to Plato or Aristotle, Doutreleau informs us (SC 84.574–75), it is of frequent occurrence in classical literature.
46. Pss 85.10; 31.5; 4.1; 1 Sm 2.3.

The Lord almighty says this: Let your hands be strong, you that have been listening in these days to the words from the mouth of the prophets from the day the foundations have been laid of the house of the Lord almighty and the Temple has been rebuilt (v.9). The Lord almighty bids the hands of the people dedicated to the Lord almighty be strong, according to the words of the Lord God almighty, when the foundations of his house have been laid, according to the former time when the Temple has been built. Now, those hands grow strong with piety and holiness of truth, according to the words of what was said by the mouth of the prophets when the foundations of the house of the Lord have been laid and the holy Temple built. Hands grow strong by words when the moral teachings are put into action; it is then that the active hands of the soul are put into operation, when the deeds of virtue are interwoven with words, and listeners to the Law are not hearers only but also doers of deeds.[47]

Now, when is there sincere and reverent zeal if not when God's people act and think with a word of piety when the foundations of the divine house are laid and the Temple rebuilt as in former times? The foundations of the Lord's house are laid and the Temple is rebuilt when the statement in Proverbs to this effect is fulfilled: "Wisdom built herself a house, and erected seven pillars." In reference to this house and Temple, the Lord incarnate says to the Father, "A body you have fashioned for me."[48] Once the aforementioned house with its foundations is built like a holy temple, *the hands*—that is, the active faculties—are strengthened according to the ancient illuminating insights, called *days.*

There is need to examine whether the house with foundations laid and the Temple built are the Church in her glory, which the apostle refers to in writing to his disciple Timothy: "If I am delayed, you may know how one ought to behave in God's

47. Some uncertainty arises from the tense of the verbs and the meaning of οἰκοδομέω being either "build" or "rebuild" as to which period Zechariah has in mind; but Didymus is interested rather in the verse's spiritual meaning.
48. Prv 9.1; Heb 10.5. The citations, one Christological, seem simply to come to the surface for a moment without developing the thought consistently. Diodore would find the hermeneutical procedure arbitrary.

house, which is the Church of the living God, pillar and bulwark of the truth." Also suggestive of this interpretation is the prophetic verse of Isaiah to this effect: "He who says of Jerusalem, You will be rebuilt, and I shall lay the foundations of my holy house." When will this happen if not when all those accepting the Gospel in mature faith and virtue "will be built upon the foundation of the apostles and prophets, with Jesus Christ himself as its cornerstone, to form a holy temple in the Lord, a dwelling" for the Trinity? In addition to these considerations, each of the devout is also a house with foundations laid and a temple built, according to the testimony of Christ, who says, "If anyone loves me, they will keep my word, and my Father will love them, and we shall come," my Father and I, "and make our abode with them."[49]

The hands of the disciples of Christ grow in strength when they do what the Gospel prescribes. The savior fulfilled the Law and the Prophets when the foundations of the house were laid and the Temple built, with the coming of the Holy Spirit upon the most holy virgin Mary, and the power of the Most High overshadowing her. It was then, in fact, that the words of the prophets of former times were fulfilled, and their oracles attained fulfillment. After all, how do the hands of those who hear the prophets' words not grow in strength with the birth from the virgin of the one whose name is "God with us"? When the Lord is with us, you see, then our hands grow in strength so that we sing praise in loud tones, "The Lord of hosts is with us, the God of Jacob is our protector." Since in fact our protector is the almighty, the God of the one who spurns evil—namely, Jacob—we are in possession of supernatural force; so let us shout aloud triumphantly, "God is with us. Be aware, nations, and submit; give heed everywhere, to the end of the earth. Even if you are strong, you will still be overcome; and whatever word you speak will not remain in you, because the Lord God is with us."[50] When will these righteous victories happen if not when our hands grow in strength, with the foundations of the house

49. 1 Tm 3.15; Is 44.28; Eph 2.20, 22; Jn 14.23.
50. Lk 1.35; Is 7.14; Mt 1.23; Ps 46.7, 11; Gn 27.36; Is 8.8–10.

COMMENTARY ON ZECHARIAH 8 175

laid and the Temple built, according to all the interpretation given of the prophetic text in hand?

Because before those days people's wages will be of no benefit, there are no payments for cattle, and there will be no relief from distress for the one leaving or the one arriving. I shall dispatch all people against their neighbors (v.10). He had made many predictions to the people benefiting from them of the glorious restoration to come and the rise of the holy city Jerusalem, with the foundations of the holy house laid on it and the Temple rebuilt to the benefit and satisfaction of the people. Their hands grow in strength with the prophetic words. This was before the days of the promise, when the city was deserted owing to its submission to the captors. People's wages were of no benefit, their efforts in vain, and their work fruitless. In addition to the futility of people's efforts, there are no wages or profit for cattle, either, whether exerting effort or bearing burdens. People's wages are of benefit, and are given also for cattle, when the foundations of the house are laid and the Temple built; it is at that time, in fact, at that time that for both the one leaving and the one arriving there is relief from distress, namely, from the sweat and toil endured for the betterment and fruition of efforts. But there is no relief from distress for the one leaving or the one arriving, he says, and the work of people and cattle is futile and profitless. Vain will be the wage for mortal beings who are rational, and none for the cattle, since people are ranged *all against their neighbors,* all concord and harmony banished on account of the ferocity and hostility arising from anger and implacable enmity.[51]

It is possible in a spiritual sense that the efforts and exertions of people who appear to have the use of reason are futile and so their wage brings no benefit, whereas for those who are more like cattle in their silliness it does not even exist. Scripture censures their irrational silliness and ferocity in saying, "Be

51. The time reference in the text continuing to be unclear, Didymus does not specify the historically different conditions obtaining at one time rather than another. Cyril tries harder, as does Theodore, who finds support in Haggai, being unable to take refuge in a spiritual interpretation, as Didymus proceeds to do.

not like horse and mule, since they have no understanding"; after all, how could there be wages for what has no understanding, doing everything irrationally? So even if in some cases
some people seem to be human, yet because they do everything
deceitfully, their actions are without reward or result, and their
wages are of no benefit for the reason that "wisdom does not
enter their deceitful soul, or dwell in a body enslaved to sin,"
only the wages of virtue and piety being of benefit. It is thus to
the soul that produces "food lasting to eternal life" and putting
into practice the holy commandments that God in "making
payment" says, "There is payment for your works." In terms similar to this reward Paul the apostle in Christ writes of those
whose work is beyond reproach, "All individuals will receive
their own payment according to their work."[52] Consider carefully whether only what is given in return for commendable actions is called *wages*, while the return for sins is referred to as
punishment, not wages.

Now, the consequence of there being no benefit in people's
wages and no wages for the cattle is that there is no relief from
distress for the one leaving and the one entering, since people,
though sent by the king who reigns peaceably, are ranged *all
against their neighbors*, constantly slaying and harassing one another. Describing such a ferocious attitude, the psalmist in the
twelfth psalm says, "All people spoke vain things in their hearts,
lying lips were in their hearts, and in their hearts they spoke."
To similar effect Jeremiah also says in reference to those of
this disposition toward each other, "Beware of friends, and put
no trust in family, because every family member is a supplant-
er, and every friend acts deceitfully; they will not speak the
truth, their tongue has learned to tell lies." Of such people the
sacred psalmist, David, also cries aloud, "Though to me they
spoke of peace, in wrath they frame plans"; and the prophet
says again, "All speak of peace to their neighbors, and have
hostility in their hearts"—namely, the lying and deceitful ones.
In the case of those who go to such pains and perform "the
works of the flesh,"[53] even if seeming to be human beings, their

---

52. Ps 32.9; Wis 1.4; Heb 11.6; Jer 31.16; 1 Cor 3.8.
53. Ps 12.2; Jer 9.4–5; Ps 35.20; Jer 9.8; Gal 5.19.

wage will be of no benefit, nor will that of those who are more like cattle.

In this verse *cattle* is to be taken as those who are pleasure-seeking and sensual, and *people* as those elders who profess the "so-called knowledge" and "the wisdom of this age and its rulers,"[54] for which the wages are of no benefit to the worker or for survival beyond this age and life of its kind. When the true light shines in the next life, you see, every deceitful sophistry and irrational pleasure will pass away, with the result that their wages, which are only in appearance, will no longer exist or be of benefit; the one leaving or entering will no longer enjoy relief from the overwhelming distress, all people being sent against their neighbors so as to pillage and abuse them.

At this time I shall not deal with the remnant of this people as in former times, says the Lord almighty. Instead, I shall let peace emerge: the vine will yield its fruit, the land will yield its produce, and heaven will give its dew. I shall give all this as an inheritance to the remnants of my people (vv.11–12). Disposed as he is to beneficence, the cause of all good things promises no longer to treat the survivors of the people as in former times when the enemy, who had prevailed over those whom they had taken captive, were in power. I shall grant peace, he says, there will be good seasons and abundant crops, the vines will bear much fruit, the land will be fertile in growing crops, heaven will give its dew, and all of this God will give as an inheritance to the remnants of this people. In a literal sense he promises the aforementioned things for the time of the return of the captives, when those who enjoyed them said in thanksgiving, "When the Lord reversed the captivity of Sion, we were like people enjoying consolation." Then God no longer treats the remnants of the chosen people as in former times when Jerusalem was desolate: he provided peace in the future in response to the prayer the people offered in saying, "Lord, our God, give us peace."[55]

On the other hand, the spiritual sense of this splendid restoration emerged when he came who said, "The Spirit of the Lord is upon me, and hence he anointed me; he sent me to bring good news to the poor, to proclaim release to captives

54. 1 Tm 6.20; 1 Cor 2.6.   55. Ps 126.1; Is 26.12.

and sight to the blind, to heal the broken-hearted." He makes the same promises also in Amos the prophet, "I shall reverse the captivity of my people Israel, and they will rebuild the cities that have been destroyed, and I shall plant them there."[56] Once these divine graces and gifts are bestowed by the generous giver, there will be peace, which will spring up with righteousness at the time of the coming of the king who receives judgment from God; it is said of him, "In his time he will make righteousness arise and an abundance of peace," such that there is no limit to his peace, which will come not to a single nation but to all the nations and the whole world ruled by him, who said to the disciples and those willing to serve under him, "My peace I give you."[57] A deep calm will prevail, and instead of treating the remnant of Israel as in former times, he shall ensure an unmatched abundance, with the vine producing its fruit, the soil its produce, and heaven its proper dew.

Now, a vine bearing its particular fruit is the spiritual contemplation of truth and the rational nature that is conformed with it, which has grown out of the true vine by way of sharing. Of this process the savior said in the Gospel, "I am the vine, you the branches; every branch abiding in me the Father prunes so that it may bear more fruit." Of these branches that contain the beginning of productivity, it is written in the Song of Songs, "Our vines are in blossom, they gave off fragrance." When the fruit grows and reaches maturity, it is plucked, thrown into the vat, and crushed, and it turns into a drink that cheers the heart of the drinker, as is said in the Psalms, "Wine gladdens the human heart."[58] In reference to the spiritual plucking there were songs written for the wine-pressing, like Psalms 8, 81, and 84, these three psalms being the only ones of the one hundred and fifty to bear the title "for the wine press."[59]

---

56. Is 61.1; Lk 4.18; Am 9.14–15. Characteristically, Didymus feels no obligation to note that Amos is speaking in the eighth century about a possible restoration of the northern kingdom.

57. Ps 72.1, 7; Is 9.6; Jn 14.27.

58. Jn 15.5, 2; Song 2.13; Ps 104.15.

59. Whereas modern commentators profess ignorance of the phrase in the Heb. which they render "for the Gittith," the LXX thought to see there *gat*, "wine press."

In accord with the spiritual sense of the vine giving its fruit, the soil also will yield its produce, causing the seed that Jesus cast in it to germinate so as to produce a hundred-, sixty-, and thirty-fold, in keeping with the interpretation of the parable: the savior interpreted the good soil as the good heart in possession of righteousness. Now, this produce of the soil is given to the one sowing the divine seeds in tears—that is, in sweat and toil—so as to reap them in rejoicing; it is to those who sow, not in a material but in a spiritual sense, that one of the Songs of the Steps refers, "Those who sow in tears will reap with rejoicing. They wended their way and wailed as they bore their seed; on return they will return in joy as they bear their sheaves." In reference to such abundance, spiritual as it is, the divine word also in the prophet Hosea gives the order, "Sow to grow righteousness for yourselves, harvest to reap a harvest of life, shed the light of knowledge for yourselves, seek the Lord as long as the produce of righteousness comes forth."[60]

The aforementioned vine produces its nourishing and cheering fruit and the good soil its produce when heaven gives its dew. We shall understand what this dew is if we know what heaven, which gives it, is, namely, nothing else but the person who bears "the image of the man of heaven," whose "citizenship is in heaven."[61] There is abundant reference in the nineteenth psalm to all those conformed to the heavenly savior: "The heavens recount the glory of God, the firmament proclaims the work of his hands." In the great song in Deuteronomy it is also written of them, "Rejoice, heavens, together with him"—the savior, obviously; after all, how could it not be with him that they exult and rejoice when conformed with him, according to the teaching of the sacred apostle Paul, who at one time writes of those faithfully and sincerely reverencing God, "Those whom he foreknew he also predestined to be conformed to the image of his Son," and at another time, "Let us bear the image of the heavenly man"?[62]

Those who are thus conspicuous for their moral and con-

---

60. Mt 13.8, 23; Ps 126.5–6; Hos 10.12.
61. 1 Cor 15.49; Phil 3.20.
62. Ps 19.1; Dt 32.43 LXX; Rom 8.29; 1 Cor 15.49.

templative virtue, "united in the same mind and the same purpose," it must be said, are one heaven in harmony, giving spiritual dew. As well, however, all such people give their own dew,
in a similar manner to what is said by Moses the revealer, "May
my utterance be awaited like rain, and my words descend like
dew." Yet even if it is given by heaven in the manner explained,
it is still supplied in particular by the Lord of the heavens, according to the inspired verse of Isaiah in these terms: "The
dead will rise, those in the tombs will be raised up, and those
on earth will rejoice, for the dew that comes from you will be
healing for them." And since those in the ground who receive
it rejoice at the healing quality of the spiritual dew, it must be
said that the dead who are risen and issuing from the tombs
also share in it especially at that time when, at the consumma-
tion when one comes face to face with truth, partial vision
through a mirror comes to an end with the victory of the one
seen in full vision. In reference to the dew taken this way one
can cite also the blessing given to Jacob by Isaac, which begins
thus: "Of the dew of heaven and the fatness of the earth."[63]

All the gifts were given to the people on their redemption
from Babylon when the Lord gave them as an inheritance. And
since it is in a passive sense that he expressed God's giving
everything as an inheritance to the remnants of the people—
namely, the fruit of the vine, the produce of the soil, and the
dew of heaven—it must be understood in both ways, actively
and passively. In an active sense the meaning is as follows: Israel
is referred to as God's portion and inheritance for the simple
reason of the virtues it possesses, which have voluntarily and
willingly been acquired by action and contemplation. The following verse also has the same sense: "Ask of me, and I shall
give you nations as your inheritance," all peoples being given as
an inheritance by the savior for pious faith and works of virtue.
If, on the other hand, a passive meaning is suggested by the
verb in question, namely, "will give as an inheritance," this will
be the meaning: God will give as an inheritance all the aforementioned gifts, bestowing them in the manner of an inheri-

63. 1 Cor 1.10; Dt 32.2; Is 26.19; 1 Cor 13.10, 12; Gn 27.29.

tance on the remnants of his people, those who say in the prophet Isaiah, "If the Lord of hosts had not left us a seed, we would have become like Sodom and have resembled Gomorrah"; and further on, "Even if the number of the sons of Israel were like the sand on the seashore, the remnant will be saved." In citing these prophetic words, the apostle makes the following addition to them: "At the present time there is a remnant, chosen by grace, not on the basis of works; otherwise, grace would no longer be grace."[64]

Now that the text cited has been clarified to the best of our ability, let us proceed to what follows. *Just as you were a curse among the nations, house of Judah and house of Israel, so I shall save you and you will enjoy blessing. Have confidence and be strong in your hearts.*[65] *Because the Lord almighty says this: Just as I planned to afflict you for your fathers' provocation of me, says the Lord almighty, and I did not relent, so I am ready and I plan in these days to treat Jerusalem and the house of Judah well* (vv.13–15). Falling victim to distress and curse is due to nothing other than sin and impiety, whereas blessing is given to the righteous by God on account of their upright actions and thoughts. People are independent, after all, with free and unfettered choice, and of themselves they do what brings on them either punishment or divine promises. In other words, just as they become liable to a curse, so, too, beneficence and blessing. At any rate, the cause of every good says to Judah and Israel, When your fathers were guilty of lawlessness and impiety so as to provoke me to wrath against them, I did not relent, instead inflicting what was proper for those provoking me to suffer. Now likewise I am ready and I plan to save the people of Judah and Israel, and I have not thought better of it.

It is possible to produce texts in support of this from the di-

64. Ps 2.8; Is 1.9; 10.22; Rom 9.27; 11.5–6. Again Didymus is more interested in the eschatological remnant than in the situation of the returned exiles.

65. Like the Heb., the LXX text of v.13 (found also in Cyril and the Antiochene commentators) reads "hands" for "hearts." Jerome has no qualms about adopting this singular reading of Didymus, Doutreleau informs us (SC 84.600). Fernández Marcos, *The Septuagint in Context*, 244–46, points out that the biblical text of later Alexandrian commentators does not totally correspond with that of the time of Didymus (Antioch's text being different again).

vinely inspired Scriptures. At one time the inhabitants of Nineveh also sinned and committed acts of impiety to such an extraordinary degree that the outcry at the wickedness ascended to God and demanded retribution, the result being that the provider and judge of all said, "In three days Nineveh will be overthrown." On learning of this when it was proclaimed to them by the prophet Jonah, who made the threat for the purpose of giving guidance, the guilty people had recourse to repentance, and so made confession and performed actions canceling their previous wickedness. The one who had forecast retribution against them relented on their repenting, therefore, taking it as a reason for beneficence. This did not happen in the case of the Sodomites for the reason of their persistence in impiety and sin, despite the merciful God's wishing to find in them grounds for benevolence; he said, in fact, "The cry of Sodom and Gomorrah is magnified, and their sins are exceedingly grave. I shall therefore go down and see if their actions match the report of their wickedness ascending to me, and if not, I shall know." In other words, Since the cry of their grave sins has summoned me, I shall descend, the purpose being that if they are found still to be committing the grave sins, they will suffer the predicted retribution for doing so; but if they have obediently moderated their impious thoughts and forbidden practices, I shall recognize them as my own in keeping with what is written, "The Lord knows those that are his, and let everyone who calls on the name of the Lord turn away from wickedness."[66]

It is in this sense that Paul, the vessel of election, writes to the Galatians, "Whereas at that time, when you did not know God, you were enslaved to what are by nature not gods, now you know God, or rather are known by God." In other words, he knows those who know him, not that he began to know them at that time, but to judge them as one knows people already known, though this does not happen to villains still persisting in their wickedness. It is therefore said by the savior to

66. Jon 3.9, 4 (the LXX reading "three days" for "forty," probably under the influence of v.3); Gn 18.20–21; 2 Tm 2.19; cf. Nm 16.5.

those persisting in their vices up to the time of the end of the world and the manifestation of the judge of all, namely, himself, "Depart from me, you workers of iniquity: I never knew you"[67]—in other words, you never had any experience or share of me, nor I of you. I mean, if you were to understand "know" in a literal sense to mean the same as "understand," how would he know they were workers of iniquity?

There is therefore a twofold sense of knowing and not knowing conveyed in the divinely inspired Scriptures. In one sense the God who knows the heart has an understanding of everyone, righteous and sinners; for instance, when the king coming to "judge the living and the dead" "is seated on the throne of his glory," he will separate righteous people from sinners so as to introduce into the kingdom those practicing righteousness and holiness to receive it as an inheritance, but to dispatch to punishment people guilty of iniquity and wickedness for not loving their neighbor as themselves, his words being, "Depart, you that are accursed, into the everlasting fire that has been prepared for the devil and his angels." In the sense of "understanding," the one "who knows hidden things" and "understands the mind of everyone" says to some people, "I know that your sins are many," and likewise in the Gospel, "You are those who justify yourselves in people's sight, but God knows your hearts, because what is lofty in people's eyes is an abomination to God." In this interpretation we must also take the saying that frequently occurs in the Gospel, "Jesus knew their thoughts," namely, villains'; being of malicious and vicious disposition, they thought they would escape "the one who understands the mind of everyone."[68]

As it is knowing in the sense of understanding, to which not knowing is the opposite, likewise one can know and not know through experience as well. For example, when Paul writes of the savior that "he did not know sin," we take the expression to have the same force as not having experience of sin in action or

67. Gal 4.8–9; Mt 7.23.
68. Acts 15.8; Mt 25.31; 2 Tm 4.1; Mt 22.39; 25.41; Dn 13.42 LXX; Jb 7.20; Am 5.12; Lk 16.15; 5.22.

thought: having an understanding of its power and by what act of choice it is committed, he therefore came to take it away from the world. This distinction extends also to the case of human beings. In Ecclesiastes, for example, it is said, "The one who keeps the commandment will not know an evil word,"[69] that is, will not be inclined to an evil word: to the one keeping the divine commandment, which is God's word, the evil word is known in the sense of being understood; since there is one single understanding of opposites, the person who knows the good word understands also its opposite.

Scripture also applies the twofold sense of knowing in reference to Adam when it says he understood what was the nature of the woman: when the creator gave her after her formation, Adam said, "This is bone of my bone and flesh of my flesh; she will be called woman." He later knew her in the sense of experience, the text saying, "Adam knew his wife Eve, she conceived and gave birth to Cain." This is applicable to every married man, both in common parlance and in divine teaching; for example, of the father of the prophet Samuel the text says, "Elkanah knew Hannah his wife, and she conceived and gave birth to Samuel." There is a reference in this sense to Rebekah: "She was a virgin, no man knew her." And the virgin Mary, who had no experience of marriage, said to the mighty angel Gabriel on hearing of conception of a child, "How can this happen to me since I do not know a man?"[70]

We consider that it is not without benefit to have digressed from the prophetic text in hand: it has been done for the sake of clarifying that obscure text, "I shall go down and see if their actions match their cry reaching [me]; if not, I shall know." There was need, you see, to determine in what sense the statement was made by God, "I shall know."[71] Now that we have

69. 2 Cor 5.21; Jn 1.29; Eccl 8.5.
70. Gn 2.23; 4.1; 1 Sm 1.19; Gn 24.16; Lk 1.34.
71. Though Didymus excuses himself for digressing on the grounds that the "text in hand" needed clarifying, that text (Gn 18.21) is itself part of a digression about different kinds of knowledge, the "prophetic text in hand" from Zechariah being at a further remove. But he tries quickly to suggest he had Zechariah in mind all the time. He might more honestly have admitted that his hermeneutic-by-association often leads him far off the track. Cyril will pick up

shown which of the people provoking him God planned to afflict and exhibit as the object of curse without relenting, and instead persisting in his verdict against them, it is time to see which are those to whom he decided instead by his innate goodness to give a second chance. He did not go back on his promise to bless Judah and Israel, since they had persevered in the way of virtue they had undertaken at the urging of God and his Law. It is said in one of the Psalms, remember, "The lawgiver will give blessings," that is, to those who keep his divine Law. In another psalm also there occurs the statement of equal relevance, which begins thus: "Who will ascend to the mountain of the Lord, and who will stand in his holy place? The person who is stainless in hand and pure of heart, who has not set his soul on vanities nor sworn deceitfully to his neighbor. This person will receive blessing from the Lord, and mercy from God his savior." Note that to the question, "Who will ascend to the mountain of the Lord, and who will stand in his holy place?" a response is given that describes the person in question, that he is stainless in hand—that is, in actions—on account of purity of heart, never setting his soul on vanities or swearing deceitfully to his neighbor, and destined to receive for these noble deeds both blessing and mercy from God his savior. There is a similar statement also in Proverbs: "The Lord's blessing is on the head of the righteous."[72]

The person who has adopted this salvific course will not forfeit the promise after being made a party to the divine promises by the one who says, I am ready to bless Judah and Israel, and shall not decide against it, persevering in my good will so as to treat them well and lead to eternal salvation those for whom my decision is not changed, since I have confirmed what I promised. Even if your fathers provoked me by sin and impiety, and a curse took effect, without my relenting from the threat by your providing grounds for a change in my attitude to you by repenting of your evil behavior, nevertheless let your heart have confidence in expecting gifts from me. They will, in fact, defi-

just the slightest hint of this long digression on "knowing" without being distracted.

72. Pss 84.6; 24.3–5; Prv 10.6.

nitely be given, since I am willing and ready to bless you; then you will prosper, you the members of Judah, the one who confesses, and of Israel and Jerusalem. After all, it is as one who "wishes everyone to be saved and come to the knowledge of the truth"[73] that I threaten, I chastise those opposed to knowing the truth of eternal salvation, submitting them for a time to hardship in my wish for them to improve and prosper. In this way, you see, they will easily profit and be saved, since I am irrevocably committed to saving the chosen ones and treating them well, so that they may be my portion and inheritance.

If we, too, want God to be merciful so as to treat us well, let our thinking (the meaning of *heart*) be positive, and let us be devoted to good works. Thus the course of our contentment and unending salvation will be beyond risk or question, once the curse that was briefly in force is canceled and totally deleted. Have unshakable confidence, therefore, in looking forward to what is promised by God, who is reliable; since it is he, in fact, who says, *Have confidence* (v.15), there is no doubt of our receiving the goods we hope for.

The second volume on the prophet Zechariah has been compiled to sufficient length; so let us conclude it and begin the third when God, who also shed everlasting light on the prophet, "provides a message by the opening of my mouth."[74]

God, who is reliable in being fountain and father of truth, never ceases to instruct and teach those who have made themselves ready for the coming of the gifts of the Holy Spirit. He provides without delay, for instance, a word of wisdom and a word of knowledge to those longing to receive them; it is said, in fact, in the epistle of James, "If any of you is lacking in wisdom, ask God, who gives to all generously and ungrudgingly, and it will be given you. But ask in faith, never doubting." Of similar import is the proverbial saying that goes, "The Lord

73. 1 Tm 2.4. Didymus repeats his (questionable) etymology of Judah; cf. n. 36 on chapter 1.

74. Eph 6.19. Since division of τόμοι is determined by length rather than movement of the prophet's thought, Didymus at this point simply moves from one volume to the next within the one chapter, engaging in parenesis by way of closure and introduction.

gives wisdom, and from him come knowledge and understanding." The person shown to be wise in God-given wisdom is thrice blessed, having the God of all as teacher; Scripture says, "Blessed the one whom you instruct, Lord, and teach from your Law." A longing to have this teacher was felt by those to whom the Lord and savior said, "You call me Lord and teacher, and you are right: I am."[75]

This gift will be ours, too, as a result of unceasing prayer by those offering it for us, the gift of wisdom and "a message by the opening of the mouth," so that we may faultlessly and properly interpret the following verses of the prophet before us, beginning at this point. *These are the directions you will carry out: speak the truth, each of you to your neighbor, deliver a peaceable judgment in your gates, do not ponder evil in your hearts, each of you towards your neighbor, and do not entertain a false oath, because I loathe all this, says the Lord almighty* (vv.16–17). Of God's directions those to do with moral and practical virtue can be put into effect, whereas those to do with knowledge of exalted mysteries refer to contemplation on the part of mystical and contemplative men. For example, when God gave many commandments through Moses the revealer for the performance of virtuous actions, those who understood the instructions that were given professed aloud their commitment to putting into effect what was ordered, saying to the minister of the divine oracles, "All that God has said we shall do and heed." Since, however, the moral directions required action and also understanding for justice to be achieved justly, temperance temperately, and bravery and wisdom bravely and wisely, this being the way to proceed in an understanding manner to the performance of the virtues in practice, there is consequently need also to heed and carry out the directions of Jesus, who makes this declaration: "Whoever comes to me and heeds and carries out my directions will be like a wise man," and so on.[76]

---

75. 1 Cor 12.8; Jas 1.5–6; Prv 2.6; Ps 94.12; Jn 13.13.
76. Ex 19.8; Mt 7.24. As the previous verses of Zechariah had led to a digression on different kinds of knowledge, vv.13–15 (this time with some justification) lead Didymus to develop the different kinds of directions given in the Bible.

Now, instructions are put into practice by those who heed them at that time especially when the teacher does what he tells others to do; of such a person the Lord says, "Whoever practices them and teaches them to people will be called great in the kingdom of heaven,"[77] whereas the one not doing what he bids others do is the least [meritorious], especially if while saying not to commit adultery he is guilty of it, while forbidding theft he is involved in it, and even while abhorring idols he ransacks temples. Does that person not ransack temples who through scandal brings harm to those consecrating themselves to divine service like living statues of the divinity? After all, the one who brings harm to such people by vile behavior and an irreligious attitude truly ransacks temples by breaking the law of which he seems to boast, thus dishonoring God. Lest you be a wicked teacher, then, give evidence in your actions of the moral lessons you teach; you will thus be "a worker who has no need to be ashamed." The apostle adopts this attitude in writing to his disciple to "have integrity, gravity, and sound words that cannot be censured":[78] does he not have "sound words that cannot be censured"? In practicing what he recommends to others and entertaining thoughts he leads others to adopt, he has sound words of teaching that cannot be censured.

It is in this life—the active and the contemplative, I mean—that the next prophetic work after the one in hand, by name Malachi, wants the true servant of God to take part. Its text runs as follows: "The lips of a priest will guard knowledge, and they will look for the Law in his mouth"[79] in their longing to learn from a godly teacher what they should know—orthodox teachings, mysteries of the kingdom, the law forbidding injustice and delivering the teachings on virtue. Having learned which instructions are to be put into practice by those receiving them, let us study which are those that lead to knowledge and truth. In teaching that "in the beginning God made heaven and

---

77. Mt 5.19.
78. Rom 2.21–23; 2 Tm 2.15; Ti 2.7–8. Scandal given by religious teachers (perhaps even the clergy, to judge from what follows) moves Didymus strongly; it is not only a recent phenomenon.
79. Mal 2.7.

earth,"[80] Moses spoke these words so that we might truly know creation and its creator; and all the other words recorded in Genesis were spoken, not for us to put them into action but for us to contemplate them, and this instruction is confirmed in all of Scripture, inspired as it is by God. The savior himself in the Gospels, for example, sometimes gives directions that are to be put into practice, and sometimes transmits what we should know and contemplate. His saying, remember, "Learn of me, for I am gentle and humble in heart, and you will find rest for your souls," and again, "If you want to come after me, deny yourself, take up your cross and follow me each day," are said with a view to being put into action, as also, "Be merciful, and you will obtain mercy," and all other directions to this effect. On the other hand, the verse, "I am in the Father, and the Father in me," and "I and the Father are one," and yet again, "Whoever has seen me has seen the Father," and all other expressions of the true doctrine of God in both testaments were spoken and recorded for us to contemplate and to have a true and religious knowledge [γνῶσιν] of them.[81]

After showing which directions must be put into practice, the Holy Spirit enunciates each in particular and in its category: the verse *Speak the truth, each of you to your neighbor* was written down for the purpose of its being put into practice. To clarify it, Paul in Christ recommends the observance of the commandment to the faithful, saying quite plainly, "Abandon falsehood and speak the truth, each of you to your neighbor." And before the apostle, the savior gave instructions for telling the truth without oath-taking: "I tell you not to swear at all: let your word be Yes, Yes, or No, No."[82] This is observed especially when all people speak the truth to their neighbors; in this way every false word and oath will disappear, the consequence being mutual regard of the most precise and perfect kind.

---

80. 1.1 of the book (Genesis) that Didymus knows as Κοσμοποιΐα.

81. Mt 11.29; Lk 9.23; Mt 5.7; Jn 14.10; 10.30; 14.9. Didymus sees distinction in biblical composition between oral teaching and written record, at least in the case of Moses and Jesus. Doutreleau, SC 84.621, assures us there is nothing esoteric about Didymus's use of γνῶσις.

82. Eph 4.25; Mt 5.34, 37.

In addition to all people's speaking the truth to their neighbors, there will also be *a peaceable judgment* when people are no longer at odds or anxious to be grasping or unjust. After all, how could they still think of stirring up quarrels and injustice when all are telling their neighbors the truth? The peaceable judgment is the same as the just one; study of it at length was conducted in what went before. Now, it is not only here but also in other writings that Scripture mentions this kind of judgment being delivered in the gates of the Hebrews; it is said in another prophet, "They hated the one who reproves in the gates, and abhorred a holy word"—the impious, that is, of whom the oracle in Proverbs declares, "Do not reprove the wicked lest they hate you."[83] Their abhorrence of a holy word, in fact, is something not true of those beginning to enjoy wisdom: they welcome the one who reproves and informs the person anxious to be righteous of what should not be done. And since they constantly hate those entrusted with reproving in the gates, the text guarantees that judgment in the gates will cause a change and bring about a return to what is good and beneficial.

Now, you might inquire why judgments and reproofs are delivered in no other place or part of the city than in its gates. To this the acceptable and plausible reply should be given that since it was through the gate that departure from the city and entrance to it was made, it was natural for the judges to sit there in examining the lives of the citizens so as easily to expel those convicted of the charge against them, while those of an untarnished record established by the evidence stayed inside and went even further inside the city. In a spiritual sense, those people are accorded this position and the seat of judgment who receive from Jesus "the keys of the kingdom of heaven"[84] so as to cast out those who are guilty of acts deserving bondage, and on the other hand to give admission to those not shackled in the bonds of sin but free of them.

83. Am 9.10; Prv 9.8.
84. Mt 16.19. Didymus is relishing this moral passage in Zechariah, and moving through it more systematically than he does in commentary on historical details of the text. Jerome follows him slavishly, Doutreleau notes (SC 84.622–24).

Now, the *peaceable judgment* is delivered at that time in particular when people *do not ponder evil in their hearts, each towards your neighbor,* practicing instead total forgetfulness of grudges. There is a twofold form of *evil:* one sense of the word is the opposite to virtue, a highly malicious disposition, and the other is evil behavior, as occurs in the verse, "Is there evil in the city which the Lord has not caused?"[85]—in other words, ill treatment. God causes it for the conversion of those suffering it, curing the ailments of the soul surgically, as by the use of burning and cutting. The word *evil* suggests a malicious disposition, and on this basis God said about the Ninevites, "The cry at their evil has risen up to me." The same sense appears also in the apostle's statement about impious people to this effect: "As they did not think fit to acknowledge God, God gave them up to a debased mind and to things that should not be done; they were full of every kind of wickedness, evil," and so on. The people heeding the Law of God, therefore, do not ponder evil against their neighbors in either sense, "not returning evil for evil,"[86] not showing a hostile disposition to the one disposed to ill-treat them. Instead, they do not ponder anything against their neighbor, even the form of evil indicated, that is, readiness to be grasping and unjust in return.

After mention of people bent on holding grudges in their hearts against their neighbors, there follows *entertaining a false oath* with the intention to commit perjury. Having forbidden all that followed, the giver of the divine Law revealed the reason for delivering these pronouncements: *I hated all this.* After all, how does he not hate the person taking a false oath when he had commanded, "You shall not take the name of the Lord your God in vain"? As with perjury, he deplores and has revulsion for the other sins as well, expressing hatred for people's not speaking the truth to their neighbors, for the ones causing trouble and not delivering peaceable judgments, for the wrathful and morose people who ponder evil against their neighbors

<hr />

85. Am 3.6, a text that had Theodoret struggling to vindicate divine holiness, and that Chrysostom cited as one popularly misused to justify lack of moral accountability.

86. Jon 1.2; Rom 1.28; 12.17.

in their hearts. In Malachi also he speaks in terms similar to
what is written here: "You kept doing all I hated." Likewise, in
Proverbs there is an obscure reference among others to the
one guilty of many sins: "He is undone by his soul's impurity,
since he takes pleasure in all God hates."[87] The one who takes
satisfaction in what the Father of goodness hates is undone by
his sin, the guilty one's soul and mind being impure.

*The word of the Lord almighty came to me: The Lord almighty says
this: The fast of the fourth, the fast of the fifth, the fast of the seventh,
and the fast of the tenth will be an occasion of joy and happiness and
of beneficial celebrations for the house of Judah; be glad, and love truth
and peace* (vv.18–19). The word of the Lord almighty that came
to me, says the prophet, bade me fast on the *fourth, fifth, seventh,
and tenth*—month, that is, there being no tenth day of the week,
as we also remarked before. In any case, it was natural that the
Lord almighty would give this order in respect of the seventh
month in the Hebrew calendar, since that was when the so-
called Day of Atonement and Humiliation was celebrated,
which Jews observe publicly and refer to as a fast, and when
those coming to the public fast on the fourth, fifth, and seventh
days purify themselves. The different forms and the manner of
fasting in accordance with the divine Law were explained in
what preceded;[88] it should further be stated here as well that
there was an obligation to give up tasty delicacies as well as
foods that were harmful and injurious in an allegorical sense.
Well-being, in fact, will come to those making confession (the
sense of *house of Judah*); *joy, happiness, and beneficial celebrations* to
those celebrating with good sense and the performance of
duty, as is said in the Psalms, "Sounds of happiness and confession, a roar of celebration," and again, "Hold a feast with the

87. Ex 20.7; Mal 2.13; Prv 6.16 LXX.
88. Didymus made some (largely spiritual) comments on fasting in the
(much mutilated) commentary on the opening verses of chapter 7. It is unclear
why these months are mentioned for fasting, Cyril looking to dates given in Jer
52 and 2 Kgs 25 for the fall of Jerusalem, and Theodoret making a rare reference to the alternative versions to verify his text, of which the Heb. is itself subject to emendation. Didymus has in mind the mention of fasting in the legislation for the Day of Atonement in Lv 23.26–30; he later defends his nomination
against possible queries, and may be familiar with Jewish observance of this day.

garlands as far as the horns of the altar." Consistent with this is what is announced in another song to this effect: "Human pondering will confess to you, and a remnant of pondering will celebrate you."[89]

Now, feasts are celebrated to our benefit when the spiritual Jerusalem ("vision of peace") lives peaceably, since the feasts are not held with good cheer when enemies are in power. When the latter is the case, in fact, God will say, "I hate, I reject your feasts, and I will not smell the scent of your festal assemblies"; and he heightens his threat still further, "I shall change your feasts into mourning, and your songs into dirges."[90] May the congregation of the faithful be far from these troubles so that in response to the call to joy and happiness we may hold *beneficial feasts* and divine assemblies, loving profound peace and also truth; undisturbed thinking and a tranquil state of soul are found there, the charm of truth and its beauty emerge there. Now, truth manifests itself especially when in the wake of the virtues tranquillity gives the lead and peace is in charge; those who have attained such a wonderful state of well-being enjoy happiness and good cheer.

Someone would probably raise a question about the basis of our conjecture that in the Hebrew calendar it was the seventh month of which the fourth to the tenth days were the times prescribed for fasting. The basis is the passage at the end of the prophet Zechariah, the work at present under examination: "Celebrate a feast of Tabernacles," which is prescribed by the Law for no other month than the one mentioned, as also are the feast of the trumpets and the fast. Clear proof that the new moon of the seventh month is the date of festal assembly can, in fact, be gained from the psalm, which puts it this way: "Sound the trumpet on the new moon, on our festival day of good omen."[91]

---

89. Pss 42.4; 118.27; 76.10.
90. Am 5.21; 8.10.
91. As observed in n. 88, there is room for doubt as to the feast(s) suggested in v.19. While confirming his option for Atonement in the seventh month, Didymus notes a later mention of Tabernacles in Zec 14.16, another feast in the seventh month, a festal time as shown by the blowing of the trumpet (he cites Ps 81.3). He thus seems to be recognizing three principal feasts: New Year ("feast

The Lord almighty says this: Many peoples shall yet come, the inhab-
itants of many cities. The inhabitants of cities[92] *will assemble in one*
city, saying, Let us all go together and entreat the favor of the Lord and
seek out the favor of the Lord almighty; I, too, shall go. Many peoples
and many nations will come to seek out the favor of the Lord almighty
in Jerusalem, and to win the favor of the Lord (vv.20–22). At the literal level the prophet foretells, when the word of the Lord
almighty has come to him, the future restoration that is an occasion of exultation and festive assembly for the Hebrew
crowds, the cities of Judah, and its capital, Jerusalem. Through
Moses God had given orders to all of Israel to celebrate a feast
for him for three days of the year in a place of his choosing,
which was to be none other than Jerusalem. Hence the enthusiasm to assemble from all the cities and towns of Judah in the
capital, where all the holy and festive rites were celebrated. All
this came to an end with the captivity, when almost all the Hebrews were expelled from the mother-city. Deploring this
pitiable and distressing situation, God's prophet Jeremiah says
in the book of Lamentations, "The streets of Sion are in
mourning because no one comes to the feast; all its gates are
destroyed, its priests are groaning."[93] After all, how could the
streets of Sion not be in mourning when deprived of their traf-
fic, with no one anxious to show zeal for celebrating and assembling in Jerusalem, its gates destroyed and pulled down by
those wielding tyrannical power? It was an inevitable consequence that the priests would groan at the deprivation of the
fine [rituals], seeing that there were no grounds for any joyful
enthusiasm at the time they should have been serving the God
who chose them.

Zechariah foretells that these unpleasant events are coming
to an end when he says, *Many peoples will yet come*—to Jerusalem,
that is: the seventieth year of the captivity had now been
reached, as we know from his saying to God in prayer, "How

of the trumpets"), Tabernacles, and Atonement ("the fast"). Modern scholars
are not in agreement as to whether there was a distinct OT feast of New Year.

92. Didymus is reading "cities" where the Heb. has "one" (as in Theodore's
text) and the LXX "five cities" (as in Cyril's and Theodoret's).

93. Lam 1.4.

long will you have no mercy on Jerusalem and the cities of Judah? This is the seventieth year."[94] Since the Lord almighty acceded to the prayer immediately, Jerusalem's return in peace was revealed to the one who offered it: many peoples would still come as before to seek out the face of the Lord almighty. The requirements are once more in force: "Three times a year every male shall appear before me," and "You shall not appear before the Lord your God empty-handed,"[95] that is, You shall bring the offerings for worship as well as other gifts and what is required for festive good cheer.

The purpose of the ritual performed with such zeal was to seek out with entreaties and holy prayers a manifestation of the Lord almighty, appearing and manifesting himself to a transparent mind that shares in holiness according to the statement given by the savior in the beatitudes, "Blessed are the pure in heart, for they shall see God." In keeping with this insight the divinely inspired Paul writes to the Hebrews to "pursue peace and holiness, without which no one will see the Lord," especially since he manifests himself to those who do not lack faith in him and appears to those observing his commandments. In the Wisdom of Solomon, remember, there is a verse to this effect: "Think of the Lord in goodness, and seek him with sincerity of heart, because he approaches those who do not put him to the test, and manifests himself to those who do not lack faith in him." And in the Gospel the savior says this: "Those who have my commandments and keep them are those who love me; and those loving me will be loved by my Father, and I shall love them and manifest myself to them."[96] It was to *seek out the favor of the Lord almighty* in this way that the many peoples came to Jerusalem, not to find God living in that place in the Temple, but to offer up acceptable prayers and have pious thoughts and an upright attitude about seeking out and winning over the Lord almighty.

94. Zec 1.12.
95. Ex 23.17, 15; 34.20. In giving his initial, literal (πρὸς ῥητὸν) comments on the verses, Didymus is spending longer than usual within an OT perspective (where Cyril makes no effort to do so) before moving πρὸς ἀναγωγήν.
96. Mt 5.8; Heb 12.14; Wis 1.1–2; Jn 14.21.

Each of the prophet's words should in a spiritual sense be applied to the glorious Church sanctified by the sovereign savior, which in the times of persecution thought that it had lost all vestige of joy and peace as far as depended on the persecutors. The many nations returning to it and inhabitants of many cities are the churches in the different districts, and those of pious attitude and irreproachable life living everywhere in the aforementioned cities will converge from many cities into one so as to attract and win over the favor of the Lord and seek it out through acceptable prayers and requests to have a vision of God.

And since what was forecast was desirable and much to be longed for, the prophet personally entertained that desire for the object of hope, and hankered after accompanying the many peoples and inhabitants of many cities converging on the one place, saying, *I, too, shall go.* The masses generally have trust in oracles to the point of ardently looking forward to them when the person delivering them is the first to show interest in what is foretold. It is possible[97] that the words *I, too, shall go* are said on the part of the savior: when he goes, those follow him to whom the promise was made in the verse, "When the Lord averts the captivity of the people, Jacob will rejoice and Israel be glad," as the Father also says to him, "I raised him up as king; he will build my city, and reverse the captivity of my people, without even payment or bribes."

What will happen once the beautiful city is rebuilt and the people brought back from captivity? From all directions many peoples and many nations will come to win the favor of the Lord almighty and seek his favor, which is the "image" of him, that is, "of the invisible God," and "the imprint of his substance." The result is that the one who approaches him with a pure mind sees the Father—in other words, the invisible God; "the one who has seen me has seen the Father," remember. The angels also have a desire to see the Son; it is said in the Gospel

----

97. The phrase represents a more than usually candid admission that the commentator feels encouraged to develop a more adventurous and gratuitous line of interpretation. The following citation of Ps 14.7 and especially Is 45.13 (the reference by Second Isaiah being to Cyrus, in fact) likewise seems tendentious.

that the angels of those who are in the Church "always behold the face of the Father in heaven"; and those longing to see it say with the saints among human beings, "Show your face and we shall be saved." With the acceptance of this entreaty by the one asked, the Holy Spirit says in prophecy, "The God of gods will be seen in Sion."[98]

Having searched for his face and found it, thanks to the Father's revealing it, let us rejoice in being the objects of mercy by his appearing to us after a sufficient search for him. There is need to study how it is that those who are the objects of mercy come together *from cities to one city*, the Jerusalem on high, in their search for the Lord's favor. Observe also whether those who took the initiative in making great progress in the virtues and the knowledge of the truth are from many cities and then passed on to the mother city, as it were, the perfect knowledge of God, living in the heavenly Jerusalem. Flight, grief, pain, and distress will give way to eternal joy, he is saying, in the company of countless angels and the firstborn of the Church, as the apostle writes, "You have come to Mount Sion and the city of the living God, the heavenly Jerusalem, to countless angels in festal gathering and the assembly of the firstborn enrolled in heaven."[99]

The Lord almighty says this: In those days ten men of nations of all languages will lay hold of the hem of a Jewish man and say, We shall come with you because we have heard that God is with you (v.23). The prophecy describes the time when many peoples and many nations will come to win the favor of the Lord almighty and seek it out, which is none other than that of the coming of the savior to humankind, when Emmanuel was born of the virgin, God then being with us.[100] When in those days he is seen on earth and lives among human beings, there will be a call for people everywhere, as the prophetic text in hand suggests, *In those days ten men of nations of all languages will lay hold of the hem of a Jewish man.*

98. Col 1.15; Heb 1.3; Jn 14.9; 1 Pt 1.12; Mt 18.10; Pss 80.3; 84.7. The πρόσωπον in the text of Zechariah, of course, may be rendered "face" or "favor."

99. Heb 12.22–23.

100. Mt 1.23; Bar 3.37.

To grasp the intent of the prophetic text in hand, there is need to consider first who is the single Jewish man referred to in particular. In my view he is no other than the one the apostle suggests in writing to the Hebrews, "It is obvious that our Lord was descended from Judah" to command and reign over those who are Jews beneath the surface, in spirit but not in the letter, circumcised not in the flesh but in the heart; we take as a reference to him what is said in the hymns by every person of discernment, "Judah my king." The same interpretation is implied also in the blessing given by Jacob in these terms: "Judah, your brothers will praise you," and further on, "Government will not depart from Judah, nor rule from between his thighs, until he comes to whom it is assigned, himself the expectation of nations." The blessed expectation, note, is not of one nation but of them all, when there will be fulfilled the prophecy that is given as follows about the calling of all people: "The root of Jesse will come, and the one who rises to rule nations, and in him nations will hope."[101] It is the hem of the robe of this man, the true Jew, rising from the root of Jesse and emerging from Judah, that ten men of nations of every language will touch, saying to him as ruler and general—or, rather, high priest and sovereign, *We shall come with you because we have heard that God is with you.* It is obvious that this applies to the Jews in the spiritual sense, those adoring God in spirit and truth, not in Jerusalem or on the mountain of the Samaritans. After all, as it is not in any place that the angels adore the Son of God, of whom the Holy Spirit says, "All the angels of God will adore him," so, too, those human beings who adore God do not adore him in any place, doing so spiritually, "in spirit and in truth."[102]

After prior consideration of this, the sequel requires us to determine how it is that *ten men of nations of all languages* will lay hold of the hem, that is, the body, of the spiritual Jew. The

101. Heb 7.14; Rom 8.28–29; Ps 60.7; Gn 49.8, 10; Is 11.10; Rom 15.12.
102. Jn 4.20–23; Ps 97.7 LXX. While it is instinctive for Didymus to adopt a spiritual interpretation to the Jew mentioned in the text, Theodore equally instinctively and studiously avoids taking such a view or citing any such NT references. The less blinkered Theodoret, however, without mentioning his Antiochene predecessor, refuses to stay at the level of type or shadow.

number ten occurs here, too, mystically in accord with allegory, as also in other divinely inspired texts that we shall refer to in what follows.[103] We shall say first that it is impossible that from all the nations and all their languages and countless numbers of people only ten men—if we take the number literally—followed Jesus, he being the true Jew descended from Judah. Surely it is therefore possible that all the vast numbers of different nations and languages coming to the Gospel to live in accordance with it and have knowledge of the holy Trinity are ten in a mystical sense, in a manner similar to what is said in Matthew by Jesus in the form of a parable, "At that time the kingdom of heaven will be like ten virgins,"[104] where the ten virgins represent all the faithful by the following interpretation.

Every person, as a living being, has five senses: sight, hearing, smell, taste, touch. In addition to these he has as well their equivalent on a spiritual level: eyes enlightened, and hearing of which the prophet says in giving thanks to the generous giver, "He fitted me with an ear for hearing." Of a similar kind to sight and hearing beneath the surface is also a sense of smell, which one needs to perceive "the sweet odor of Christ" and the scent of his spiritual fragrances. There is also a taste and touch beyond the ordinary by which it is possible to taste that the Lord is the messiah, and to touch and feel the Word of life.[105] All those, then, who are disciples of the Gospel and have senses that are pure, both external and internal, are ten virgins ruled by Christ. By contrast, if any people from carelessness lose the senses of the interior man and act only by the mortal ones, they will become five foolish virgins, relying on material things only, and so their light will not be maintained, being quenched through lack of oil.

In the manner mentioned, the ten men of all languages and

103. Didymus has already developed this allegorical approach to numbers in comment on 1.7, and will do so again on 13.8–9. Cyril simply observes that "ten is a symbol of perfection," and moves on.
104. Mt 25.1 (Jesus immediately mentioning, however, that only five of the virgins were wise).
105. Is 50.4; 2 Cor 2.15; 1 Pt 2.3; 1 Jn 1.1. Doutreleau (SC 84.648) traces the notion of the spiritual senses back to Origen, who also cites 2 Corinthians and 1 John.

nations who are traveling with the true Jew are those who keep both kinds of senses unaffected and pure, in accord with what was said by the apostle, "Grace and peace will be with those who have an incorrupt love for Christ our Lord." Those attached to the letter probably think that the ten men are those who put into practice the Decalogue conveyed by the great revealer. Or even Christians, those with the name of Jesus; it begins with the tenth letter in both Greek and Hebrew, the letter *i* being the tenth in both alphabets, Greek and Hebrew. Now, while many examples can be produced, even from the divinely inspired Scripture, to show that the learned theory of numbers does not seem forced,[106] it suffices for the present to borrow expressions from Paul the apostle and John the disciple beloved by Jesus. The former writes to the Romans, remember, that God had said, "I have kept for myself seven thousand men who have not bent the knee to Baal"; and the latter, "There follow the Lamb"—that is, the savior—"a hundred and forty-four thousand virgins undefiled by women," these texts not being susceptible of factual interpretation. After all, how could it be that, if such a vast number of God-fearing men were in reserve, the mighty prophet Elijah was so ignorant of it as to say, "I am the only one left, and they are after my life"? And how could there literally be so many thousands of virgins, especially men, at that time in particular when the event of the savior's ascension had occurred not long before, the result being that John was still among the living?[107]

Yet each of these expressions is in accord with reality, provided that the numbers are not taken completely in a material way: the seven thousand men who had not bent the knee to Baal are those who conform in a mystical manner to the sabbath reserved to the people of God, and the number is closely related to the number 1000 and the number 7, of which it is composed. In many texts, in fact, you can see the number 1000 mentioned in a manner befitting God, as in the following state-

106. Eph 6.24. Not surprisingly, Didymus suspects that his development of number symbolism may not appeal to all readers, though Jerome repeated this statement of the significance of the letter iota; see SC 84.650.

107. Rom 11.4; Rv 14.3–4; 1 Kgs 19.10, 18.

COMMENTARY ON ZECHARIAH 8

ment about God: "He was mindful of his covenant forever, of a word he commanded for a thousand generations from Abraham"; there is no suggestion that there will be a thousand generations to the end of the world, as has previously been pointed out at greater length in other places.[108] It is on the basis of this mystical numbering that the seven thousand is composed, and in terms of it those people are numbered who sincerely revere God and genuflect before the one who alone is the cause of everything.

Likewise, the train of virgins who have not been defiled with women is counted in thousands to the number of a hundred and forty-four. The implausibility of a factual interpretation is still further indicated in the uniform inclusion from each tribe of Israel of twelve thousand men who are virgins; it was probably not possible for such a large number of men remaining unmarried for the sake of Christ to be arrived at even from the whole population when John was still living on earth. Since a literal reading of the text is out of the question, then, we claim it is on account of the virtue associated with the number that there are so many thousands of men of undefiled and blameless life; it is a squared number, with the combined factors of twelve expressed in thousands, twelve being a much-used figure, as is clear to one browsing through the Scriptures. An irrefutable explanation of this has been given in the works on the Apocalypse of John and Paul's epistle to the Romans;[109] the reader of these works will see the divine insights into numbers scattered throughout the Scriptures, both those before the coming of the savior, called the Old Testament, and those after Christ's coming here, known as the New.[110]

---

108. Heb 4.9; Ps 105.8, Didymus having written a commentary on the Psalms, partly extant. Theodoret in his commentary is content to say that the number in that psalm verse denotes simply "succession and eternity" (FOTC 102.173).

109. The works are not extant.

110. Like his successors, Didymus gives no suggestion that he recognizes the conclusion of a literary whole composed of chapters 1–8 of Zechariah, as scholars have since Joseph Mede in 1653.

COMMENTARY ON ZECHARIAH 9

N ORACLE OF *the word of the Lord in the land of Hadrach and Damascus,*[1] *because the Lord surveys human beings and all the tribes of Israel, and Hamath in its borders* (Zec 9.1–2). In their role as ministers of the divine word, the saints receive it from the God who gives it as though they are divinely possessed so as to proclaim knowledge of the future, according to the [apostle] speaking in Christ.[2] This is the manner in which Habakkuk gains access to a divine oracle and has a vision, the text about him saying, "The prophet Habakkuk saw an oracle of the Lord."[3] Here too, then, it is in relation to such divine ecstasy that *an oracle of the word of the Lord* is announced.

Now, what is the *oracle of the word,* and to what does it refer? It came, he is saying, in the land of Hadrach, Damascus, and Hamath within the borders of Damascus, with God *surveying human beings and the tribes of Israel.* Being seen by God is a blessed thing according to the verse, "The eyes of the Lord are

---

1. In these verses, where the LXX diverges from the Heb., Didymus has unaccountably omitted "its (or his) sacrifice" after "Damascus." He does not recognize signs of an editor's work in the Persian period of linking three "oracles" beginning at Zec 9.1, 12.1, and Mal 1.1 (the term λῆμμα occurring in those places), and distinguishing this collection from Zec 1–8.

2. Lk 1.2; 2 Cor 12.1–4.

3. Hab 1.1. Didymus, who already at the beginning of the work had referred to the prophet as θεοληπτούμενος (an Aristotelian term), is further encouraged to make the connection between the term in his text, λῆμμα, "oracle," and λαμβάνω, and to speak of divine possession, θεοφορία, as the model of biblical inspiration illustrated here. Theodore, in meeting the term first in Na 1.1, had likewise accepted that analogue of inspiration; Theodoret was less willing, Antioch being unhappy with a notion suggesting the behavior of a pagan μάντις, preferring to highlight the human contribution. On meeting this term for "oracle" at Hab 1.1, Cyril had simply emphasized that prophets convey God's thoughts, not their own; Jerome (CCL 76A.526) would warn that the notion of possession was a Montanist aberration. See my article, "Psalm 45: a *locus classicus* for Patristic Thinking on Biblical Inspiration."

on the righteous," and the prayer of the one prayerfully asking
to attain it, "Direct your gaze to me and have mercy on me."[4]
Give thought to whether the land of Hadrach can suggest the
mass of the people of old that found faith in the savior, who
said, "Learn of me that I am meek and humble of heart, and
you will find rest for your souls." Damascus, on the other hand,
refers to those called from idol worship, the people of Damascus being very much the adherents of superstition. Hence, as
opposed to those finding rest for their souls in the savior, who
is meek and humble of heart, in their cruelty and savagery they
are murderous to their neighbors; hence their name in Greek
means "blood drinkers" or "a bag's blood," since they are full of
slaughter. The result is that with humankind being surveyed by
the Lord almighty, some came to faith from the nations, and after them in second place others came from the tribes of Israel.[5]

All those mentioned, being savages before the divine call,
were within the borders of Damascus. While still a child, Jesus
took them as spoils, taking "the booty of Samaria and the might
of Damascus in opposition to the king of Assyria." Observe
whether this victory of the infant not yet of an age "to call on father or mother" suggests the call of the magi from the east, who
came from the east to Jerusalem to worship the king born
there, guided by a star appearing to them, as the Gospel according to Matthew recounts.[6]

*Tyre and Sidon, because they were very proud. Tyre built itself a
rampart, stored up silver like dust and amassed gold like dirt of the
streets. Hence the Lord will take possession of it, will strike its might
into the sea, and it will be consumed by fire* (vv.2–4). The calling of
all the nations is signified in the names cited, the inhabitants of
Tyre and Sidon being extreme in their worship of idols; the
verse in one of the Psalms, "Daughters of Tyre will bow down to

4. Pss 34.15; 25.16.
5. Mt 11.29. Whereas Cyril and Theodoret will try to identify the cities mentioned in the author's sequence of cities in Syria first and then in Phoenicia,
and a modern commentator like Petersen (*Zechariah 9–14 and Malachi*, 46) will
see in them a clue to the author's theme, "Yahweh's purview is international,"
Didymus moves quickly to an eschatological interpretation. He finds value
again in popular etymology rather than topographical precision.
6. Is 8.4; Mt 2.1–2.

him with gifts," suggests the call of those "with no hope" and the conversion of those "without God in the world." The same interpretation should be given also to the verse in another song, "Glorious things are said of you, O city of God. Behold, Philistines,[7] Tyre, and the Ethiopian people—they were there."[8] At that time, you see, at that time when they turned from the impiety and superstition to which they were in thrall, the Philistines, the Tyrians, and the people of Ethiopia were in the glorious city of God, and so are styled God's portion and inheritance, having renounced the error of the Philistines and the idolatry of the Tyrians and Ethiopians. We should make the effort to compare with the text in hand the words in the Gospel to this effect: "Woe to you, Chorazin! Woe to you, Bethsaida! For if the deeds of power had been done in Tyre and Sidon, they would have repented long ago in sackcloth and ashes."[9] In other words, when the powerful portents of Jesus were worked, the citizens of Chorazin and Bethsaida, Jews though they were, did not repent, whereas those of Tyre and Sidon would have repented if they had happened in their midst. But even if at that time they did not see the powerful marvels of Jesus, later on, seeing them, they found faith in the one working them and came to repentance.

At any rate, their future call is implied also in the prophecy in hand, *Tyre and Sidon, because they were very proud*, boasting of *having built a rampart* that seemed indestructible. They are facile and tendentious remarks, which led a proud city to consider itself impregnable and invincible. It is in reference to such protective measures adopted by the heretics, which will fall to those fighting under God's leadership, that the apostle writes, "The weapons of our warfare are not merely human: they have divine power to destroy strongholds, destroying arguments and every proud obstacle raised up against the knowl-

---

7. The term ἀλλόφυλοι, which in view of the mention of Tyre probably refers here to "Philistines," can also be used for foreigners in general. Cf. n. 18.

8. Ps 45.12; Eph 2.12; Ps 87.3–4.

9. Mt 11.21. Again Didymus develops the eschatological potential of the Phoenician cities of Tyre and Sidon rather than explicating hints in the text to their rise and fall in OT times.

edge of God."[10] The apostle's text, you see, does not refer to material strongholds being destroyed by arguments, that is, tendentious remarks.

It is also to Nineveh (a term meaning "charming"), very proud of the walls and ramparts it built for invulnerability, that the destroyer of such boasts says, "You will be intoxicated and will be ignored, and you will seek a refuge from the enemy. Your fortifications are fig trees with watchmen, and on being shaken they will fall into the mouth of the eater." How, in fact, will the [city] that is intoxicated on the wine of debauchery not be ignored by the provider for all things when the apostle speaking in Christ writes to forbid the drinking of it, "Do not get drunk with wine, for that is debauchery"? How, in fact, will such a person not be ignored when he sampled the vine of Sodom and the branches of Gomorrah, which Moses took to be wrath of serpents and lethal venom of asps in saying, "Our enemies are fools, their vine is from the vine of Sodom," and a little further on, "Their wine is the poison of serpents and the lethal venom of asps."[11] The city that has taken this drink to the point of intoxication is ignored by the caring God so as no longer to find a place of refuge when invisible foes advance to lay waste like powerful enemies.

Now, what will ensue from this tumult if not the weakening of its ramparts, which it thought secure and immovable, to such an extent that they are shaken like fig trees with watchmen, whose fruit falls into the mouth of the eater as a result of the tumult? The attacking enemy, you see, gaped and opened its mouth so as to be in readiness to eat those toppling off the barricades, whose fragility showed them to be vulnerable to the victorious sovereign, who gives power to walk upon the opposing forces, according to the savior's word to the disciples in the Gospel, "I have given you power to walk" beyond other things, even "on all the might of the foe, and no one will do you wrong," that is, harm you. Now, confirmation that falling into the mouth of an eater means being vanquished comes from

10. 2 Cor 10.4–5.
11. Na 3.11–12; Eph 5.18; Dt 32.31–33.

many passages, especially the one that says, "Israel was a sheep gone astray, lions hunted it; the king of Assyria was the first to consume it, and later the king of Babylon consumed its bones." Nevertheless, even if the hostile powers are strong, and comparable with the lions for ferocity, they will meet with punishment when Israel (referred to allegorically as a sheep) is freed after being devoured by them, leading the prophet to cry aloud triumphantly, "Israel is holy to the Lord, first-fruits of its produce; all who eat of it will sin; troubles will befall them, says the Lord." Scripture goes on in mockery of those intoxicated and ignored, "Draw water for yourself for the siege, strengthen your fortifications"[12] which you consider impregnable; even if at any time the arguments seem irresistible and the tendentious remarks irrefutable, once truth appears they will be refuted so as never again to be raised against the knowledge of God.

One should interpret in similar fashion the watchposts and walls thought to be impregnable by the adherents of idolatry and polytheistic error. It is rather in allegorical fashion that they are given the name of the Tyrians, which in the Greek language means "confinement" or "confined."[13] And since all evil people are that way of their own accord, no depraved person being vile by nature, Tyre also was God's inheritance along with all those of whom it is said by the Father to the savior, "Ask of me, and I shall give you nations for your inheritance."[14] Since Tyre was also one of all the nations inherited, it will in future be brought into subjection so as to repent on seeing the marvelous deeds of Jesus. In fact, if at first it was so bold as to *build a rampart, storing up silver like dust and amassing gold like dirt of the*

12. Lk 10.19; Jer 50.17; 2.3; Na 3.14. Once again Didymus has developed a spiritual interpretation of one city, Tyre, with a lengthy digression involving scriptural statement about another, Nineveh. He concedes it is time to return to Tyre, if not to Zechariah's thought.

13. Though Jerome, who should know better (his familiarity with Heb. deriving from time spent in Chalcis a decade before), will adopt this version (*angustia*), Didymus's popular etymology rests on a confusion of Heb. final consonants.

14. Ps 2.8. The Antiochenes would concur with Didymus's insistence on the goodness of human nature and the correlative imputability of human depravity (a favorite theme of his, which Doutreleau further documents; see SC 84.664).

streets, its might was cast down into the storms of human life, referred to allegorically as *sea*, when the silver stored up was of no benefit, being compared with *dust* of the earth for its amount and worthlessness, nor did the gold amassed avail for its security, being compared to *dirt of the streets*. In other words, even if the adherents of impiety [develop] countless arguments and ideas, their efforts will be consigned to ruin. After all, how would the wealth of those raging against the truth not be compared with dust when they "bear the image of the man of dust,"[15] the gold they amass also being as valueless as the dirt of the streets? Those following the impious teachings, in fact, are treading on dirt, thus being subject to countless falls.

Nevertheless, even if Tyre resists for long in its path of opposition, it will experience punishment by way of fire, after which the savior said also of it, "I have come to cast fire on the earth: would that it were already alight," so that every pernicious growth will be consumed, whether thorn, prickle, or weed. It will actually be good for Tyre to suffer this kind of consumption by fire, according to the expression of the savior, "Everyone will be salted with fire."[16] It will also be beneficial for all its might to be cast into the sea, in which are found both silver that is stored like dust and gold that is amassed and that resembles dirt of the streets. When its overweening might is thrust down into the sea and it is consumed by fire, the underlying substance[17] that remains will become an inheritance of the Lord, being his own creation. All the nations, in fact, will become his inheritance when they abandon all superstition and polytheistic error.

Everything said about Tyre should be applied also to Sidon: its evil and impiety are identical, as also its repentance and conversion to God. Sidon has much in common with Tyre for its worship of idols.

Ashkelon will see it and be afraid; Gaza, too, and will feel intense anguish; Ekron, too, because its hope was put to shame. A king will perish from Gaza, and Ashkelon will not be inhabited. Foreigners will

---

15. 1 Cor 15.49.

16. Lk 2.49; Mt 7.16; 13.5, 40; Mk 9.49.

17. This Aristotelian expression is one of many philosophical terms found in Didymus.

dwell in Ashdod; I shall destroy the arrogance of Philistines and remove their blood from their mouth and their abominations from between their teeth. And they, too, will be left for our God, and will be like a commander in Judah, and Ekron like the Jebusite: I shall provide my house with an elevation to prevent going and coming; no one will invade them any longer to drive them off, because now I have seen with my eyes (vv.5–8). On seeing the disasters befalling the Tyrians, Ashkelon took fright, dreading that it might meet the same fate; Gaza also felt great distress, whereas Ekron for its part felt shame at the frustration of its hope. What was the cause of the great distress felt by Gaza if not the loss of its king, and of Ashkelon's being afraid if not its inhabitants' meeting with disaster? One should interpret in similar fashion also the fate of Ekron and Ashdod and the Philistines in general.[18]

Such being the literal sense, there is need to divine the spiritual interpretation. Ashkelon, being something esteemed for its precious character and sound foundation, and adopting a watchful attitude, *will see*, no longer blinded by extremes of pleasure and the other passions, and thus adopt such reverence as to be numbered among the possessors of this virtue, to whom the proverbial oracle about wisdom and her father refers, "He will protect the way of those who revere him." The prophet in question urges all people to this praiseworthy condition—or, rather, the word in him urges them in the expression, "Let all flesh be reverent before the Lord" almighty.[19] Since the text in hand presented Tyre as experiencing not only disasters but also a change for the better, Ashkelon perceived this and exhibited perfect reverence emerging from this text: "The fear of the Lord surpasses everything," and from this: "Nothing is lacking to those who fear the Lord," filled as they are with every benefit, "since those who seek the Lord want for no good." In the wake of Ashkelon, which was frightened by a perceptive

18. The ambivalence of ἀλλόφυλοι allows Doutreleau (SC 84.658–59) to deny Didymus the credit of recognizing the cities in these verses as Philistine rather than simply "foreign," even if he does not pause to explore any historical basis to the fate Zechariah accords them (which Petersen, *Zechariah 9–14 and Malachi*, 51, suggests may be portrayed as beneficent, not punitive).

19. Prv 2.8; Zec 2.13.

gaze on the commendable transformation of Tyre, Gaza also will suffer extreme pangs in the manner of the one who is grief-stricken with repentance and says, "Each night I shall drench my bed, with my tears I shall bedew my couch." When will Gaza undergo this experience of grief if not when by knowing itself it knows its potential, the force innate within it, given it naturally by the divine word?[20]

With such provisions made for Gaza in her extreme grief, shame will be the lot of Ekron—"sterility," in other words, this being the meaning of the name—when her hopes are frustrated. Fecundity in a spiritual sense has a double meaning: one is the case with those who can say to God, "From fear of you we have conceived in the womb, felt birth pangs, and given birth," and this insemination deserves praise where the Word is spouse. That which involves adulterers is culpable; of such an offspring and its mother, at any rate, it is said by the Lord of all, "I shall have no pity on her children because they are the children of prostitution; their mother was a prostitute, the one who bore them brought shame on herself."[21] Since the birth of children differs in this twofold fashion, it is a blessed thing to suffer with sterility when ruin comes from birth resulting from unseen partners that are evil; being sterile is all to the good. Fecundity has its source in God when it results in a brood of saving offspring; the bride who is the object of such benefits so as to become mother of many children dwells in the house of her husband, of whom it is said in the Psalms, "He gives the barren woman a home, the mother rejoicing in her children," and in another passage there is mention of many children and a large family after sterility, "A barren woman had seven children." It is of her—or, rather, to her—that the prophet Isaiah cries aloud, "Give vent and cry aloud, you who felt no birth pangs, because

20. Sir 25.11; Pss 34.9–10; 6.6. The Heb. text involves some wordplay between homophones, Ashkelon and the word for "fire," Gaza and "force"—hence Didymus's final comment. For Jerome the homophones actually represent the meaning of the city names. Both commentators see Heb. "sterile" in Ekron, and, *pace* Zechariah, Didymus develops at length the spiritual potential of that notion.

21. Is 26.17–18; Hos 2.4–5.

the abandoned woman has more children than the woman with a husband."[22]

Now, the texts cited make particular reference to the two callings, to those from the circumcision and those from the nations: the former had the Law as husband and had children by it, while the latter was barren and bereft of children through being godless and absolutely "without hope in the world," according to Paul's letter about the idolaters. This was the case when the true bridegroom made his appearance: by him the sterile woman became mother of divine offspring to that number of seven we cited on account of the incorruptibility and purity associated with it, qualities identified with the mystical number seven. Despite everything, the barren woman had seven children, and was established in her home by her husband as mother of happy children.[23] On the other hand, "the mother with many children became weak," since her offspring were "many" not so much in number as in rapid growth, an implication made also in the Gospel text where those traveling by the broad way which leads to ruin are said to be many. In this interpretation, too, the sons of Israel ruled by the tyrant of the spiritual Egypt were many and "extremely prolific."[24]

To distinguish himself and those entrusted with the same ministry as his from the many referred to of this kind, the apostle writes, "We are not peddlers of the Lord's word like so many." Consistent with this interpretation is the psalmist's statement in the hymn, "Many will say to my soul," and again, "Many rise up against me." While the synagogue of the circumcision grew weak as a result of its prolific issue of children, despite having the Law as its husband, that which was called from the nations, despite formerly being barren, became a mother of children to the number of seven (in the sense indicated),

22. Ps 113.9; 1 Sm 2.5; Is 54.1.
23. Gal 4.21–31; Eph 2.12; Ps 113.9. The significance of the number seven is explained in line with Philo's number symbolism rather than the Semitic notion of completeness—neither of which, however, is Zechariah's focus.
24. 1 Sm 2.5; Mt 7.13; Ex 1.7. The distinction Didymus is making may be related to the jibe Theodoret is aware of in the first of his *Questions* on Exodus, where he may be referring to Clement's rhyming of Ἰουδαῖοι and χυδαῖοι, the latter term used in Exodus and by Didymus.

"born anew, not of perishable but of imperishable seed, through the living and enduring word of God." The result is that now the barren woman's children are more numerous than those of the woman living life by the Law, allegorically called her husband.[25]

Such are the differences in children and their birth emerging from the divine instruction. It is all to the good for the soul at risk of giving birth to children of perdition to be sterile, whereas it is destructive and harmful for the one ready to conceive by the seeds of the divine word to be sterile. One should therefore pray to be delivered from the latter sterility so as to give birth to sound and lovely children. This is the interpretation given in commentary on Ekron, which means "sterility," [a city] so sterile as to cast off its hopes and expectation of large numbers of useless children.

While Ekron was in this situation, with its expectation frustrated, *the king of Gaza perished;* who he was we were told in what went before. The one governing it, whether anger or reason, was its king: if he was the ruler before the reform in life and conduct, its ruin was welcome; but if he came after the reform and the turn for the better, . . .[26]

. . . the flesh of the dragon, but also those "who bite and consume one another," with *abominations in their teeth and blood in their own mouth.* If they are removed, *there is left for the Lord* those rid of their murderous insolence; once every evil is removed that befalls humankind, there is left what is in accord with the image and likeness of God by which they were created. "Though enjoying a state of honor," you see, "man did not understand," reducing himself to the status of cattle, "so as to be likened to senseless cattle"; but once the condition of dumb animals and wild beasts was removed, there is left for our God the honor, since the rationality emerges of the man who becomes upright with the removal of many convoluted arguments. Though "God made human beings upright," remember, they

25. 2 Cor 2.17; Ps 3.1–2; 1 Pt 1.23; Is 54.1; Gal 4.27.
26. At this point two pages of the manuscript are missing, presumably commenting on vv.5–6: "Ashkelon will not be inhabited. Foreigners will dwell in Ashdod. I shall destroy the arrogance of the Philistines."

went in search of idle arguments, which were numerous on account of their prolific development.[27] In any event, in the prophetic text in hand, with the removal of the obstacles affecting the people of Ashkelon, the citizens of Gaza, and the inhabitants of Ekron, those made in God's image and likeness will be left, sincerely confessing our God, so as to be styled *commanders of Judah* (Judah meaning "the one who confesses"). Everyone who by free will makes a confession is a commander. As well, *Ekron will be like the Jebusite,* which in translation means, "trampled underfoot."

After this happens, God builds for the recipients of his favors an edifice with a lofty watchtower so that by remaining within it they may be secure, lest by going hither and yon they may become disorderly and return to the sins they abandoned instead of "forgetting them and straining forward to what lies ahead so as to attain the prize of the heavenly call." When they have gained these achievements—or, rather, God's gifts—there are no longer enemies to drive them out, since all fierce opposition is routed. In olden times the tyrant of the spiritual Egypt harassed God's people to the point of saying boldly and proudly, "I shall pursue and overtake, I shall divide spoils, I shall satisfy my soul, I shall destroy with my sword, my hand shall dominate." But while still making these proud boasts, he was drowned, all his arrogant words thwarted, so that he could not continue his pursuit. The king of the Assyrians also suffered the same fate: after making countless bold threats, he was suddenly annihilated and his great army wiped out in one fell swoop by a single angel, so that Scripture's report of it says that a single angel destroyed "a hundred and eighty-five thousand," with the result that there was no one capable of driving out the people of God.[28]

In short, the benefactor and source of everyone's blessed salvation is saying, Hence *no one will any longer drive them off, because now I have seen with my eyes,* that is, with the watchful powers, of whom the apostle writes in these terms: "All things are

---

27. Gal 5.15; Gn 1.26; Ps 49.12; Eccl 7.29.
28. Phil 3.13–14; Ex 15.9; 2 Kgs 19.35.

naked and laid bare to God's eyes" and word. It must be said, secondly, that God's eyes that see are the guardian angels that survey human affairs, of whom the psalmist says, "His eyes are fixed on the nations."[29] It is not unlikely, on the other hand, that God's eyes are also contemplative men, whose divine insight has been described; since the whole Church of the saved is the body of Christ, perceptive people are its eyes, as the text from the apostle indicates. In accord with all the interpretations of the text, then, since the eyes see those who are watching, no one will come to drive the people out. Another interpretation of the prophecy, however, might be as follows: since the eyes have seen the savior coming for the benefit and salvation of all, everyone driving them out has been overcome, "power being given to walk on snakes and scorpions and all the power of Satan";[30] following the passage in hand the savior's victorious coming is presented in these terms: *Rejoice exceedingly, daughter Sion; proclaim, daughter Jerusalem,* and so on, which we must cite textually as follows.

Rejoice exceedingly, daughter Sion; proclaim, daughter Jerusalem: lo, your king comes to you righteous and saving; he is gentle, riding on a beast of burden and young foal. He will destroy chariots from Ephraim and a horse from Jerusalem; a war bow will be destroyed, and a multitude, and peace from nations. He will rule waters as far as the sea and the sources of the earth's rivers (vv.9–10). The evangelists claim that the prophecy in hand was fulfilled with Jesus riding on an ass and a foal that had been let loose and brought into the neighboring town. With God's grace may this be made clear by those explaining the Gospels, of which we, too, have spoken to the best of our ability in the work on the Gospel according to Matthew.[31] Now is the time, then, to interpret as well the words of the prophet in addition to that.

29. Heb 4.13; Ps 66.7.
30. 1 Cor 12.27; Lk 10.19.
31. The commentary on Matthew or other Gospels is not extant. The evangelists unanimously speak of Jesus riding a foal on the occasion of his entering Jerusalem, Mt 21.5 and Jn 12.15 citing this verse from Zechariah. While the Johannine passage rationalizes into one Jesus' apparently double mount mentioned here, Didymus will proceed below to exploit the eschatological potential of the two. And whereas Theodoret will accept the Christological interpreta-

He bids the daughter of Sion to rejoice promptly and exceedingly, and the daughter of Jerusalem to announce also the
coming of the savior king, righteous and saving, gentle and riding on a beast of burden and young foal, whose intention is for
chariots from Ephraim and a horse from Jerusalem to be destroyed along with a war bow, a multitude of nations, and
peace. With this achieved, the one who is to come will rule waters as far as the sea and the sources of the rivers of the earth.
Our next step is to explain the meaning of each of these items.

The *daughter of Sion* is the soul with an eye for the finer
things, attentive to what is invisible because eternal. Sion, in
fact, means "observatory and commandment put into practice":
how does the soul with an eye for truth not put the divine commandment into practice, implementing it so as to say with confidence, "The commandment of the Lord is clear, giving light
to the eyes," and again, "Your commandment is all-embracing,"
"and your servant loved it"? Just as such a soul is *daughter of Sion*
in the way defined, so it is also *daughter of Jerusalem*, being a soul
that sees "peace that surpasses all understanding."[32] Clearly the
verse gives a direction to both, to one to rejoice exceedingly in
the coming of the one who is truly king, to the other in her elevated position to make the announcement of the sovereign who
is coming. Jerusalem, you see, has precedence over Sion, and
hence does her daughter over the other's daughter, rejoicing
alone being bidden in the one case, but announcing as well in
the other. In other words, the one who lives the active life of
righteousness can simply rejoice, whereas it is the one with the
gift of contemplation who announces as well through possession of the supernatural gift of the Holy Spirit, which is the
word of wisdom and knowledge.[33]

The prophetic text gives an order to rejoice exceedingly and

tion, even the rabbis by his time recognizing a messianic reference in v.9,
Theodore ("stupidly," in Theodoret's view) prefers to see Zerubbabel as its immediate fulfillment.

32. Pss 19.8; 119.97, 140; Phil 4.7. In commentary on 1.14 Didymus had given his (disputed) etymologies of Sion and Jerusalem, which he takes as distinct
entities, as are their daughters as well, whereas the city alone is the referent in
all cases. He proceeds at once to a spiritual interpretation of these verses.

33. 1 Cor 12.8.

make an announcement at the coming of a king, who is both *saving and righteous*, and who is no one else but Jesus. After all, who is to such an extent saving and savior of the world as "Emmanuel, God with us," born of a virgin who had no experience of man, fulfilling the prophecy that ran as follows: "Lo, a virgin will conceive, and bear a son"? An angel gave the name Jesus to this child born of a virgin without a man's involvement, supplying also the reason for the name of this kind: this is the reason for his being called Jesus, he said, "because he will save his people from their sins." At any rate, when Mary had given birth at Bethlehem, a mighty angel appeared, saying, "Today there is born to you a savior, who is Christ the Lord, in the city of David."[34] It is regarding the birth of Christ that the order was given to those foretelling his coming down here, according to the verse in Isaiah, "Tell daughter Sion, Lo, a savior has come to you," and he is no other than Jesus, who said of himself, "The Son of Man has come to seek and to save what was lost," and again, "There is no one righteous and saving but me." After all, how could he not save, he who was raised up by the Father as a horn of salvation in the house of David, as was said by Zechariah, father of John the Baptist, when filled with the Holy Spirit, "Blessed be the Lord, the God of Israel, because he has looked favorably [on his people] and redeemed [them]; he has raised up a horn of salvation for us in the house of David"?[35]

The king who comes, as well as being righteous and saving, is also gentle, riding upon a beast of burden and a foal; he says of himself in the Gospel, remember, "Take my yoke upon you and learn of me that I am meek and humble of heart, and you will find rest for your souls; for my yoke is easy and my burden light." Each of those bearing the easy yoke is a beast of burden on whom the gentle king rides; and since he is savior not only of those saddled with his easy yoke but also of those recently called, he is riding a young foal as well, still untamed and chafing at the bit, so as to tame it as well, excellent horse-breaker as

34. Mt 1.23; Lk 1.34; Is 7.14; Mt 1.21; Lk 2.11. As noted before, Didymus gives particular attention to the virgin Mary, going out of his way here to highlight her virginity (not a concern of Zechariah, needless to say).

35. Is 62.11; Lk 19.10; Is 45.21; Lk 1.68–69.

he is.[36] In addition to this interpretation, both peoples that are called are implied by the text: one from the circumcision, saddled according to the letter and shadow with the yoke of the Law, referred to as a heavy yoke; and one lately called from every form of idolatry and extreme superstition. Because those saddled according to the letter with the Law bore a heavy burden, the apostles said of it in the book of their Acts, "Neither we nor our fathers were able to bear" the heavy yoke of the Law. Paul, speaking in Christ, writes in similar terms to the Galatians, who wished to undergo physical circumcision despite receiving the Gospel, "Stand firm, then, and do not submit yourself to the yoke of slavery again."[37] After all, it was not logical for the disciples of the Gospel to submit themselves any further to the burden and heavy yoke after having come to faith in the one who said, "My yoke is easy."

Likewise, the gentle king was riding also on a young foal that was mentioned, "so that he might create in himself one new humanity"; in this way one people and one Church will develop from both callings. To similar effect there is mention in the Gospels of the foal being let loose from the town opposite for it to come to Jesus so that the savior might tame it and ride on it. It says, note, that no one had yet sat on it, the suggestion in the text being that those from the nations had not yet undergone transformation by any word of teaching, godless as they were in the world and without any real hope. Even if they were an unbridled foal before coming to faith, yet once Christ, who dawned from Judah, shone on them, they gained an expectation, according to what was said of him, "He will be the expectation of nations," and again, "Nations will hope in him."[38]

Whereas the two peoples who were called gained great benefit from being ridden by the righteous, saving, and gentle king, *chariots from Ephraim and a horse from Jerusalem* are destroyed,

---

36. Mt 11.29–30. While Jn 12.15 rationalized the apparent mention in the LXX of two animals, Didymus exploits it to develop an eschatological significance.

37. Acts 15.10; Gal 5.1.

38. Eph 2.15; Mt 21.2; Mk 11.2; Lk 19.30; Eph 2.12; Heb 7.14; Gn 49.10; Is 11.10; Rom 15.12.

and with them the bow of the cruel and fierce enemy, which dispatches "the burning shafts of the evil one," inflicting licentious love, the result being that those driven to extremes and inflamed with shameful passions are set on fire. The chariots from Ephraim are the assemblies of the heretics and their irrational teachings; it has often been shown that heresies often emerge under the banner of Ephraim on account of Jeroboam's being the first to lead a schism, and he was from the tribe of Ephraim. In fact, just as the savior bears the name of Judah on account of his descent from the tribe of that name, and he is leader of the Church, so the word that initiates the false teachings is Ephraim, promising much fruitfulness on account of its success with its dupes. In reference to the destruction of the chariots, the army of the truth says in the Psalms about their cavalry and charioteers, "Some rely on chariots, some on horses, whereas we shall boast in the name of the Lord our God. They were entangled and fell, while we got up and stood straight."[39] . . .

. . . they were in accord with sin and impiety. To everyone of this attitude the sovereign Law says, "You shall not join a large number in evildoing, nor conspire with a mob to become an unjust witness." In reference to this baneful attitude disposed to evil, wickedness personified in Proverbs, whoever she be, called out shamelessly and boldly to each of her dupes, "Mine is a sacrifice of peace, today I pay my vows."[40]

With all that has been commented on done away with by the mighty king, this also will take place: *He will rule waters as far as the sea*, suggesting they are salty and not potable, *and the sources of the rivers of the earth*, waters conducted as far as the sea. Coming from that source, on account of its saltiness, impious teachings spoil the sweetness of the earth's potable rivers at their sources. They are like the waters by which Pharaoh settled and of which he boasted in the words, "Mine are the rivers, I made them." Drinking from them was forbidden by God in Jeremiah

39. Eph 6.16; Ps 20.7–8. The popular etymology of Ephraim as suggestive of fruitfulness, based on Gn 41.52, is repeated also by Jerome. At this point in Didymus's text two pages of the manuscript are missing.
40. Ex 23.1–2; Prv 7.14.

the prophet: "What use now is it to you to be in the land of
Egypt and drink the water of Gihon? What value is it to be in
the land of Assyria and drink the water of the rivers?"[41] By the
issues of the rivers of the land reference is made, on account of
their seeming to be sweet to the taste, to the plausible and subtle arguments about them.

*And as for you, by the blood of the covenant you dispatched your
captives from a waterless pit. You will take your place in a fort as prisoners of the assembly, and for one day of your sojourn I shall repay you
double* (vv.11–12). After giving orders to Sion and Jerusalem, respectively, to rejoice exceedingly and to announce the coming
king, saving and strong and gentle, the word in the prophet—
or, rather, God—directs his attention to the one coming, and
says, *And as for you, by the blood of the covenant you dispatched your
captives from a waterless pit.* After all, where should the captives
have been if not in a waterless pit restrained by their persecutors? You can find large numbers of holy men cast into waterless pits by people scheming and plotting to take their lives.
Joseph, for instance, was envied for his goodness, and those unjustly envying him threw him into a waterless pit; likewise, the
most wise Daniel, too, God's friend, the Babylonians cast into a
waterless pit, the lions' living in it suggesting it was waterless, as
they could not stay alive if it was full of water; Jeremiah, too, for
example, the great prophet, his adversaries threw into a pit full
of mire.[42] And none of these objects of scheming remained
helpless, since their God delivered them unharmed from the
waterless pit. Since these events occurred by way of symbol,
note whether the waterless pit suggested by the symbols is the
Hades of impious and sinful people, where there is no life-
giving water, since in that place there is no welcome dampness.
For example, when the rich man clad in purple and linen . . .[43]

41. Ezek 28.9; Jer 2.18. While the final phrase of v.10 in the LXX puzzles
commentators, Didymus passes over Zechariah's reference to arrive at a spiritual meaning.
42. Gn 37.24; Dn 6.16; Jer 38.6: all corroborative examples—but how do
they relate to the situation Zechariah is describing?
43. Lk 16.19. There follow two pages of Didymus's manuscript in fragmentary condition (SC 84.698, 700–701). At least the fragments of the pages
(which Doutreleau, unlike others, does not try to reconstitute) allow us to see

. . . "If the blood of goats and bulls, with the sprinkling of the ashes of a heifer, sanctifies those who have been defiled so that their flesh is purified, how much more will the blood of Christ purify our conscience from dead works to worship God living" and true.[44]

Now, what their fate will be and what kind of security will be given to the captives released from the waterless pit the sequel reveals, as the text says, They *will take their place in a fort*—evidently a reputable one—those *prisoners of the assembly*, the glorious Church, which no longer has any "spot or wrinkle."[45] The watchtowers ensure salvation; there the prisoners of the assembly take their place at rest after removal from the waterless pit. In what went before, the text made clear what were the detestable fortresses that Tyre and Nineveh built. On the other hand, let us see what are the reputable ones now mentioned in which the prisoners of the divine assembly are at rest under protection. In the divine book of Proverbs reverence is described as a fortress for those who practice holiness and righteousness: "The fear of the Lord is a fortress for the holy one." The one protected in the fear of God goes beyond this protection, praying to be protected by God himself, and saying to him in prayer, "Become for me a protector God, a secure place to save me," and again in the thirty-second psalm, "You are a refuge for me from the onset of tribulation; my joy, rescue me from my pursuers." To similar effect also in the thirty-first psalm the one begging to attain an impregnable fort said, "Become a protector God for me, a place of refuge for my salvation." Likewise the one who has fought the good fight, finished the good course, and kept the faith is himself kept by it; and to show that it is securely fortified and impregnable, he cries out in thanksgiving with like-minded people, "Lo, a fortified city and our salvation; he will erect wall and rampart." What, in fact, is the way to interpret the impregnable wall and fortified city? It

---

Didymus tracing the phrase "blood of the covenant" to Ex 24.7–8 and NT eucharistic contexts that cite it, like Mt 26.28, Lk 22.20, 1 Cor 11.25. Jerome again followed his lead in this; see CCL 76A.832.

44. Heb 9.13–14.
45. Eph 5.27.

is the Church, with a wall composed of the spiritual law and mystical contemplation, on the one hand, and on the other a fortification beyond the secure wall, namely, Scripture taken literally and factually.[46]

In yet another sense the wall of the beautiful city is faith in the Trinity and the only-begotten Son of God, God's Word, God's truth and wisdom, while the fortification in terms of this interpretation is the doctrine of the Incarnation and birth of the child of Mary, the virgin who had no experience of marriage. It is possible to say that the wall guarding the Church is its religious thinking in respect of the doctrines of the truth, while the fortification is the moral teaching and observance of the commandments. It could also be said in a different manner that the strong city is principally fortified by the intelligent grasp of spiritual and incorporeal things, which has as a fortification the knowledge of the material things of the visible world and its parts as well as of the divine providence governing it.

The person who, as a captive of Christ, resides in this city and the reputable fortifications associated with it lives without fear in the expectation of receiving a double portion of consolation and comfort for the tribulations suffered. The text proceeds, in fact, to say to the great number who have received favors, *For one day of your sojourn I shall repay you double,* since the consolation for past tribulations is doubled. As a concrete example of this interpretation, take the story of the valorous Job: in the same way as restoration was made to him twofold for all he had lost, so those left completely deprived for piety's sake "have a promise of life here below and to come," not a life that is passing, leaving in a miserable condition those who hope in it alone, but one that is possible for believers here below, according to the saying of the savior, "Whoever believes in me has

46. Prv 10.29; Pss 71.3; 32.7; 30.2; 2 Tm 4.7; Is 26.1. Once more one gets the impression that the Zechariah text is only an occasion for Didymus's own thoughts on Christian teachings; and so he feels free to move on to a long series of "possible" interpretations of τεῖχος and περίτειχος, terms not occurring in Zechariah here, the development bringing out the priority the commentator gives to kinds of scriptural interpretation, Christian dogmas, levels of reality (in Stoic terms). Had he been able, he might have noted the alliterative play in Heb. on "Sion" and "fortress," an item that would not be the result of eisegesis.

eternal life," and again, "This is eternal life, knowing you, the true God, and Jesus Christ, whom you have sent." May the one who has this life have it many times over when the end comes and truth is seen face to face.[47]

The following more elementary interpretation may also be given. When death passed to all human beings through the transgression of the first human being, the body was separated from the soul, which as expected was distressed by the loss of its long-time companion and resultant exile.[48] While this lasted a single day, in compensation God made double repayment, raising up its body and returning it to the soul, the result being that it not simply recovered it but also in place of a corruptible, dishonorable, weak, and physical body, it received one that is incorruptible, strong, and honorable—namely, a spiritual body.[49] Anyone attentive to the reading of the divinely inspired sayings will also gain further understandings of the double recompense by God for being deported for a single day. At a literal level this one may also be stated: the people who were deported into enemy hands by the norm of captivity were not simply restored, but they also dominated their oppressors. By this happening, those subjected to brief hardship enjoyed double satisfaction.

Hence I have stretched you, Judah, like my bow; I have filled Ephraim. I shall stir up your children, Sion, against the children of the Greeks, and stroke you like a warrior's sword. The Lord will appear over them (vv.13–14). The Father stretched the savior, who sprang from the tribe of Judah, like his bow, with which he dispatches arrows that inflict wounds that are salutary.[50] Note the difference: the destructive bow of Ephraim is called an enemy

47. Eph 3.1; Jb 42.10; 1 Tm 4.8; 1 Cor 15.19; Jn 6.47; 17.3. Didymus adds a (rare and) brief parenesis.

48. Rom 5.12. Didymus is predictably uncertain of the meaning of double recompense in the text, where Zechariah is promising a doubling of the restored city's population. So again he offers the reader more than one possible interpretation, in the course of which he makes a clear statement of the reality of the Fall and its consequences. He does not see it as a cue for moralizing, as a preacher might.

49. 1 Cor 15.42–44.

50. This time Didymus makes no attempt to summarize the historical reference in the verses, launching at once into a Christological interpretation and generating an unusual image of the Son as the Father's stretched bow.

because of the enemy's use of it. There is therefore mention in the seventy-eighth psalm of the hostile powers of Satan and all the heretics: "Sons of Ephraim aiming and dispatching arrows were turned back on the day of battle," weakened and routed, obviously because their defenses were crushed. It is said, in fact, "May their sword enter their own heart, and their bows be broken." The broken bows are the warriors' hearts, from which issue evil remarks like sharpened arrows, of which the divine word says, "Their tongue is a deadly arrow, deceitful the words of their mouth." In other words, the words of those promising the "falsely named knowledge" are full of lethal venom, dealing death to those who receive them.[51]

The shafts of the mighty savior, on the other hand, are not like that; of them it is said in the forty-fifth psalm to the blessed man who is a skillful archer, "Your arrows are sharp, O mighty one," which instill divine love in those struck by them, such that the divine bride who is happily in love says, "I am wounded with love." Note the unusual feature, where the savior in person is bow, bowman, and arrow: in the prophetic text in hand it is said to him by God, *I have stretched you, Judah, like my bow*, and in the psalm those who sing his praises say, "Your arrows are sharp, O mighty one," whereas he says of himself in Isaiah, "He used me like a chosen arrow, hiding me in his quiver." After all, how could the one who causes those whom he wounds to be chosen not be a chosen arrow, hidden in the quiver, namely, the flesh he received from Mary?[52]

Once this divine bow was stretched, and arrows were aimed from it and dispatched to inflict divine love, Ephraim *was filled*, routed and shown to be weak, according to the verse just now cited from the psalm, "Sons of Ephraim aiming and dispatching arrows were turned back on the day of battle," though God in his great generosity *stirred up the children of Sion against the*

51. Pss 78.9; 37.15; Jer 9.7; 1 Tm 6.20. If the Christological conceit proves unsustainable, Didymus feels no qualms about taking another tack; the text itself is not an inhibiting factor for him.

52. Song 2.5; Ps 45.5; Is 49.2. Christ, previously the bow, is now an arrow in the quiver, an analogy one is prepared to find rather in later Antiochenes not totally committed to the complete union of natures in the person of Jesus.

children of the Greeks. The offspring of the Greeks in this text means those who profess the "falsely named knowledge" and all those guilty of impiety that leads them to release their impious words like lethal arrows against those who have not taken up "the shield of faith."[53] The children of Sion, stirred up by the God who reigns over them, are those who profess the truth. Now, Sion, the mother of the children stirred up by God, is none other than the one commented on just above, whose daughter was bidden to rejoice exceedingly and promptly at the appearance of the strong king who saves.

God strokes Judah *like a warrior's sword,* bringing salvation in two senses: in one case, a bow is stretched to deliver a blessed wound of love; in another, being an excellent general he strokes his sword as a warrior to cut down his opponents. In the forty-fifth psalm it is also written of him, "Gird your sword on your thigh, O mighty one, in your charm and your beauty, for the sake of truth, gentleness, and righteousness; your right hand will guide you in marvelous fashion." After all, how will his right hand not guide in marvelous fashion the mighty one with girded thigh who strikes the stricken in a remarkable manner? It is possible, then, to hear him saying to those overtaken by his divine might, "You, Ethiopians, are wounded by my sword"; wounded by the one saying this, and rejecting the life of Ethiopians, they will be invested with immortality so as to say in thanksgiving, "The splendor of the Lord our God will be upon us." When the source of every good washed us clean, we emerged shining and white, according to the one speaking with confidence, "You will wash me, and I shall be whiter than snow." Now, how did those who were wounded to good effect so as to die to impiety become Ethiopians, if not by being born of the devil and choosing to do his will? In fact, it is said of him that he is black as a result of the darkness of his ignorance and

53. Ps 78.9; 1 Tm 6.20; Eph 6.16. Having declined to give even the briefest paraphrase of the historical reference in these verses, Didymus again avoids the historical basis of the mention of Greeks at this point (which admittedly some modern commentators would like to excise as an anachronism), though he might have thought of Jl 3.6. As to the meaning of Sion, he refers the reader to his previous comments on 9.9, where he understood Sion to have a daughter.

malice, as indicated in the book of repentance called *Shepherd* and in the *Epistle of Barnabas*.[54]

May we for our part also be stricken to salutary effect by the word that is living and active, of whom Scripture says, "The word of God is living and active, and sharper than any two-edged sword," so that, put to death in the flesh, we may be brought to life in the spirit. May we also be wounded by the chosen arrow dispatched by the stretched bow, this being the way for us to be stirred up as children of Sion against the offspring of the Greeks. Numerous as they are, the children and sons of the Greeks showed zeal against the doctrines of the true religion so as even to leave behind voluminous writings. Yet they were destroyed when God stirred up churchmen against them who rebutted their polemical discourse so as to say with confidence, "The weapons of our warfare are not merely human, but have divine power to destroy arguments and every proud obstacle raised up against the knowledge of God." When the children of Sion are stirred up against those of the Greeks, the Lord responsible for it *will be against them,* joining in unity those raised up with those against whom they are raised up, his purpose being to reign over them once brought together in one mind and one will, creating one new humanity out of Greek and Jew.[55]

And his arrow will go like lightning; the Lord almighty will sound a trumpet blast and issue forth brandishing his threat. The Lord almighty will protect them (vv.14–15). When God stretches Judah like a bow, his arrow will go like lightning, causing wounds and blows that instill the love of God in the perfect soul or the glorious Church, making it the light of the world and capable of saying, "I am wounded with love." It is not only here that there is mention of the luminous arrows dispatched from the divine

---

54. Ps 45.3–4; Zep 2.12; Pss 90.17; 51.7; Jn 8.44. Though the NT as well as other literature of the early Church like the *Shepherd of Hermas* and *Epistle of Barnabas* develop the theme of the opposition of darkness and light, Didymus gives it a racial dimension—not an element in Zechariah's thinking.

55. Heb 4.12; 1 Pt 3.18; 2 Cor 10.4; 1 Cor 1.10; Eph 2.15. The Antiochene commentators do not follow Didymus in taking the opening clause of v.14 in conjunction with v.13.

bow: in Habakkuk also these words are said to God: "Your arrows will go like light, like the lightning gleam of your weapons."[56] Now, there is no difference between the plural and the singular expression: we are understanding in general terms the expression *an arrow going like lightning*, and particular arrows take many forms. The word that inflicts a wound leading to desire in those who adopt different forms of virtue and different forms of teaching is that *arrow* in general, whereas the words about individual virtues and individual teachings are particular, and hence are referred to as arrows in the plural. The single arrow goes like lightning, and the multiple arrows like light according to Habakkuk, all of the arrows being bright that are dispatched from the bow stretched by God. Now, the bow is Judah. It was explained previously that these things are announced in reference to the savior, who springs from the tribe of Judah.

When the divine arrow has gone forth like lightning for the enlightenment of the interior man and the eyes of the heart, the Lord almighty will sound the trumpet to stimulate also the interior sense of hearing, the result being that the person who senses the ensuing benefit will utter a cry of thanksgiving, "The Lord's instruction opens my ears," especially as he has given me ears for hearing. Note whether what is given by God is called "trumpet" and "lightning" for different reasons: what is announced in a clear, piercing, and audible fashion is compared to a trumpet, whereas what enlightens the understanding, the soul's eye, resembles lightning.[57]

Now, just as to those who receive them willingly and to the best of their ability all the divine benefits are luminous and au-

56. Song 5.8; Hab 3.11.
57. Is 50.5. The precision, ἀκρίβεια, that Didymus displays in distinguishing between arrow and arrows and between trumpet and lightning as employed by the author compares favorably with his modern counterpart Petersen's observations: "The careful reader notes, however, that unlike the multiple lightning strokes [*sic*] of the thunderstorm (Hab 3.11), the poet has focused on a single arrow, which will strike like lightning. It is as if the poet were emphasizing the singularity of the deity's act by this use of the lightning-arrow simile. . . . The second and unusual element, related to the first, involves the claim that Yahweh trumpets with a horn. . . ." (*Zechariah 9–14*, 64). Needless to say, though thus appreciating the author's imagery as Didymus does, Petersen does not adopt his spiritual interpretation.

dible, so a threat is delivered against those who live indifferent lives. Hence it is logical that after the arrow going like lightning and the sounding of the trumpet by the Lord almighty, he proceeds to say that the benefactor makes a threatening move. Great kindness emerges, however, from God's taking action in a threatening manner without its having full impact, since the threat eventually effects reform, as happened in the case of the Ninevites. In delivering the threat, remember, "In three days Nineveh will be overthrown," he gave the impression not of actual punishment but of a threat of being roused and removing himself from them so as to give them the occasion of repentance and deliver them from the threat when they stopped what they had been doing. By this means, of course, Adam also, immediately on hearing the words of his wife, who was deceived by the serpent, gained such a sense of the lawgiver's reaction as to say, "I heard the sound of your feet when you were walking," when before the Fall he grasped his presence and the sound of him.[58]

God did not distance himself from the Jews, therefore, when they sincerely observed the Law and worshiped its giver, nor was it to abandon them completely that he issued forth brandishing his threat in the words, "I left my house, I parted from my inheritance." His leaving is clearly presented in the words of Jesus in the Gospel, "Your house is left to you."[59] That his purpose and goal were the good of those abandoned is shown by the sequel to the statement, The Lord almighty will issue forth brandishing his threat, namely, *The Lord almighty will protect them*. In other words, when he gave the impression by his threat of distancing himself from them, then it was that he came to their help, holding out his invincible shield over them, of which it is said in the hymns to the object of his favor, "His truth will surround you like a shield."[60]

---

58. Jon 3.4 (the LXX, probably under the influence of the previous verse, putting "three" for the Heb. "forty"); Gn 3.10, where Didymus's insertion of "feet" is seconded by Gerhard von Rad, "*Qôl* here does not mean voice but (as in II Sam. 5.24) the rustle of God's step." See von Rad, *Genesis. A Commentary*, trans. John H. Marks (Philadelphia: The Westminster Press, 1961), 88.

59. Jer 12.7; Mt 23.38.

60. Ps 91.4.

Since the claim was made just now that in blowing the trumpet in a piercing and loud manner the Lord almighty conveys his favors, we should support it with scriptural references. The Holy Spirit bids the herald of truth raise his voice like a trumpet so that the teaching he offers may rouse to battle God's soldiers against their opponents, but also as a summons to festive assemblies. Mention of this occurs in the divinely inspired sayings, sometimes obscurely, sometimes in factual description. Sufficient proof that the sounding of a trumpet suggests publicity lies in what was said by Jesus to those intent on self-glorification in doing good works to the neighbor, "In giving alms do not sound a trumpet before you"; in other words, he wants this virtue in particular to be performed in secret since its public performance is due to a growth of vainglory and vanity. As well, the commandment is transgressed which forbids it, "Do not do to another what you hate":[61] taking credit from the misfortune of the needy, as it were, is not a favor to the recipient, and consequently the giver is responsible for what he would not like to experience. When, then, the Lord almighty illumines those benefited by him, he sounds a trumpet to publicize the gifts he gives, protecting those well-disposed so that they remain proof against scheming and harm, and surrounding them with an invincible shield once they have put on all the armor of their ruler and king. May it be our lot, too, to "put on the armor of light" and "take up the shield of faith" so as to be able to say with confidence, "You are my help and shield; O my God, do not delay."[62]

They will consume them, overwhelm them with slingshot stones, drink their blood like wine, and fill the altar like bowls. The Lord will save them on that day, his people like sheep, because holy stones roll on his ground (vv.15–16). When God has stretched Judah like a bow, and stirred up the sons of Sion against the children of the Greeks, victory will be theirs; the offspring of the Greeks will be consumed by those stirred up against them, who accurately stone them like skillful slingers so that they are overwhelmed

61. Is 58.1; Mt 6.2; Tob 4.15.
62. Eph 6.11; Rom 13.12; Eph 6.16; Ps 40.17.

by being covered with stones. Their blood is avidly drunk by the slingers, who also fill the altars like bowls. When the sons of the Greeks suffer the fate nominated, that is, being overwhelmed by stones and their blood being drunk, then the Lord will save those protected like sheep, who have become his people, since the stones able to be used in construction of the divine foundation will be easily moved so as to *roll on God's ground*, being light and easily moved by the one who removes from them their weight and stony character. By thus rolling upon God's holy ground, in fact, they will incorporate themselves into the building, fixed suitably into the walls of the holy city and the structure of God's Temple.[63]

Now, we must study the deeper meaning of those being overwhelmed by the slingstones who are consumed by those protected by God almighty. Words that involve a verdict of punishment, like stones accurately dispatched by slingers, will consume sinners, with the result that they will no longer be enemies of God, when the wickedness that made them resistant to God's graces is consumed, since they have been covered under the slingstones and proven by them. In other words, just as "love covers a multitude of sins," not allowing the sins it covers to exist any longer because they are completely obliterated, so the words of reproof and censure that come against those under assault from slingers will overwhelm them and become their cover.[64] Their blood will be drunk like wine, the drinkers thus growing merry and light-headed, so that the altars then become like bowls, vessels productive of merriment. After all, how could the one who offers a sacrifice of praise and righteousness not partake of the divine draught? In fact, just as those who do not worship in the manner required cover with

63. Of verses that are obscure in both Hebrew and Greek, Jerome (CCL 76A.836) declaring them "convoluted," Didymus makes an honest attempt to do justice to the literal sense before turning to the spiritual.

64. 1 Pt 4.8. The "cover," κάλυμμα, referred to here is, in Doutreleau's opinion (SC 84.726–27), a reference to the cover of the chalice mentioned also in the liturgy of St. John Chrysostom. "It is this image which Didymus will have retained and which provides him with a way of moving to the blood drunk like wine to the point of merriment and to altars transformed in bowls of joy"—a rare reference by Didymus to the liturgy of the period, he observes.

tears the altar of the one who directs these words of censure to them: "You covered my altar with tears. Am I still to have regard for your sacrifice, or accept a gift from your hands?"[65] On the one hand, then, let this warning be given to those who sacrifice in an impious manner, but on the other, the promise to those devoutly performing their sacrifices appropriately that the altars will be bowls of merriment, and that since they worship in this fashion, they will be saved, emerging in a luminous condition occurring on that spiritual day when they will be saved through transformation from sheep into God's people like sheep. The first condition of those who make a good beginning as they should, you see, is to be led like a flock by the excellent shepherd with the result that after being sheep they will emerge as a people and will have as their king the one who was formerly their shepherd. After being styled people of the almighty, they will also form part of the city built by the Lord of hosts.

The *holy stones rolling on God's ground* on account of their lightness and weightlessness become . . . Peter, leader of the apostles, writes, "Come to him, [a living stone, though rejected by mortals yet] chosen and precious in God's sight, and like living stones let yourselves be built into a spiritual house, to be a holy priesthood, to offer spiritual sacrifices pleasing to God through Jesus Christ." If in reference to such people . . . "If they keep silent, the stones will cry out" . . . bowing down to him, according to what is written in the Psalms, in one case, "Praise the Lord, all the earth," and in another, "Let all the earth bow down to you and sing to you" . . . seven books . . .[66]

Because anything good is his, anything beautiful is from him, grain for young men and fragrant wine for maidens (v.17). Anything very special belongs . . . in the epistle of his, "Every generous act of giving and every perfect gift is from above, coming down from the Father of lights, with whom there is no variation or shadow

65. Mal 2.13.

66. Commentary on the "rolling stones" in v.16, which diverges considerably from our Heb., survives only in fragmentary condition, and includes reference to 1 Pt 2.4; Lk 19.40; Pss 96.1; 66.4; and the seven books of *The Captivity of the Jews* of Josephus.

due to change." Hence he alone . . . "gives good things to those
who ask him" . . . the Lord "who satisfied your desires with
good things." It should be understood . . . says, "Do good" . . .
the articulate Isaiah, "Learn to do good" . . . in the apostle's
words, "Test everything, hold fast to what is good, abstain from
every form of evil" . . . *Because anything good is his, anything beautiful is from him,* accordingly . . . *grain for young men, fragrant wine
for maidens . . .*[67]

. . . the physical man not only fails to perceive the things of
the spirit, but considers them foolishness, because the senses
of the interior man are impaired. After all, how could the sense
of smell and taste not be impaired in the case of the one who
has not tasted the Lord in the sense of the saying, "Taste and
see that the Lord is good," as well as that which allows recep-
tion of the sacred breath of his name, according to the verse,
"Your name is perfume poured out, therefore the maidens
loved you"?[68]

67. Commentary on v.17 is also fragmentary, including reference to Jas 1.17;
Mt 7.11; Pss 103.5; 34.14; Is 1.17; 1 Thes 5.21. At this point two pages of the
manuscript are missing.
68. 1 Cor 1.14; Ps 34.8; Song 1.3.

COMMENTARY ON ZECHARIAH 10

SK FROM THE LORD *timely rain, early and late. The Lord caused visions and winter rain, and will give to each one a plant in the field.*[1] *Because the diviners spoke of trouble and the seers spoke of false visions and false dreams, they offered empty consolation. Hence they dried up like sheep, and were abused because there was no healing. My anger is roused against the shepherds, and I shall have regard for the lambs* (Zec 10.1–3). Owing to the prevalence of wickedness, drought often occurs at God's decision. Hence in such circumstances there is need for the one to be propitiated who is angry with the people for falling into godlessness to the extent of appeasing and winning over demons instead of God and so accepting oracles and divinations from them.

Such a plight befell the Hebrews in the time of the great prophet Elijah, when there was no rain on the earth for three years and six months, so that there was a complete dearth of produce and as a result people were close to death, and the other living creatures were worse off as a result of shortage of necessities. In view of the prevalence of this wickedness, it would have been logical for Israel, who had frequently been the object of beneficence in such circumstances, to cling to God and beg rain from him so that prosperity might return. It did not do so, because a false belief held sway that the idols were able to grant the petitioners what was asked of them, and in fact they were unable to provide. The source of the folly was Jezebel, wife of the king of the Hebrews, who was so very devoted to idol worship that her husband was also caught up in it. In

1. Didymus's commentary shows that he has divided the verse this way. The LXX further complicates the meaning by reading Heb. "[thunder]clouds" as "visions."

231

her time, accordingly, there was a growth in numbers of the prophets of Baal, idol of the Sidonians, and there were seers, diviners, and likewise dreamers peddling their dreams, always bold enough to give false prophecy of future developments they claimed to foretell. When good times came, they took a different tack and claimed there was no longer need to beg rain from "the one who makes the sun rise on good people and bad, and who sends rain on righteous and wicked."[2]

Since those under such an influence fell into such awful ignorance, therefore, God had pity on the people in this situation and suggested to the prophet to say, *Ask for timely rain* in good season "from the one who makes clouds rise from the ends of the earth and turns lightning into rain," according to the prophetic announcements in Jeremiah.[3] To instill confidence in those it urged to ask for rain in season, the verse went on, *The Lord caused visions and winter rain;* rain would have come not once but many times if the impiety dominating the Hebrews had not brought them to the point where they were rendered unworthy of God-given favors. Since it is God who always allows the land to drink for the sake of human beings, he is the one to be made propitious when drought comes, and not the false seers[4] . . . the story from Kings.

Now that the text of Zechariah has in my view been sufficiently developed at a literal level, there is need to study it also spiritually. The spiritual sense of the rain as God-given teaching appears in Scripture thus: "Let the clouds rain down righteousness," clouds that have been given the command not to shed rain when . . .[5]

The apostle in Christ, himself also a cloud in the spiritual sense, writes to the Hebrews, "Ground [that drinks up] the rain

2. 1 Kgs 17–18; Lk 4.25; Mt 5.45.
3. Jer 10.13.
4. The notion of drought enters the LXX text by a misreading of the verb "wander" in v.2. In a commentary that is now in fragmentary condition, Didymus continues to refer to historical precedents (the reference to the request for rain not being clear even in the Heb. text) such as the Elijah cycle in 1–2 Kings, citing also Jas 5.16–17; Ps 143.9.
5. Is 45.8. There follows a section of the commentary in fragmentary condition, where it is possible to recognize citations of Dt 32.2; Eph 4.14.

repeatedly falling on it [produces] growth" . . . the apostle's statement, "Ground that drinks up the rain repeatedly falling on it and produces growth useful to those for whom it is culti-vated receives a blessing from God, whereas if it produces thorns and thistles, it is worthless and close to being cursed, and its end is burning." Lest you think he wrote this in a factual sense, he proceeded, "We are confident in your case, beloved, of better things that bear on your salvation,"[6] that is to say, be-cause you bear fruit as a result of the *early and late rain* that falls, whereas those who receive only one or the other do not bear perfect fruit. Those from the circumcision received only early rain and did not attach themselves to the Gospel, since they did not come to faith in the savior. Likewise, after the coming of the savior, the heretics partook only of the late rain, never en-joying the early rain, and they and their teaching emerged as imperfect, since the apostolic Church alone bears perfect fruit that is sweet and edible as a result of having a perfect drink from both rains. This interpretation is suggested also by the prophecy of Hosea that runs as follows: "Let us press on to know the Lord; we shall find him in readiness like the dawn, and he will come to us like early and late rain on the earth."[7]

Early rain should be taken in another sense in reference to the doctrine of the Incarnation of the savior, and the late rain in reference to his divinity.[8] Those who enjoyed both draughts say, "The Word was made flesh, and dwelt among us; we have seen his glory, glory as of the Only-begotten of the Father, full of grace and truth." What was written by Paul to the Corinthi-ans also has this sense: "Even though we once knew Christ in the flesh, now we no longer know him in that way." In refer-ence to the former interpretation, the one concerning the two testaments, use could be made of the verse, "Paul, a servant of Jesus Christ, set apart for the Gospel of God, which he prom-

6. Heb 6.7–9.

7. Hos 6.3. The implication of Didymus's development of the notion of twofold rain is that heretical teaching is deficient because it is out of touch with the Old Testament.

8. By θεολογία, which can mean also "true doctrine of God," Didymus here and in commentary on 1.8 seems to refer to Christ's divine nature.

ised beforehand through his prophets in the holy Scriptures, the Gospel concerning his Son, who was descended from David according to the flesh and declared to be Son of God with power according to the Spirit of holiness."[9]

A third sense should also be given: early rain can be taken as what is known and prophesied "in part" in this life, whereas the late rain is what will be seen "face to face" in the world to come. One could also go so far as to claim that corrective moral instruction and the corresponding practice of virtue are the early watering, and the doctrine of the knowledge of the mysteries of God the late. This twofold rain will come, God willing, when we advance in the process of knowing the Lord by prayer and study of the divinely inspired Scriptures and the practices proper to the most elevated insight; when this is performed in advance, the Lord whom we seek will be found "ready like the dawn," having become early and late rain on the earth that has received Jesus' sowing. This, in fact, is the way it will bear the fruits indicated in what follows—resurrection, life, perfect knowledge—as the same text just cited suggests in these words: "He will come to us like early and late rain on the earth. And we shall rise and live; we shall stand before him and know him."[10]

Filled with these good things stemming from divine inspiration, the person who has sought the Lord will avoid as abominations *the utterances of the false seers*, who relate dreams rather than interpret them. This is what they are like who implant heresies in Christianity, "understanding neither what they are saying nor the things about which they make assertions," "paying attention to deceitful spirits and teachings of demons, through the hypocrisy of liars whose consciences are seared with a hot iron." Those people are in the grip of false dreams who decline to stay sober and alert, overcome by numbness as if sleeping at night and intoxicated; Scripture says of those who dream and are always wanting to doze off, "Sleepers sleep at night, and drunkards get drunk at night," deprived of the true

9. Jn 1.14; Rom 1.1–4.
10. 1 Cor 13.9, 12; Hos 6.2–3.

light.[11] Hence, even if they ever promise consolation, their consolation is futile: from their so-called inspired predictions there will come no pasture or growth that gives nourishment. Hence they *dry up* like sheep without pasture, of whom the holy one said, "The Lord shepherds me, and nothing will be wanting to me; he settled me in a green pasture." Now, this lush pasture is available to the one who enters and leaves by the door that is no other than the savior, who says, "I am the door: anyone who enters by me will enter and leave and find pasture."[12]

Since they are deprived of it, those who are caught up in dreams and false oracles will dry up like young animals without food, the result being that there is no *healing* for them in their severe plight. God's anger is so far aroused against the worthless shepherds on account of their neglect of the flock that the lambs experience God's anger along with the shepherds; the chastisement will extend also to them, and fat lambs will be punished and chastised so that even they *dry up* along with the sheep herded together in flocks. Harm comes to the flock on account of the shepherds' fall into godlessness, God himself saying of them, "The shepherds acted impiously towards me, and went after things of no value," giving heed to oracles and seers and peddlers of false dreams, with the result that the sheep also suffered harm and met with ruin. The harshest censure has therefore been delivered by the one who cares for all: "My people have become lost sheep; their shepherds have driven them off,"[13] so that the very lambs have been abused, no longer enjoying the benefits of rich pasture.

Yet even if they were reduced to this condition of their own fault, through the kindness of the good shepherd the lamb of God was sacrificed to take away the sin of the world. Of him the prophecy states, "He was led like a sheep to slaughter, and like a lamb silent before its shearer"; the Baptist, who was more than a prophet, said in identifying him, "Behold the lamb of

11. 1 Tm 1.7; 4.1–2; 1 Thes 5.6–7.
12. Ps 23.1–2; Jn 10.7, 9. The LXX of Zec 10.2 is reading Heb. "wandered" as "dried up," and Heb. "shepherd" as "healing," a flawed basis for spiritual development of the text.
13. Jer 2.8; 50.6.

God who takes away the sin of the world."[14] Once the sin of the world was removed, the sheep in receipt of such benefits suffer no drying up or similar plight, nor do the lambs who felt chastisement from the one who said, *My anger is roused against the shepherds.* We, too, should make every effort to be subject to the good chief shepherd, who leads to a green pasture those shepherded by him, so that they come in and go out, thus applying themselves to the divine sayings in both an internal and an external sense, and experiencing a life that is blessed and everlasting.

The Lord God almighty will attend to his flock, the house of Judah, and will make them like his handsome warhorse. From it he looked down, from it he drew up, from it his bow in anger, and from it will issue forth everyone driving forth in it. They will be like warriors trampling mud in the streets in time of war and will be deployed, because the Lord is with them (vv.3–5). After being angry, the Lord God, almighty as he is, will to their advantage heal those fallen victim to his wrath and attend to his flock, namely, the house of Judah, or the one who confesses, Judah meaning "the one who confesses."[15] The Lord God, almighty as he is, will attend to his flock; of him it is said also in Micah, "He shall stand and see, and shall shepherd his flock in the strength of the Lord,"[16] who is savior. Now, the fact that the only-begotten Son of God is the Lord God almighty has been proved in what went before; since the Trinity is of one being, and the one who is generated is of one being with the one who generated him, the savior is Lord God almighty from Lord God almighty. After all, how is the one "who was in the beginning with God" not Lord God? And just as "it was through him that all things were made,"[17] so, too,

14. Is 53.7; Mt 11.9; Jn 1.29.

15. From its first appearance in comment on 1.13, this dubious etymology of Judah is often paraded by Didymus, not always with relevance.

16. Mi 5.3.

17. Jn 1.2–3. The terminology of the creed of Constantinople of 381, including ὁμοούσιον, leaves its mark on Didymus's work a few years later. The fact that he makes little effort on this occasion to find a historical basis for the verses, preferring to involve himself in theologizing, reflects the obscurity of some of the Heb. terms, which present too great a challenge for the LXX. Theodore will even decline to cite the verses, simply seeing Zerubbabel in focus, as usual.

he controls and reigns over them, and so is in this respect almighty.

This person, recognized as God, therefore, came on earth to find and save the human race, the sheep that had gone astray from the hundred rational ones; as an excellent shepherd he "laid down" his life for the sheep he came to save, and thus attended to his very own flock. They are the house of Judah, of whom it is said, "Judah, your brothers will praise you." And since the transformation of those given this favor is swift as a result of the change, he will draw up those constituting his flock to be like a single handsome horse, "all united in one mind and one purpose," so that he will turn from shepherd to skillful rider guiding them to salvation. Now, this benefit occurred when those with a longing for his coming sent a delegation and said, "Mount the horses, and your riding will be salvation."[18]

From this house of Judah, from a flock turned into a handsome horse, he looked down and drew from it a bow, from which he discharges arrows, the words of punishment and threat. In reference to them the one who drew the bow said, "I shall make my arrows drunk with blood," and again, "My arrows will put paid to them." He had already said, in what went before, that the punishments in a deep sense are called arrows; in the seventh psalm likewise there is mention of the judge of all, both living and dead, "He stretched his bow and readied it, and with it he made ready instruments of death; he forged his arrows with fire."[19] Now, what will happen, when the Lord God almighty looks *down from* Judah and from it draws a war bow, is that those from Judah who have received suffering from him will become battle-hardened warriors. There will issue forth at the same time the one driving forth in readiness for war so as to trample mud in the streets, many being struck down and mud being formed from the blood. This happens in the case of the victors, not the vanquished: the latter are put to flight, pur-

18. Lk 15.4; Jn 10.11; Gn 49.8; 1 Cor 1.10; Hab 3.8. The literal sense of the verses being unclear, Didymus falls to consulting his mental concordance for lexical similarities.

19. Dt 32.42, 23; Ps 7.12–13. The LXX of Zec 10.4 has lost the cornerstone and tent peg (or some such items) suggested by the Heb.

sued, and hunted down, while the former run after and hunt
down those who in fear turn their backs, and trample down the
blood of the slain like mud, accelerating the pace of the flight
like horsemen.

After these achievements the Lord their God will be on their
side to fight for them, and so they will say in gratitude, "The
Lord of hosts is with us, the God of Jacob is our protector," and
again, "With God we shall exercise power, and he himself will
reduce our oppressors to naught." Having God with them, they
will confidently be deployed against those on whom they wage
battle and war, so that each of them says in thanksgiving, "The
Lord is my light and my salvation: whom shall I fear? The Lord
is the protector of my life: whom shall I dread? When evildoers
pressed upon me to devour my flesh, my persecutors and my
foes themselves fainted and fell. If an army were deployed
against me, my heart would not fear; if war broke out against
me, I would still hope." With the same boldness the singer of
the third psalm also had the confidence to say, "I shall not fear
countless numbers of people encircling me." To those prepared for battle in this way Scripture says encouragingly, "One
of you will pursue thousands, and two will put to flight myri-
ads," not only human adversaries but unseen ones as well; in
their contest with them the soldiers of Christ are clad in his armor, and say, "Our contest is not with flesh and blood, but with
the rulers, the authorities, the cosmic forces of this present
darkness, and the spiritual forces of evil." It is, in fact, despite
being encircled by all these foes that the one with confidence
in the name of God like an invincible shield says, "They surrounded me in a circle, and I took vengeance on them in the
name of the Lord." And the prophet utters the same victorious
cry as this: "Lo, the Lord will help me: who will harm me?"[20]

And the cavalry will be confounded. I shall strengthen the house of
Judah and save the house of Joseph, and shall settle them, because I
loved them, and they will be as though I had not turned them away. Be-
cause I am the Lord their God, and I shall hearken to them. They will

20. Pss 46.7; 60.12; 27.1–3; 3.6; Dt 32.30; Eph 6.12; Ps 118.11; Is 50.9: am-
ple documentation of a single thought.

be like the warriors of Ephraim, their heart will rejoice as though from wine, their children will see and be glad, and their heart will rejoice in the Lord (vv.5–7). Those who put great reliance on ranks of cavalry are covered in confusion when the fortunes of war are at variance with their expectation, and they learn from experience that "worthless is a horse for salvation." Of those who wage war in this fashion, the band of holy ones says, "Some rely on chariots, some on horses, whereas we shall rejoice in the name of the Lord. They were entangled and fell, while we got up and stood straight." Like them, the tyrant of Egypt and everyone deployed with him were confounded when overwhelmed in the Red Sea, so that the hymn was sung against them that begins this way: "Let us sing to the Lord, for he has been splendidly glorified, horse and rider he tossed into the sea." Of these riders it is said also in one of the Psalms, "At your rebuke, O God of Jacob, those riding the horses fell into a sleep."[21]

Now, there is need to grasp who these men are. If the horses are taken to be human bodies because of their restless and skittish behavior, their riders are the souls that fail to tame with discipline and skill the horses on which they are mounted—hence the shame in which they are covered and have to endure, as the prophetic verse states, *The cavalry will be confounded.* Understood in another sense, the horses can be people who are boastful and deceitful, on whom are mounted wicked powers that proceed in disorderly fashion because they are unskilled in the use of the reins and are traveling in a blind rush. Because they wildly spur on the four-legged passions, they will be ashamed; they come to grief through sleeping and dozing. Those who ride in a salutary manner do not suffer shame; the soul that mortifies and keeps in control the body in which it is contained is not simply mounted or seated, but is a rider skilled as a horse-breaker. Likewise, some divine powers who ride excellent men with equestrian skills proceed as horsemen do, carried along by the force of divine teaching, having as guide and leader the one whose riding brings salvation; Scripture says of

21. Pss 33.17; 20.7–8; Ex 15.1; Ps 76.6.

him, "Mount your horses, and your riding will bring salvation."[22]

A certain sage of ancient times distinguished horseman from rider, calling the latter worthless and the former commendable: the one who rides without skill, not holding the horse in check, is a mere rider, as the aforementioned sage made clear, since it is only the one riding with equestrian skills who is rightfully referred to as a horseman. For example, when the mighty prophet Elijah was taken up, God's interpreter Elisha cried aloud, "Father, father, chariot of Israel and its horseman!"[23] The one who rode in excellent fashion, keeping his particular chariot under control, of necessity was a horseman, not a mere rider. Since this is the difference between horseman and rider, it is not horsemen but riders who will be put to shame for dozing in the course of being mounted on the horses, whereas the cavalry who control their mounts in a sober and alert manner ride with skill. Hence they achieve victory and emerge victorious, while those riding the worthless horses are put to shame.

The people of Judah are strengthened, and the house of Joseph lives and will be saved by the sovereign God. Joseph and Judah respectively stand for the incarnate savior in that he sprang from Judah and distributed grain to those suffering hunger and thirst, the result being that they then had plenty of bread with the arrival of abundant supplies. It is therefore said in the case of Mary's giving birth that they were filled with good things, those who previously were starving as a result of their scorn for spiritual nourishment, which their spiritual Joseph had provided. He made available such a profusion of food that even in the wilderness he satisfied the need of a large crowd for food with just a few loaves.[24]

After *strengthening the house of Judah and saving the house of Joseph*, God promises to *settle them* for no other reason than that

22. 1 Cor 9.27; Hab 3.8. Didymus is wringing every spiritual drop out of the mention of cavalry, irrespective of Zechariah's point, and he is not finished yet: Scripture having little to say on the subject, he turns to Philo.

23. 2 Kgs 2.12.

24. Lk 1.53; Mk 6.35–44 and parallels.

he *loved them.* Now, this will happen only when they receive the promises of which . . . he convinced them, of which Scripture says in these terms: "What no eye has seen, nor mortal ear heard, nor the heart conceived, what God has prepared for those who love him." These promises will come to them *as though I had not turned them away,* but watch over and regard them, being the Lord their God. I shall therefore hearken to them if they bear much fruit in accord with the name Ephraim, which means "fertility."[25] The result is that their contemplation will be a source of satisfaction and joy, like wine made from the true vine, on which sufficient comment has already been made. Now, what will come of drinking the divine wine if not rejoicing in the perception of the mysteries of the kingdom of heaven and everything else that requires elevated perception, since after it you will see God with a pure heart in attending to "the imprint of his being" in such a way that he who is the "image" and "imprint" of the unseen God says, "He who has seen me has seen the Father."[26]

Those to whom the promises were made will not be the only ones to enjoy the sacred visions; as well, there will be the children they have generated by godly instruction and imitation of a good life. The apostle in Christ therefore writes to Corinthians and Galatians: to the former, "I gave you birth through the Gospel"; to the latter, "My children, for whom I am again in the pain of childbirth until Christ is formed in you." Peter, leader of the apostles, likewise writes as though to his own children in a letter he dispatched, "Like obedient children, do not be conformed to your former ways." Barnabas, likewise, who along with Paul was himself appointed apostle for the uncircumcised, sent a letter to those with faith in the Gospel, and directed it to his sons and daughters, as it were. The psalmist also addresses those born of him in regard to virtue, "Come now, children, listen to me, I shall teach you the fear of the Lord. Who is it who wants life and loves to see good days?"[27] Upon seeing them, the

<hr/>

25. 1 Cor 2.9. The etymology of Ephraim Didymus had arrived at in commentary on 9.10 with the support of Gn 41.52.

26. Heb 1.3; Col 1.15; Jn 14.9.

27. 1 Cor 4.15; Gal 4.19; 1 Pt 1.14; Ps 34.11. The *Epistle of Barnabas* is an

children of the aforementioned will rejoice in spirit (referred to as "heart"), thanks to none other than the Lord their God, who says to each of those living according to the divine Gospel, "Enter into the joy of your Lord."[28]

I shall send them a signal and welcome them, for I shall ransom them and they will become as numerous as they were before. I shall sow them among peoples, and those far off will remember me. They will raise their children and bring them back. I shall bring them back from the land of Egypt and welcome them from Assyria; I shall bring them into Gilead and into Lebanon, and none of them, not one, will be left behind (vv.8–10). Though he is inclined to welcome back those deported by the norms of captivity, the Lord does not do so in one fell swoop, instead signaling his favor to its recipients. This thought occurs in a particular way in the Gospels: in his wish to give rest to souls, Jesus says, "Come to me all you who labor and are burdened, and you will find rest for your souls. Take my yoke upon you, and learn of me that I am meek and humble of heart; for my yoke is easy and my burden light." Having decided . . . to welcome them back to him so that they may take his yoke, easy as it is, and his light burden, he signals this to them by saying, "Come to me and I shall give you rest."[29] This divine exhortation is found also in Isaiah, where the Holy Spirit cries aloud, "Shine, shine, Jerusalem, for your light has come upon you, and the glory of your God has risen upon you. Lo, darkness and gloom will cover the land and the nations, but the Lord will appear over you." In fact, to signal the fact that there is need to be enlightened by the savior, the true light, he went on, "The Lord will shine on you, and the glory of your God will become visible on you." The result is that the royal souls will advance, since the sovereign rules over them with the light of the one who welcomes them, accompanied by the nations called to

---

early work by an author called Barnabas whom Didymus (but not Origen) thought to be Paul's associate. We have observed how Didymus is always anxious to highlight Peter's position of eminence.

28. Mt 25.21.

29. Mt 11.28–30. Didymus finds the briefest of references in these verses to the historical situation of the exiles' promised return before taking an eschatological interpretation.

the Gospel by the splendor of the glorious Church, which is the
spiritual Jerusalem because it sees "the peace of God surpassing
all understanding" on account of its perfect elevation and royal
eminence.[30]

Now, the reason for his signaling and welcoming them back
he appropriately proceeds to state, *for I shall ransom them and I
shall make them as numerous as they were before.* He ransoms them
when cruel and implacable tyrants took them off by the norms
of captivity from their own way of life. There is mention in other scriptural passages of the manner and way in which the
restoration to freedom occurs; one of the holy ones, for instance, cried aloud to the benefactor, "My joy, ransom me from
my persecutors," and again, "You ransomed me, Lord God of
truth." Peter, the head of the disciples of Christ, indicates the
return of those rescued from the former misfortune when he
writes to the faithful, "It was not with perishable things, gold or
silver, that you were ransomed from the vain ways received
from your fathers, but with the precious blood of Christ the innocent and spotless lamb."[31]

Having rescued them and made this promise, the savior necessarily proceeds, *I shall make them as numerous as they were before,*
not so much in size and number as in degree of honor, like the
blessing spoken to Abraham by God, "I shall make him increase
and multiply him; I shall bless him and he will be blessed, proving to be father of many nations by God's gift." Now, he became
father of many nations not only in the flesh but also in the spirit, that is, with his children and sons doing his works and having his faith. The savior himself accordingly addresses the most
severe censure to those claiming to have Abraham as their father in the flesh when he says, "If you are children of Abraham,
do the works of Abraham." It is in this sense that the vessel of
election, the apostle Paul, writes to the Church, explaining how
the sacred patriarch is father of the nations: "All who are of
faith are sons of Abraham" and "blessed with him." The same

30. Is 60.1–2; Phil 4.7.
31. Pss 32.7; 31.5; 1 Pt 1.18–19. In preference to considering the historical
content of the passage, Didymus immediately turns to "other scriptural passages" dealing with restoration of freedom.

interpretation is suggested by the prophetic statement that occurs in Isaiah, "The least of them will turn into thousands, and
the smallest into a large nation."[32] Taken in a physical sense this
prompts ridicule, since many holy personages had no children
at all: Elijah, for instance, and Elisha did not have any children,
nor John the Baptist, and yet no one was greater than he in
commendable behavior and holy knowledge. So a spiritual interpretation must be given to the multiplication of those with
the promise of becoming *as numerous as they were:* it is not at this
point that the righteous began to be multiplied and become
numerous in the sense explained, for they were numerous even
before the present life.[33]

Since these people were numerous, he scattered them like
seed among the peoples so that they might share in their
virtue. In other words, just as seeds sown in the ground affect
the surrounding soil for the production of crops and fruit, so
those sown among the peoples and the nations bring those
among whom they are sown to their peculiar fertility so that
they become imitators of their virtue. You would not be wrong
in claiming that those who heard Jesus were in receipt of seeds
from Jesus: "Go and make disciples of all the nations"; and likewise those in John's Gospel, "I appointed you"—that is, determined and designated you—"so that you should go and bear
much fruit," and your fruit will be glorified. I believe that it was
in this way that the holy ones were taken into captivity with the
peoples to both Babylon itself and Assyria,[34] the purpose being

32. Gn 17.20; 12.2; Jn 8.39; Acts 9.15; Gal 3.7, 9; Is 60.22.
33. Having shown little interest in explaining the verses in a literal sense,
Didymus becomes quite forthright in arguing for a spiritual interpretation
when he may reasonably have admitted mere hyperbole. It is one thing to err in
favor of one line of interpretation; it is another to show heat in disqualifying the
alternative when reason recommends it. Editor Doutreleau (SC 83.81–82) is
prepared to admit that, though an isolated remark, the final clause here does
suggest an acceptance of Origen's condemned views about the pre-existence of
souls. The fact highlights the irony of Didymus's heated rejection of the obvious
(and irreproachable) sense of the verse.
34. Mt 28.19; Jn 15.16. In this detail Didymus adverts to a feature of the
text, the mention of both Babylon and Assyria, which also strikes modern commentators: is there simply a general reference to Mesopotamia, or a particular
mention of Israelites deported to Assyria like those specified in 2 Kgs 17.6? It
does not, however, indicate a general shift of focus for Didymus.

that they would share their virtue like seeds of salvation and produce ear and crops. It naturally follows from this that those at a distance from the Lord owing to sins and infidelities would remember him.

These promises apply in particular to those coming to faith from the nations. It is said of them, for instance, in the twenty-second psalm, "All the ends of the earth will remember and will be converted to the Lord, and all the clans of the nations will bow down before him, because kingship is the Lord's and he rules the nations." After all, how does he not govern and rule those who are mindful of him and have turned towards him so as to bow down and glorify their ruler and benefactor? Now, what will follow for those mindful of the sovereign if not the constant recollection of "the city of the living God," which is a heavenly city according to the verse, "You who are at a distance, remember the Lord, and let Jerusalem come into your heart."[35]

Those shown kindness by the savior have large families and many children in a spiritual sense, and will bring up their children with a share of the spiritual nourishment, so that it may be said of each of them in terms of the text of the divine Proverbs, "A righteous father is good at educating." In addition to the spiritual meaning it can also happen in a literal sense: Zechariah, being a righteous father, properly reared his child John the Baptist, as Abraham did Isaac, and Isaac Jacob. The divinely inspired Paul, too, as a father gave a useful and commendable education to those to whom he gave birth through the Gospel; listen, at any rate, to his letter to the Corinthians: "I gave you milk to drink." In similar terms, too, Peter writes to the faithful among the diaspora, "You who have been born anew, not of perishable but of imperishable seed, through the living and enduring word of God, long as newborn babes for the spiritual milk so that by it you may grow into salvation." In this sense also the evangelist John, after giving birth by means of instruction to his disciples, writes to the whole Church, "Children, keep yourselves from idols."[36]

35. Ps 22.27–28; Heb 12.22; Jer 51.50.
36. Prv 23.24; 1 Cor 4.15; 3.2; 1 Pt 1.23; 2.2; 1 Jn 5.21.

In addition to rearing their children, dedicated fathers will also direct them by advice and godly admonition against their being any longer in the company of evildoers in the places of infidels, God willing, as the author says, *I shall bring them back from the land of Egypt and welcome them from Assyria.* The hope is that they would no longer suffer hardship under the spiritual tyrant of Egypt or be under the control of the ruler of the Assyrians, referred to as "great cleverness" on account of his villainous and twisted schemes, which not everyone censured— only those saying with God's wisdom, "We were not unaware of his schemes." It is possible to refer to the princes of Egyptians and Assyrians as the same tyrant in one sense or another; but if distinct evil powers are indicated by different names, there is no problem: such a usage is not impossible, there being many "principalities and authorities of this present darkness as well as cosmic powers and spiritual forces of evil."[37]

After freeing from Egypt and Assyria the fathers who properly rear their children and who give them birth, the giver of generous gifts promises to lead them *into Gilead and Lebanon,* with no evil king to annoy them further. Note whether he leads into Gilead those anxious to have the transfer of witness,[38] the transfer from vice to virtue: one who repents transfers from sin to righteousness, from impiety to piety, while in another sense righteous people transfer from the elements of instruction to further advancement, and from there to what comes next, and so on to the end, after which there is no further good, this being the goal of all desires. It is in this sense that the psalmist says of those changing abode, "They will go from strength to strength." There is a transfer also from the shadow of the Law to its reality by those who bypass the death-dealing letter and reach the life-giving Spirit. We need to examine

---

37. Is 10.12; 2 Cor 2.11; Eph 6.12. Didymus gives a spiritual dimension to Zechariah's mention of the people's return from both Assyria and Egypt, whereas Petersen would take it to mean that "the prophet emphasizes the truly international scope of Yahweh's activity" (*Zechariah 9–14 and Malachi,* 76).

38. In Gn 31.37 Laban's "mound of witness" is called Gilead in Heb. by his partner in the covenant, Jacob. Didymus draws the long bow in giving this place name a spiritual dimension, as he proceeds to do also with the name Lebanon.

whether a transfer also occurs from knowing and prophesying in part;[39] there will be witness of transfer or transmigration, which is achieved indisputably because of containing the proof in itself.

Those led by God into Gilead are led also into Lebanon after being divinized, Lebanon meaning "divinity" in the statement by the divine bridegroom to the godly bride, his partner, who is a godly soul and the "glorious Church" adorned with such sanctity as no longer to show "spot or wrinkle or anything like that," namely, "The scent of your garments is like the scent of Lebanon." This could be said in reference to each of those who have been divinized by participation in the word of God, for it is to them that reference is made by the savior: "He gave the name gods to those to whom the word of God came."[40]

"The scent of your garments is like the scent of Lebanon." "Garments" in the plural are the particular types of virtues that adorn "the queen placed on the right" of the royal groom. It is said by the sages that the incense offered by the magi to the child born of Mary along with gold and myrrh signifies divinity in the following sense: since the one born of the virgin is both God and man as well as being king, it was right that in recognition of his divinity a gift of incense be offered, and with this incense an offering of gold be made to recognize him as king. It is said, at any rate, in the seventy-second psalm that the one who has come is king and that gold is offered to him, "O God, give your judgment to the king," and later, "He will live, and to him will be given some of the gold of Arabia."[41] Having become man in reality and not in appearance only, the one who is glorified for becoming mortal and being destined "to taste death for the sake of everyone by God's grace" was offered myrrh along with the other gifts. This gift indicates the burial of the one

39. Ps 84.7; 2 Cor 3.6; 1 Cor 13.9. We are clearly at some distance from Zechariah's thought.

40. Eph 5.27; Song 4.11; Jn 10.35.

41. Ps 45.9; Mt 2.11; Ps 71.1, 15. Didymus is playing upon the meaning of λίβανος as "incense," and on the fact that, despite its title in reference to Solomon, Ps 72 was used in the liturgy of the Epiphany, as it was applied also in the targums to the messiah.

who died for all; at any rate, Joseph and Nicodemus embalmed the body of Jesus when it was taken down from the cross.[42]

Once the munificent God had led into Gilead and Lebanon those redeemed from Pharaoh and Assyria, none of the enemies was left—not by existing no longer, since it is impossible for a rational being to be reduced to nothing, despite being guilty of every sin and awful impiety—but by no longer being foe and adversary of those redeemed by God. This will be particularly so when "God has become all in all," "when all come to maturity, to the measure of the full stature of Christ," "when they are united in the same mind and the same purpose." This will happen when the Son says to the Father, "Grant that they may be one in us, as I and you are one." Clearly, when all receive the fullness of divinity, there is no one left who is cut off from this unity, outside and alone; then all "grief, pain, and groaning will disappear," and likewise in place of great numbers all will be combined in one single man.[43]

They will cross by a narrow sea, and strike waves in the sea, and all the depths of the rivers will dry up. All the arrogance of the Assyrians will be done away with, and the scepter of Egypt will be removed. I shall make them strong in the Lord their God, and they shall boast in his name, says the Lord (vv. 11–12). Constantly in the divine words earthly existence and life in this world are referred to as a sea. The Gospel parable of the net, for instance, suggests nothing material, describing everything in a spiritual manner:[44] the net cast into people's life for catching fish, referred to allegorically, is the divinely inspired Scripture, woven together in various ways by "God's wisdom in its rich variety." The sea is the condition of each of us, extended and broadened for pleasure-loving and passionate people who are in a condition almost of immobility; fish utter no sound, of course, and have no clear impression because their senses are dull. And if the fish that swim in it

---

42. Heb 2.9; Jn 19.38–40.

43. 1 Cor 15.28; Eph 4.13; 1 Cor 1.10; Jn 17.21; Is 35.10; 51.11. Doutreleau (SC 84.779) detects here traces of Origen's condemned doctrine of apocatastasis.

44. Mt 13.47, a parable that Didymus turns into an allegory for his moral purposes. He proceeds to give lengthy development of the "allegory" in place of analysis of the Zechariah text.

have no clear perception on account of the impoverishment of their soul and senses, by contrast the saints as good anglers in pursuit of the fish ply their skills in the vastness of the water of the sea. It is regarding them, at any rate, that it is written in the divine hymns, "Those who go down to the sea in ships, plying their skills in many waters, have seen the works of God and his wonders in the deep."[45]

The souls launch out in boats that are human bodies into the surging, salt-filled billow of human life by plying skills in deep water, fishing while controlling the tiller; each intelligent person keeps control, one of the charisms of the Holy Spirit. Scripture says, remember, that "support and control" are a gift of the Holy Spirit. In addition to being in control, the intelligent person is also a fisherman, possessing that skill of which Jesus said to the disciples, "Come after me and I shall make you fishers of men." Those plying their skill in deep water see "the Lord's works and his wonders in the deep," applying themselves as far as possible to the deep, which is God's judgments: even though they are unsearchable, yet those with the Spirit of God who penetrate his depths see in the deep God's marvels and works.[46] Note also another task of those launching into the sea that is announced by the prophet Isaiah: "They will be spread out in ships of foreigners, and will plunder the sea as one," by foreign ships referring to their bodies on account of their being of a different nature from the souls that have embarked, since they are spiritual beings and actually created in God's image and likeness. They plunder the sea, taking as booty the dragon in it, wresting from its clutches souls it had deceived with argumentative and deceptive teaching. The fact that the dragon lives in the sea the psalmist in the one-hundred-and-fourth psalm proclaims, "The sea itself, vast and wide; ships sail there, small animals along with large, the dragon itself whom you formed to play in it."[47]

---

45. Eph 3.10; Ps 107.23–24.
46. Prv 1.5; 1 Cor 12.28; Mt 4.19; Ps 107.24; Rom 11.33; 1 Cor 2.10.
47. Is 11.14; Gn 1.26; Ps 104.25–26. Again Didymus forsakes the text of Zechariah to choose a similar one in Isaiah, which in fact is rendered obscure in the LXX.

It should be noted that here on the one hand the sea is vast and wide for those that live with the dragon, while on the other it is *narrow* for those anxious to be beyond it. In other words, just as for the righteous the gate is narrow, and the way is obstructed for those seeking eternal life by living uprightly, whereas the gate is broad and the way wide for depraved and pleasure-loving people, with the result that many fall to their ruin, so the sea in an allegorical sense is found narrow for those who for their reverence for God "are afflicted in every way but not crushed" and so able to say with confidence, "Through much affliction we must enter the kingdom." The billows of the sea in the way interpreted are struck by the one who is its lord and its master; to him the holy ones say with acclaim, "You are in control of the sea's power, and you calm the tossing of its billows." Jesus did just that in a material and a spiritual sense when he rebuked the sea that was boiling against the apostle's skiff and the wind that was stirring up its waves, with the result that at once all became calm and peaceful, once water and air were settled.[48]

As well as the rebuking of the billows of the sea taken allegorically, the depths of the rivers were also dried up. It was with reference to them that in his conceit the king of Egypt, referred to as a dragon on account of his lethal venom, boasted and haughtily claimed, "The rivers are mine, it is I who made them." Those with experience of the narrowing of the sea, the striking of its billows, and the drying up of its deep rivers have recourse to the one who achieved this and gratefully utter a hymn of praise expressed in these terms: "He turns the sea into dry land, they will cross the river on foot,"[49] obviously because the very depths are dried up and the sea's billows stricken. With the sea's billows stricken and all the depths of the rivers dried up, *the arrogance of the Assyrians* will be no more and *the scepter of Egypt* will be done away with, no longer to reign; the arrogance of the Assyrians . . . will suffer the same fate. Their insolence, in fact, took a double form, being abusive on the one hand, and on the other showing arrogance and haughtiness in being insolent.

48. Mt 7.13–14; 2 Cor 4.8; Acts 14.22; Ps 89.9; Mt 8.23–27.
49. Ezek 29.3, 9; Ps 66.6.

With their adversaries brought to naught, those proceeding by a narrow sea *are strengthened* by the Lord their God, and thus each of them says in gratitude, "The Lord is my strength and my celebration, and the Lord has become my salvation," and again, "I shall love you, O Lord, my strength." In similar terms Jeremiah also says to God, "My strength, my help, and my refuge, O Lord my God." The same sentiments as those of the psalmist and the prophet Jeremiah are expressed forcefully also by Paul speaking in Christ when he writes, "I can do all things in him who strengthens me."[50] With the insolence of the Assyrians removed and the kingdom of the Egyptians done away with, they are fortified by the name of their benefactor and they utter *boasts* against those who are routed, as if each of them were saying, "As for me, God forbid that I should boast of anything but the cross of Christ, through whom the world is crucified to me and I to the world." In other words, with the world crucified so as no longer to be active, prevented from going where it wills and doing what pleases it, the slave of Christ is crucified to it so as no longer to be active, feet and hands being bound, and will boast blamelessly in the words, "I have been crucified with Christ."[51]

The person who genuinely has this confidence in Christ boasts in these terms: "Let the one who boasts boast in the Lord," not boasting of anything physical or corporeal to which he could lay claim, nor of anything external. All such things, in fact, are forbidden: "Let the wise not boast of their wisdom, nor the strong of their strength, nor the rich of their riches; instead, let the one who boasts boast of this: of understanding and knowing the Lord and practicing mercy and justice in the midst of the land." This sentiment the mother of the prophet Samuel also uttered in giving thanks for the birth of the child born against hope, except that she replaced "wisdom" with "prudence."[52] With God's help good deeds will also be our doing, so that we may give thanks to the one who as a generous giver makes them possible.

50. Pss 118.14; 18.2; Jer 16.19; Phil 4.13.
51. Gal 6.14; 2.19.
52. 1 Cor 1.31; Jer 9.23–24; 1 Sm 2.10, where the Jeremiah verses occur again in the LXX.

Now that the third book on the prophet Zechariah has also been sufficiently developed, let us call a halt to it, beseeching God, who multiplies visions, to "put a word in the opening of my mouth"[53] so that I may if possible explain also what follows, if that is his will.

53. Hos 12.10; Eph 6.19. Thus, for reasons of length, closes Didymus's third tome at this point.

COMMENTARY ON ZECHARIAH 11

HE GODLY SAGE who has an intellect that is developed and very focused "understands a proverb, obscure discourse, sayings of clever men, and riddles." Words that make announcements in a hidden manner are riddles. The text of the prophet before us, for example, is phrased in the manner of a riddle and proposes an obscure teaching . . . There is a riddle in the phrase *Open your doors, Lebanon* (Zec 11.1): it is not to the material mountain, lifeless as it is, or the trees on it, removed from sense and imagination, . . . that the command is given for the doors of Lebanon to be opened and the pines to lament the fallen cedars, but to proud and arrogant men fallen into unlawful idol worship of "the rulers of this age."[1] The incorporeal powers . . . the rational mortal beings and the other rational beings guided by reason. When, on the other hand, trees and wild . . . the human being, in the image and likeness of God, enjoyed a dignity from the creator compared with the unintelligent cattle . . . Of such creatures the prophetic text says, "They became like stallions in a frenzy for females, each neighing for his neighbor's wife" . . . and the divine command, "Be not like horse or mule that has no understanding,"[2] since in a spiritual sense the man who wrecks others' marriages and in a frenzy mates with others' wives is a horse. Mule is the name given to the one proven to be without issue, sterile in what is good, and especially the soul who makes promise of virginity without God-given intelligence; such a person is stupid, even if seeming to be pure in body, being a mule and not a bride of the Word.

There are many names of animals that are applied pejora-

---

1. Prv 1.6; Zec 11.1; 1 Cor 2.8. This page of the text has suffered the ravages of time.

2. Jer 5.8; Ps 32.9.

tively to human beings, asses and camels being the terms rightly used of those who bear the burdens of vice, loaded down by
vengeful demons and hostile powers. Of such people the great
prophet Isaiah, who was divinely possessed, . . . said that the offspring of asps carry "their riches on asses and camels," a statement that is not literal, having rather a spiritual sense. The savior, too, in directing his disciples "not to give what is holy to
dogs or cast pearls before swine," gives the direction in allegorical fashion, dogs and swine being the flatterers and pleasure-
lovers who take satisfaction in the impure mire. . . .[3] The dog,
remember, is a low-slung animal given to intemperate leaping
when enraged by a wasp, fawning and barking. Does not the
person bark who abuses his neighbor, as it were deafening him
with his accusations? Of such people the loud-voiced Isaiah
cries out, "They are all dumb dogs, ignorant of sound thinking,
evildoers." As such people are dogs, then, returning to their
vomit in addition to their other vices, those people would be
swine who, after being cleansed of the mire of their passions,
once more wallow in them. In reference to those of this attitude, that mighty disciple of Christ, Peter, writes, "It would have
been better for them not to have known the way of righteousness than, after knowing it, to turn back from the holy commandment passed on to them. The proverb has proved true in
their case, 'A dog returns to its own vomit, and a sow is washed
only to wallow in the mire.'"[4]

The savior forbade the giving of what is holy to such people
on account of their returning to the evil they had vomited up,
because after seeming to repent they returned to the sin they
had rejected. Just as one should not share with such people by
communicating to them the holy knowledge of the mysteries of
the kingdom of heaven, so one should not cast before swine
the divine pearls which are the words of the sages, the ornament of the interior man and his sense of hearing. Do not
these pearls adorn the person who believes in the one who says,

3. Is 30.6; Mt 7.6. Predictably, Didymus is not in accord with the opinion of a
modern commentator like Petersen, who writes, "It would be improper to treat
the poem as an allegory" (*Zechariah 9–14 and Malachi*, 81).

4. Is 56.11; 2 Pt 2.21–22; Prv 26.11.

"Give your ear to the words of the wise," and to God the Word, who says, "Incline your ear to the words of my mouth"? The lovely pearls that are so precious, which the merchant of the kingdom seeks and hunts down, the possessor must not cast before the swine in this sense, lest they trample them underfoot in their ignorance of their value and beauty.[5]

Sufficient texts have been cited as proof of the pejorative comparison of human beings with mindless beasts. There is now need to adduce passages showing that human beings are also likened favorably to behavior and movements of some animals. Are they not also referred to by the savior [saying], "My sheep listen to my voice," and again, "I am the good shepherd, and I give my life for my sheep"? Christ's sheep are those who behave equably and gently, and of their number the flock is composed, of whom the Holy Spirit says through the prophet, "The Lord will stand and see, and he will shepherd his flock in strength." In a similar spiritual sense the vessel of election, Paul, speaking in Christ, quoted the law, "You shall not muzzle an ox that treads the grain," and after quoting it went on, "Surely it is not for oxen that God is concerned? Is it not solely for our sake that he speaks"—that is, for the apostles? "Because the one who ploughs should plough, and the one who threshes should thresh in the hope of taking a share."[6]

Countless other such examples can be found by the person who attends to the reading of the divinely inspired Scripture; but lest the treatment be protracted needlessly, we should pass on to the text in hand about Lebanon and its trees that goes as follows: *Open your doors, Lebanon, and let fire consume your cedars. Let the pine lament because the cedar has fallen, because the mighty were in severe difficulties. Lament, oaks of Bashan, because the dense forest has been felled* (vv.1–2). The word Lebanon in an allegorical sense sometimes means "idolatry," sometimes "arrogance and conceitedness." In the Song of Songs, remember, the

5. Prv 5.1; Ps 78.1; Mt 13.45. Doutreleau (SC 85.808–9) finds "surprenante" the expression "God the Word" (redolent rather of the Antiochenes), and would like to amend it.

6. Jn 10.16, 14; Mi 5.4; Dt 25.4; 1 Cor 9.9–10 in Didymus's own text. He then rightly admits he is at risk of needlessly prolonging this preface to the chapter.

church from the nations is summoned by Christ her bridegroom: "Come hither from Lebanon, my spouse, you will come
and advance from the beginning of faith";[7] in other words, having received Christ's word from the beginning, she comes to
the one who calls her from the practice of vice to virtuous
morality, and from ignorance and disbelief to the knowledge of
God and a faith that has grown with her maturity. Just as, however, the text cited refers to Lebanon as the most impious cult
of idols and demons, so it highlights its arrogance in the verse,
"Lebanon will be transformed into Mount Carmel," that is to
say, conceitedness and presumption will be brought to the
knowledge of circumcision, which is called that of the heart
through the spirit (Carmel meaning "knowledge of circumcision").[8] The person who has this knowledge practices humility,
having learned from Jesus to be lowly in heart and spirit.

To this Lebanon in its twofold sense the inspired prophet—
or, rather, the Lord through him—gives the word to *open its
doors* so that the cedars within its doors may be devoured by fire.
The cedars are sinful demons and arrogant people, smashed by
the voice of the Lord, as is said in the twenty-ninth psalm in
these terms: "Voice of the Lord smashing cedars, the Lord will
smash the cedars of Lebanon." Against these trees, which are
wild and bear no edible fruit, it is written in Isaiah in addition to
other things, "The Lord of hosts has a day against all that is
proud, arrogant, lofty, and elevated," and a little further on,
"and against every cedar of Lebanon that is lofty and against
every oak tree of Bashan." These trees that are so wild are grown
for idolatry and arrogance, but are smashed and consumed by
fire along with those who bring arguments to their defense, according to the further saying in Isaiah, "Lebanon will topple
along with its lofty ones." In other words, idolatry will collapse
along with its advocates, demons, and argumentative people;
and likewise arrogant people along with their conceit will fall

7. Song 4.8, where the LXX has read the Heb. for "the crest of Anan" as "the
beginning of faith."

8. Heb 6.1; Is 29.17, where again the LXX reads the generic term for an or-
chard or fruitful region as the proper name Carmel (Didymus coming up with
another case of creative etymology); Rom 2.29.

when God resists the proud, according to the sentiment in the text in the divine Proverbs, "God resists the proud." In reference to such boastful people those who practice humility offer prayer to God, expressing it this way: "Raise your hands against their arrogance forever," and later in the same psalm, "The arrogance of those who hate you rose up constantly to you."[9]

To Lebanon as explained in the twofold sense the divine word gives the order to open its doors. Once arrogance and idolatry are opened and extended, in fact, the fire of punishment will devour *the cedars*, both the boastful people and also the arrogant demons, who are none other than "the rulers of this present world," and also human—or as Scripture puts it— "earthly wisdom," which gives instruction in "proud obstacles against the knowledge of God." When the cedars are consumed by fire, *the pines lament*, since the mighty (referred to as cedars) are fallen. Perhaps, on the one hand, the incorporeal powers of evil are called cedars, and, on the other, the people under their influence are known as pines, namely, heretics and sages of this world and age.[10] The obscure expression is clarified by the following phrase: *The mighty were in severe difficulties.* They are the ones glorying in their rule, not only human beings but also the incorporeal rulers of this age. In reference to these arrogant leaders, in Nahum, the seventh of the Twelve Prophets, there is a statement to Nineveh: "They will cast lots for your glory, and all your dignitaries will be bound in shackles," lest with unshackled and unfettered hands they commit forbidden actions. It is good, in fact, if "hands involved in injustice" be shackled.[11]

With the oaks of Bashan in severe difficulties, *the dense forest is felled.* Now, a forest is a place for wild trees that bear no nourishing fruit. It is felled, consumed by the fire because its foliage is dense. The oaks that are lamented, far from being inanimate plants, are in an allegorical sense human souls that are conceited and hostile powers. We should not be unaware that "oaks" in

9. Ps 29.5; Is 2.12–13; 10.34; Prv 3.34; Ps 74.3, 23.
10. 1 Cor 2.6; 2 Cor 1.12; 10.5. Having decided to take the opening verses allegorically instead of as a taunt to foreign nations, Didymus is forced to speculate about the meaning of each particular item mentioned.
11. Na 3.10; Ps 58.2.

the material sense refers at times to all trees, at times to a particular kind of tree; when we call all trees "oaks" [*drues*, δρύες], we speak of the one who fells them as a *druotomos* [δρυοτόμος] and what is made from them as *druina* [δρύινα], and hence we call the assemblage of timbers *druphaktoi* [δρύφακτοι] and fruits from trees *akrodrua* [ἀκρόδρυα]. In addition to the generic reference, there is a particular kind of tree that is an oak, as there is likewise a cypress, a silver fir, a box tree.

The doors of Lebanon which the divine word bids open, vile as they are, are the same as the doors of death, to which the psalmist in the ninth psalm refers in speaking of God: "He raised me from the gates of death." In reference to these, which belong to evil, the command is given to the sage in Proverbs, "Do not approach the doors of her house," and again in reference to all false thinking and impiety, "The foolish and audacious woman comes to need a morsel; she has no sense of shame, sitting as she does on a seat at the door of her house, brazenly inviting the passersby to the public places." The person who distances himself from these doors hammers on the doors of which the savior spoke, "Knock and it will be opened to you," to which Wisdom in Proverbs refers, "Blessed is the man who hearkens to me, and the one who will keep my ways, watching daily at my doors, observing the doorposts of my entrance."[12] The one who watches daily at these doors goes nowhere near the doors of what is personified as a loose woman of no sense, nor to those of Lebanon, which must be opened with the relaxation of their semblance of security so that what is kept within may reveal its unsightliness, be loathed and abandoned, with no one on the alert wishing to see it.

Now, the fact that the mention of different trees does not refer to inanimate things can be perceived from many texts, especially prophetic ones, which have to a degree been already cited. It suffices to recall one, that of the prophet Ezekiel, where Pharaoh and Assyria occur as trees, as it were. They are evil powers, tyrants respectively of Egypt and Assyria, with roots and

---

12. Ps 9.13; Prv 5.8; 9.13–15; Mt 7.7; Prv 8.34. The situation of the returned exiles does not enter Didymus's mind.

with branches growing high, thanks to abundant water; out of
envy they strive to emulate the trees of God's garden of delights, to have large boughs like those of firs and pines. I mean,
how could such tyrants be understood as rivaling even in thickness and imitating material trees, in whose branches and limbs
all the birds make their nest and where the wild beasts give
birth? For the prophecy to be easily comprehensible, however,
let us quote part of it to this effect: "Lo, Assyria, a cypress in
Lebanon, with beautiful branches, dense foliage, and great
height, its summit reaching to the very clouds. Water nourished
it; the deep made it grow tall, brought its streams round its
trunk, and dispatched its tributaries to all the trees of the plain.
This is why its growth outstrips all the trees of the plain, its
limbs are extended, and its branches elevated, thanks to abundant water. As a result of its growth all the birds of heaven nest-
ed in its branches, and under its limbs all the beasts of the plain
had their young, while in its shadow the whole multitude of nations made their dwelling. It was beautiful in its height on account of the vast number of its limbs, because its roots were
sunk into abundant water. Many cypresses and pines in God's
garden were no match for its branches, and there were no silver firs like its limbs. No tree in God's garden could match it
for beauty on account of the vast number of its limbs, and the
trees of God's garden of delight envied it."[13] The same or similar things as are said of Assyria are said also of Pharaoh.

We should not ignore the fact that most of our brethren see
in Pharaoh and Assyria a reference to the devil, who is presented allegorically in different senses, sometimes as Pharaoh,
sometimes as Assyria. Let those who adopt this interpretation
explain which trees of the garden resemble the devil—obviously not inanimate things but beings that are rational. It is not
surprising if names of trees stand for rational beings when even

---

13. Ezek 31.3–9. Doutreleau (SC 85.819) notes some differences in this text
from the major forms of the LXX. One might have thought that Didymus had
adequately made his point that the Zechariah text should be taken allegorically
without proceeding to this lengthy quotation of one of Ezekiel's celebrated allegories. He will admit below that he intended to write a commentary on Ezekiel
(apparently never composed).

God's wisdom is spoken of sometimes as a true vine, sometimes as a tree of life.[14]

A sound of shepherds lamenting the reversal of their greatness, a sound of lions roaring at the reduction in the Jordan's insolence (v.3). Those who in a priestly or a teaching role guide the people considered as sheep are their shepherds, while those who govern them as kings or tyrants are lions. And since the two types of rulers are called shepherds and lions, it necessarily follows that their subjects are referred to as sheep and other domestic animals—as sheep by allusion to those pasturing them, and as other domestic animals by allusion to the lions. It is said, for instance, in Proverbs, "A lion is stronger than domestic animals; he is not put to flight, nor does any animal scare him."[15]

The misfortune of those subjected to the teachers—or, rather, false teachers—and to the tyrannical masters is lamented by the shepherds, not out of pity for the flocks but because they were deprived of base gain and culpable pleasures, fearing that they might serve the God who gave the Law and who commissions them to govern rather than minister to their own belly. In reference to the heretics, the divinely inspired apostle writes in guidance to the peoples of the Church, "Do not be carried away by all kinds of strange teachings: it is good to be strengthened by grace," and again, "For such teachers serve, not Christ, but their own belly, and by smooth talk and flattery they deceive the hearts of the innocent," since in their simplicity they are animals easily led.[16]

These people who are in difficulties, then, lament the pleasures they long for, since there is *a reversal of the greatness* they were deceived into thinking they possessed. Likewise, too, those who rule in wrath roar aloud, since there is a *reduction in the Jordan* where they hunted and lay hidden, thinking they had

14. Jn 15.1; Rv 22.14. By the "brethren" Doutreleau (SC 85.820) thinks Didymus has in mind commentators generally. In his commentary on this chapter of Ezekiel, Theodoret, PG 81.1124, does allow for some reference to the devil after seeing Pharaoh and Assyria principally in focus; he possibly has Didymus in mind.

15. Prv 30.30.

16. Acts 20.29; Heb 13.9; Rom 16.18.

protection and security on account of their ferocity. With many trees already cut down and felled, as has just been said, the dense forest has been laid low. You can find much in Scripture suggesting the cruelty and ferocity of those governing in wrath, who are rightly called lions. For instance, in the prophet Jeremiah the cruel ruler of Babylon and the tyrant of Assyria are referred to as lions; the prophetic text goes this way: "Israel is a straying sheep, lions pursued it: first the king of Assyria consumed it, and later the king of Babylon its bones."[17] It is in this sense that the passage in the fifty-eighth psalm about people and evil powers should also be taken: "They have anger in a way similar to a serpent, like an asp that is deaf and stops its ears, that will not hearken to the command of the charmer, drugged with drugs from a sage. God smashed their teeth in their mouths, the Lord broke the lions' molars." We do not believe, in fact, that there is anyone so naïve as to suppose that only the molars of the material lions were smashed while the rest of their bodies remained unharmed.[18]

The Lord almighty says this: Shepherd the sheep of slaughter. Those who acquired them killed them without repenting, and those who sold them said, Blessed be the Lord, we are rich. And their shepherds were unaffected by them (vv.4–5). Of those appointed for instructing and shepherding the rational flock, some govern according to the will of God, others with impiety and deceit. It is possible to adduce texts from Scripture in reference to both groups of shepherds. It is said by God about those who commendably perform the commission assigned them, "I shall give them"—the flocks, that is—"shepherds after my own heart, and they will shepherd them by being shepherds with knowledge." Of such knowledgeable leaders of the flock the Christ-bearing apostle makes mention as people appointed in the Church

17. Jer 50.17. A modern commentator like Petersen takes a similar view of this "reduction in the Jordan" as the loss of natural vegetation, and likewise sees a relationship with earlier material in Jeremiah (though rather with Jer 25.34–38); see *Zechariah 9–14 and Malachi*, 82.

18. Ps 58.4–6, verses that Dahood classes as "some of the most difficult phrases in the Psalter" (Anchor Bible 17, 57). Yet Didymus is prepared to make the lengthy quotation of a difficult passage to reinforce his point (that hardly needs further reinforcement) of scriptural allegory.

along with apostles and prophets, teachers and evangelists.[19] Perhaps apostles and prophets, teachers and evangelists are those who with knowledge and understanding instruct the assembly of Christ, while the shepherds are those who are involved in the active life and preside over good works, transmitting in an uncomplicated way the faith and counsels of Christian people. Those who on account of their depravity are the direct opposite of the knowledgeable shepherds are the ones called impious; it is of them and of those responsible for other evils that God says, for instance, "Priests have not said, Where is the Lord? Those in possession of my Law have not known me, and the shepherds acted impiously towards me," and so on.[20]

People so impious are also promiscuous: while they are perhaps guilty of licentious behavior, they have relations in particular with the demons that introduce devious and novel teachings and with "the clever ideas of the rulers of this age." For instance, "those who did not see fit to acknowledge God and were given up to a debased mind are guilty of improper behavior, having lustful desires for one another, males committing shameless acts with males, females exchanging the intercourse natural to females for unnatural, and women having lewd desires for women." In addition to licentious behavior in a physical sense, the shepherds who act impiously towards God have relations also with evil powers, as is said in the Psalms to the source of piety, "Lo, those keeping their distance from you will perish; you destroyed everyone who was unfaithful to you. For me, on the contrary, it is good to cleave to God." In reference to the impious pastors the statement is made in Jeremiah to the unfaithful soul, "To your shame you have taken to yourself

19. Jer 3.15; Eph 4.11; 1 Cor 12.28. Didymus does not gain the impression felt by some modern commentators that this prophecy (Zec 11.4–5) is the most enigmatic in the Old Testament; to him it refers simply to good and bad pastors in the Church, even if their roles have to be distinguished from those the NT acknowledges. He does not, however, spend time distinguishing among the roles of sellers, buyers (or owners), and shepherds, as the text requires. Jerome, interestingly, contests both responses: it is a *manifestissima prophetia*, and *superflua est tropologiae interpretatio* (CCL 76A.850).
20. Jer 2.8.

many shepherds," and again, "You prostituted yourself with many shepherds, and hypocritically you kept returning to me, says the Lord."[21]

Once the good shepherds are separated from the bad, a command is given to the knowledgeable ones to this effect: *Shepherd the sheep of slaughter,* that is, those already slaughtered, or due to suffer that fate, or objects of unjust plotting. These last are referred to in the forty-fourth psalm, where those whose death is plotted say to God their benefactor, "For your sake we are being put to death all day long, we are reckoned as sheep for slaughter," and again, "You gave us like sheep for eating." They are, in fact, slaughtered by the lawless governors for no other purpose than to be food for those of whom it is said, "When people rose up against us, then they would have swallowed us alive." But their murderous frenzy was frustrated, with the result that those who were rescued said in gratitude, "Blessed be the Lord, who did not give us as a prey to their teeth."[22] Those who give the impression of being owners, and not shepherds of the flock committed to them, slaughter the sheep with a blade (namely, their subtle argumentation that masks their impious ideas) without caring or repenting of their deeds of murderous robbery; they therefore sell what is not theirs as though their own, of course, brazenly boasting without shame of becoming rich. The pastors who are anxious to please the sovereign who has entrusted the flock to them do not slaughter or sell, for the purpose of getting rich from avarice or base gain, the rational sheep committed to them.

Lest such an abomination happen through negligence on the part of the leaders of the Church, Peter, the head of the apostles, writes in these terms: "I urge the elders among you to shepherd the flock in your midst not reluctantly but willingly, not lording it over those in your charge, so that at the coming of the chief priest and shepherd Christ Jesus you may be award-

21. 1 Cor 2.6; Rom 1.26–28; Ps 73.26–27; Jer 3.3, 1. The picture of clerical behavior (in Didymus's own church?) is bleak, though the relevance of the Jeremiah citation depends on the misreading by the LXX of similar Heb. forms for "friend" and "shepherd."
22. Pss 44.22, 11; 124.2, 6.

ed the unfading crown of glory." Clearly, those who lord it over Christ's sheep as negligent shepherds sell God's sheep for base gain, and so cry aloud, *We are rich*, devouring those whom they do away with by their scandal. When the people (referred to allegorically as sheep) were harmed and abused, the falsely named shepherds *were unaffected by them*, not suffering with the flock like the one who says, "Who is weak, and I am not weak? Who is made to stumble, and I am not indignant?" The godly teachers are encouraged to have this love by the savior, who is a model for them, so that the evangelist John, a sharer in divine wisdom, proclaims to those with reverence for God in the style of Christ, "He"—namely, Christ—"laid down his life as a ransom for us, and we ought to lay down our lives for one another."[23] People with this attitude towards those of the same dispositions, who with brotherly love think and feel alike, oppose those who slaughter the sheep entrusted to them, who claim with audacity, *We are rich*, for base gain we have acquired sheep, *and are unaffected* after devouring them.

Hence I shall no longer spare the inhabitants of the earth, says the Lord. Lo, I shall surrender all people into the hands of their neighbors and into the hands of their king. They will destroy the earth, and I shall not rescue them from their hand. I shall shepherd the sheep of slaughter in the land of Canaan (vv.6–7). Since those entrusted with the care of the rational sheep scorned them to the point of having no feeling or concern for their welfare, and even selling them to strangers for base gain, the Lord almighty threatens to have pity no longer on the earth—that is, those who live there. The weaker ones will be surrendered to those who lord it over them by the cruelty and power they think they have, with the result that all those on earth will be laid low, all being surrendered into the hands of their neighbors and their king, who governs no longer lawfully but despotically.

God delivers this in the style of a threat so that through fear of what is expected those for whom the threat is meant may stop sinning. In fact, God will never cease having pity on his creatures, as the Wisdom of Solomon in all its virtues says, "You

23. 1 Pt 5.1–4; 2 Cor 11.29; Mt 20.28; 1 Jn 3.16.

spare all things, Lord, in your love for souls, loathing nothing you have made, nor hating what you have created"; "for you created everything to have existence, and the generative forces of the world are wholesome." Having experienced this surpassing goodness of the one who sustains everything and shows universal providence, his servants intercede for the people in the words, "Have pity on your people, Lord, and do not expose your inheritance to the shame of being in the power of the nations, lest the nations ever say, Where is their God?"[24]

The one who is the cause of all and their provider showed such pity for the human race as to surrender to death for the sake of everyone his own Son for the redemption of the dead from being under the reign of death. Introducing people to this surpassing salvation, the apostle writes of God, "Far from sparing his own Son, he surrendered him for us: will he not also give us everything else with him?" To spare us, he did not spare his Son; whereas he is impassible and proof against all harm, we are mortal and vulnerable to passions. Hence, if he had spared his Son by not giving him up "to taste death on behalf of everyone,"[25] we would have remained in the grip of ruination through transgression of the divine commandment. Instead, for us to become free, in his providence he surrendered his own Son, who was not due to incur the harm of dying, but who proved to be savior of all by being surrendered for them.

This being so, if God says, *I shall no longer spare the inhabitants of the earth*, he admonishes by instilling fear through a threat to prevent their incurring punishment, and instead for them to elude the power of sin, thus no longer being subject to punishment. He reveals the manner of his no longer sparing them by saying that he will *surrender all people into the hands of their neighbors and into the hands of the* evil *king* they have chosen, with the result that they *will destroy the earth*, since those opposed to one another will "die like mortals." These are the people who by quarreling and jealousy walk according to the flesh;[26] people like that are surrendered into the hands of demons who pos-

---

24. Wis 11.26, 24; 1.14; Jl 2.17.   25. Rom 5.14; 8.32; Heb 2.9.
26. Ps 82.7; Rom 13.13.

sess their neighbors on the score of their love of pleasure and
their materialistic attitude. It is then, in fact, that they can
be admonished, when surrendered to those they considered
friends and neighbors, and experiencing their cruelty and ferocity; they will also flee the tyrannical ruler on experiencing
his hardheartedness. The Hebrew people at one time, of
course, likewise longed to be free from the Egyptians' audacity
in the knowledge of the hardship and harsh government imposed by them.

With the earth destroyed—that is, with those upon it at odds
with one another—God *shepherds the sheep of slaughter in the land
of Canaan*, the retribution prepared for them. It was said before
as well that *the sheep of slaughter* were those ready for suffering
and those already slaughtered, when we quoted the statement
made to their benefactor by those in distress, "You have given
us like sheep for eating," and again, "We were reckoned like
sheep for slaughter."[27] Take note as to whether there is something commendable in the shepherding of the sheep for
slaughter in the land of *Canaan*, which means "prepared," perhaps because those treated with abuse are brought to a safe
haven, which is not to be regretted and is the result of the hardships imposed for their instruction. The divinely inspired apostle Paul describes it in writing, "Godly grief produces repentance that results in salvation and brings no regret, whereas
worldly grief produces death"[28]—hence the latter is to be avoided, and to be replaced by [the grief] that is godly and brings
not regret but salvation from God.

*I shall take for myself two staffs; one I called Beauty, and the other I
called Cord; I shall shepherd the sheep. I shall remove three shepherds in
one month. My soul will be depressed by them; their souls roared at me.
And I said, I shall not shepherd you* (vv.7–9). In the person of the
savior the prophet Zechariah reports the facts about two staffs

27. Ps 44.11, 22, cited in comment on 11.4.
28. 2 Cor 7.10. Though Didymus is apparently taking the phrase in his text
(lit., "to the Canaanite") to mean "to the land of Canaan," this latter phrase appears only in the Antioch form of the text as read by Theodoret. Despite his
conjectured etymology of Canaan, modern versions (NRSV) and commentators
see "merchants" (or here specifically sheep dealers) in the term.

he took for himself. Nothing more is signified by the two staffs in the present text than scepters of government, or rather of kingship, of which they are symbols. Since, then, the whole human race is divided into the people of the circumcision and the Church called from the nations, the God of Jews and gentiles,[29] being together their savior and king, took the two scepters for himself so as to produce one kingdom from the two.

Now, the interpretation of the prophecy will be gained from the text of the Gospel: just as one kingdom under one king emerged from believers from nations and Jews, so, too, there is one flock under the one true shepherd, who gave his life for the sheep. The Gospel statement made by the savior runs as follows: "I have other sheep that are not of this fold; those, too, I must gather, and they will hear my voice, so that there may be one flock and one shepherd," meaning that the other sheep are not from the Jewish fold, but are the believers in the Gospel from the nations. The two flocks under one shepherd are the same as the two scepters held by the same king. This will be accomplished when effect is given to the statement, "Rejoice, nations, with his people."[30]

A different interpretation could be given to the verse, "I have other sheep that are not of this fold," the sheepfold referring to this earthly world in which those with a body still live, whereas souls freed from it live for the time being in the nether regions and were gathered by the good shepherd, who came to them when "he died for everyone" "so as to be lord of the living and the dead."[31] If, then, there is one lord of dead and living with royal power and pastoral skill, the two flocks and kingdoms will emerge as one. When this happens, the multiple rule will cease, with the true shepherd removing *the three shepherds* ruling wickedly *in one month*, that is, all together at one time.

Now, there is need to inquire who are the three leaders of

29. Rom 3.29. The continuing obscurity of reference of the Zechariah text encourages Didymus to proceed immediately to an eschatological interpretation. He does well for the moment not to dwell further on the symbolic value of the staffs, their names suffering at the hands of the LXX, as will emerge.

30. Jn 10.11, 16; Rom 15.10; Dt 32.43 LXX.

31. 2 Cor 5.14; Rom 14.9.

the flock who are due to be removed. The priestly caste of the Jews, those wrongly called prophets by them, and those who reigned after Jeroboam: they were all responsible for harm to those they ruled. It is said, for instance, in Hosea, "Priests hid the way of the Lord, they murdered Shechem, they committed iniquity in Israel," and again in the same prophet, "Israel will be abused like the deranged prophet." It is possible to find many things written as well about the lawless reign which has rent the people of God, including the following verse: "Hear this, you priests, and give ear, house of the king, for against you is the judgment that you have been a snare for the summit, and like a net spread over Tabor." Against those who gave poor leadership, the holy Jeremiah also cries aloud in severe censure in the person of the sovereign God, "Priests did not say, Where is the Lord? Those who handle the Law did not know me, the prophets gave wrong prophecy, and the shepherds committed impiety towards me and took useless directions."[32]

We should examine whether the three shepherds behaving impiously towards him refer to the other kings of Israel as well as the priests and prophets. We should not ignore the fact that the false teachers are also called shepherds behaving impiously towards God. Interpreted this way, the three shepherds are removed in one month by "the truly great high priest, Jesus, who has passed through the heavens," a true prophet, of whom a divine prediction says, "The Lord God will raise up for you a prophet from your brethren." In addition to being high priest and prophet, he is also king, and thus the Father says of him, "I raised him up as king, and all his ways are straight; he will build my city, and will reverse the captivity of my people without ransom or gifts." So it is he, the one who builds the spiritual city of God and ransoms the people, who says of himself, "I was established as king by him on Sion his holy mountain, I announce the Lord's command."[33]

32. Hos 6.9–10; 9.7; 5.1; Jer 2.8. Though Didymus could not pass up the temptation to identify the three shepherds, for whom commentators have nominated any number of possibilities (as does Theodore with a disclaimer about the significance of numbers; Sprenger ed., 381), he confines himself to one or two.
33. Heb 4.14; Dt 18.15; Is 45.13 (in reference to Cyrus); Ps 2.6–7.

In addition to the interpretations given of the three shepherds, it should be noted that the three culpable pastors being removed are those who behave impiously to the Trinity: some of them are greatly inclined to show impiety to the Father, others to the Son, and others to the Holy Spirit. On the one hand, those of the Son-Father opinion have false ideas of the Father, depriving the Father (to the extent of their impiety) of the only-begotten Son, who is God the Word of both wisdom and truth. Others have false ideas about his origins in particular, thinking he is created from nothing. And there are those who contest the Spirit, believing he is one of the created things. The three groups of people in error have ungodly ideas about the Trinity, although each reveals a particular kind of impious tendency, as has already been remarked. The shepherds guilty of such impiety *will be removed in one month;* in other words, for the period of the present life the false teaching makes promises, which will be brought to nothing when perfect illumination comes from the true light after the present evil age and temporary life. Those who hope in it alone are more to be pitied than anyone.[34]

The removal of the three lazy leaders of the flock happens when the soul of the king making these threats *is depressed by them,* especially since they do what is hateful to him. His *soul* is explicable in many ways. One way, which is the literal one, is what he has as a perfect human being,[35] and he lays it down so as to take it up again. On the one hand, then, he lays it down in giving it as a ransom for many, so that it is described in these terms by John, who introduces us to truth: "He laid down his life for us, and we ought to lay down our lives for one another." On the other hand, he took it up in rising from the dead "without its being abandoned to Hades." By another interpretation the soul of the savior saying these things is every person so

---

34. 1 Jn 2.8; Gal 1.4; 1 Cor 15.19. Didymus has in mind the views of Sabellians and Pneumatomachians, who disputed the status of Son and Spirit.

35. Doutreleau (SC 85.848) sees this observation as a precaution against charges of Apollinarianism, Apollinarius having denied a human soul to Jesus, a denial that Kelly, *Early Christian Doctrines*, 290, declares "a permanent feature in the Alexandrian tradition."

closely related to him as to be styled a person "in Christ," so that there is no difference in referring to him as a man of God or a soul of God; Elijah, remember, styled a man of God, could also be called a soul of God, and likewise Moses the revealer and anybody else sharing in the same holiness and virtue.[36] There is no need of many testimonies at present, however, as the proof has been given many times already; it suffices to cite the word of Paul and Peter: the former wrote, "Let every soul"—that is, every person—"be subject to the governing authorities," and the latter, "That is, eight souls were saved,"[37] referring by eight souls to those saved in the ark in the flood: Noah, his three sons, his wife, and the three partners of his sons.

What is referred to as God's soul *is depressed* by the three shepherds who were removed in one month, and is indignant along with the savior who removes them. Their removal occurs on account of *their souls roaring* like lions through savagery at the true shepherd. After the description of the shepherds' cruelty, the good leader of the flock says to the sheep lost by the lazy pastors, *I shall not shepherd you,* by way of a threat, especially because they were still subject to the harmful ones, who were not yet removed. The clause, *I shall remove three shepherds,* in fact shows that they were still in charge of the flocks deceived by them.

Now, how and why one staff was called *Beauty* and the other *Cord* will be clarified in the texts not yet cited. With God's help, we should continue. *Let the dying die, the faulty fail, and let the ones who are left eat the flesh of their neighbors* (v.9). With the good shepherd in charge of the flock, each of the sheep is cared for in the proper way. The Lord Jesus says, for instance, "My sheep listen to my voice and follow me, and I give them eternal life, and they will never perish." The result is that each of those making up the divine flock cries aloud in reference to the leader of the flock, "The Lord is my shepherd, and there is nothing I shall want. In a green place is where he settled me;

36. Mt 20.28; 1 Jn 3.16; Acts 2.31; 2 Cor 12.2; 2 Kgs 1.9.
37. Rom 13.1; 1 Pt 3.20.

with restful waters he fed me; he revived my soul. He guided me on the paths of righteousness for his name's sake."[38]

Though the rational nurslings are cared for in this way, they are left to their own devices by the one who says, *I shall not shepherd you.* So quite the opposite fate happens to the flocks: now *the dying die,* being at a distance from the shepherd who says of his sheep, "I have come that they may have life, and have it in abundance, since I lay down my life for my sheep."[39] In addition to the death of the dying, the *failing will fail* because of being deprived of protection, and so all of those bereft of their particular pasture will devour the flesh of their neighbors, taking a turn to savagery. When the church of the Galatians succumbed to this cruelty, these words were rightly addressed to it by the apostle Paul: "If you bite and devour one another, take care you are not consumed by one another." The psalmist sings about ferocious enemies of his, "When evildoers pressed upon me to devour my flesh"; yet despite their being of such dispositions, he remained unhurt and said, "Those who distressed me and my foes themselves fainted and fell." And the prophet Jeremiah says of those who like wild beasts are bent on harming the devout, "Israel is holy to the Lord, the first-fruits of his produce; all who devour it will sin, trouble will befall them, says the Lord."[40]

Now, it is also to the good that the verse says that they *eat the flesh of their neighbors,* not the soul or spirit of the neighbor. The person rescued from this cruelty cries aloud in gratitude for himself and his familiars, "Blessed be the Lord, who has not given us as prey to their teeth."[41]

I shall take my beautiful staff and cast it aside to cancel my covenant that I made with all the peoples of the earth. It will be canceled on that day, and the Canaanites will know, the sheep that are protected, because it is the word of the Lord (vv.10–11). With the abandonment of the people of the circumcision by the shepherd on account of their impious behavior to him, they encountered disasters befalling them, the result being that *the dying died and*

38. Jn 10.27–28; Ps 23.1–3.   39. Jn 10.10, 15.
40. Gal 5.15; Ps 27.2; Jer 2.3.   41. Ps 124.6.

the faulty failed, and the remnant were so overwhelmed that *they ate the flesh of their neighbors.* A calling comes to the church of those of the nations who found faith in Christ, [the church being] referred to as a commendable staff—that is, a kingdom— when he says, *I shall take my beautiful staff.* This happens when the Father says to the Son, "Ask of me, and I shall give you nations for your inheritance."[42] When the royal scepter was *cast aside* by the one who receives all the nations as an inheritance, *the covenant made with all the peoples was canceled;* it is said of it in the great song in Deuteronomy in these terms: "When the Most High apportioned the nations, when he dispersed the sons of Adam, he fixed the boundaries of the nations according to the number of God's angels."[43] When this covenant was canceled by Christ, and the angels of the nations were no longer in command, all the nations became the heritage and portion of the one who cast aside the beautiful staff to dissolve the covenant with all the peoples.

This excellent achievement was effected on the day arranged by the sun of justice, which the father of all the believing nations, Abraham, was most glad to see. That is to say, everyone who composed the nations was blessed in his offspring, provided they had his faith, which was reckoned as righteousness. In reference to this day the whole band of saintly people and also angels sing in these terms: "This is the day the Lord had made; let us be glad and rejoice in it." They are its sons, and the savior said to them, " You are the light of the world"; "the day has come, let us conduct ourselves soberly as in the daylight."[44] With the completion of these divine acts of power, *the Canaanites will know, as the sheep that are protected, that it is the word of the Lord,* which has to do with the matters in hand—the staff and the covenant with all the peoples, which should be understood as suggesting the great supernatural mysteries. The Canaanites should be understood as those from

42. Ps 2.8. All commentators, ancient and modern, are at a loss to explain how these verses apply to Zechariah's time.

43. Dt 32.8.

44. Mal 4.2; Rom 4.3, 16, 17; Jn 8.56; Ps 118.24; 1 Thes 5.5; Mt 5.15; Rom 13.12–13.

the nations "prepared" to become the inheritance of the Son of God on account of their adoption of the humility of the one who said, "Learn of me that I am gentle and humble of heart, and you will find rest for your souls."[45]

I shall say to them, If it is good in your sight, set my wages, and give them or decline. They set my wages at thirty pieces of silver. The Lord said to me, Throw them into the smelter and see if it proves true in the way I was tested for them. I took the thirty pieces of silver, threw them into the house of the Lord, into the smelter (vv.12–13). The prophetic verses, which are stated in an obscure fashion, all of a sudden pass from the person of the speakers to those to whom they refer; their interpretation can be established and proven from reference to many passages in Scripture. To avoid prolonging the treatment, however, the text from Jeremiah should be cited in the person of God that reads as follows: "Run through the streets of Jerusalem and see if there is someone practicing faith and mercy" (or "judgment," in one of the manuscripts), "and I said, As the Lord lives, they say; hence they do not swear with falsehood." In other words, after God says to the holy men, "Run through the squares of Jerusalem and see if there is anyone doing such things there," and those in receipt of the order reply, "As the Lord lives, they say," and God says to them, "Hence they do not swear with falsehood."[46] Notice how many changes of speaker there are in these few successive phrases, differentiated not in the text but by the meaning. As this is the case in the text quoted, then, so is it also in the verse cited from Zechariah: the savior speaks (he being the one who gives voice to the words before us about the removal of those of the circumcision), and continues by making reference to the calling of the nations who at that time were idol-worshipers. He then begins afresh on another topic: In reply I said to them, namely, the Jews: *If it is good and just in your sight, give me as my wages* what you have *set*, that is, determined; but if not, *decline*, rejecting my terms. They agreed that *my wages* are *thirty pieces of silver*.

45. Mt 11.29. For Didymus's conjectured etymology of Canaan, see n. 28.
46. Jer 5.1–2. Didymus adjusts the text to suit, and even looks to manuscript variants, a rare piece of textual criticism. As often, he prefers to subject the illustrative text to exegesis rather than the set reading.

Now, the wages and the silver should be taken in a spiritual sense. In many places in the divine teaching, in fact, words and discourse are referred to by this term: "The words of the Lord are pure words, silver tested by fire in the earth, seven times purified." And again it is said in Proverbs, "The tongue of the righteous is silver tested by fire," speech being referred to by the word "tongue." And since not all silver in an allegorical sense is commendable but also base, God therefore says to the false teachers of Israel, "Your silver is impure," blame falling not on material coinage but on deceitful talking. And in reference to those guilty of it God says to people of insight, "Call them rejected silver, because the Lord has rejected" the generation responsible for it, that is, for deceitful and forbidden behavior. Capable of this interpretation is the oracle in Proverbs that goes as follows: "Silver given with deceit is to be regarded as a potsherd." The misleading and contentious arguments proposed deceitfully by the sophists, even if seeming to deal with important subjects referred to as "elevated topics raised against the knowledge of God," should likewise be regarded as a potsherd. An example is what "people of an earthly mentality" propose, who, Isaiah said, "raise their voice from the earth."[47]

There is thus a difference in the kinds of spiritual silver: those from the circumcision set at thirty pieces of silver the wages of the one who suffered for them, and the Father says to the one receiving the thirty pieces of silver, *Throw them into the smelter and see if* the silver given them *proves true in the way I was tested for them.* This, in fact, is the way it will become clear if they provided a recompense commensurate with the hardship I underwent for them, "laying down my life and giving it as a ransom for many." When the Father had said this, namely, *Throw the thirty pieces of silver into the smelter,* the one "who was obedient

47. Ps 12.6; Prv 10.20; Is 1.22; Jer 6.30; Prv 26.23 LXX; 2 Cor 10.5; Phil 3.19; Is 8.19. The Heb. term (which the NRSV renders as "treasury") appearing as "smelter" in the LXX ("potter" in the Syriac) leads Didymus off into notions of true and false doctrines, no reference being made to its applicability to Zechariah's situation. He will make mention more than once of a potsherd, as though aware of the occurrence of the term in prophetic texts in reference to potters and pottery.

to the point of death"[48] immediately discharged the order, saying, *I took the thirty pieces of silver and threw them into the house of the Lord, into the smelter.*

When this was accomplished, it was revealed that the recompense of the Pharisees and the others from the circumcision was false, thus being considered a potsherd by those scrutinizing the Scriptures that testify to the savior, who uttered them. In many places in the Gospels, remember, censure is directed against those accused of false words, such as in the verse, "This people honors me with their lips, but their heart is far from me; in vain do they worship me, teaching human precepts and doctrines," while canceling God's commandment for the sake of their pernicious tradition. They are likewise censured for mounting a false case about the obligation to pay tribute to Caesar or not, the result being that they were convicted of deception on this and their claims and of speaking with utter trickery; in dialogue with them the savior said, "Show me a coin, and tell whose image and inscription it is." When they said, "Caesar's," they were severely censured by being told, "Render to Caesar what is Caesar's, then, and to God what is God's."[49]

It is not only the Jews who accosted Jesus to test him that are guilty of false discourse, however, but also those within Christianity, heretics teaching false doctrines, "practicing cunning and falsifying the word of the Lord," mistaking and distorting the meaning of the divinely inspired sayings; there is need to give them a wide berth, treating like a potsherd their false words, which are worthless silver. Are not the words worthless of those who posit two uncreated principles, a good and an evil (these people being the Manicheans)? and of those who claim the Son is a creature, and who separate the Holy Spirit from Father and Son? and the words of those who show no reverence for the Incarnation of the savior, maintaining that the savior came in appearance and not in reality?[50]

48. Mt 20.28; Phil 2.8.
49. Mt 15.8, 6; Is 29.13; Mt 22.17–21.
50. 2 Cor 4.2. Didymus applies the idea of dross to a wide range of heretical

It is not only the false silver, however, that will be revealed by the smelter of the house of God, but also the true silver bearing the image and stamp of the sovereign savior, "purified seven times"; we must hold on to it and be enriched by possessing it. There are those who take the view that the thirty pieces of silver which Judas got from the Jews to betray the Lord are suggested also by the text in hand, and that it is the severest condemnation of the Jews for giving and of Judas for taking the thirty pieces of silver for the betrayal. In fact, they should have given them as recompense to the one who suffered for their salvation and that of the whole world, and not have "the one who gives life to everyone" done away with.[51] The blasphemies which the Jews uttered against the savior when he was crucified for all creation should be cast into the house of the divinely inspired Scriptures and the smelter within it for their dissonance to be proven or, rather, their opposition to the prophecies about Christ and his cross.

I cast aside the second staff, Cord, to cancel the covenant between Judah and Israel (v.14). Our savior and Lord had taken up two staffs, one of which he called *Beauty* and the other *Cord;* in first casting aside the one named *Beauty* he revealed the mysteries already clarified. In now casting aside the one referred to as *Cord* he canceled the covenant between Israel and Judah. It is possible to learn again from the great song what the staff called *Cord* is. The verses of the song cited before go this way: "When the Most High apportioned the nations, when he scattered the sons of Adam, he set the boundaries of the nations by the number of God's angels; Jacob was the Lord's portion; his people, Israel, the cord of his inheritance." This refers to the whole of the Hebrew nation as one staff and one portion. The nation survived for a long time in its entirety, being styled one staff, in keeping with the statement in the Psalms to the king and provider of all: "Remember your congregation, which you acquired from the beginning; you redeemed a staff of your inheritance." This one

---

positions within Christianity: Manichean, Arian, pneumatomachian, docetic. He will proceed to include the gnostics.

51. Ps 12.6; Mt 26.15; Neh 9.6.

kingdom was divided into two governments, with the result that one was called Judah and the other Ephraim, those remaining in Jerusalem being governed by those of the tribe of Judah, who had succession from the house of David, while the others went down to Samaria and had as their leader Jeroboam from the tribe of Ephraim, who led Israel into sin.[52] The unfortunate division continued for a long time, since the king of Judah and the tyrant of Samaria stood aloof and had their differences until God had pity, re-establishing the twelve tribes as a single kingdom with Judah alone in control as before the division.

There is mention of this restoration in Hosea the prophet, where the sovereign says, "The sons of Israel and the sons of Judah will be brought together, and will establish for themselves one government and will come up from the land, because great will be the day of Jezreel."[53] There is need to give attention to this prophecy, revealing as it does that those established in a single kingdom will come up from the land—those, that is, who are below in the land in the sense of being at odds with one another when separated from a unifying government. The covenant of the division[54] was in force for a time between Judah and Israel, and its rupture and dissolution happened by permission of the savior, the purpose being that, with the removal of the difference in the divisions, the staff called *Cord* might be held as before by a single king, the one with succession from Judah, so that there would be one flock and one shepherd under the legitimate king ruling the whole nation.[55]

There is reference to such a restoration of two kingdoms into one legitimate government also in the prophet Ezekiel. The prophetic passage goes as follows: "A word of the Lord came to me in these terms: Son of man, get yourself a staff and write on it, Judah and the sons of Israel associated with it. You are to take a second staff and write on it, For Joseph (the

---

52. Dt 32.8–9; Ps 74.2; 1 Kgs 14.16. This time, by contrast, Didymus endeavors to explore the historical situation hinted at by the analogy in the text.

53. Hos 1.11.

54. Doutreleau (SC 85.868) finds the phrase unclear, suggesting a version "for the division" or "before the division."

55. Jn 10.16.

staff of Ephraim) and all the sons of Israel associated with it. You will join them together so as to bind them into one stick, and they will be in your hand. When the sons of your people say, Are you not telling us what these things mean to you? you will say to them, The Lord, the Lord says this: Lo, I shall take the tribe of Joseph from the hand of Ephraim and the tribes of Israel associated with him, and give them to the tribe of Judah. The staffs on which you wrote will be in your hand before them, and you will say to them, The Lord, the Lord says this: Lo, I am taking the whole house of Israel from the midst of the nations where they have gone, and shall assemble them from all those round about them, and shall bring them into the land of Israel. I shall make them one nation in my land and on the mountains of Israel; one ruler will be king over them all, and they will no longer be two nations, and no more divided into two kingdoms." And further on, "I shall purify them, and they will be my people, and I shall be their God. My servant David will rule in their midst, and there will be one shepherd over all, because they will walk in my commands, and observe my judgments and perform them. They will dwell in their land, which I gave to my servant Jacob." And a little further on: "My servant David will be their ruler forever. I shall make with them a covenant of peace; it will be an eternal covenant with them, and I shall establish my sanctuary in their midst forever. My habitation will be among them; I shall be their God, and they will be my people. The nations will know that I am the Lord who sanctifies them by the presence of my sanctuary in their midst forever."[56]

With the clarification of the consistency of the obscure prophecy with the division of one government into two kingdoms and their restoration to a single government in keeping with the prophecy of Hosea, we should proceed from the literal sense to understand in a spiritual sense the two staffs that the Son of man took for himself. That is to say, we should accept

56. Ezek 37.16–28. Still pursuing the historical situation in the mind of Zechariah, Didymus not surprisingly sees a connection with the Ezekiel passage, for which in Petersen's view "some commentators have argued too quickly" (*Zechariah 9–14 and Malachi*, 97).

that what is signified by them is the callings of the two peoples, from the nations and from the circumcision, united in a single royal scepter, in keeping with the sense of the apostolic writing which runs as follows: "He is our peace, making both groups into one and breaking down the dividing wall so as to create in himself one new humanity in place of the two," the Greek and the Jew. You see, since one acted as Jew and the other as Greek, there were two staffs and two men arising out of the difference in religion, making it impossible for them to serve one king. But when the true leader appeared to whom the saints say, "Your kingship is a kingship for all the ages," then all men became visibly one people, called to serve one God and king who "brought the good news of peace for those far off and peace for those nearby,"[57] so that together in the Spirit they might be made into one kingdom serving one God and king.

The people called from the nations is the staff on which is written "Judah," "the one who confesses," while that from the circumcision is the scepter dedicated to Joseph. Each of the two staffs in the obscure passage would be clarified in detail in each case in the work on Ezekiel if God in his goodness were to call us to treat of this subject.[58] As present needs require, however, we employ allegory. When the two governments became one staff, the one raised up by God in the flesh from David was raised by the Father; he has become the eternal shepherd and king by the Incarnation, recognized as the mediator of an eternal covenant of peace, and will reign without end in stability and peace forever, his reign never to end.[59] It is in keeping with this peaceful condition obtaining among the subjects that holy gifts of God's kingdom are given—namely, sacraments—by the generous giver himself who dwells in the midst of those who are both saved and sanctified. Such a great and marvelous good was made available at the time of the Incarnation, when the

57. Eph 2.14–15; Ps 145.13; Eph 2.17.
58. Such a commentary on Ezekiel (which seems not to have been completed), Didymus implies, would delve further into the historical situation lying behind this figure of the two staffs, whereas for the moment he has to be content with an allegorical interpretation and move to a New Testament fulfillment.
59. 2 Tm 2.8; Rom 1.3; Lk 1.33.

Word became flesh and dwelt among his own familiars so that they might further advance and perceive "his glory, glory as of the Only-begotten of the Father, full of grace and truth."[60]

It would not be out of place for a clarification by way of digression to be given (to the extent possible) of the two scepters that the Son of man took for himself so as to bind and fasten them together and make them into a single staff. This good will reach perfection when "the full number of the nations has come in" to the summit of beatitude and "all Israel is saved."[61]

The Lord said to me, Furthermore take for yourself shepherd's gear of an unskilled shepherd because, lo, I am raising up a shepherd for the land: what has failed he will not take note of, what is scattered he will not go after, what is hurt he will not heal, what is sound he will not guide. The flesh of the chosen he will eat, and their knuckles he will twist (vv.15–16). Since the rational sheep of their own accord fell foul of serious error and harm, the good shepherd declared, *I shall not shepherd you.*[62] For these flocks, left leaderless by their own choice, given over by the desires of their hearts to impurity, disgraceful passions, and a base mentality, God, who abandoned them to their wishes, raises up a shepherd, who without skill or care pastures those thus abandoned—or, rather, brings harm on those that are themselves responsible for it. He has no interest in the one abandoned, straying, and wandering from the assembly and restoration of the divine flock from which it fell away, nor does he ward off further harm. In fact, *he does not go looking for what is scattered, does not heal what is hurt, does not guide what is sound,* his interest and enthusiasm being to cause evil, not good. Accordingly, he does everything for base gain and his own advantage; so *he eats their flesh and twists the knuckles* of those placed under him.

This is not the case, however, with the skillful shepherds, appointed to the flocks by God's gift, so that the God of every benefit says, "I shall give you shepherds after my own heart, shepherding you with skill." After all, how could they not be

60. Jn 1.14. Is it in fact to the sacraments as the eschatological gift that Didymus is referring by his use of μυστήρια?

61. Rom 11.26.

62. Zec 11.9.

good pastors whose head "gives his own life for the sheep," "good shepherd" as he is? It is of him that the chief of the apostles writes to the leaders of the assembly of the faithful, "I exhort the elders among you to tend the flock in your midst not under compulsion but willingly, so that when the chief shepherd appears, you will win the crown of glory that never fades." None of those pasturing the sheep with which they have been entrusted lords it over those received by lot,[63] which is what they do who *eat the flesh* of the sheep, looking for pleasure at their expense, believing they gain credit for shame and actions productive of it; by indiscriminate eating they make a god of their own belly, thus serving it and not the Lord Jesus, so that the letter from the apostle himself refers equally to them in saying, "they serve not the Lord Jesus but their own belly."[64]

Whereas false teachers and false pastors are of this attitude, the good shepherds have as payment for their teaching only simple and frugal nourishment, relying as they do on the one who appoints them to this task. "The laborer deserves his nourishment," and so they confidently say and write, "We are content with what there is," namely, food and shelter. They also say to their disciples, for example, in recommending this, "We brought nothing into this world, because we can take nothing out of it, either; we have food and shelter, and shall be content with that." People of such virtue have confidence in proclaiming, "Silver and gold we have none." [65]

Teachers that bring such benefit do not grasp at the flesh of those in their charge, longing only in their spirit and anxious to preserve with them "the unity of the Spirit in the bond of peace." Hence, they do not *twist their knuckles*, either, but guide and encourage them to run in the straight ways of the Lord and do their duty, keeping in healthy condition also the *knuckles* of their hands. Now, I said their hands have *knuckles* under instruction from the all-wise Daniel. Possibly there is a force in the *twisting of the knuckles* similar to the statement of the mighty

---

63. Jer 3.15; Jn 10.14–15; 1 Pt 5.1–4.
64. Phil 3.19; Rom 16.18.
65. Mt 10.10; Heb 13.5; 1 Tm 6.7; Acts 3.6. Didymus speaks with some feeling, perhaps with experience of both models in mind.

prophet Elijah to the irresolute people who took two paths, "How long will you limp on both hamstrings? If the Lord is [God], follow him; if Baal, follow him."[66]

After making the threat to raise up a shepherd in the land who would not show care for the abandoned sheep or go after the lost, not binding up or healing the one that is wounded, and would be uninterested in guiding the healthy so as to make them still healthier, clearly and openly he orders the prophet to take the gear of *an unskilled shepherd*, who had neither the skill nor the experience of a good pastor, the purpose being for him to convey to those for whom his prophecy was intended the force of what he was ordered. People not understanding the words, you see, do not grasp the actions performed by the teacher. So since the listeners needed an understanding of an unskilled, inexperienced shepherd, the divinely inspired holy man in full view took the designated gear so as to speak about it when asked what it meant by those witnessing his taking shepherd's gear of someone not skilled but unskilled. Many such provisions are reported in the prophets, especially in Ezekiel. It is not unlikely that the mention of the shepherd who was so ruinous is a foretelling of the Antichrist, as is found in many parts of Scripture.[67]

He mentions the *chosen* sheep whose flesh he eats—not those definitively and truly elect, but those chosen as friends and familiars by the one who eats their flesh.

---

66. Eph 4.3; Dan 5.24 Theodotion; 1 Kgs 18.21. The reference to the "ankles/knuckles," ἀστράγαλοι, is puzzling to all the commentators (Petersen seeing the phrase indicative simply of total consumption; see *Zechariah 9–14 and Malachi*, 99); Didymus consults his concordance, and finding the term in Theodotion in reference to the hand that wrote on the wall in the presence of King Belshazzar, and perhaps forgetting that Zechariah is talking rather of sheep, prefers "knuckles," a choice hardly supported by his reference to 1 Kings. Doutreleau (SC 85.880–81) takes the exercise as a further illustration of the absurdity of a literal approach to obscure texts encouraging the commentator to adopt a spiritual interpretation; but, to his credit, Didymus worried this bone at some length before doing so.

67. Theodoret, with Didymus possibly open before him, like Jerome approves of this nomination of the Antichrist after (typically for an Antiochene) considering the possibility of Antiochus IV. Didymus himself is reserved about such a reference. He also acknowledges the occurrence of prophetic signs and actions in the Bible.

O those who shepherd futile things and desert the sheep: a sword is on his arm and his right eye. His arm will completely wither, and his right eye will be completely blinded (v.17). The divine word blames—or, rather, threatens—the false pastors for deserting and abandoning the sheep, going after *futile things,* namely, base gain and consumption of the flesh of the nurslings confided to their care. To each of them, or to one in place of them all on account of their being cast in the same evil mold, he says, *a sword is on his arm,* that is, his actions. It has often been demonstrated that by allegory "arm" suggests actions.

What in fact is the sword that is *on the arm and eye* of the guilty shepherd, if not the word of punishment, in reference to which God says in Isaiah to those subject to the Law, "If you are willing and obedient to me, you will eat the good things of the earth; but if you are not willing and obedient to me, a sword will devour you"? Of this avenging blade God likewise says in Jeremiah, "I shall stretch my hand over all the inhabitants of the earth" for them to suffer these hardships. In another interpretation the sword of God may be the word that rescues from evil ways those embroiled in them. The savior, for example, says in the Gospels, "Do not think that I have come to bring peace on earth; rather, a sword"—in other words, Gospel teaching does not result in our being at peace with earthly things and the earth, but in those people being at odds with it who have an earthly frame of mind and bear the image of the man of dust.[68] This sword was given to Abraham under the form of an oracle in order to remove him "from the land, from his kindred and his father's house," by "land" meaning the body with which he was clad, by "kindred" those of identical pursuits and way of life, and by "father's house" the word uttered by the mind, in the commentary of one of the sages on the Mosaic teaching. In a sense similar to the oracles to Abraham is what is said by the divine bridegroom or, rather, his father, "Listen, daughter, look and incline your ear, forget your people and your father's house, because the king has desired your beauty, and he is your Lord."[69] For individuals to forget their own people and their fa-

---

68. Is 1.19–20; Jer 6.12; Mt 10.34; Phil 3.19; 1 Cor 15.49.
69. Gn 12.1 (the sage in question being Philo); Ps 45.10–11.

ther's house is the same as leaving their kindred and their father's house when invited to do so.

The aforementioned avenging sword on arm and eye—that is, on the practical and contemplative faculties—withers the shepherd's avenging arm, removing all moisture and fatness that could wreak harm, so that it dies. It also afflicts with blindness now and in the future the eye that seems to be on the right to its possessor, but in reality is not so, being instead on the left, ill-omened, and worse, if that is possible. These words could also be understood in reference to the Antichrist, described as having a strong and lively right arm on account of the signs and portents he works, false though they are, and a right eye, since he shares in the sight of the king of Assyria, taken in a spiritual sense, of whom the Lord himself said, "I shall inflict on the lofty mind, on the king of Assyria," who proudly boasted, "I shall plunder the force of the nations, and with the wisdom of intelligence I shall abolish the frontiers of nations; with my hand I shall occupy the whole world." Being son as to impiety of this vain person who boasted, "There is no one who will escape me or resist me," the Antichrist boasted of having a strong arm and right eye, an arm that was withered by the sword as interpreted before, and an eye that it blinded by gouging out its awful sight. Paul writes specifically about this to the Thessalonians: "Until the lawless one comes whom the Lord Jesus will destroy by the breath of his mouth and will annihilate by the manifestation of his coming."[70] His right eye represents each of the heretics peddling the "falsely named knowledge,"[71] while his arm represents every charlatan pretending to work portentous marvels. Both come to nought, one withered like an arm, the other blinded like an eye by the aforementioned sword.

It is possible to adduce clear testimony to this from the book of the Acts of the Apostles. By performing works of a charlatan

70. 2 Thes 2.9; Is 10.12–14; 2 Thes 2.8. Modern commentators also admit the ambiguity of the reference in this woe oracle to the "guilty shepherd," finding the prophet himself the probable candidate; so Didymus not surprisingly opts instead for the Antichrist.

71. Cf. 1 Tm 6.20. Still a further heresy to be added to the conventional arsenal listed earlier.

and proposing teaching, a magician with the name of Elymas had the intention of undermining the adherents to the faith; he represented himself as a wonderworker and a mind-reader, and took pride in powers he thought he had. Accosting him with bold accusations and divine resolution, the godly Paul said, "O son of the devil and enemy of all righteousness, full of deceit and every villainy, will you not stop making crooked the straight ways of the Lord? Lo, the hand of the Lord is upon you, you will be blind and unable to see the sun for a while." The same form of impiety as that of Elymas was shown also by Simon the charlatan, whom Peter also unmasked with God's power, though his right arm did not wither nor was his right eye blinded.[72]

With sufficient clarification given, in my view, according to our ability, to the account of the unskilled, wicked shepherd, we must take up the rest of the prophet beginning with a different passage.

72. Acts 13.8–11; 8.9, 18–23.

COMMENTARY ON ZECHARIAH 12

N ORACLE OF THE WORD *of the Lord on Israel. Thus says the Lord, who stretches out heaven, lays the foundation of earth, and forms a spirit of a human being in it: Lo, I am making Jerusalem like a shaken threshold for all the peoples round about and in Judah; there will be a siege against Jerusalem. On that day I shall make Jerusalem a stone trodden on by all the nations; everyone who treads on it will mockingly mock it, and all the nations of the earth will gather against it* (Zec 12.1–3). The prophet Zechariah prophesies the fate of Judah and Jerusalem and its inhabitants after the crucifixion of Jesus, receiving his message from the creator of everything, *who stretches out heaven, lays the foundation of earth, and forms a spirit of a human being in it.* It was remarked above that the divinely inspired prophets are in a state of possession when in receipt of the word in virtue of which they prophesy the future. Not to repeat the same information many times, we should be content with what was already said.[1]

God *stretches out heaven and lays the foundation of earth,* bringing from non-existence to existence these primordial created realities which comprise in themselves the other beings, as the great revealer says, "Heaven and earth and their whole universe were complete." In beginning Genesis, at any rate, he clearly said, "In the beginning God made heaven and earth,"[2] that is,

---

1. Predictably, Didymus does not resonate with those modern commentators who would see the beginning of a new piece of composition at this point, signaled by the very feature of the text Didymus is implicitly highlighting, the occurrence of "oracle," λῆμμα, as occurred also at 9.1. The term encourages him again to speak of the prophets as θεοληπτούμενοι (as he had done at the beginning of the work without that encouragement), to which he adds κάτοχοι, both terms implying possession. He makes no attempt to develop any (admittedly obscure) historical situation that Zechariah may have in mind.

2. Gn (here Κοσμοποιΐα) 2.1; 1.1. Doutreleau (SC 85.892–93) points out that Didymus will employ in comment on these verses a series of Stoic terms. Jerome will (not surprisingly) reduce this detailed excursus.

he stretched out heaven and laid the foundation of earth. There has been frequent explanation already of the manner of stretching out heaven and laying the foundations of earth when commentary was given on such texts where God says, "I alone stretched out heaven," and the psalmist on the creator, "He set the earth on its firm foundations, it will never be over-turned."[3] He who unfolded heaven by stretching it out and set earth on its foundations also created the human being, *Forming in it its spirit,* that is, combining and uniting the soul with the body, to the extent possible, so as to produce one complete living being composed of soul and body.

Now, the spirit of the human being is formed not simply but *in it:* it is of a nature that is not bodily but rational. Beforehand, however, the human being's body was formed, as was said by Moses, "God formed the human being from dust of the earth." The spirited and courageous Job was aware of this manner of creation when emboldened to say to the creator, "Remember that you formed me from mud, and you turn me back to the earth." Yet he also says of the origins of what is composed of soul and body, "Your hands made me and formed me,"[4] the body being "formed," the soul "made"; the latter being called "spirit," he formed it in the human being to partake of the faculty of sense as a result of its composition, so that the whole person emerges as ensouled, sensate, alive.

In addition to this way of seeing it, there is another way of putting it. The *human being's spirit formed in it* is what the apostle describes in writing: "What human being knows what is truly human except the human spirit that is in it?" The spirit is something different from the rational soul, called "the human being hidden in the heart." Its formation is not like that of the body, however: it is what the holy psalmist prays to occur in his own heart: "Create a pure heart in me, O God." It is a pure heart that is formed when it is shaped according to virtue and holi-ness in other forms in such a way as to act and think with clarity and harmony. This was the attitude of the woman who slew the

3. Is 44.24; Ps 104.5.
4. Gn 2.7; Jb 10.9, 8. Didymus feels the need to justify the author's use of the verb "form," πλάττειν, of the soul.

cruel tyrant Holofernes, the noble Judith, to whom the wise
elders said in commendation, "The formation of your heart is
good."⁵ The terms "form" and "formation" are the same as
those applied to the body; while they suggest some resistance to
being formed on the part of the material subject, the formation
of the spirit occurs through an impression of thoughts and rational representations.

The one *who stretches out heaven, lays the foundation of earth,
and forms the spirit of the human being in it* threatens to devastate
and destroy the city and region of the Jews on account of the
crimes committed by those guilty of godless deeds against the
savior who has come. They inflicted cross and scourging, remember, on the one who gave his life as a ransom, removing
the sin of the world—and this despite his coming for the salvation of all.⁶ Now, what is the awful fate he forecasts for the
Christ-killers? *Lo, I am making Jerusalem like a shaken threshold
and Judah for all the peoples round about* so that they will no longer
have a basis and security because they will be abandoned by the
one who laid its foundation and protects it. The prophecy of
Isaiah made in the manner of a threat is fulfilled, "Daughter
Sion will be abandoned," and in Jeremiah by the one who rejects it on account of its bouts of impiety in the words, "I abandoned my house, I dismissed my inheritance, I surrendered my
beloved soul into the hands of its foes." Before the abandonment and surrender, remember, the city to which this refers
was a house and inheritance and beloved soul; but later he said
of it because of its impiety towards him, "Lo, your house is left
to you in ruins." Now, it is right that the threshold and not the
doors will be affected: it is not the complete security that is undermined—only what is in shadow and the letter, which is an
introduction to the externals of the Law, referred to as "regula-
tions for the flesh imposed until the time comes to set things
right."⁷

The awful fate that was threatened befell both the material

5. 1 Cor 2.11; 1 Pt 3.4; Ps 51.10; Jdt 8.29. Didymus cites most of the deuterocanonical books, while like the Antiochenes not citing Esther.

6. Mt 20.28; Jn 1.29.

7. Is 1.8; Jer 12.7; Mt 23.38; Heb 9.10.

Judah and its capital, which in fact was destroyed to the point that there was no longer stone standing on stone.[8] So the neighboring peoples of foreign nations, who were not allowed to enter and set foot on the sacred floor, will trample upon it in the way a common and ordinary stone is trampled on when people walk on it with unwashed feet. Contemplating this harsh plight with prophetic gaze from a distance, weeping and wailing over the city that had fallen foul of such misfortune, Jeremiah exclaimed mournfully, "How lonely sits the city that was thronged with people! She is reckoned as a widow, once the most populous city among the nations!" On approaching Jerusalem the savior had said this would happen to her: "Jerusalem, Jerusalem, if even you had only recognized the things that make for peace. But now they are hidden from your eyes: your enemies will come upon you, surround you, and throw a rampart around you," so that you will be abandoned and dashed to the ground, with all the hostile nations encircling you, and so you will be seen to be desolate. "When you see Jerusalem surrounded by armies," Scripture says, remember, "you will know that its devastation has come near."[9] The killers of the Lord had actual experience of this when the Romans overpowered them, destroyed their cities, and enslaved them; they were taken off into captivity or, rather, uprooted from their motherland, and so no longer had their own land or country, but were taken to every quarter of the earth.

In reference to the wrath that had at last befallen Judah and its inhabitants, an historian, one individual from those who actually experienced it, wrote an account in many volumes of them and their places,[10] so that the fulfillment is indisputably visible both of what the savior said and of what Zechariah uttered in prophetic mode, beginning with the verse *I am making Jerusalem like a shaken threshold.* When the threshold was reduced to shaking and the city subjected to a siege, all the foreign na-

---

8. Mt 24.2.

9. Lam 1.1; Lk 13.34; 19.42–43; 21.20.

10. The *Jewish War* of Flavius Josephus, in seven volumes written in the 70s. Josephus was leader of the Jewish forces in Galilee in the war with Rome, and was defeated in 67; so hardly just a private citizen, ἴδιος.

tions scornfully entered and trampled on it like an unclean stone, no longer approaching it as a shrine and sacred surface, showing no respect or performance of due rites of expiation and purification. Hence they *mockingly mocked it* like a ruin, with everyone from that time coming to it to "plough it like a field."[11]

In addition to the literal sense,[12] it could be taken also in the spiritual sense: all the heretics through their evil thoughts and actions "build Sion in blood and Jerusalem in wrongdoing." I mean, how could they fail to build Sion in blood when they scandalize and pour blood on those they deceive? Hence they also build Jerusalem in wrongdoing. Now, the fact that those tricked by the tricksters are wronged is clearly indicated by the reference to such people in the divine Proverbs, which has this to say: "They will be filled with their own impiety; for wronging infants they will be killed, and examination will spell the end of the impious."[13] The word of God *shakes* the threshold of the wretched city that has been built so that they may be overthrown by severe accusations and so be trampled down by the neighboring peoples that trample down the falsely named Jerusalem like a stone that has been defiled, just as they *mockingly mock* the "falsely named knowledge"[14] in their recognition of its impurity and uncleanness, professing as they do the reality and the mysteries of the kingdom of heaven.

And since it is not a few who mockingly mock it for its descent into insignificance, but all the nations, he was right to say that all the nations were assembled in it. Jerusalem is trampled underfoot like a stone when the sun of justice rises and brings about the marvelous spiritual day referred to many times before.

On that day, says the Lord almighty, I shall strike every horse with

---

11. Jer 26.18.

12. Didymus has hardly focused on any historical point of the Zechariah passage, let alone recognized its apocalyptic character, which leads a commentator like Smith, impressed with the sweeping scenario and the doxology of the Lord as cosmic creator, to gasp, "This is Armageddon, the last great battle of earth" (*Micah to Malachi*, 275).

13. Mi 3.10; Prv 1.31–32 LXX.

14. 1 Tm 6.20.

panic and its rider with shock, whereas on the house of Judah I shall open my eyes and strike all the horses of the peoples with blindness (v.4). In what we looked at before in the prophet, comment was made on horses and their riders in a variety of ways; hence at this point we should leave aside most of it, and mention only that interpretation which meets our present need. Deceitful people who use the support of contentious arguments are "horses that are worthless for salvation," having as horsemen and riders the spirits of error and the lying, hypocritical demons whose teaching they dispense, proposing "the wisdom of this age and its rulers." Horses of this kind God strikes on the day of his making, in keeping with the statement given in blessing to the person enlightened, "For you the Lord will be an everlasting light." The wicked horses, however, God does not strike with the intention of their never existing any longer, but for them to understand what they are saying and asserting, since they have lost their wisdom and forfeited their intelligence.[15] When this happens, the rider of every such horse will *be shocked.*

When this plan has been put into effect, God will *open* his *eyes on the house of Judah,* which is "the Church of the living God." Reigning over it is the savior, who sprang from the tribe of Judah, and to whom those who share in God's wisdom say, "Judah, may your brothers praise you; your hands are on the back of your foes, and the sons of your father will bow down to you." On the house of this Judah the beneficent one will open his eyes, his powers of observation and surveillance, so that each of those in receipt of the light and grace will say this manner of prayer: "Set your gaze on me and have mercy on me." All the righteous receive this gift, since their sovereign "sets his eyes on them and gives ear to their petition."[16]

In addition to the horse in question being *stricken with panic and its rider with shock, all the horses of the peoples will be stricken with blindness* by the one who exercises providence over everything. These are the people who have been affected with the sting of

15. Ps 33.17; 1 Tm 4.1–2; 1 Cor 2.6; Ps 118.24; Is 60.19; 1 Cor 1.19; Is 29.14.
16. 1 Tm 3.15; Gn 49.8; Pss 86.16; 34.15.

adultery and fornication, the prophecy saying of them, "They turned into horses besotted with females, each one neighing after his neighbor's wife." It is for their own good that the neighing beings are stricken with blindness, lest they be enticed further to licentiousness. The soul's gaze is, in fact, lifted up to self-control in consequence of this deprivation of eyesight, so that it now sees what must be done and ought to be practiced. The magician Elymas, for instance, whose vision was malicious, was blinded for a time, losing a charlatan's sight, so that later he might regain his sight and behold "the sun of righteousness." It was not without purpose, in fact, that mention was made of his being without sight of the sun "for a time": it would be seen when his blindness was succeeded by vision of the light.[17]

All the commanders of Judah shall say in their hearts, We shall find for ourselves the inhabitants of Jerusalem, in the Lord almighty their God (vv.4–5). Judah, the praiseworthy one to whom it was said, "Judah, may your brothers praise you," is the sovereign and holder of power over all. *The commanders* serve under him, designated as "eyewitnesses from the beginning and ministers of the word"—namely, the apostles of Christ. We should also examine whether all men who bear the Spirit, prophets and all others who serve under Judah, teachers, evangelists, those thus nominated as *commanders,* seek in an effort to find no others than the inhabitants of that Jerusalem that sees "the peace that surpasses all understanding" and God's heavenly city of which the vessel of election, Paul, speaking in Christ, writes, "You are making your approach to Mount Sion and city of the living God, the heavenly Jerusalem." The faultless, law-abiding citizen who resides in this beautiful city, resolute in holiness and all the rest of divine virtue, is unshakable, in keeping with what is said in one of the Songs of the Steps, "The inhabitant of Jerusalem

17. Jer 5.8; Acts 13.11; Mal 4.2. It was in commentary only a few verses previously that Didymus had mentioned Elymas in similar phrasing. Though there blindness, in keeping with Zec 11.17, had been highlighted as an affliction, here the commentator also makes a point of showing its positive effects. Doutreleau (SC 85.906–7) observes that Didymus can never be quoted expressing regret for his lack of sight.

shall never ever be moved." He inhabits it, remaining forever subject to its king.[18]

The aforementioned commanders find inhabitants of the divine city, whose architect and creator is God,[19] sons and disciples of theirs. Paul found Silvanus and Timothy, the evangelist Luke and the other familiars of whom mention is made in his epistles and the Acts of the Apostles. Peter likewise, the savior's genuine disciple, found Mark the evangelist and many others. Likewise John, the disciple beloved by the Lord; there is mention in the book of his Acts of inhabitants of Jerusalem he found.[20] And all the key figures who lead the apostolic Church with right teaching find like-minded people, citizens of the true and spiritual Jerusalem, who thus inhabit it. Of the aforementioned commanders *the Lord almighty* is their master and king.

On that day I shall make the commanders of Judah like a firebrand in wood and like a burning lamp in stubble, and they will devour all the peoples round about on the right and on the left. Jerusalem will dwell by itself. The Lord will save the tents of Judah as in the beginning lest the boasting of the house of David be exaggerated and the conceit of the inhabitants of Jerusalem over Judah (vv.6–7). At the time referred to as *day* on account of the light, the commanders of Judah find for themselves the inhabitants of Jerusalem. They are appointed by God *as a firebrand in wood and as a burning lamp in stubble* so that *all the peoples round about on the right and on the left* may be consumed.

The commanders of Judah in a spiritual sense are appointed as a firebrand in wood and a lamp in stubble, the purpose being for them to devour with their ardent and brilliant word the wills that are fruitless and materialistic. Trees that do not produce good fruit, after all, are cut down and the wood thrown into the fire, consigned to punishment, so that their worthless quality may be consumed; likewise chaff, being stubble and not

---

18. Lk 1.2; Phil 4.7; Acts 9.15; Heb 12.22; Ps 125.1.

19. Heb 11.10.

20. Most of these works and characters occur in the New Testament. The relationship of Peter and Mark is an exception, but the tradition is important for the church of Alexandria. Jerome balks only at mention of the Acts of John, an apocryphal work.

grain, is consumed by fire. It is mentioned in the Gospel,[21] remember, that when Jesus clears the threshing floor with the winnowing fork in his hand, the grain—namely, righteous men—is deposited in the storehouse of the promises, whereas the chaff is burnt in unquenchable fire to the destruction of the malicious will of those found fruitless by their own will.

There is reference to such people by the savior in Micah the prophet: "Woe is me! I have become like someone gathering stubble in the harvest and like the gleanings in the vintage, with no bunches left to eat, no new fruit." After referring obliquely to the current fruitlessness, he explains it in what follows: "Alas, my soul, the faithful have disappeared from the land, and there is not one upright person left; everyone is bent on bloodthirsty vengeance, everyone inflicts distress on his neighbor. They put their hands to evildoing." How are they not destined to punishment, in fact, devoured by the fire of retribution, these people in the grip of the aforementioned crimes? To one of the commanders commented on, the Lord says, "I have put my words like fire in your mouth, and this people like wood, and they will be devoured" for the fruitlessness they have chosen to have. The oracle in Isaiah also has this sense: "The light of Israel will be like a fire, it will consume the wood like grass, consume it from soul to flesh," that is, from evil intention to base action (referring to the intention by "soul" and to actions by "flesh"). The commanders appointed as a firebrand perform the same role as the coal taken from the spiritual and heavenly altar with the tongs by one of the seraphim; by bringing it to the mouth of the prophet he wiped out his transgressions and purified his lips.[22]

Now, it is time to say what the firebrand and the burning lamp consume *on the right and the left.* The familiar position of impious and sinful things is on the left, while what is falsely decked out as virtue is reckoned as being on the right. To condemn both, then, the divine word says, "Keep straight the paths for your feet, and set your ways right; veer neither right nor

---

21. Mt 3.10–12.
22. Mi 7.1–3; Jer 5.14; Is 10.17–18; 6.6.

left";[23] fail neither by excess or by defect, each being a vice. Whereas liberality, the willingness to share, is commendable, miserliness is a veering to the left, while prodigality in wasting money is thought to be on the right when it is spent not on what is necessary and proper but on the pursuit of base pleasures. Since both the miser and the wastrel are censurable, then, the firebrand and the lamp set alight to both. In the treatment that we have entitled *On the Virtues,* it has been amply shown by us that, whereas the virtues are in the middle, veering to right and left of them, that is, defect and excess, are vices. *Right* and *left* in question here, though found to be applicable to almost all human beings, refer to *all the peoples round about.*[24]

When the peoples surrounding the holy city undergo punishment, then it will regain its occupants, protected by the one who built and chose it, in accord with the saying about its security, "Mountains around it, and the Lord around his people." In reference to such protection there is also a statement in the prophet in hand that the "Lord almighty will be like a wall of fire" around it, as was commented on at the beginning of Zechariah. Jerusalem will be reoccupied, and those surrounding it with hostile intent will be put to flight in keeping with the statement by the one inhabiting it, "All the nations surrounded me, and by the name of the Lord I warded them off," and so on.[25]

Now, an appropriate addition in reference to the reoccupation of the holy city itself is the statement that *The Lord will save the tents of Judah as in the beginning,* tents that are nothing other than the kinds of virtue. The oracle in Proverbs declares of them, "The tents of the upright will stand firm"; and the psalmist sings of the love they attract, "How lovable are your tents, Lord of hosts"—in other words, how desirable they are, full of people celebrating. A cry of joy, you see, and of a sound

23. Prv 4.26–27.
24. A phrase that Petersen regards as simply "a classic case of hyperbole" (*Zechariah 9–14 and Malachi,* 116) prompts Didymus to a précis of a hitherto unknown work of his on virtue and vice that bears the clear influence of Aristotelian thinking. See Aristotle, *Ethica Nicomachea* 2.1106a20–1109b26.
25. Ps 125.2; Zec 2.9; Ps 118.10.

of confession is uttered nowhere else than in the tents of the righteous. *The Lord saves the tents of Judah as in the beginning* before the vice and impiety of human beings gain control. It is possible to take *tents saved as from the beginning* as the bodies in which we are clothed; salvation will happen when our corruptible body, dishonorable and weak, will put on incorruptibility, which is glory and power, becoming a spiritual body after being a physical body.[26] In many places in the narratives tents imply progress, being dwellings for travelers, and are saved with God's power as from the beginning, when the perfect state of virtue is achieved.

The good things mentioned will come to pass with God's grace so that each of the saved will boast in the Lord, and none will count on themselves, but on the source of the perfect goods. *The boasting of the house of David* will no longer be *exaggerated nor the conceit of the inhabitants of Jerusalem* when everyone sings, "It is better to trust in the Lord than to trust in man, it is better to hope in the Lord than to hope in a ruler." Presenting this virtue as modesty, in Jeremiah God gives the direction, "Let the wise not boast of their wisdom, nor the strong of their strength, nor the wealthy of their wealth; instead, let the one who boasts boast of this: knowing the Lord, and practicing justice and mercy in the midst of the earth." On giving birth against the odds, the mother of Samuel gratefully uttered the same words, simply replacing the phrase "the wise boasting of their wisdom" with "Let the prudent not boast of their prudence." All boasting is forbidden because it is culpable and harmful, and as a result James writes about it all in general in his letter, "All such boasting is evil," because it involves shame and reproach, and hence Jeremiah speaks with severe censure to the conceited, "Be ashamed of your boasting and reproach" all day long. To the person in the grip of such vanity and vainglory the word says, "Why do you boast of evil, mighty one, of lawlessness all day long?" Now, the boasting of the house of David is exaggerated, as also the conceit of the inhabitants of Jerusalem against the savior who springs from Judah. This oc-

26. Prv 14.11; Pss 84.1; 42.5; 118.15; 1 Cor 15.44, 46.

curs when those who seem to be members of the Church think they practice virtue by their own power and not by the grace of the one who says, "Learn of me that I am gentle and humble of heart."[27]

On that day the Lord will be a shield over the inhabitants of Jerusalem; the infirm among them will be like the house of David on that day, and the house of David like the house of God, like an angel of the Lord before them (v.8). On the day when the doughty deeds of the commanders of Judah are performed, the Lord in his magnificence *will be a shield for the inhabitants of Jerusalem.* For each of them the saying will be fulfilled about "the one dwelling under the protection of the Most High": "His truth will surround you with armor." And in another psalm the Lord will be a shield for those who fear him, so that each of them says, "Because you are my protector, into your hands I commend my spirit." The inhabitants of the spiritual Jerusalem will be able to take up and don God's livery, girding their loins in truth, protecting their feet with sandals in preparation for a peace befitting God, then putting on a breastplate of righteousness, and above all taking up the shield of faith with which the fiery shafts of the evil one are extinguished.[28]

Since the king of all creation protects the inhabitants of the great city of Jerusalem with his own shield, there will be such force and power that the person in their midst who was previously weak will receive the strength of the house of David, "the Church of the living God," which is God's temple. Thus each of those in possession of the Church's knowledge and virtue will cry aloud in a hymn of praise, "The Lord is my strength and my song, and has proved to be my salvation."[29]

And since those saying this have their citizenship in heaven while walking on earth, and are thus not yet of equal status with angels in being risen from the dead, it follows that *the house of David,* a word meaning "strong of hand," would be an angel of God. It has the gift and the eminence of the one born of the

---

27. 1 Cor 1.31; Ps 118.8–9; Jer 9.23–24; 1 Sm 2.10 LXX; Jas 4.16; Jer 12.13 LXX; Ps 52.1; Mt 11.29.
28. Ps 91.1, 4; Prv 30.5; Ps 31.4–5; Eph 6.13–16.
29. 1 Tm 3.15; Ps 118.14.

immaculate virgin Mary, called "angel of great counsel," as was
said in the person of the choir of holy ones by Isaiah, who often
foretold his descending hither, "A child was born to us and a
son given to us, and his name will be angel of great counsel."
We should study the precision of the prophecy that reveals to
us the infant's birth from Mary and the giving of the only-
begotten Son from the bosom of the Father. A son was not giv-
en without a child's being born for us, as is impiously supposed
by the docetists, nor again was the child born of a virgin without the Father's giving the only-begotten Son, as taught by Paul
of Samosata, Photinus the Galatian, and their equally impious
companions Artemas and Theodotus.[30]

While these people were banished from the Church for being recognized as completely impious, then, we by contrast
hold fast to the ancient position of the assembly of the faithful,
and confess that God the Word came down, assuming the human condition complete with soul, body, and spirit. The fact
that the Father gave the Son for the child to be born John the
evangelist makes very clear in showing the incarnate one saying
of himself, "God so loved the world as to give his only-begotten
Son, so that everyone believing in him might have eternal life."
What is sent to the Romans by the Christ-bearing Paul in these
words has the same meaning: "God sent his own Son in the likeness of sinful flesh so as to condemn sin in the flesh."[31] This
had to be said by me on account of the aforementioned Photinus and his teacher Marcellus, who claim that the Son who was
sent is flesh, the Son nowhere being referred to by them as God
the Word. At greater length in other works a refutation has
been made by us of their "falsely called knowledge," where
there was occasion to refer to the Son of God—I mean, God
the Word and his Incarnation.[32]

30. By citing a popular etymology of the name David, and invoking Is 9.6,
Didymus arrives at a litany of heretics from various periods linked by their false
ideas of the Incarnation, to whom he will proceed to add Apollinarius (implicitly) and Marcellus of Ancyra.

31. Jn 3.16; Rom 8.3.

32. 1 Tm 6.20. Doutreleau (SC 85.925) sees here a reference to Didymus's
Commentary on John, not extant.

In another interpretation it is possible to say that the one born of Mary is the house of the one who is "strong of hand," creator of all things, and is angel in the sight of recipients of his favors, inhabitants of holy Jerusalem. He became an angel in their sight to reveal God's mighty designs.

On that day I shall seek to do away with all the nations advancing on Jerusalem. I shall pour out on the house of David and the inhabitants of Jerusalem a spirit of grace and compassion (vv.9–10). On that day, which approaches after the night of ignorance and evil is far gone, of which the apostle writes in the words, "The night is far gone, the day approaches; let us live honorably as in the day," the beneficent Lord then *seeks to do away with all the nations advancing* in revolt and a warlike manner against the city of the great king, *Ierosoluma*, otherwise called Jerusalem.[33] Now, he is seeking to do away with all the nations at odds with truth and reverence for God, not to the extinction of all human beings—something impossible—but for them to be no longer evil and wicked. After all, had he wanted to destroy humanity completely, he would not have *sought* to do it, capable as he is of reducing everything in an instant to nothingness; since he had drawn things from non-existence and called them into existence, it would have been much easier for him to remove them from existence.

But that was not his intention—hence the saying of the all-wise Solomon about him, "He brought everything into being, the generative forces of the world are saving, and there is no baleful poison in them." You see, just as our Lord and savior came to seek our race, which was lost, and saved it, so in seeking to do away with all the nations advancing on Jerusalem he saves them. He destroyed the causes of harm coming from them as a result of lawless behavior and deviant views, so that peace held sway and the nations no longer advanced on divine Jerusalem, forsaking their rebellious manner and hostile attitude. The word *advance* indicates that the invaders are foes and

33. Rom 13.12; Mt 5.35. Doutreleau (SC 85.926; 84.636) is at a loss to account for the introduction of this form of the name, which is not in the Zechariah text, though frequent in the NT.

foreigners, as the proverb says to the person of peaceable life, "When you lie down, your sleep will be sweet, and you will have no fear of attacks by impious invaders."[34]

Now, because the removal of the nations sought by the savior, who exercises providence over all, is achieved, the text proceeds to say that, on the day indicated, he who promises good things *will pour out on the house of David and the inhabitants of Jerusalem a spirit of grace and compassion* in his capacity as "father of compassion" and giver of the Holy Spirit. This, in fact, emerges from the divinely inspired Scriptures: of this gift Paul, for one, writes, "The love of God has been poured out in our hearts through the Holy Spirit who is given to us." Solomon, for his part, says in his book of Wisdom, "Who has traced out what is in the heavens, unless you have given wisdom and sent your holy spirit from on high? Thus the paths of those on earth were set right, and people were taught what pleases you." And the actual source of the spirit says to someone in Isaiah, "I gave my spirit to you," and again he says to others about such a person, "I gave my spirit to him."[35]

To clarify what the generous gift is, the one who offers it says, *I shall pour out a spirit of grace and compassion,* as is possible to learn also from other statements: God says, "I shall pour out some of my spirit on all flesh," implying the rich gift, as also does the statement, "God's love has been poured out in our hearts." It emerges from the apostle's statement that the "spirit of grace" is the Holy Spirit, when he writes, "Anyone violating the Law of Moses dies without mercy on the testimony of two or three witnesses. How much worse punishment do you think will be deserved by the one who spurned the Son of God, profaned the blood of the covenant, and outraged the Spirit of grace, by which he was sanctified?" In keeping with the Holy Spirit's being the Spirit of grace is the statement in another text of the apostle in these terms: "There is a variety of gifts but the same Spirit," and again, "To one is given through the Spirit the utter-

---

34. Wis 1.14; Lk 19.10; Prv 3.24.

35. 2 Cor 1.3; Rom 5.5; Wis 9.16–18; Is 42.1. Doutreleau (SC 85.930–31) has difficulty identifying the penultimate Isaian citation, but Jerome had no qualms about allowing it to be Isaian.

ance of wisdom, to another the utterance of knowledge, to another faith in the same Spirit," and there follows the listing of the various gifts.[36] The Spirit of grace is also the Spirit of compassion, given by "the Father of compassion." Comment has been made on this text in another commentary, that it is the God of all who is the compassionate Father of God the Word and <giver> of the Holy Spirit.[37]

As we know from the text who it is who generously bestows the Spirit of grace and compassion, we are consequently aware of what the house of David is and who the inhabitants of Jerusalem are. Each can represent the Church, which is both Jerusalem and house of David, as is about to be made clear.

They will look on me because they have maltreated me, and show grief for them as for a loved one, and feel pangs as for a firstborn (v.10). Having fallen foul of grievous misfortune, the Jews, after gaily murdering the Lord, were in the grip of severe pangs of grief as if grieving for a dear departed and lamenting a firstborn son; "wrath has overtaken them at last,"[38] the result being that their homeland has been ruined and they have been enslaved and forced to wander throughout all the earth. It is possible to learn from the present text itself that it was by the decree of God's providence that they were subjected to this for the sacrilege they committed in subjecting the savior of all to crucifixion; the one who suffered at their hands says, remember, *They will look upon me because they maltreated me.* Did they not treat him in an impious and unholy manner when they mocked Jesus when he was suspended from the gibbet by saying, "Aha, you who destroy the Temple of God and in three days raise it up! He saved others, himself he cannot save." "If you are the Son of God, come down from the cross."[39]

36. Jl 2.28; Rom 5.5; Heb 10.28–29; 1 Cor 12.4, 8–9.
37. 2 Cor 1.3. Fragments of Didymus's *Commentary on 2 Corinthians* are extant, but throw no light on his final statement here, where Doutreleau has had to insert "giver" to resolve difficulties in the thought, already object of attention by ancient scribes; see SC 85.932–33.
38. 1 Thes 2.16.
39. Mk 15.29–31; Mt 27.40, 42. The following Johannine citation leads Didymus to ignore any historical reference in the verse to Zechariah's time, and to focus immediately on the crucifixion, always a ready rationale of Jewish misfortunes.

They were guilty of these mocking words and many others; and the evangelist records the accomplishment of the prophecy which goes as follows: "They will look on him whom they have pierced," which except for a difference in wording is the same as the verse *They will look upon me because they maltreated me.* Those with a good knowledge of Hebrew claim, in fact, that the text of Zechariah was translated as the Gospel verse, either from the evangelist's translating it, since he was a Hebrew, or from the transmission of it by another translator, like Aquila, Theodotion, or someone else, who rendered the Hebrew text into Greek. Now, we have been induced to say this as a result of the attempts of some people to find where in the prophets the verse occurs, "They will look on him whom they have pierced," which is not found anywhere in the available forms of the Old Testament.[40]

There are good grounds for thinking it is the killers of the Lord who feel grief for a loved one and pangs for a firstborn, since a harsh fate befell them for killing Jesus, a Son who was firstborn and beloved. The two senses of *beloved* have often been examined, worthy of being loved and also only-begotten Son. Both are applicable to Jesus Christ, who is beloved Son— of God, that is, of whom it is written, "God is love"[41]—and also only-begotten, being only Son, only-begotten of the Father and of the holy virgin Mary.

On that day the mourning in Jerusalem will be magnified like the mourning for a pomegranate cut down in the open field. The land will mourn tribe by tribe, each tribe by itself and their women by themselves: the tribe of the house of David and their women by themselves; the tribe of the house of Nathan by itself and their women by themselves; the tribe of the house of Levi by itself and their women by themselves; the tribe of the house of Shimei and their women by themselves; all the remaining tribes, tribe by tribe, and their women by themselves (vv.11–14). Taken

40. Jn 19.37; cf. Rv 1.7. The discrepancy Didymus notes in verb forms in the Johannine citation and Greek biblical texts he is using or knows of arises from a misreading, or alternative reading, of the Heb. Didymus could be thought somewhat naïve in supposing John did his own translating or had access to versions by Aquila and others that are generally thought less antique. At least he admits his own lack of Hebrew.

41. 1 Jn 4.8.

allegorically, the trees in Scripture refer to independent beings, sometimes bearing good fruit by choice, sometimes harmful and noxious. For example, the people of Israel, to be sure, though planted by God as "a fruit-bearing vine of excellent stock, reverted to being a vine of bitter grapes," and thus proved worthy of being cut down since it produced "bunches that were tart and grapes of bitterness"; as the saying goes, "Every tree that does not bear good fruit is cut down and cast into the fire."[42]

Just as the vine producing good fruit changed and bore bad fruit, therefore, so the pomegranate plants that turned from good to bad suffered the fate of being cut down, as the present text declares. It is said likewise by Christ the bridegroom in the Song of Songs about cultivated plants bearing edible fruit, "I went down to see among the growth of the torrent, to see if the vine had budded, if the pomegranates had blossomed." In other words, on going down into the trial posed by life (referred to anagogically as a torrent), he saw the vine and the pomegranates beginning to show fruitfulness as suggested by the blossoms. After the blossoming and the yield of mature fruit, the bride of the Word (the Church betrothed to him) felt a longing to take her fill of the drink provided by the groom, saying to him accordingly, "You will give me a drink of fragrant wine, of my pomegranate juice." Pomegranate juice not only slakes the thirst, but when offered as potion also benefits the drinker. The fruit of this tree, covered with a skin, is nicely compact and suitably thick, such that the groom says to his companion, "Your cheeks are like the skin of a pomegranate, my bride,"[43] since a modest blush appears on your countenance along with the fruit under the skin that is orderly and compact.

42. Jer 2.21; Dt 32.32; Mt 3.10.

43. Song 6.11; 8.2; 4.3. The LXX has had difficulty with the Heb. phrase "like the mourning for Hadad-rimmon in the plain of Megiddo" in Zec 12.11, seeing a reference to pomegranates, as modern commentators also debate the precise reference. Whereas Theodoret will call on his botanical knowledge to rationalize this version—never thinking the Heb. text might mean something quite different, the basis of the Armageddon that appears in Rv 16.16 as the site of the cosmic battle in the end-time—Didymus sees spiritual value in the reference, confirmed by the mention of pomegranates in the Song of Songs. Zechariah's historical situation is not a factor in his thinking.

Trees understood in this fashion, when given up to indiffer-
ence, are cut down by their own fault when "the axe is put to
the root," like the vines that produce no fruit that is praiseworthy and beneficial, leading the savior to say, "Every branch that
does not abide in me is cut down and cast into the fire." Now,
the cutting down will be extensive only when *a pomegranate is
cut down in the open field.* When this penalty is applied, the tribes
of the earth will be affected with weeping and wailing as their
pomegranates suffer a change for the worse. The "cutting
down" that is mentioned should be taken in similar fashion: as
the trees are toppled from their very roots, so the tribes of the
earth are "cut down" in a different sense, dealing blows to their
chest with their hands.[44]

The text directs that this be done by the separation of wives
from husbands; it was inappropriate, even if they did not sense
the impending disaster, for partners to have intercourse for having a family with the threat in place when it was time for praying. Even apart from such a specter of wrath, the Christ-bearing
apostle forbids husbands to approach their wives at times of
prayer; in his letter he tells married people to abstain from marital intercourse especially at the time when they should pray
and implore God: "Deprive one another" (of customary intercourse, that is) "for a time to devote yourselves to prayer."[45] If
this happens for the sake of purity and at a period when nothing fearsome threatens, then, let purity be a greater concern
when danger is involved. This, in fact, was also one of the points
in the teaching before the coming of the savior. When the nations were ranged in warlike fashion against Israel to plunder
and enslave it, the divine word gave orders for the practice of
fasting and self-denial to the people threatened by the assault of
the foe: "Sanctify a fast, proclaim a solemnity," and a little further on, "Let the bridegroom leave his chamber and the bride

44. Mt 3.10; Jn 15.2, 5, 6. Didymus is here invoking the different senses of
the verb κόπτω so as to harmonize Zechariah's thought about mourning tribes
with the analogy of the pomegranate trees.

45. 1 Cor 7.5. Didymus notes the provision for separation of the sexes in the
Zechariah text, and tries at length to account for it without belittling the value
either of women or of marriage.

her bridal chamber. At the altar step the priests will weep and say, Spare your people, Lord, and do not give your inheritance to the shame of their domination by nations, lest the nations say, Where is their God?"[46] Note how shameful and inappropriate it would be for the newlyweds to dwell in the actual chamber and bridal chamber with disaster pending, while the priests were in mourning at the altar step.

In the history of ancient times there are also prohibitions similar to this one. An ark was built by Noah in view of the fearsome deluge, remember, at the bidding of the one who cares for everything, the purpose being that Noah and his household would be preserved from all harm. When the onslaught of rain was already threatening, the Lord said to the righteous man, "In you go, you and your sons and your wife and your sons' wives," so that the men might be by themselves in the vessel apart from the wives, with no marital intercourse occurring at a time of annihilation of the human race, with everyone swept away except for the four couples who had gone into the ark. The men and their partners did not continue living apart when the land dried out at the cessation of the flood, and they came out of the ark at God's command for "Noah to leave the ark with his wife, and their sons and their wives."[47] The threat to human beings had been offset, you see, and cohabitation was restored so that growth in the human race might be assured by natural increase.

In a manner similar to our reading of the story of Noah and of the prophecies of Joel, in this case as well the text recommends *mourning* in speaking of men mourning *by themselves* and similarly women when the impending calamity is perceived. Note also, at any rate, the precision of the command in preserving not only the distinction of one tribe from another, but also men of one tribe from their wives and vice versa, the text saying, *tribe by tribe, and their women by themselves.* By *the tribe of the house of*

---

46. Jl 2.15–17.

47. Gn 7.1, 7; 8.18. The provision Didymus sees in the Genesis text for husbands and wives to observe abstinence in the ark Doutreleau notes (SC 85.942) is found also in Isidore of Pelusium (in the 5th century) and, predictably, in Jerome.

David it refers to those who are in this category as a result of acting regally and bravely by exercise of their strength. And since
men are distinguished from women not only in a literal sense
on the score of men's begetting and women's giving birth, but
also spiritually, men may rightly refer to the souls that spread
teachings to other souls in the process of instruction, whereas
in allegorical fashion those may be called women who receive
the teaching from others instead of generating it of themselves.

Likewise, too, in the case of Nathan, Levi, Simeon, and the
remaining tribes, the distinction between men and women is to
be made literally and spiritually. The tribe of Nathan and that
of Levi represent, respectively, those of a prophetic knowledge
and way of life and those who attend on God, Nathan being a
prophet, remember, and Levi a priest; even in a literal sense it
is from the latter that the men who attend on God as priests are
descended. Simeon differs from both, his name meaning
"heeding" or "hearkening,"[48] which refers to those heeded by
God when he grants their petitions for the particular reason
that they for their part heed the divine commands. Just as in
the tribes specifically named, then, the men are apart and the
women stay by themselves, so, too, the remaining tribes, who
are in a similar situation in their mourning.

There was a precise indication that the mourning had to occur in no other city than Jerusalem, and from this fact the command is shown to have a reference that is spiritual above all;
the people were still in captivity, remember, when the prophet
said these words. There is need to examine whether it is in accord with such a purpose—at the approach of the world's end
as John's saying goes, "It is the final hour," and the human race
has reached its maximum—that the apostle writes, "The time
has grown short; it is now for those with wives to be as though
they had none"[49]—men keeping their celibacy, women living as
widows for Christ's sake, and people opting for virginity to live
apart so as to devote themselves to prayer generously and unin-
terruptedly.

48. Cf. Gn 29.33. Didymus can capitalize on an etymology, we have seen, beyond the intention of the original author.
49. 1 Jn 2.18; 1 Cor 7.29.

COMMENTARY ON ZECHARIAH 13

N THAT DAY *every place will be open in the house of David and the inhabitants of Jerusalem for transformation and aspersion* (Zec 13.1). *On that day*—a term already frequently commented on—this is what will happen in addition to the other events: every place will be opened in the house of David in Jerusalem, a *transformation* occurring with a view to a godly *aspersion*. Now, the place opened to the house of David is the divinely inspired Scripture, in particular the Scripture before the coming of the savior; and the place opened to Jerusalem is the Jerusalem on high, mother of the righteous and "heavenly city of the living God." The *place* in the text, however, is to be understood not as what circumscribes and limits a body, but the one distinguished with a view to propositions and arguments. On the opening of the places determined this way there will follow a transformation from the letter to the spirit, from the shadow to the reality, and—to put it in a nutshell—from the temporal to the eternal, and from the visible and earthly to the lofty and invisible.[1]

What follows on the transformation is nothing other than the sprinkling that confers perfect purification. This aspersion is performed with the savior's divine blood, about which the chief of the apostles, Peter, writes in making this prediction to those to whom he sends the letter, "Grace to you and peace in abundance for obedience and sprinkling with the blood of Jesus Christ." The divine blood is sprinkled on the conscience of the worshipers of the living God, "ransoming" the participants "from the futile ways inherited from their ancestors," as is stat-

1. Gal 4.26; Heb 12.22. Didymus has not detected the LXX's reading a similar form "place" for Heb. "fountain," which Theodoret will arrive at by consulting the alternative versions; and so he proceeds to develop the faulty notion by recourse to Aristotelian categories of place.

ed in the same letter from the wise spiritual guide, "You know that you have been ransomed not with perishable things like silver or gold, but with the precious blood of Christ, like that of a lamb without defect or blemish." Those sprinkled in this way to obtain a pure heart appeal constantly and incessantly to the one capable of conferring the purification, and thus say as one, "Wash me, and I shall be whiter than snow." It is to this purity, "religion pure and undefiled," that the sacred verse urges us in its exhortation, "Wash, make yourselves clean."[2]

If we also are affected by a longing for this aforementioned sprinkling, let us show interest in living as citizens of the spiritual Jerusalem with David as our king, so that *the place* in the sense explained may be completely opened to us for an aspersion after moving from shadowy realities to the perception of wisdom that is original and real.[3]

On that day, says the Lord, I shall eliminate the names of the idols from the land, and there will be no further remembrance of them; I shall remove the false prophets and the unclean spirit from the land (v.2). When the aforementioned transformation takes place with a view to the aspersion and the truth, then the fictions of the heretics (referred to figuratively as *idols*) will be eliminated from the land; people will no longer be deceived, idolatry in a figurative sense will be shown up by the manifestation of truth, and all the false prophecy will be removed as well as the *unclean spirit* responsible for it that was found in the human being before faith in Christ. It is also possible that there is reference in *elimination from the earth* to material statues and the demons associated with them. Proof that the images are suggested by this term can be gained from the psalmist's statement, "The idols of the nations are silver and gold; they have feet but do not walk," and so on. And the fact that the one term is used for the actual shrines and the demons lurking within them the prophet Isaiah confirms in a passage beginning thus: "Bewail, carvings in

2. 1 Pt 1.2; Heb 9.14; 10.22; 1 Pt 1.18–19; Ps 51.7; Jas 1.27; Is 1.16.
3. Didymus makes a rare exhortation of his own, unfortunately based on the LXX's mistranslation. At no stage has he given a baptismal interpretation to the aspersion (perhaps because that was not the style of baptizing in his church) as will the bishop of Cyrus.

Jerusalem and in Samaria: what I did to Samaria and its idols I shall also do to Jerusalem and her idols."[4] Carven and molded idols that bewail are not the work of artisans, which does not naturally bewail. Bewailing is an action belonging to living things; it is an involuntary cry uttered by a living being affected by natural distress. This thought is developed in many places in the work on Isaiah with support from the Wisdom of Solomon, which has this to say: "The impious and their impiety are equally hateful to God; the action will be punished along with the guilty one." This statement of the sage refers to the artisan and the wood sculpted by him in the likeness of a living being; just as what has no soul cannot bewail, as has been pointed out just above, so it is also incapable of being punished. Hence the verse should be taken to refer to the demons attached to the lifeless images.[5]

With the elimination of the idols from the earth, there will be removed from it the false seers and in short those promoting false foreknowledge, rightly referred to by the divine instruction as *false prophets*. Their fate will be the same as that of the unclean spirit; after all, how could the spirit of the seers and the augurs not contain the uncleanness of impiety? This text could also be taken to refer to the leaders of the heresies, who are full of demons and deceitful spirits; it is of them that the divinely inspired Paul writes in these terms: "Some people will renounce sound faith by paying heed to deceitful spirits and teachings of demons through the hypocrisy of liars, whose own consciences are seared with a hot iron." It is not surprising if there is reference in the prophet to the *unclean spirit* in the singular and to "the deceitful spirits" in the plural in the apostle's letter: taken together in general fashion they refer to one spirit.[6]

Elimination of the idols' names so that there will be no further remembrance of them, of their boasting and stupidity, was well put,

4. Ps 115.4, 7; Is 10.10–11.
5. Wis 14.9–10—a helpful citation for Didymus's case? Jerome confirms that he composed a commentary at least on Second Isaiah.
6. 1 Tm 4.1–2. Once again Didymus shows his precision as a commentator in noting textual details that may worry a reader.

no relic remaining even of their name, let alone their power.

If individuals still prophesy, their fathers and mothers who bore them will say to them, You shall not live, because you spoke falsehood in the name of the Lord; and their fathers and mothers who bore them will bind them hand and foot when they prophesy (v.3). If despite the removal of the false prophets and the unclean spirit from the land someone still presumes to prophesy under the influence of sleep or madness, he would be so absurd and so open to criticism that not even his parents would believe him, even condemning him to death in the words, *You shall not live, because you spoke falsehood in the name of the Lord,* being not a prophet but a false prophet. With his *father and mother* accusing the false prophet, they hasten to *bind him hand and foot,* accusing him of specious and deceptive arguments.

Since the expression *those who bore them, when they prophesy* can be taken two ways, there is need to distinguish the two senses. One of the senses is to this effect: being human parents of a human being and maintaining towards him the attitude of parents, they will bind him hand and foot and condemn him for speaking falsehood in the name of the Lord. The other interpretation is this: his father and mother will bind him hand and foot, having generated his prophesying by giving birth to him as a false prophet, generating him by birth and upbringing by way of imitation and instruction, since they themselves obviously had leanings to false prophecy.

It is not idly or to no purpose that such a person is called a human being: walking according to the flesh "in quarreling and jealousy," he wrongly bears the title of human being in a way similar to those of whom it is said, "But as human beings you die," and like those whom the Lord classes as undeserving of the divine Spirit: "My spirit shall certainly not abide in these human beings on account of their being flesh."[7]

On that day the prophets will be ashamed, each of his own vision when he prophesies, and they will put on a hair shirt as a penalty for false prophesying. He will say, I am no prophet, and a human being brought me up from my youth. I shall say to him, What are these

---

7. Rom 13.13; Ps 82.7; Gn 6.3.

wounds between your hands? He will reply, I received the wounds in the house of my beloved (vv.4–6). People who promise knowledge of the future incur shame through the failure of their predictions. So since the censure of the false prophet comes not only from strangers but even from those who bore him, for this reason he is covered in confusion, his prophecy called into question, with the result that he now reproaches himself and falls to lamenting, *clad in a hair shirt.* Accordingly, he admits he has been a human being from his youth, the term *youth* in this case suggesting not age but juvenile and superficial behavior; the wretch, you see, who lacks mature wisdom, venerable years, and a spotless record, lives in ignorance, according to the proverbial saying, "Folly is bound up in the heart of a youth, and the rod of discipline drives it far from him." The person who surpasses this deplorable condition directs an appeal to God, "Remember not the sins of my youth and my ignorance."[8]

The person convicted of telling lies when prophesying is ashamed of the stupidity of his visions, which are characteristic rather of seers than of prophets, and he confesses he is no prophet and has been brought to this role without coming from the stock of prophets. And since he is clad in a hair shirt, and denies being a prophet under pressure and not for the sake of truth, it is put to him, *What are these wounds between your two hands?* His reply is, *I received the wounds in the house of my beloved,* my parents so far from supporting my claim to be a prophet as even to inflict blows on me. It is possible to say that the *house of the beloved* of the false prophet is the crowd loved by him, who condemned his pronouncements to the point of submitting him to abuse. The text should also be applied to dissident thinkers in Christianity.[9]

The feigned repentance of the false prophet clad in a hair

8. Wis 4.8; Prv 22.15; Ps 25.7. Didymus does not know that our Heb. has the false prophet *not* wearing the garment, which itself is a matter of debate by modern commentators as also by Theodore and Theodoret. He will proceed to correct the impression that wearing sackcloth is not a commendable penitential exercise.

9. We have seen abundant evidence of Didymus's preoccupation with a range of heretical groups in the Christian community, a concern not so evident in Cyril (before Nestorius's accession) or the Antiochenes.

shirt is mentioned also by Isaiah in connection with those who
fast and pray to no purpose; a censure is delivered against hypocrites, "If you bow your head like a ring and lie down on sackcloth and ashes, even so do not call it an acceptable fast." Now,
I am not saying that no one benefits from a hard regimen and
an austere life, since benefit comes from its performance accompanied by repentance. After much wickedness the Ninevites, for example, repented at the preaching of the prophet
Jonah and escaped the threat of the dire overthrow of their
city. The psalmist is also in agreement with this when he says,
"When they harassed me" (his foes, that is, visible and invisible), "I donned sackcloth and humbled my soul in fasting," and
in another psalm, "I took sackcloth for my clothing, and became a byword to them." When this harsh condition gives way
to possession of good things, the recipient of them moves to a
sense of joy, saying, "You turned my grief into happiness for
me, you rent my sackcloth and clad me in happiness."[10]

Sword, rise up against my shepherd and against his fellow citizen,
says the Lord almighty. Strike the shepherd, and the sheep will be scat-
tered, and I shall raise my hand against the shepherds (v.7). It is from
this prophetic verse that the evangelist Matthew has borrowed
the statement in his gospel where it says, at the capture of Jesus
and the flight of the disciples, who were scandalized, "So that
what was said by the prophet might be fulfilled, 'I shall strike
the shepherd, and the sheep will be scattered,'" meaning by
strike and *wound* the death for the sake of the rational flock of
the true shepherd, "who laid down his life for the sheep," "giv-
en as a ransom for many." It is possible to hear the good shepherd himself saying to the Father in reference to the plot
hatched to pierce his hands and gouge his feet, "They persecuted the one whom you struck, and added to the distress of my
wounds."[11] Those who slew the Lord, in fact, added to the distress of his wounds by striking the one whom God handed over
for them, aggravating their plot by persecuting him.

. . . [Aware] of the guilt rashly incurred by the villains, the

10. Is 58.5 (our Heb. speaking of a bulrush in place of a "ring"); Pss 35.13;
68.11; 30.11.
11. Mt 2.23; 26.31; Jn 10.15; Mt 20.28; Pss 22.16; 69.26.

one who had let his own shepherd be offered for the sheep orders that *a sword rise up* against his own shepherd and his fellow
citizen, that is, the Hebrew people. Yet while the sword raised
up killed the fellow citizen, it actually did no harm to the pastor
who accepted death out of pity for the flock; after all, how
could he fail to remain free of all harm who says to God, "Deliver my soul fróm the sword"? This verse occurs in the twenty-
second psalm, where the sentiments are all expressed in the
person of the savior.[12] Whereas the soul of the one uttering the
prayer was delivered from the sword, his fellow citizen fell victim to the punitive blade, as is said in Amos the prophet, "All
the sinners of the people will die by the sword." The same retribution is hinted at in what is said by God in the prophet Zephaniah, "You for your part, Ethiopians, are felled by the sword."[13]
Those struck by God's sword are Ethiopians in that they share
in the devil's evil and sin, getting their name from his blackness; in the *Shepherd* and in the *Epistle of Barnabas,* remember,
Satan is called black, falling away from the splendor and virtue
and spiritual whiteness that only the person whitened by God
can completely possess.[14]

When in the sense mentioned the shepherd is struck and as
a result *the sheep are scattered,* he extends his hand over the shepherds, the chief priests, elders, and Jewish teachers of the Law,
who conspired against the good shepherd, who laid down his
life for the sheep for them to gain salvation. *Scattering* befalls
the shepherds and the sheep under them when God's hand is
extended against them.[15]

12. Ps 22.20, thus classed a messianic psalm—something Theodore will not
concede, who would not acknowledge even the evangelists' citation of Zec 13.6.
For his part Didymus is having the same difficulty as the Antiochenes in establishing the probity or otherwise of the shepherd, not prepared like some modern commentators to resort to transposition of verses.

13. Am 9.10; Zep 2.12 (where Theodoret will also account for the admittedly puzzling inclusion of Ethiopians on the basis of spiritual blackness; see PG
81.1852).

14. In the ninth similitude of the *Shepherd of Hermas* the righteous and the
wicked are clad in white and black, respectively, while in the *Epistle of Barnabas,*
which speaks of the two Ways of Light and Darkness, the devil is referred to as
the "Black One." Doutreleau (SC 85.965) notes that Jerome does not replicate
Didymus's references to these early compositions.

15. Unlike the Antioch form of the LXX, Didymus's text does not contain

With the fourth book developed to sufficient length to the point where God says, *I shall extend my hand against the shepherds,* we shall with the help of the generous giver make a start to the fifth with the next verse, beginning thus.

On that day, says the Lord, two parts will perish and fail, while a third will be left in it. I shall pass the third through the fire, and fire them as silver is fired, and test them as gold is tested. He will call upon my name, and I shall hearken to him and say, This is my people. They will say, The Lord is my God (vv.8–9). By mention of the day a time is referred to that suggests when two-thirds of the people of captivity will perish and fail, while the third [part] will be proven to be acceptable by passing through the fire, having been fired like purified silver and proven like gold.[16] The third of the captives that is thus purified and proven will call on the name of God, and will find God giving heed and salvation; the appropriate consequence will be that the beneficiaries will be styled the people of him who gave them heed and who now shows himself their God in the way he was God of Abraham, Isaac, and Jacob. Though as creator, of course, he is God of all other people, he is in a special way God of the patriarchs who serve and reverence him.

After making these general comments, we should proceed to see who are the two-thirds that *perish and fail,* and the third that undergoes reform and is brought to salvation. We should begin with the division into three of the people of the Hebrews in captivity. Many of those deported from their own country and homeland into that of their conquerors by the norm of captivity completely abandoned the worship of God and served idols, thus being in thrall to . . . and adoring Baal and the dragon as well as the dumb image of the tyrant Nebuchadnezzar. While others did not go so far, they practiced Judaism apart from the Law and in an improper way; of such a kind were the elderly villains of adulterous tendencies and those of like mind

---

the word "little (shepherds)," though his comment is similar enough to the An-tiochene commentators' to suggest he may know it. Length requires him to close the fourth volume at this point.

16. Didymus is making some attempt to relate the verses to the situation of the captive population Zechariah has in mind.

in condemning the chaste Susanna. In addition to those who practiced idolatry and lived Judaism apart from the Law, there was another group who were commendable and reverent in captivity, not superstitious, not transgressors of the Law, but holy and pleasing to God. Their number included many holy men, such as the prophet Zechariah, on whom we are commenting, Daniel and the band of Azariah, the prophet Ezekiel, the high priest Joshua son of Jozadak, and many others, who were familiar with the practice of virtue and knowledge of the truth and of God.[17]

The impious two-thirds, pagan and Jewish, deserved punishment for their crimes, and *perished and failed,* so that by a harsh fate they might undo the damage they incurred. With that done, by a verdict of divine providence the third part was kept apart from the other two, and was sanctified and reformed by the giver of good things, God the Word, by being brought through fire that purified and made them "fervent in spirit." Of this fire the savior of all himself says, "I have come to cast fire on the earth, and how I wish it were already kindled," and again, "Everyone will be salted with fire." The mighty John, than whom "no one greater has arisen among those born of women," also teaches regarding himself, "I came to baptize with water for repentance," whereas regarding the savior of all, "He will baptize you with the Holy Spirit and fire"[18]—that is, sanctifying and purifying some by the Holy Spirit, others by fire, or them all by the Holy Spirit and by fire. Those who have passed through fire, the third of the captives that are reformed, whose call God heeds, say in their own person to the one who offers salvation, "You have proved us, O God, tested us in the fire as silver is tested, led us into the trap, laid troubles before us" (or "on our back," the reading in many manuscripts), "you put people over our heads. We passed through fire and water,

17. To Didymus's mind the survival of a remnant and the mention of purifying fire recall the contents of the book of Daniel and its additions, The Prayer of Azariah and the Three Jews, Susanna, Bel and the Dragon, as well as prophets supposedly of the period, and the account of the restoration in Ezra.

18. Rom 12.11; Lk 12.49; Mk 9.49; Mt 11.11; 3.11.

and you brought us into refreshment."[19] To the same effect in Isaiah as well the benefactor says to the beneficiary, "Fear not, because I am with you; even if you pass through water, the torrents will not overwhelm you; even if you pass through fire, the flame will not burn you, because I am with you." And when do people pass through fire and remain unharmed if not when they receive the voice of God, of which it is said, "Voice of the Lord who cuts a way through the fiery flame"?[20] In other words, just as the Red Sea was divided by the holy rod and the people passed through without loss, so the fiery flame was cut and divided, and the crossing was achieved without scorching by flames.

The third of the Hebrew population that remained after the two-thirds perished and failed were proved like the spiritual gold and silver that pass through the fire. This is stated in similar terms in Wisdom:[21] "As gold and silver are proved in the furnace, so are chosen hearts by God." The same sense is found also in what the apostle Peter writes in his letter, urging people to bear nobly and magnanimously the tribulations, especially those for the faith; his text goes as follows: "In this you rejoice, even if you have to suffer manifold trials, so that the quality of your faith, which is more precious than gold proved by fire, may be found to result in praise and glory." James is also of similar mind in communicating the Gospel to the disciples: "Consider it all a joy, beloved brethren, when you encounter manifold trials, aware as you are that your testing produces endurance, and let endurance have its full effect so that you may be mature and complete, lacking in nothing."[22] These, in fact, are the dispositions of those to whom the text is addressed, fired like silver in their speech and tested like gold in their thinking, and so they will find God responsive when they call on his name, thus being styled people of the benefactor, as he is their God.

19. Ps 66.10–12. Didymus is aware of, and takes the trouble to cite, an alternative reading that the Antioch text incorporates.
20. Is 43.1–2; Ps 29.7.
21. Actually, Proverbs; Didymus has erred.
22. Prv 17.3; 1 Pt 1.6; Jas 1.2–4.

We should scrutinize the text in hand in a different sense as well. In the Church of Christ there are some people who are superstitious and others by contrast with them who are of a Jewish mentality; again, there are some who show genuine reverence for God, and it is among these who are mature that the apostles "speak wisdom," since they have all advanced to the point of reaching "maturity to the measure of the full stature and fullness of the knowledge of the Son of God." The two-thirds will perish and fail so that they will no longer practice superstition or Jewish ways like those of the Ebionites.[23] Once this happens, only mature members of the Church *will be left in it* so as to be styled *God's people,* and he may be confessed as *their God.*

We should give careful consideration to seeing if a third interpretation can be read in the text in hand. Each of the virtues lies between two vices, excess and defect—for example, boldness and self-control, the former between audacity and cowardice, the latter between licentiousness and torpor; likewise the excess of piety is superstition, the defect is impiety. Similarly, a readiness to share and give things away is an admirable disposition, whereas the excess is wastefulness and the defect miserliness.[24] And since some people sin by excess in being guilty of audacity, superstition, and wastefulness, while others sin by defect in being guilty of impiety, cowardice, and miserliness, consequently these two kinds and groups perish and fail when they undergo punishment. The third group is mature, being tested and proven like silver and gold, which are speaking and thinking, and they overcome defect and excess by being proven and mature as a result of the virtues being intertwined.

It could further be claimed that there is also another sense to be grasped. Those who "bear the image of the man of dust,"

23. 1 Cor 2.6; Eph 4.13. Didymus adds to his list of Christological heresies this further group found in the early Church with Jewish reservations about the divinity of Jesus. Jewish sympathies were a concern also in other parts of the Church, as Chrysostom and Jerome testify.

24. Didymus developed this Aristotelian notion of virtue above in comment on 12.6–7. It is notable that he first did his best to relate 13.8–9 to the situation of the exiles, only then moving to an ecclesiological meaning for the verses and now to a moral—and on to a further moral one.

being impure and endowed with material tastes, resemble what is called by some people an Indefinite Dyad.[25] In Scripture, for example, the unclean animals embarked two by two, whereas the clean animals, being related to the chaste virgin seven, entered the ark seven by seven. And since those bearing the image of the man of dust are a dyad, their quality fails and perishes, so that the third kind—those "bearing the image of the man of heaven"—emerges proven.[26]

To each of these explanations the wise person will apply each passage of our text. The third group can be understood to *be left* on *the day* when these prophecies come to pass.

25. Doutreleau (SC 85.976–77) identifies this term as the Pythagorean designation for the principle of multiplicity.

26. 1 Cor 15.49. In the Genesis narrative of the Flood, the numbers of animals embarking vary between two (6.20; 7.2, 9) and seven (7.2), depending on the author of the verses; but Didymus is interested more in Pythagorean principles and Philo's understanding of numbers already cited in commentary on 9.5–8. Did his readers appreciate an interpretation of Scripture given in the light of the thinking of Aristotle, Pythagoras, and Philo? Antioch preferred the principle of Aristarchus, "Clarify Homer from Homer."

COMMENTARY ON ZECHARIAH 14

O, DAYS OF THE LORD *are coming, when your plunder will be divided in your midst. I shall assemble all the nations against Jerusalem to battle; the city will be taken, the houses ransacked, and the women defiled; half of the city will go off in captivity, but the remainder of my people will not perish from the city* (Zec 14.1–2). There is reference to *days of the Lord* when harsh and punitive actions are taken on the guilty, a sense you can find confirmed in many places. In Isaiah, for instance, the moment of retribution is called the day of the Lord in this way: "The day of the Lord comes, dire, full of anger and wrath, to render the whole world desolate and destroy the sinners from it."[1] Since he announces a terrible fate for those with whom God is angry for being in thrall to impiety and other sins, therefore, it is right to describe as *days of the Lord* those on which there will be a lamentable misfortune for both Jerusalem and its citizens. After all, what could be so lamentable and dire as the division in its midst of the spoils which the enemy seized in their attack as a result of weakness? This does not always happen, however: there are times when the plunderers take their booty and divide it far from the city, or rather the district, fearing that by dividing it in the city they may be obstructed by the captives finding new heart.

After the verse saying, *Lo, days of the Lord are coming, when your plunder will be divided in your midst,* the Lord immediately

---

1. Is 13.9. As we have, on the authority of Paul Hanson, reached "full-blown apocalyptic" with this chapter, it is high time for Didymus to note at least this index of the genre, which has been to the fore throughout Deutero-Zechariah. Petersen appositely remarks, "Any commentary on Zechariah 14 must work with a provisional judgment about the nature of the literature." (See P. D. Hanson, *The Dawn of Apocalyptic,* 369, and Petersen, *Zechariah 9–14 and Malachi,* 137.) Didymus is not deterred by the fact that his text (like Cyril's) differs from most forms of the LXX in reading plural "days."

says *he will assemble all the nations against them to battle,* as happens on a day of engagement; the nations are assembled for military action in the assault on Jerusalem. It is to it, in fact, the announcement is made of the division of its plunder in its midst, and, further, the ravaging of the houses of its inhabitants and the defilement of their women. After all, as distressing and extremely taxing as it is for the division to be made by the conquerors in the sight of the inhabitants, especially when not only common and public property is affected but also each person's by the sacking of their houses, what is more grievous and burdensome than all this is the shameful defilement of the women while their partners witness it but are powerless to prevent the lawless act; their inability is such that half the inhabitants are snatched from their own city. Nothing of the sort happens to those under the protection of God's right hand, these constituting the third mentioned as being saved when the two-thirds perished and failed.

In Isaiah also the divine word threatens such a cruel pillaging; the prophetic text reads as follows: "All who are assembled" (people huddled together) "will fall by the sword; they will rend your children before your very eyes, plunder your houses, and take your wives for themselves." The outrage of women being violated by the uncontrollable enemy in the sight of their husbands, with whom they live, is described also in what is said to the vile priest Amaziah by Amos, the prophet with piercing vision, "Your wife will be a prostitute in the city, and your land divided up by line."[2] Both dire threats impart anguish to husbands who see their partners within the city, not outside it, the laws of marriage being abused by the ruthless foe and their own land divided up by line in the presence of the owners, who are powerless to prevent the injustice.

Such things befell them, resembling the savagely inhuman fate of the inhabitants of Jerusalem and Judea when the Jews were captured by the nations on account of the guilt incurred by the killers of the Lord. "The nations raged, the peoples

2. Is 13.15–16; Am 7.17 (Didymus's reference to the prophet's "piercing vision" perhaps arising from the opening verse of that book where Amos is said to "see" words about Israel—like Habakkuk).

formed vain and futile plots, the kings took their stand, and the rulers came together in concert against the Lord and against his Christ. God ridiculed and mocked them, in wrath speaking against them and in his rage confounding them." So the apostle writes to the same effect about those who killed the Lord and the prophets and persecuted the apostles: "God's wrath has overtaken them at last."[3] It was noted above as well that a Jewish historian, Josephus by name, truthfully and precisely described the disasters befalling the nation, including starvation and other misfortunes much worse than that; the searcher after good can meditate on it if interested in reading directed to learning and the fear of experiencing the same fate.[4]

The text says that the survivors were not snatched away from the city by the cruel tyrants; they were those whom God tests by fire, as he proves silver and gold so as to bring to light their glory and honor.

The Lord will issue forth and go into battle among those nations, like a day of battle formation on a day of war. On that day his feet will stand on the Mount of Olives facing Jerusalem on the east. The Mount of Olives will be split in two, half of it to the east and half of it to the sea, an immense abyss (vv.3–4). Incorporeal as he is, or, rather, transcending every spiritual being, God is not the subject of corporeal attributes—namely, colors or forms or size—and so he is invisible. It is quite necessary, you see, for the visible being to have form, size, color, and other properties associated with it, whereas God is invisible, as many expressions in the Scriptures confirm, since he is a spiritual being, not moving by change of place nor in any way situated in a place. For the present it suffices to quote texts that go as follows: "He is the image of the invisible God," and again, "To the king of the ages, God incorruptible and invisible." Gospel texts suggest the same as the apostolic ones, one saying this: "No one has ever seen God; it is God the only Son, who is close to the Father's heart, who

3. Ps 2.1–5; 1 Thes 2.16. Theodoret, PG 81.1952, will take a cue from this passage to adopt an eschatological interpretation of "the Day."

4. Didymus had referred previously to the *Jewish War* of Flavius Josephus in comment on 9.15–16 and 12.1–3—brief references, as here, which he encourages his readers to follow up with a view to learning and moral improvement.

has made him known," and again, "Not that anyone has seen God except the one who is from the Father."[5]

Since these are the correct statements and ideas about God, then, there is need to take in a spiritual way befitting God the statements made about him in the divine Scriptures in a more corporeal fashion as part of his plan. This is the way, in fact, he himself says in the prophet, "I do not change," and among the sacred authors speaking to the same effect the psalmist in one case says to the object of his praise, "You, on the contrary, are the same," and, "You will abide," and in another case James writes about his being impassible and unchangeable, "Every generous act of giving and every perfect gift, is from above, coming down from the Father of lights, with whom there is no variation or shadow due to change."[6] And in the way we take and interpret the expressions about his repenting and his wrath and similar things, so, since he is incorporeal, we take the expressions about his going up and coming down, going out and coming in, in a way appropriate to this understanding of him. Hence when there occurs in the text in hand *The Lord will issue forth,* we do not imagine movement from place to place, such movements being true of bodies.

Accordingly, since it is not appropriate to attribute them to an invisible being, and yet they occur in the divinely inspired sayings, there is need to examine how they should be understood in pious fashion. Being the fount of goodness and "full of grace and truth," in descending to those who are part of his plan, the source of all things in some fashion comes from himself. In the Gospels, for instance, our Lord and savior says of himself, "I came from God, and now I am here; I did not come on my own—he sent me." In the same sense the prophet Habakkuk declares to him, "You came forth for the salvation of your people to save your anointed ones." And as he comes and is here for those being saved, so much more when he is wrath-

5. Col 1.15; 1 Tm 1.17; Jn 1.18; 6.46. This well documented essay on scriptural anthropomorphisms is prompted by Zechariah's mention of movement on God's part and his going to war and having feet. Doutreleau (SC 85.984–85) lists other cases where Didymus has lectured on divine transcendence.

6. Mal 3.6; Ps 102.27, 26; Jas 1.17.

ful and goes to war; it is written in Micah, for example, "Lo, the Lord issues from his house; he will be a witness among us and will come down," and in Isaiah, "The Lord of hosts will issue forth and crush the enemy, he will awaken his jealousy and cry aloud against his foes with strength."[7]

With these texts being interpreted in a way befitting God, here God is said to go out *against the nations, so that he is in battle formation against them on a day of battle* when *his feet will stand on the Mount of Olives facing east.* After all, where should the feet stand of the one who no longer advances menacingly as was said above, "The Lord will sound a trumpet blast and issue forth with a threat of his wrath"? In similar fashion, after his transgression Adam heard the sound of God's feet in the evening, thus gaining the impression that the one who had previously accompanied and conversed with him had forsaken him and moved away from him. In this sense the savior in the Gospels said to the Jews who had strayed from the truth, "Lo, your house is left to you," and previously in the prophet, "I have abandoned my house, left my inheritance" and so on.[8] But even if he was far from those who were abandoned on account of impiety, yet his feet stood firmly on the mountain where there is a garden plot bearing fruit that sustains and preserves the divine light and heals diseases and pains. They stand not on a low-lying garden plot, however, but one situated on a high mountain, to the east of the divine light of the sun of justice.[9]

Now, what happens when the Lord's feet are standing to the east of the Mount of Olives? The divine garden plot is divided so that the part of it that had put down roots on the east stayed firm, and the rest moved to the sea, whence an *immense abyss* was formed. And since you can find in Scripture olive trees deserving praise and blame gathered in the same place, let us see which of them is in the light facing east and which turned towards the sea. The holy psalmist in his loud chant announces in reference to himself, "I, on the other hand, am like a fruitful olive tree in the house of God." And in one of the Songs of the

7. Jn 1.14; 8.42; Hab 3.13; Mi 1.3, 2; Is 42.13.
8. Zec 9.15; Gn 3.8; Mt 23.38; Jer 12.7.
9. Mal 4.2.

Steps it is said of the person who practiced reverence, "Blessed
are you, and it will go well with you. Your wife like a vine flour-
ishing in the recesses of your house, your sons like olive shoots
around your table. Lo, this is the way the person who fears the
Lord will be blessed. May the Lord bless you from Sion, may
you see the good things of Jerusalem and see your sons' sons."[10]

No one honestly reading this psalm would be so dull and
simple as to think that all these promises accrue to every pious
person; many people without having any material goods at all
possess fear of God, which perfects the one who has it, according to the text, "Nothing is lacking to those who fear him," that
is, God.[11] The great prophet Elijah, for example, and Elisha, his
disciple, and—what am I saying?—John the Baptist, "than
whom no one is greater among those born of women," had
none of what was listed in a material sense: they were not married, they had no children physically speaking. But even if they
had no share in these material things, they still had sons and
grandsons in a spiritual sense; they were blessed by God in Sion
and saw the good things of the true Jerusalem, having made
their approach to Mount Sion and the heavenly Jerusalem,
which is the city of the living God.[12] The olive trees in this sense
and their offshoots are planted on the Mount of Olives facing
east, being transplanted to the garden that God planted in
Eden in the east. The statement is not surprising: if the brigand
who repented by confessing the savior to be king was told by
him, "This day you will be with me in paradise," how is it not
more the case that those who lived their whole life, or most of
it, in this fashion will be granted this promise so as to say with
confidence, "Our citizenship is in heaven," and again, "Though
groaning on earth, our life is in heaven."[13]

With this blessed garden plot spiritually understood, there
should be placed also the wild olive tree grafted on to the holy
root in its richness so as to become a cultivated olive tree such
that it can claim with the same confidence as the psalmist: "I,
on the other hand, am like a fruitful olive tree in the house of

10. Pss 52.8; 128.2–6.   11. Cf. Sir 15.13.
12. Mt 11.11; Heb 12.22.
13. Gn 2.8; Lk 23.43; Phil 3.20; cf. 2 Cor 5.1–2.

God."[14] The branches that are pruned away for unbelief—the Jews who killed the Lord—are found lying towards the sea, obviously because of the storm-tossed and salty waters of worldly affairs, whence arises an *immense abyss*. In the same sense as the apostle in reference to the branches pruned away, in Jeremiah also God speaks at length to the community of the circumcision: "Why has my beloved committed abominations in my house? Surely prayers and sacrificed meat will not divert troubles befalling you, or let you escape in this way?" After the one who sees in secret had accused it of committing abominations in his house, the divine word said to it, "The Lord called you a shady olive tree because of your shape, but your branches have become useless." After all, how could branches cut off because of their own infidelity be anything but useless, especially when exposed to the tempest of life that brings a tidal wave and a vast volume of salty and bitter water? In addition to their going to the sea, the disbelieving branches are cast down into an *immense abyss*. In reference to this city that is the cause of its own fate—the Jewish city, I mean—it is said by God in another prophet, namely, Micah, "I shall cast down its stones into an abyss and uncover its foundations."[15]

Since this harsh retribution befell the wretched community of the Jews, it should be a concern of ours, believers in the savior, to be a fruitful olive tree in the house of God facing east on the Mount of Olives, so that by the grace of God we may pass into the godly paradise, having become imitators of Christ, of whom it is written, "Lo, a man, east is his name."[16]

Half of the mountain will face the north and half of it the south. A valley of my mountains will be filled in, and a valley of the mountains will be joined together as far as Azal in the way it was filled in at the time of the earthquake in the days of Uzziah king of Judah (vv.4–5). Half of the mount (of olives, clearly), he is saying, will face the

14. Rom 11.17, 24; Ps 52.8. As often happens with Didymus, a tangential commentary on olive trees has developed by way of association, highlighting Jewish infidelity—hardly Zechariah's principal focus (obscure though this is). Antioch again would feel the direction being followed to be arbitrary.

15. Jer 11.15–16; Mi 1.6.

16. Zec 6.12, where we noted the LXX had misread as "east (or Dawn)" the Heb. for "shoot."

north away from what faces the sea and the abyss, while the other half goes to the south. The meaning of *north* and *south* we
can learn from the Song of Songs, where the Church is compared with a bride saying to her bridegroom, "Awake, north
wind, and come, south wind, blow across my garden and let my
fragrance be wafted." In this passage *north* means the power of
evil, or rather Satan in person, whereas the savior is called
south, he being the bridegroom. When the north wind that is
mentioned blows, it is very cold, and the wafting of the divine
fragrance is hindered, since the pores of the plants are con-
stricted as a result of the coldness and harshness of the north
wind. Hence the bride keeps it at a distance and invites the
south wind so that the spiritual pores are dilated by its warmth,
and there is a wafting of the fragrance, of which mention is
made in reference to the groom by his spiritual partner, "The
scent of your perfume surpassed every fragrance." I said the
south wind is warm and fragrant, aware that it is . . . and came
to cast fire upon the earth, as he himself announced in the
words, "I came to cast fire upon the earth, and how I wish it
were already kindled."[17]

The direction "Awake, north wind" should be not only recit-
ed but put into effect so that it may be dispatched to a distance.
Now, the faithful soul gives effect to the direction "Awake, north
wind" in the case of the teacher who says, "Desist from evil and
do good," and the apostle writing to the whole Church, "Test
everything, hold fast to the good, avoid every kind of evil," since
avoidance of every kind of evil and desisting from evil drives off
the north wind and encourages the south wind to come by making an approach to it with pious faith and the practice of virtue.
This, in fact, is the way that the provider of all good things
comes to purified [souls] who are thus pleasing to him, as the
sacred author James wrote, "Approach God, and he will approach you." The [soul] with longing for his presence, as in the
verse, "Come, south wind," says in the actual wedding ceremony,

17. Song 4.16; 1.3; Lk 12.49. Didymus's commentary is affected by the fact
that his text differs (from other forms of the LXX and) the Heb., making attention to Zechariah's thought less likely and encouraging an immediate (and acknowledged) spiritual interpretation.

"Come, my nephew, let us go out into the fields."[18] Similar in effect to the verse, "Awake, north wind, and come, south wind," is the verse, "Approach God, and he will approach you; resist the devil, and he will flee from you," since it is no one but the person who resists the devil who says to him, "Awake, north wind," and approaches God with the invitation to the south wind to come to him, God the Word, of whom in the song of the prophet Habakkuk, in place of "God will come from Teman,"[19] it is said in one of the translators, "God will come from the south," since the Father comes from the south, that is, the bridegroom, according to the statement by him in the Gospel, "The one who receives me receives the one who sent me." In other words, in the way the one who sees him sees the Father, so the one who receives him receives the Father, who abides in him,[20] since it is in him that the Only-begotten is found.

What will transpire when the Mount of Olives in the sense explained faces north and south? The *filling in of the valley of God's mountains and its joining together as far as Azal.* Now, the valley and its joining together are to be understood only by grasping what God's *mountains* are. In one sense his mountains are to be understood as the prophets, not only for their characteristic loftiness of knowledge and wisdom but also for the superiority of their life in practice. It is in reference to them, in fact, that the psalmist exclaimed to the creator of all things, "You shed light marvelously from everlasting mountains"; after all, how could they fail to be everlasting mountains when it was from them that God marvelously shed the light of the knowledge of truth and in short granted illumination about the Trinity, since they have an insight into eternal things not seen, according to the apostolic exhortation?[21]

18. Ps 33.14; 1 Thes 5.21–22 ("to the whole Church"?); Jas 4.7; Song 4.16 (where the LXX has inadequately rendered the Heb. as "nephew," a version Theodoret has to work hard to rationalize throughout his *Commentary on the Song of Songs*).

19. Jas 4.7; Hab 3.3, a passage where Theodoret will acknowledge these two translations or interpretations known to him (possibly from Didymus, whom Jerome again reproduces).

20. Mt 10.40; Jn 14.9–10.

21. Ps 76.4; 2 Cor 4.18. By προφῆται Didymus may mean rather OT

The *valley* of these mountains is the profound obscurity of what is stated obliquely in Scripture, which the one coming to fulfill the Law and the Prophets has filled in, leveling by his teaching and presence the rough and uneven bottom of the puzzling sayings so that it may be easily negotiated in its smoothness. When this was done, the valley of the mountains was joined together in obvious concord as far as Azal, the one who was said to be "fleet of foot" like a sharp-eyed gazelle because of his swift running (this animal having keen sight, as is indicated by its name, derived from the verb "to see clearly"). Hence the joining of the mountains will extend to Azal in that it is recognizable to those of keen sight.[22]

The filling in of the ravine between the mountains happened in the same way as in the days of the earthquake in the reign of Uzziah, king of Judah. We did not find that a real earthquake had happened in the reign of Uzziah, neither in the books of Kings nor in the Chronicles. Hence the reference to it in the text should be taken spiritually.

Note whether a disturbance occurred when Uzziah wanted to wrest the priesthood; he entered the Temple of God, approached the holy altar, and endeavored to offer sacrifice on his own and not by means of the priests. The priest on duty that day, with the support of the other ministers, vigorously resisted this bold presumption, saying, "It is not for you, Uzziah, to offer sacrifice to the Lord—only the priests." He was upset, and stretched out his hand in anger to have the priests arrested by his bodyguards so as to do them harm; but immediately his hand became leprous, the result being that at once the tyrant was cast out of the Temple. The sanctuary had been defiled by his temerity and violence in wanting to appropriate a role that was not assigned to him but reserved to the priests resident in the Temple.

---

authors in general; in either case Theodore would contest any such grasp of the Trinity in the OT.

22. The Azal that Didymus finds in his text is one of several LXX forms representing the obscure Heb. term. He sees a connection with the Asahel who was one of the sons of Zeruiah (2 Sm 2.18) and who had a reputation for the speed of a gazelle, an animal whose large eyes gave it its name. All things considered, a

In addition to the failure of his wish to wrest authority he
was impeded from exercising kingship by the impurity of lep-
rosy; so his son, who was due to succeed him in charge, then
acted in that role.

In the days of the earthquake resulting from this fusion, a valley
was joined together with the mountains in the days *when Uzziah
was king of Judah.* The earthquake mentioned at this point occurs also at the beginning of Amos the prophet: "The words of
Amos, which came from Tekoa, two years before the earthquake in the days of Uzziah." What is here called an earthquake was, according to a Jewish tradition that circulated, the
vision Isaiah had, of which the text says this: "In the year that
King Uzziah died, I saw the Lord seated on a throne elevated
and lofty. Seraphim were in attendance around him, each with
six wings," and a little further on, "One called out to another,
Holy, holy, holy is the Lord of hosts; heaven and earth are full
of his glory."[23] Heaven and earth were full of God's glory at the
death of Uzziah after the offense he committed; after all, how
could there not be a tumultuous movement greater than any
other, when God appeared for the purpose of heaven and
earth being filled with his glory, of removing the iniquities of
the one who feels compunction on seeing the divine vision,
and of forgiving the sins of the entire people? In the days of the
death of Uzziah, who was bent on violating the divine laws,
bent on usurping the priestly functions not proper for him, the
breach in the laws he had opened was rejoined. Once again the
priest performed his proper role in the Temple unhindered,
and the king was attentive to the protection of his subjects without getting involved any further in priestly functions, since
priestly worship did not fall to him.

As to the Azal mentioned here being a place name, the per-

---

contrived attempt to find spiritual significance—not that modern commentators do much better.

23. Am 1.1; Is 6.1–3. The account in 2 Chr 16.16–21 of Uzziah's effrontery,
as Didymus rightly observes, does not make mention of an earthquake (though
archaeologists claim there is evidence at ancient Hazor of such a quake in his
reign—hence perhaps Amos's remark); but Didymus by his usual method of intertextual association concludes Isaiah is referring to it (with the support of "a
Jewish tradition," probably arising from a similar logic).

son who has taken the trouble to study the topography of Judea will inform us of what he finds to be the precise situation.[24]

The Lord my God will come, and all his holy ones with him. On that day there will be no light; there will be cold and ice for one day. That day is known to the Lord. Not day and not night, and at evening there will be light (vv.5–7). The text in hand may signify the second and glorious coming of the savior, of which John in Revelation spoke in the following elevated terms befitting God: "Lo, he is coming with the clouds, every eye will see him, even those who pierced him." This understanding is suggested by what the savior said of himself: "Tribes will see the Son of Man coming on the clouds of heaven with great power and glory"; after all, how could the one who arrives in royal fashion not be resplendent with great glory? He comes also with great "power," however, because *holy ones* accompany him, not men only but also angels. It is logical, in fact, that "those who have been his eyewitnesses and servants" and "ministering spirits assigned to his service" by him should with him be resplendent, so that he should be acknowledged as their king, and they as his powers, that is, his forces.[25]

On the day the Lord God will come, *there will be no* visible *light,* since the true and eternal light will provide the daylight, according to what is foretold in Isaiah about the perfect light in these terms: "The sun will not provide you with light of day, nor will the rising of the moon light up the night for you; instead, the Lord will be an everlasting light for you, and your God will be your glory." It could also be put this way: those who are not light have need of what enlightens them, but do not require it when they themselves become light. So since in the age to come ("day" being used allegorically) "the righteous will shine like the sun in the kingdom of their Father" and emerge as light illuminating themselves, they live *on that day* without need

24. For Doutreleau (SC 85.1006) there is reference here to a visit to Didymus by Jerome, who had made a tour of the whole of Palestine with expert guides, thus confirming 387 as the likely date of this commentary.

25. Rv 1.7; Mt 24.30; Lk 1.2; Heb 1.14. Regarding "the holy ones," Petersen agrees that "one may anticipate that they might have a military role"; *Zechariah 9–14 and Malachi*, 143.

of light from another source. In this life, in fact, those who illuminate themselves with the light of knowledge so as to hear from the savior, "You are the light of the world," live in a resplendent condition, not from another source but from their being light and day themselves; the choir of holy ones cries aloud about this, "Let the splendor of the Lord our God be upon us." To this spiritual Jerusalem in its profound holiness the prophet says, possessed by God and enjoying the Holy Spirit, "Shine, shine, Jerusalem: your light has come to you, and the glory of your God has arisen upon you. Lo, darkness and gloom will cover the earth among the nations, whereas on you the Lord will shine, and the glory of your God has arisen on you. Kings will come to your light, and nations to your splendor."[26] After all, how could that light which is in receipt of these promises not be bright and luminous when it results from being illuminated to the point of displaying divine splendor?

We should examine whether it is also possible to apply in the following way the prophetic text in hand. When the Lord almighty comes with his holy ones, the condition of those being judged will be such as to be without light through their ignorance of their own situation, the result being that they need him "who sheds light on the hidden things of darkness and uncovers the thoughts of the heart," so that on "appearing before the tribunal of Christ" they may be given the recompense of their deeds, both good and bad, while in the body. And since alarm and panic will strike those being judged in their confusion and disturbance, *there will be cold and ice on one day,* with people frozen at the prospect of harsh and distressing developments, as the Gospel declares.[27]

The day of the Lord, being continuous and uninterrupted by intervention of night, will be *known to God,* who is "light without darkness," and so for this reason it will be *not day nor night* but everlasting day. It will no longer be the sun providing daylight nor the moon illuminating the night, since according to

26. Is 60.19; Mt 13.43; 5.14; Ps 90.17; Is 60.1–3.
27. 1 Cor 4.5; 2 Cor 5.10; Lk 21.26. Our Heb. speaks of *no* cold and ice, as do some forms of the LXX.

the prophet, as has just been said, it is the Lord who is everlasting light. In fact, even if the day seems to some people to come to an end, *at evening there will be light,* with God enlightening everything. The *day,* understood in this way and proving to be so, will be known to the Lord, being worthy of his knowledge, as suggested by the statement in Scripture, "The Lord knows those who are his."[28] This verse does not contradict the following Gospel passage: "No one knows about this hour and this day, neither the angels nor the Son—only the Father." Sufficient reflections have been made about the Gospel passage in the work on Matthew in a previous composition, with which a studious reader will be familiar. For the present it need only be said that one should apply "knowing" and "not being known" to different sorts of days, and take "being known" and "not being known" in different senses.[29]

On that day living water will come out from Jerusalem, half of it to the first sea and half of it to the last sea. It will be like this in summer and spring. The Lord will be king over all the earth (vv.8–9). On the day known to the Lord living water will come out from Jerusalem, "the heavenly city of the living God,"[30] half of which will go to the first sea, the other half reaching the last sea. This happens not only in summer but also in spring, the Lord reigning over all the earth, that is, all people.

Since the prophecy connotes nothing physical or factual, it should all be taken spiritually.[31] *The living water coming out from* the spiritual *Jerusalem,* which is the Church envisioning peace, is the spiritual law or, rather, the knowledge of the mind of the Church, which on reaching the sea sweetens it and induces tranquillity, expelling and eliminating every tempest. This interpretation, of course, was the object of clarification when we

28. 1 Jn 1.5; 2 Tm 2.19.

29. Mt 24.36, a text quoted by the Arians to uphold their subordinationist position. Didymus's Matthew commentary, of which Jerome speaks, is not extant.

30. Heb 12.22.

31. This is not a rule of thumb for Didymus: he has shown some interest in looking (perhaps where he should not try, as in this "full-blown apocalyptic"; see P. D. Hanson reference in n.1 above) for an αἰσθητός or ἰστορικός reality in Zechariah's text before taking it κατ᾽ ἀναγωγήν.

commented on the following verse in Isaiah: "The whole earth was filled with the knowledge of the Lord in the way deep water covers the sea"; in other words, just as divine love—both God's love for the objects of his favor and the love of the beneficiaries for the generous gift—"covers a multitude of sins,"[32] making them disappear without keeping count of them, covering up shameful exploits, so the knowledge of God, being *living water,* "covers the sea" by changing it into a sweet drink. This is the sense in which the living water coming out of Jerusalem to the first and last sea expels every tempest and tidal wave, salty taste and bitterness, and produces calmness, tranquillity, and a pleasant taste, so that there are no longer . . . seas. The living water divided into two: half of it was dispatched to the first sea, the other half to the last sea, not only in summer but also in springtime.

There being such great benefit, *the Lord will be king over all the earth,* as is said in the Psalms, where in one case, "The Lord is king; let the earth rejoice," and in another, "Say among the nations, The Lord is king; he set the world in place, and it will not be moved."[33] Now, the world was set in place so as to remain unmoved when *the first sea* was sweetened, that is, the Jewish synagogue, and the *last,* namely, the calling of the nations. Both these seas were filled with tumult and tempests before accepting the Gospel and faith in the savior, or rather in the holy Trinity.

There is need to examine whether it is possible that the living water was apportioned to the two covenants, the New and the Old, at the time when the water issued from Jerusalem. It came from it at the time when the utterance of the words of God reached "all the earth" and "his statements to the end of the world," the result being that everywhere there are sacrifices and a clean oblation offered spiritually to God, especially since the Lord emerges as mighty king among all the nations.[34]

---

32. Is 11.9; Jas 5.20. Didymus this time does not think intertextually; if he did, he might have cited Jl 3.18, Ezek 47.1–20, or Gn 2.10–14 on the flowing streams of water. Nor does he take a sacramental interpretation, as will the bishop of Cyrus (Theodoret, PG 81.1956).

33. Pss 97.1; 96.10.   34. Ps 19.4; Mal 1.11.

When the living water was apportioned, half to each covenant, . . . was within Jerusalem, guarded—or, rather, overshadowed—by the shadow of the Law and "the old written code" at the depths of winter. But when spring followed on, and flowers blossomed on earth, and the turtledove was heard in the land, in the words of the Song of Songs, "the fig tree put forth its figs, the vines blossom, the winter has passed, the rain has gone and taken itself off, the flowers have appeared in our land."[35]

Hence, when spiritual springtime comes and then the month of first-fruits, we celebrate the feast of the crossing, called Pasch in Hebrew, in which Christ is immolated so that we may be sated with his spiritual flesh and sacred blood and "celebrate the festival with the unleavened bread of sincerity and truth." After this festival we shall celebrate also the feast of Weeks, called Pentecost, in which we shall harvest ripened sheaves and fully grown ears of corn that have flowered in the spring.[36] In praise of God for both the seasons the holy one said, "You it was who established sun and moon, summer and spring; you it was who made them; remember your creation," all the earth (humanity, I mean), you, the only king, who destroyed death, which reigned from Adam to Moses, as well as the devil with his power. Confirmation that the living water is the draught from the divine word is to be found in the Gospel, where the savior says, "Those who drink from the water that I shall give them will have a spring of living water gushing up to eternal life," and again, "As Scripture says, From the heart of anyone believing in me rivers of living water will flow."[37] In other words, just as those who drink from the water Jesus gives will have in themselves a spring of living water, so rivers of living water will flow from the heart of those who drink it.

On that day the Lord will be one, and his name one, encompassing

---

35. Rom 7.6; Song 2.11–13.

36. 1 Cor 5.7. The reference to Easter and the Eucharist is a rare liturgical allusion, as Doutreleau notes (SC 85.1019). Didymus makes a point of highlighting the Jewish background to the Christian feasts. His accent on spring would have been less pronounced had he been aware that (our) Heb. reads rather "winter."

37. Ps 74.16–18; Rom 5.14; Heb 2.14; Jn 4.14; 7.38.

*all earth and the desert from Geba as far as Rimmon south of
Jerusalem; Ramah will remain in its place; from the gate of Benjamin
as far as the first gate, to the corner gate and to the tower of Hananel, to
the king's winepresses they will occupy it [Jerusalem]. There will be no
further curse, and Jerusalem will abide confidently* (vv.9–11). When
by the grace of God the aforementioned events occur, then
polytheism will disappear, and only the sustainer of all things
will be known and confessed. In former times there were differences between the last sea and the first, between the calling of
the Jews and of the Greeks (this being the sense given to
"seas"), and there was not confession by everyone that there is
one God: the idolaters thought there were many gods, the Jews
one. With the coming of the Gospel, however, people acquired
the knowledge of one sole creator, so that Paul, speaking in
Christ, writes, "Surely God is God also of gentiles, and not only
of Jews? Yes, also of gentiles, since God is one"—a clear indication that God is one. *On that day,* accordingly, when he comes
who is expected, the only-begotten Son of God, when all error
and false belief is done away with, there will be confession of
one sole true God. The result will be that those with knowledge
of the truth will bow down and serve him alone, since the gods
made by human hand are no more, as the divine word says,
"Gods that did not make heaven and earth will perish from the
earth and from under heaven."[38]

It has been said in our text above that the Lord will destroy
from the earth all wooden idols, removing from it the unclean
spirit, the result being that the demons will no longer be
thought to be gods. Of them the sacred author to whom "the
hidden mysteries of wisdom" were revealed by the ruler of all
says, "All the gods of the nations are demons." It is not only
when these falsely called gods disappear, by the cessation of acceptance of them as gods, that God will alone be known, when
those attached to the idols are "converted from them to the
service of the living and true God." It will also happen through
the pious insight that neither the world nor any of its parts is
God, when people will no longer serve or reverence creation

38. Rom 3.29; Jer 10.11.

instead of its creator, thus no longer bowing down to the sun and the moon or serving them. [39]

Thus God will be one, and, on the day that the sun of justice makes[40] and reveals, *his name will be one* as well: when everyone is in agreement in having a precise and pious understanding, he will be referred to by one name. Thus will be fulfilled the saying in the hymns, "How wonderful your name in all the earth," and again, "You magnified your holy name over all," and further, "As your name, O God, so also your praise to the ends of the earth." In keeping with the psalm is what the prophet Habakkuk says about the true God in these terms: "The earth is full of your praise."[41] Since the name of the one God is everywhere on earth shouted aloud and glorified, there is no other name signifying God. Now, this happens particularly when the prayer said to God comes into effect (not to mention others), "Hallowed be thy name." In some fashion, you see, God's name is dishonored by being blasphemed and profaned among the nations in the case of those whose thoughts and actions are not in conformity with him, whereas it is hallowed when the name of God is raised without dishonor over all who prove to be good and honorable, and so God becomes all in all at the end of things.[42] The name of God is hallowed also at the time when no longer applied to idols and demons and creation, the name of God thus being *one* in everyone's mouth.

There is need to examine what is the consequence of acknowledgment of God's being one and his name one. On all the earth round about and in the desert, the Lord and his name will be confessed. By *desert* here should be understood the Church from the nations, and by *earth* the people of the circumcision; both peoples will serve one Lord, knowing no other God than the one who says, "No other God than me will you know," only my name being exalted over everyone. In professing God to be one, however, we [do not recognize] the Trinity

39. Zec 13.2; Pss 51.6; 96.5; 1 Thes 1.9; Rom 1.25; Dt 4.19.
40. Ps 118.24; Mal 4.2.   41. Pss 8.1; 138.2; 48.10; Hab 3.3.
42. Mt 6.9; Rom 2.24; 1 Cor 15.28.

in such a way as to think divinity is true of the Father but not of Son and Holy Spirit: there is one divinity of Father, Son, and Holy Spirit, as has been demonstrated in many places in the work on the Son.[43]

With the acknowledgment of one Lord and his one name encompassing all the earth as far as the desert, the understanding had a beginning *from Geba,* which in translation means "testimony," the testimony of which the savior spoke in the Gospel in the words, "You search the Scriptures, because they give testimony to me." To similar effect the apostle Paul also writes, "The righteousness through faith in Jesus Christ is testified to in the Law and the Prophets." From the divine testimony there comes knowledge that God is one and his name is one *as far as Rimmon,* which means "lofty" or "elevated." In other words, to what point was there need for the divine testimony to go if not to the lofty and elevated mind, since the testimony is in effect a demonstration? The text tells us where: the testimony and the elevation exist and are found *south of* the spiritual *Jerusalem;* reference to the south was just now made in citing the passage from the Song of Songs, "Arise, north wind, and come, south wind."[44] Hence, to avoid repeating the same point over and over, we should be content with what was said then, and proceed to what follows. *Ramah will remain in its place,* not moving from place to place, its name meaning "elevation" or "elevated." Now, where must it remain elevated on account of its extreme eminence, if not in a lofty place, not sinking or moving? In other words, it is appropriate and beneficial for those to remain in holiness who have made great progress towards the goal, [the progress] that is perfection in itself.

43. Hos 13.4; Ps 138.2. In his introduction Doutreleau, SC 83.18, discusses the authenticity of a work on the Trinity discovered in the eighteenth century and attributed to Didymus; no work on the Son is known. He also notes that Didymus at this point is rebutting the charge of Sabellianism raised by the Arians against those insisting on the "one divinity."

44. Jn 5.39; Rom 3.21; Song 4.16. The author's thought is obscured by the LXX; further, Didymus is less interested in the location of the places, preferring to look for spiritual meaning in supposed etymology and to develop that. Etymology pays off in the case of "Ramah," which the LXX has rendered as a place name for the Heb. "high."

The gate of Benjamin, a name meaning "son of the right" or "of days," implies initiation into the divine mysteries and teachings on the right way, by which he enters who does and understands everything aright and with illumination, being called son of the right and of days. There is need to examine whether a son of days is the "son of light" to whom the savior refers along with like-minded people, "The sons of this age are more shrewd in dealing with their own generation than the sons of light," and of them it is written, "Live as children of light."[45] *From the gate* (of those enlightened and on the right, which is *first* insofar as an initiation) *as far as the corner gates. The corner gates* can be taken two ways: one way as praiseworthy . . . for making a junction of the walls, whose head—Christ the cornerstone—is recognized as foundation and completion. "The stone which the builders rejected has become the cornerstone," being also the foundation of those built on it, who are addressed by the wise architect who appointed the head of the Church and writes as follows: "Built on the foundation of the apostles and prophets, with Christ Jesus as the cornerstone." Paul was able to call the savior a cornerstone, having previously quoted for his purposes from the prophecy of Isaiah the prophetic statement in the person of God, "Lo, I am laying in Sion a cornerstone, a chosen and precious stone as its foundation, and the one who believes in it will not be confounded." And Peter the disciple of Christ put in his letter that the Lord as a living stone is foundation and head of the sacred building, the Church.[46]

One can, on the other hand, take the corners in another way as "liars"; it is there where hypocrites stand to pray, are conceited and vainglorious . . . give the impression of piety. The same corners, in fact, which begin at the first gate, are no longer salutary, a corner being nothing other than a rupture of a straight line . . .[47] It is at these corners and worse places than

45. Lk 16.8; Eph 5.8. While it is from Gn 35.18 that Didymus derives the former etymology for Benjamin, Jerome repudiates the latter in citing it, as Doutreleau notes (SC 85.1028).

46. Ps 118.22; Eph 2.20; Is 28.16; 1 Pt 2.4; 1 Cor 3.10–11; Eph 1.22; 2.21.

47. Mt 5.5. Some lines in the manuscript are defective at this point. Again, though not ignoring any of the place references in the verses, Didymus is not

they that the whore parades in the streets . . . : "Her feet are not content to stay at home," Scripture says, "sometimes she roams outdoors, sometimes she stations herself at every streetcorner" until she leads astray the foolish young man. It is, in fact, only this brainless youngster that she with her small talk can ensnare, never accosting the man grown old in good sense who to his honorable old age has led a stainless life.[48]

Since, however, there were corners to be seen in Scripture worthy of both blame and praise, let us study how they differ so as to see which it is best to avoid and which not. The gates after the gate of Benjamin, the first in honor, are the corner gates, entrances for people at harmony and accord, which it is good to enter, being entrances of righteousness. The order is given about them, "Open the gates, let the people observant of truth enter," and so on; of them the psalmist cried aloud, "Open for me gates of righteousness, I shall enter by them and confess to the Lord." The corners that are not good are not called simply corners but specifically streetcorners, not streets where Wisdom feels free to roam but those . . . with width and breadth leading to perdition.[49]

The entrances that are worthy of praise reach to the *tower of Hananel,* meaning "circumcision by grace." The grace of circumcision, however, is not that of the flesh performed according to the letter, but that of the heart done according to the life-giving spirit. It is possible to take the tower of Hananel as the way of life according to the Gospel and interior Judaism;[50] it was of it that the savior spoke in instructing the disciples, "If any of you wants to build a tower, does he not first sit down and determine if he has what is needed to complete it, lest having laid its foundation he is unable to finish it, and those who see it begin to mock him in the words, This man began to build but could not finish?" There is reference under the form of a parable to the active and the contemplative life. People with grace

---

concerned to identify their location, simply responding to their scriptural echoes and exploring their spiritual applicability.

48. Prv 7.11; Wis 4.9.
49. Is 26.2; Ps 118.19; Prv 1.20; Mt 7.13.
50. Rom 2.29.

in place of circumcision, however, are not like that: after laying the foundation they complete the building by erecting both house and parapet; in other words, after planning to build their life like a tower, they finish it by making of it a refuge and secure lifestyle with a view to spying out enemies who advance from afar. Having finished this building, the psalmist says in gratitude to his fellow worker, "You guided me because you became my hope, a strong tower in the face of the foe."[51]

The one who goes as far as the tower of circumcision—of grace, that is—and reaches *the winepresses of the great king,* Christ, dwells on a hillside so as to gather the grapes of harvest from the true vine and its fruitful branches for the making of wine that brings joy to a person's heart.[52] Songs and psalms have been written about wine vats with such an interpretation; surely, after all, our mind is not so confined to earth as to believe that spiritual people under the inspiration of the Holy Spirit have referred to material winepresses and vats, and not instead to lofty spiritual interpretations. In accord with the idea of dwelling near winepresses of this kind, there is in the Song of Songs the saying by the bride to the companions of the groom, "Conduct me to the house of wine, bring me love."[53]

When what is implied by the prophecy at hand comes to fruition, *there will be no further curse, and Jerusalem will abide with confidence in the king,* having learned that "it is better to have confidence in the Lord than in a human being," and the proverb that says, "The one with confidence in the Lord is blessed."[54] There is need to inquire, however, how it is that when these things happen, there will be no further curse. The word is used in a twofold manner, suggesting on the one hand what is forbidden for the defilement it brings, and on the other what is consecrated and dedicated to God. To be taken in reference to the former is the following text: "If any do not love the

---

51. Lk 14.28–30; Dt 22.8; Ps 61.3.
52. Jn 15.1–2; Ps 104.15.
53. Song 2.4. Didymus would be impatient with commentators who assure us that the royal winepresses, like the other Jerusalem sites, can be easily identified.
54. Ps 118.8; Prv 16.20.

Lord, let them be accursed," and the one that goes, "No one speaking by the Spirit of God says, Jesus is cursed." In this sense Paul wanted "to be accursed for the brethren and kindred according to the flesh." For the latter sense . . . of the word *curse* many texts can be assembled from the historical books of Scripture, which a scholar will find for himself.[55]

So when *Jerusalem will abide with confidence,* there will be no one in it under curse, nor any idol, since carved and graven images will have been abolished from it. When these are done away with, in fact, it will abide confidently because it will be enjoying spiritual security, of which Jeremiah the prophet said in these words: "Blessed is the person who has confidence in the Lord."[56]

This will be the downfall with which the Lord will strike all the peoples who attack Jerusalem. Their flesh will wither while they are still on their feet, their eyes run from their sockets, and their tongues rot in their mouths (v.12). This is the downfall affecting those attacking it and surrounding it with stakes. Now, what are the [misfortunes] that he predicts for those besieging the beautiful city of Jerusalem? *Their flesh will wither while they are still on their feet,* either from extreme starvation or from dread of the expected abuse and hardship. The withering of their flesh will be so extreme that *their eyes will run* and leave their sockets, *and their tongues rot in their mouths.*

This misfortune did not affect to the same extent those besieging and plundering the material Jerusalem as the people persecuting Christianity and the Church of Christ, which is Jerusalem taken anagogically. Christian history recounts all the calamities truly . . . inflicted on those who ravaged the servants . . . and places of assembly to the point of razing them and consigning the divine books to the flames. There is fuller treatment of these things in many places in our work on Isaiah, and we urge studious readers to peruse it.[57]

---

55. 1 Cor 16.22; 12.3; Rom 9.3. Didymus is much more at home with psalmists and prophets, evangelists and apostles, than with the OT historical books.

56. Jer 17.7.

57. In commentary on 8.6 Didymus had referred in similar terms to the

God strikes those encircling Jerusalem with hostile intent so that they may desist from the awful condition they adhere to in being devoted to their superstitious service. When their *downfall* occurs for their own good, it will be followed by a recovery and stable condition that win exceeding commendation. In reference to this prophecy the righteous Simeon, filled with the Holy Spirit, took into his arms the infant born of Mary without marital intercourse and gave witness in the words, "Lo, this is the one who is set for the downfall and rise of many."[58] It is thanks to him, in fact, that people who are . . . and carnal fall so as to arise in keeping with God's holiness and prove secure, solidly established in faith and other virtues, as is written by the apostle to Church members, "Stand firm in faith." This stand happens thanks to the savior Jesus; we can learn from his words, "There are some standing here who will not taste death." Those who have received this benefit reject a carnal way of thinking and eyes with evil vision, and so are no longer in the flesh but in the Spirit, no longer living in a vicious and adulterous way but virtuously and with self-control, putting to death by the Spirit the works of the body, turning their eyes from vanities by raising them towards God so as to exclaim, "I raised my eyes to you, who dwell in heaven," and again, "My eyes are always turned to the Lord."[59]

An attempt should be made to understand in conformity with the interpretation thus adopted the saying in the Gospel by our savior reported as follows, "I have come into the world for judgment, so that those who do not see may see and those who see may become blind." In other words, once the eyes with sinful vision are deprived of evil sight, there will be a gift of sight that enables correct and holy vision.[60] It is possible also to

---

persecution of Diocletian at the beginning of the century, with special mention of destruction of buildings and books.

58. Lk 2.34.

59. 2 Cor 1.24; Mt 16.28; Rom 8.6; 2 Pt 2.14; Rom 8.13; Pss 119.37; 123.1; 25.15.

60. Jn 9.39. The LXX's rendering as "downfall" Heb. "plague" (v.12), which would have allowed for some effort to be made to dwell on Zechariah's (admittedly apocalyptic) scenario instead of immediately adopting an "anagogical" interpretation, perhaps accounts for Didymus's ringing the changes on the sense

take the Gospel text in another sense. Since the Jews were impious in their blasphemies by not believing in the Lord, it was fitting that they be blinded, as is said in the prophet, "God's servants were blinded," that is, those who made false promises to serve him. When this happened, those from the nations were called to faith and recovered their sight at the coming of the one who said, "The Spirit of the Lord is upon me, because he has anointed me, he has sent me to bring good news to the poor, to proclaim release to captives and sight to the blind," shedding light on them by his own wisdom, as is written, "A man's wisdom will shed light on his face." The same sense should be given also to the statement in the Psalms, "the Lord gives wisdom to the blind,"[61] the purpose being that they should no longer be blind but gain clear vision.

The eyes with evil sight fall from their sockets and are rendered ineffectual so as to be replaced in the same sockets, which are the natural thoughts,[62] with eyes that see God. These eyes a person raised towards him in the manner of the one who says, "Towards you I raised my eyes, you who dwell in heaven." So the flesh that has a hostile attitude to God will *wither*, and the eyes with impious sight will *run from their sockets* thus interpreted so as to reveal those with sharp vision, of whom the apostle writes the following sentiment: "Enlightened in the eyes of the heart." In similar fashion, then, Scripture also says that the *tongues will rot in the mouths* of those with deceptive speech even about material matters, so that what was said by the wise ruler of all takes effect, "My tongue will meditate on your righteousness alone."[63]

On that day deep astonishment from the Lord will fall on them. All will seize the hands of their neighbors, and their hands will be interlocked with the hands of their neighbors. Judah will deploy its forces in Jerusalem and assemble the might of all the peoples round about, gold

---

of sight as though under a feeling of compulsion. "An attempt should be made, . . ." he says, "it is possible. . . ." Other effects of the plague/"downfall" are passed over.

61. Is 42.19; Lk 4.18; Eccl 8.1; Ps 146.8.
62. A Stoic term, Doutreleau tells us (SC 85.1044–45).
63. Ps 123.1; Rom 8.7; Eph 1.18; Ps 71.24.

and silver and garments in great abundance (vv.13–14). On the day
when what the prophet conveyed reached fulfillment, *deep as-*
tonishment from the Lord fell upon them, with the Lord provoking it.
Astonishment here means "amazement as a result of frenzy or de-
rangement"; in the prophet Hosea, for instance, there is a text,
"The sons of Israel will return and seek out the Lord their God
and David their king; and they will be astonished at the Lord
and his good things," which suggests amazement or, as some
commentators claim, wonderment. The text in Habakkuk also
has the same sense, "I pondered your works and was astonished," the prophet meaning that astonishment in that sense
came from the Lord and was magnified in the beneficiaries.[64]

When that happens, *Judah will deploy its forces in Jerusalem.* Of
Judah, the one who confesses more than all others, it is said, "Judah, may your brothers praise you." Judah, meaning "the one
who confesses," will deploy its forces in the true Jerusalem,
whose "occupant will not be shaken forever,"[65] the purpose being for it to *assemble the might of all the peoples round about, gold and*
silver and garments in great abundance. Comment has often been
made on the other divinely inspired writings as well and in
studying the prophet in hand that the word *gold* signifies the enlightened mind and the name *silver* a precise word. Hence we
must adapt in a manner appropriate to gold and silver the *gar-*
ments, too, of which holy Judah collected a vast amount from all
the peoples round about, that is, all the nations who found
faith. Now, clothing and garments by divine anagogy are the different kinds of virtue and the actions performed in accord with
them, as well as the doctrines of piety and the mysteries of truth.
With both of these is draped . . . the queen, bride of Christ, the
Church, as the singer says in the forty-fifth psalm, "The queen
attends at your right clad in a garment of gold of a rich variety,"
and further on, "clad in golden tassels of a rich variety."[66]

I mean, surely the mind is not so blind as to think that the

---

64. Hos 3.5; Hab 3.2. Didymus admits consulting predecessors, if not on
Zechariah, at least on Hosea, in his wish to clarify this term. He does not generally refer to any.

65. Gn 49.8; Ps 125.1.

66. Ps 45.9, 14.

Holy Spirit is teaching about corporeal vesture, and not about garments covering and adorning the inner person, about whom the exhortation occurs in Ecclesiastes, "At all times let your garments be white," with which God himself clothes and dresses the soul that says in thanksgiving, "I rejoice in the Lord, for he has clothed me in a garment of salvation and a tunic of happiness." To the one taking pride in the clothes adorning her, the bridegroom who provided her with them says, "I clothed you in silk and fine linen,"[67] by "silk" referring to what is woven from inconspicuous and delicate thoughts and works, and by "linen" what is composed of physical actions and words, since linen is grown from the soil—hence the comparison with physical things. After having assembled a force of peoples round about, and deployed them in the spiritual Jerusalem, "which sees peace," Judah assembled the spiritual valuables of the peoples: gold, silver, clothing in great abundance—that is, spirit and word in the spiritual interpretation, and clothing assembled in great abundance in the sense understood.

With sufficient clarification given to the present passage, let us move on to what follows it. *And this will be the downfall of the horses, the mules, the camels, the asses, and all the cattle in those camps through this downfall* (v.15). Just as the nations came to no good from their standing firm, but on falling had a blessed and commendable rising, as has just been explained, so those who in an allegorical sense are horses, mules, camels, and asses will on falling from the condition that was theirs rise in salutary fashion for their own good. Those who became horses in a frenzy for females so as to neigh after their neighbor's mate fell from the pleasure-loving passion and adulterous condition so as to rise by a commendable rising, of which Jesus spoke to his disciples, "Rise up, let us go hence," and when he cried out to the Church from the nations that had become his bride, "Rise up, come, you who are close to me." This is the sense of the apostolic verse that goes like this: "Sleeper, awake, rise from the dead, and Christ will shine on you."[68]

---

67. Eccl 9.8; Is 61.10; Ezek 16.10.
68. Jer 5.8; Jn 14.31; Song 2.10; Eph 5.14. As mentioned above on v.12 (on which some modern commentators see v.15 following directly), the LXX's

In a way similar to the downfall of the horses, the mules will also fall, being given this name because of sterility of spirit. In reference to both these animals the divine word says to human beings, "Be not like horse and mule, without understanding as they are." Just as men who have a frenzy for women and are promiscuous are spoken of as horses, so a virgin who has a body that is inviolate but is not really pure in spirit can allegorically be called a mule. For this kind of sterility the man who has become a eunuch, not for the kingdom of heaven but to be pleasing to human beings, is also called a mule. After the downfall the horses and mules in this sense will rise up and have as their rider the one to whom the holy ones said, "Mount your horses, your riding is salvation."[69] Likewise, the mule, too, after undergoing the transformation commented on, will have David—the savior, I mean—mounted and riding in royal fashion.

In the manner demonstrated, there will fall and rise also *the camels and the asses and all the other beasts found in those camps*— that is, the people corresponding to these animals. Like the downfall of the horses and the animals listed after them, camels represent in a figurative sense people who are really devoted to the divine Law without distinguishing what is to be implemented and what is not; on the one hand, they chew the cud, crushing and reducing to powder the nourishment that is regurgitated, holding devout discourse on the Law, while on the other hand they do not have cloven hoofs or cleft feet, and so are unclean, not distinguishing what is to be done from what is not.[70] Such people include the Jews according to the flesh, who do not distinguish the spirit from the letter, the reality from the shadow, or even malicious behavior from what is done virtuously—hence the saying that they are considered "a sinful nation, a people full of sins," as it does not suffice for purity to have thoughts that are purposeless, that is, futile. As the saying goes in their regard, "Peoples had purposeless thoughts"; abandon-

---

rendering as "downfall" a form in our Heb. for "plague" allows Didymus to go off on these far-fetched comparisons and textual associations. In the process Zechariah's thought is lost.

69. Ps 32.9; 1 Cor 7.34; Mt 19.12; Hab 3.8.

70. Lv 11.4; Is 41.15.

ing the instruction of the one "who gave them birth and raised them," they all heard the statement as though addressed to each, "The son who stops observing his father's advice will turn to evil discourse."[71]

While Israelites according to the flesh are camels in bearing the stamp of being clean, on the one hand, and on the other of being unclean, idolaters are asses in being unclean, unbridled, bowed low, braying because they are deprived of intelligence and reason. And since they reached this state of their own accord, it is possible for them to fall from it so as to rise and, again bearing the image,[72] enter into the spiritual Jerusalem we have so often explained. You see, since the ass was tied to her colt in the village opposite—that is, in opposition to paradise, whence the human being was expelled for breaking God's commandment—it was a beast of burden, quite devoid of intelligence or reason. But when Jesus mounted it so as, bearing the image, to enter Jerusalem, it was transformed from an ass into the rational features of reason, so that it is said of the savior that "he ties the ass to the vine." This happened when he made the Greek and the Jew into one new man, the vine being the people of circumcision, referred to in words addressed to God, "You transplanted a vine out of Egypt, expelling the nations and planting it," and the vinedresser saying to it, "I planted you as a fruitful vine completely true."[73] It is to such a vine that he tied the people from the nations, who were devoid of intelligence before their calling, and a colt because of being recently called.

We should examine whether in another sense it is to himself, the true vine, that he has drawn and fastened the human race so as to . . . "Anyone attached to the Lord is one spirit with him."[74]

Like the aforementioned horses, the mules and all the other

---

71. Is 1.4; Ps 2.1; Is 1.2; Prv 19.27.

72. The rare Greek term behind this phrase occurs again immediately below in reference to Jesus, the term "image," ἄγαλμα, normally referring to an idol.

73. Mt 21.2; Gn 49.11; Eph 2.15; Ps 80.8; Jer 2.21.

74. Before this citation of 1 Cor 6.17 some lines of the manuscript are missing.

beasts of those camps, . . . may undergo the same transformation when tamed and brought to reason.

Through this downfall, that is, the one commented on.

As many as are left of all the nations advancing on Jerusalem will come up year by year to worship the king, the Lord almighty, and celebrate the festival of Tabernacles (v.16). The survivors of all the nations, having advanced and assaulted it [Jerusalem], go up each year to adore the king, the Lord almighty, at the time of the feast called Tabernacles, which Jews for their part observe in a factual and literal sense, while righteous men attend it as they do the other feasts. At any rate, let us first give the literal sense so that the overall and allegorical sense may appear. After the people of the Hebrews left Egypt and crossed the Red Sea, with Pharaoh and all his army drowned, the move into the holy land by those helped by God did not occur at once. As a result, they lived in the desert for all of forty years without city or towns or houses; and since it was not possible for those intending to cross into the holy land to be completely without shelter, those who had left Egypt erected tents as a covering and dwelling so that even in this way they might have a memorial of the favors conferred with the setting up of the tents each year. The Law given to them provides a clear confirmation of this devotion: Scripture says, "If your son asks you in the future, What is the meaning of these tents? You will say to him, After we were refugees for a long time in Egypt, God led us out of it into this desert, and hence we set up the holy tents so that at the sight of them each year there is no chance of the good gift being forgotten."[75] Comment should be made also as to how and when the feast of Tabernacles was celebrated: "In the seventh month," Scripture says, "on the fifteenth day take ripe fruit from the tree, palm branches, leafy branches, and willow and weeping willow branches from the brook for celebration."[76]

75. Dt 6.20; Lv 23.43. As the notion of tents had received allegorical development before his time, Didymus thinks he should first recount the historical background to tent-living and the later feast. For Christians in Alexandria, Jewish feasts would naturally be of (reinterpreted) significance.

76. Lv 23.39–40, a text which does not allow Didymus to see how an originally agricultural festival has later been given a historical perspective (like

Now, it is appropriate to say what the spiritual interpretation
is of all of this. "Tent" is the name given to progress in virtue
and wisdom since it provides covering for travelers. The interpretation is given in the forty-second psalm, where the person
with devotion to the house of God says, "I shall pass through
every corner of the wonderful tabernacle as far as the house of
God"—that is, for the one passing to the house of God there is
need for a site for a tent and remarkable progress, whereas the
one who has reached the goal after great progress resides there
and no longer lives in a tent, and so says in high spirits, "That I
may dwell in the house of the Lord for length of days," and
again, "One thing I asked of the Lord, this I sought, that I
might dwell in the house of the Lord all the days of my life, that
I might contemplate the delights of the Lord and visit his temple." In keeping with the interpretation given is also the beginning of the eighty-fourth psalm, "How lovable are your tabernacles, Lord of hosts. My soul longs and faints for the courts of
the Lord," and a little later, "Blessed are all who dwell in your
house, they will praise you forever."[77] The hymn-singing, in fact,
is performed forever by those who after making great progress
have come to the house whose foundations God laid. In reference to such tents, spiritual as they are, the sage says in his
song, "A cry of joy and salvation in the tents of the righteous,"
and the author of Proverbs says, "Houses of the righteous
abide," and "tents of the upright will stand."[78] Actually, progress
must halt at some stage when the end is reached that is referred to as a "house": it is not possible or seemly to be ever
progressing and never reach the final stage, called a "house,"
where the true servants of God perform spiritual services forever, praising and glorifying God with thanks for his judgments
that are perfect and unfailing.

Each of the tents so understood should be wreathed attrac-
tively in the prescribed decorations, "ripe fruit from the tree,
palm branches, leafy branches, and willow and weeping willow

other major feasts in the Jewish calendar). Nor does he advert to the novelty in
Zechariah's apocalyptic vision whereby gentiles also celebrate the feast.
   77. Pss 42.4; 23.6; 27.4; 84.1–2, 4.
   78. Ps 118.15; Prv 12.7; 14.11.

branches." Take note as to whether the ripe fruit comes from
wisdom, called a tree of life, as the proverbial saying goes, "It is
a tree of life to all who approach it, and security for all who de-
pend on it as on the Lord."[79] Another term used of it is a true
vine bearing ripe fruit, grapes and raisins, from which is
pressed "wine that gives joy to the heart." In addition to this
fruit, one has to take palm branches as covering for the port-
able house, that is, the tent, which always flourishes because its
heart is always on high. Branches taken from the palm help towards cleanliness when used as a broom; a woman who lost one
of the ten drachmas used it to get rid of rubbish from the
house and found the lost coin, which bore the image of the sovereign, which is none other than the person made in the image
and likeness of God. In reference to the palm whose branches
have to be taken to adorn the tent, the bride in the Song of
Songs sings, "I said, I shall climb the palm, I shall attain its
height."[80]

Beyond the palm branches there is need to take as well leafy
branches with much fruit—leafy because of the thickness and
density of foliage and fruit. The leafy branches represent the
different kinds of virtue, practical and contemplative, and the
fruitful doctrines of piety. For the adornment of the woven
tents there is need to take also willow and weeping willow
branches. Some commentators were inclined to claim that willow and weeping willow are the same, both terms referring to
the one tree, a symbol of purity and incorruption because
when its flower is crushed and mixed with water, it renders
drinkers eunuchs, as was observed also in another work.[81]

79. Prv 3.18. As often happens, in his spiritual development of Zechariah's
reference to the feast of Tabernacles Didymus in tangential fashion is commenting rather on one of the texts used for documentation, item by item. There is
spiritual potential here, he feels. And he proceeds by this process of loose
(Diodore would say arbitrary) association to palm branches to brooms to lost
coins to coins of tribute to people in God's image and likeness. Zechariah is left
far behind.

80. Ps 104.15; Lk 15.8–9; Mt 22.21; Gn 1.27.

81. The work, now lost, would be a commentary on Leviticus. In his Question 32 on Leviticus, Theodoret cites the same claim made for the willow. Is
Didymus, by citing the force of the willow, ἄγνος, for purity, suggesting this
word is related to ἁγνός? According to Liddell and Scott, the ἄγνος is the

The person who celebrates the spiritual feast of Tabernacles does so by climbing up, as the prophet in hand suggests, as those observing it in letter and shadow of the Law mark it down below. And since the chaff and straw of the shadow hides the spirit and the truth, we should take the palm branches so as to sweep away what the apostle called "rubbish" and thus have a spiritual understanding of the law regarding this festival, as we rise up to its height. This, in fact, is the way to be able to adore in spirit and in truth *the king, the Lord almighty.*[82]

In addition to the understanding already expounded, the feast of Tabernacles should be taken also another way. Our human bodies are given this name: the most holy of Christ's disciples, Peter, at any rate, writes, "The Lord Jesus Christ has shown me that the putting off of my tent is fast approaching." To similar effect also is the divinely inspired Paul, "While we are still in this tent, we groan under our burden, because we wish not to be unclothed but further clothed, so that what is mortal may be swallowed up by life." The feast of Tabernacles is principally and especially celebrated, however, by those directed to rejoice, not only men not defiled by women, but also women devoted to preserving purity in spirit and body.[83] In addition to these, they also adorn their tents who as partners in an honorable marriage keep pure and unstained their marriage bed. The feast of garlanded and adorned tents is celebrated even better on high, at the moment of resurrection we look forward to, when the corruptible body rises incorruptible and the physical body rises spiritual. Is it not a divine tent, the body sown in weakness and dishonor so as to rise in power and glory?[84]

It is worth examining how the spiritual feast should be cele-

---

"chaste-tree," associated in Hellenistic culture with chastity. Matrons spread these branches on their beds at the Thesmophoria. See Henry George Liddell and Robert Scott, *A Greek-English Lexicon: A New Edition*, revised and augmented by Henry Stuart Jones and Roderick McKenzie (Oxford: Clarendon Press, 1843; repr. 1961), 12.

82. Phil 3.8; Jn 4.23.

83. 2 Pt 1.14; 2 Cor 5.4; 1 Pt 1.6, 8; Rv 14.4; 1 Cor 7.4. That the latter citations do not reflect any pejorative attitude to marriage on Didymus's part is established by the following citation from Heb 13.4.

84. 1 Cor 15.42–46.

brated on the fifteenth day of the seventh month. It behooves
the one who celebrates the feast with tents in the sense explained to rise above the world made in six days, cease all
servile work, and observe the rest of the seventh day according
to "the law of the sabbath given to the people of God," which
Jesus alone confirmed in the words, "To all of you coming [to
me] I shall give rest," and again, "You will find rest for your
souls." They celebrate the feast on the fifteenth day of the seventh month who "have given a part to the seven and a part to
the eight," adhering to the Old and New Covenant; the Old,
you see, is signified by the seven through practice of the sabbath, and by the eight the resurrection of Christ on the eighth
day following crucifixion, and it thus became the Lord's day.[85]

All who do not ascend to Jerusalem from all the tribes of the earth to
worship the king, the Lord almighty, will be added to the others (v.17).
The spiritual Jerusalem is positioned on the heights according
to the sage remark of the apostle who writes in one place, "the
Jerusalem on high," and in another, "You have made your approach to Mount Sion and the city of the living God, the heavenly Jerusalem." The only ones to ascend to it are those who
are able to say, "Our citizenship is in heaven," and again, "He
(God, that is) has raised us and seated us with Christ Jesus in
the heavenly places." Those who still "bear the image of the
man of dust" and "have their minds set on earthly things"[86] are
the tribes of the earth, not ascending to the beautiful city positioned on the heights which sees peace. *Those not ascending will*
be added to those from all the nations who do not ascend, and
will suffer the same fate as theirs.[87] Those "who have their
minds set on earthly things" do not ascend because they are
borne down by the weight of earthly deeds. Those who strive to

85. Heb 4.9; Mt 11.28–29; Eccl 11.2. Still concentrating on the Leviticus
text rather than Zechariah, Didymus feels the need to see the Law observed
spiritually, in the process giving doubtful relevance to a text from Qoheleth that
R. B. Y. Scott paraphrases as "Don't put all your eggs in one basket"—hardly the
desirable attitude to the relation of the testaments Didymus intends. See Scott,
Proverbs, Ecclesiastes, Anchor Bible 18 (Garden City, NY: Doubleday, 1981), 252.

86. Gal 4.26; Heb 12.22; Phil 3.20; Eph 2.6; 1 Cor 15.48; Phil 3.19.

87. Our Heb. text and the Antioch version read, "No rain will fall on them,"
rather than "They will be added."

ascend to the city with foundations that are unbreakable because they were laid by the Lord, "its architect and builder," will
worship the king, the Lord almighty along with the angels; Scripture says, remember, "All God's angels will worship him."[88]

It is not the Father to the exclusion of the Son, nor the Son
apart from the Father, who is referred to as the one being
adored, *king and Lord almighty:* in the Trinity there is one kingship, the same lordship and almighty power. Hence if we have
the desire to adore the Trinity as *king [and] Lord almighty,* let us
not remain as tribes of the earth, but store up treasures in heav-
en and have our heart there. . . . Thus, being in Jerusalem, let
us adore with all rational creatures, when everyone in heaven,
on earth, and under the earth bends the knee to the king, and
every tongue confesses to the glory of God the Father that Jesus
is Lord.[89]

If the tribe of Egypt does not go up or travel there, on them will occur
the downfall with which the Lord struck all the nations that did not go
up to celebrate the feast of Tabernacles. It is the sin of Egypt and the sin
of all the nations that did not go up to celebrate the feast of Tabernacles
(vv.18–19). Mention was previously made of the exceptional
celebration in Jerusalem of the feast of Tabernacles with particular might and splendor, from which emerges the importance
of going up to that festival and the downfall awaiting those who
excuse themselves from the very important action. Not only
Egyptians but also all the other nations will by divine design be
struck and suffer downfall in order that they may perceive that
they are wrong and recover the desire to "observe the feast with
garlands,"[90] namely, the feast of Tabernacles.

Since this feast is open to two interpretations already specified, zeal should be shown through love of God to complete in
a brisk manner [our] progress in virtue "with cries of joy and
salvation." The purpose is for us to ascend as a result of this
progress to the house whose foundations have been laid by the
savior of all forever, and praise the one who has brought us to
him after great progress, so that each may say with faith and

---

88. Heb 11.10; Ps 97.7.   89. Mt 6.29; Phil 2.11.
90. Ps 118.27.

knowledge, "Lord, I loved the beauty of your house and place of habitation of your glory." By this, in fact, it becomes possible to raise such hymns of song as, "I circled about in his tabernacle and sacrificed a sacrifice of rejoicing."[91]

The person who is the recipient of this blessed and holy guidance, even if Egyptian or from another nation, will find rest as was the case also before the downfall, now that on the basis of complete and perfect virtue one occupies Jerusalem in the inner man. The sacred text says it is a grievous sin not to go up to the feast of Tabernacles in the sense explained. In the explanation given, the spiritual feast of Tabernacles has been interpreted in different ways, and in all these ways there is need for everyone to go up to it, be one Egyptian or any other nationality, as was said before, this being the way to become a genuine Israelite in whom there is no guile, thus being a Jew in hidden fashion according to the inner man.[92]

On that day, what is on the bridle of the horse will be holy to the Lord almighty, and the pots will be in the house of the Lord like bowls before the altar. Every pot in Jerusalem and in Judah will be holy to the Lord almighty (vv.20–21). On the day already explained of the holy feast of Tabernacles, when there is an obligation to go up and celebrate it so as to worship the king, the Lord almighty, *what is on the horse's bridle will be* called *holy to the Lord almighty.* Now, this is nothing other than the word that holds in check obstinate souls, devoid of intelligence and other virtues, whose frenzy and obstinacy the sage reproves in giving an order to the frenzied, "Be not like horse or mule, unintelligent; keep their jaws under tight bridle and rein if they do not come near you." After all, how would the horse be led to the spiritual rider when it had "a passion for females, neighing after its neighbor's mate," driven to frenzy by shameful passions, so that with its wanton tendencies restrained it might submit to the horsebreaker and so prove useful in battle. Hence the proverbial saying about it, "A horse is prepared for a day of battle, but help comes from the Lord."[93]

91. Pss 118.27, 15; 26.8; 27.6.　　92. Jn 1.47; Rom 2.29.
93. Ps 32.9; Jer 5.8; Prv 21.31.

Like the horse in a spiritual sense, the infertile man, who in
an allegorical sense is a mule, is pacified, bridle and rein re-
straining the jaws and [leading him] to the skillful rider, and so
he is responsive to the pull of the bridle and carries the rider in
orderly fashion. . . . is in accord with the verse from the psalm,
as blessed James wrote in his epistle, checking the rebellious
tongue that is out of control on account of a loquacity that is
guilty of words better not said. His text goes as follows: "We put
bits into the mouth of horses and guide their whole body"[94] so
that their gait may be regular and straight. How much greater
is the need to keep a check on the tongue—speech, that is—so
as not . . . only to avoid falling into the abyss but also to keep
out of harm's way, and so dedicate the bit to the Lord almighty
himself.

With the horse's bit dedicated, *the pots in the house of the Lord*
in which meat for sacrifices is cooked *before the altar* will be like
bowls in which the liturgical libations are offered. Hence in different senses pot and bowl have the same function, as do liba-
tion and sacrifice. That is to say, although in material matters li-
bation is one thing and sacrifice another, and likewise pot and
bowl, it is not the same in spiritual matters, . . . where function
and symbolism differ. The savior, for example, true high priest,
is called lamb and shepherd whereas in the material order the
lamb cannot be a high priest offering itself to God and a shepherd leading itself to pasture; the high priest is different from
the victim, and the shepherd from the sheep. Now, if this is the
case, it is in an allegorical sense that the pot is the same as the
bowl; in reference to the spiritual bowls the divine bride in the
Song of Songs says of her nephew, "My nephew came into his
garden to bowls of perfume to pasture his sheep in the garden
and gather the lilies."[95] Now, the bowls of perfume into which
the nephew of the one saying these things descended are the

94. Jas 3.3.
95. Song 6.2. Didymus has not shown an interest in ritual, let alone sacramental, details of the text; and so here in preference to investigating the relevance of horses and particular receptacles to Temple ritual, he chooses to seek
spiritual capital from a (favorite) associated text, the Song of Songs. As often
with Didymus, the subtext becomes the text.

divinely inspired Scriptures, or rather their divine meanings, in which the one who descended pastures the sheep in the garden and gathers the lilies, the flowers bearing spiritual fragrance which are called lilies.

When the pots in front of the spiritual altar become bowls of perfume, then *every pot in Jerusalem,* the holy [city], *and in Judah will be holy.* Jerusalem in these lines is to be taken as the glorious Church, and Judah as the one "whom his brothers praise and to whom his father's sons bow down."[96] Who he is has been mentioned in the prophet's words read previously.

All those sacrificing will come and take some of them and cook in them. And there will no longer be any Canaanite in the house of the Lord almighty on that day (v.21). All those who bring a sacrifice of righteousness and offer a sacrifice of praise will come to the one whom they adore and serve so as to glorify him at his invitation when he says, "A sacrifice of praise will glorify me."[97] They will join with one another in consensus so as to perform their priestly service together, taking some of the consecrated pots . . . positioned around the altar so as to cook the meat of the victims in them, as already mentioned. And since the rite of the aforementioned pots is performed with reason and informed insight, they are rightly called bowls. I mean, the fact that this kind of receptacle signifies the word is indicated in the Song of Songs; the bride, for example, imagining in her mind the beauty and charm she loves in her nephew, says, "His jaws like bowls of perfume exuding fragrance."[98] Now, "jaw" suggests the word, which, like a spring, spreads and exudes fragrance.

Since this worship is given a mystical interpretation and performed by those who come to conduct sacrifice in spiritual fashion by cooking in the holy pots the meat (understood in a spiritual sense) from heifers and rams, *there will no longer be a Canaanite in the house of the Lord almighty on that day* when restoration occurs of . . . Now, a Canaanite is a foreigner born of a womb lacking piety; there will be none, whether because of a change into "the true Israel in whom there is no guile," or be-

96. Gn 49.8.
98. Song 5.13. See n. 95.

97. Ps 50.23.

cause of expulsion from the house of the Lord almighty. *Canaanite* should be taken allegorically to mean the person who has forfeited the condition of an Israelite. Of such a kind would be one of the elders who had a passion for Susanna; the wise Daniel said to him, "Offspring of Canaan and not of Judah, beauty has seduced you and lust corrupted your heart. This is the way you dealt with the daughters of Israel, and in fear they had relations with you; but a daughter of Judah did not put up with your iniquity." To similar effect is what is said by Hosea about licentious people as Canaanites in these terms: "By partaking in idol worship, Ephraim laid a stumbling block for himself. They chose Canaanites, they prostituted themselves with prostitution."[99]

Since the licentious person in a figurative sense is a Canaanite, he is expelled from the holy house of the Lord almighty so as no longer to occupy it. In fulfillment of this the divine apostle Paul writes to the church of the Corinthians, "It is reported that there is sexual immorality among you, and of a kind that is not found even among the nations, a man living with his father's wife. And you took pride in this! Should you not rather have mourned, so that the one guilty of this would have been removed from your midst?" He was expelled from the assembly of the faithful, the purpose being that he come to a sense of the evil he had embarked on of his own free will and receive the wages of his fall. That is what happened, the result being . . . seriously repentant; thus one who put aside his sinful behavior was admitted to the Church, the house of God.[100]

Now, the fact that no one is evil by nature, as some heretics believe, and that change happens by choice emerges from the Gospel, where the Canaanite woman changes into a woman from a dog, the one who saves here styling her "daughter" when he says, "Daughter, your faith has saved you." Perhaps she was a dog before coming to faith, in fact, for the reason that

99. Jn 1.47; Susanna 56–57; Hos 4.17–18 LXX.
100. 1 Cor 5.1–2. Didymus is not making a statement of the discipline of his own church in the fourth century. He does, on the other hand, proceed to rebut contemporary heretical views of Valentinians and Manicheans about a natural inclination to evil.

she was a licentious woman, a dog being an animal that is . . .
given to coupling with others and to indulging in shameful
fawning. At any rate, there is a veto on the earnings of prostitution in the saying of the Law, "You shall not bring a dog nor the
fee of a prostitute into the house of your Lord God"; in observance of this there is no Canaanite in the house of the Lord
almighty on the day illuminated by the sun of righteousness,
the true light, the only-begotten Son of God.[101]

Since the end has been reached of the prophet we have
been elucidating, Zechariah, we also bring to a close the composition of the commentary on him.[102]

101. Mt 9.22; Dt 23.19; Mal 4.2; Jn 1.9. Didymus here, as in his comment on
11.7, is unaware of the Canaanites' reputation for (shady) commerce suggested
in passages like Hos 12.7, Prv 31.24, and Ezek 17.4. His suggestion that Jesus in
the Matthew pericope is implying the Canaanite woman was a prostitute seems
unhappily far-fetched.

102. Having begun his work with the briefest of prayers for divine help,
Didymus closes without any such acknowledgment. The task asked of him has
been completed; a lengthy peroration is not required.

INDICES

GENERAL INDEX

Alexandria, *passim*
allegory, *passim*
Altaner, B., xi, 6
anagogical, 19, 20, 24, 51, 135, 157, 332, 342
anthropomorphism, 322
antigrapha, 8, 46
Antioch, *passim*
Antony, 3
apocalyptic, 10, 23, 24, 33, 38, 39, 290, 319, 342, 349
apocatastasis, 22, 248
apocrypha, 99, 293
Apollinaris, 21, 269, 298
Aquila, 7, 8, 103, 302
Aramaic, 8
Arian, 21, 143, 276, 332, 337
Aristarchus, 13, 318
Aristotle, 10, 13, 98, 137, 172, 202, 207, 295, 307, 317, 318
Artemas, 21, 298
Augustine, 23, 79

Balthasar, H. U. von, xi, 17
baptism, 308, 333
Bardy, G., xi
Barthélemy, D., xi
Bienert, W. A., xi
Bouyer, L., xi, 24
Brisson, J., 17
Brown, R. E., 18, 93
Bruce, F. F., xi
Butler, C., xi

calendar, 31
canon, 9, 108, 134, 164, 224, 241, 288, 293, 313, 315
Cappadocian, 21
catenae, 4
Chalcedon, 29
Christological, 14, 20, 59, 70, 77, 85,

91, 122, 125, 173, 213, 221, 222, 317
Clement of Alexandria, 210
Constantinople, 3, 8, 21, 59, 236
Crouzel, H., xi
Cyril of Alexandria, *passim*

Dahood, M., 143, 261
Daly, R. J., xi, 17
Danielou, J., xi, 17
deuterocanonical, 9, 134, 164, 288
Di Berardino, A., xii
Diocletian, 3, 342
Diodore, 16, 17, 18, 22, 23, 56, 64, 99, 173
Docetism, 276
Doutreleau, L., *passim*

Ebionite, 317
Ehrman, B. D., xi, 9
Ephesus, 23
Ephrem, 4
Epicurean, 13, 97
eschatology, 13, 35, 181, 203, 204, 213, 216, 242, 267, 280, 321
etymology, *passim*
eucharist, 119, 120, 134, 334
Eunomian, 143
Eusebius of Caesarea, 8, 168
Eustathius, 17, 60, 64
Evagrius, 22
exegesis, 7–22

Fall, 221
Fernández Marcos, N., 4, 29
Frend, W. H. C., xii

geography, 5
Gnostic, 21, 46, 223, 276
Grant, R. M., 9
Greek, *passim*

INDEX OF HOLY SCRIPTURE

Old Testament

New Testament